TREASURES OF THE HEART

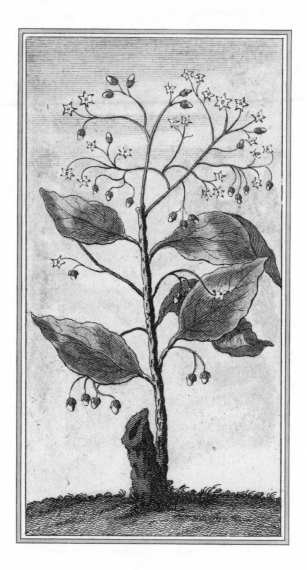

Treasures of the Heart

HOLIDAY STORIES THAT REVEAL THE SOUL OF JUDAISM

Diane Wolkstein

Schocken Books, New York

On the spine and frontispiece of the book is an eighteenth-century lithograph of a spice tree—a cinnamon tree. Its branches are used as a design element throughout the book.

Copyright © 2003 by Diane Wolkstein

All rights reserved under International and Pan-American Copyright Conventions. Published in the United States by Schocken Books, a division of Random House, Inc., New York, and simultaneously in Canada by Random House of Canada Limited, Toronto.

Schocken Books and colophon are registered trademarks of Random House, Inc.

Grateful acknowledgment is made to the following for permission to reprint previously unpublished material:

HarperCollins Publishers: The Song of Songs from *The First Love Stories* by Diane Wolkstein. Copyright © 1991 by Diane Wolkstein. Reprinted by permission of HarperCollins Publishers.

Shambhala Publications, Inc.: Excerpt from the poem "Drowned in God" from *The Rumi Collection* edited by Kabir Helminski. Copyright © 1998 by Kabir Helminski. Reprinted by permission of Shambhala Publications, Inc., Boston, www.shambhala.com

Library of Congress Cataloging-in-Publication Data

Wolkstein, Diane.
Treasures of the heart: holiday stories that reveal the soul of Judaism / Diane Wolkstein.
p.   cm.
Includes glossary, bibliographical references and index.
ISBN 0-8052-4144-2
1. Fasts and feasts—Judaism.   2. Bible stories, English—O.T.
3. Talmud—Legends.   I. Title.

BM690 .W63 2003
296.4'3—DC21   2002075856

www.schocken.com

Printed in the United States of America

First Edition

9 8 7 6 5 4 3 2 1

For Shlomo Carlebach, zt'l, whose heart was full of praise

and for Moses and Abram
Rebekah, Hannah, and Nathaniel

*"The bridegroom delivered the Torah that is bigger
than the earth and broader than the seas.
The bride consented to the covenant,
and an everlasting agreement was made.
As a dowry, the bride brought a heart
that understands, ears that listen, and eyes that see."*

16TH CENTURY SEPHARDIC MARRIAGE CONTRACT

BY ISRAEL NAJARA

Contents

Contents

Contents

Foreword

For twenty-six years, I listened to stories in my synagogue. On each holiday, our rabbi, Shlomo Carlebach, told stories that opened my heart to prayer and transformation. While Shlomo was alive, I was mostly content to receive. This is not to say that I always agreed with him. I categorically refused to refer to God as "He." Because I was raised in the Reform tradition of Judaism, I kept asking Shlomo why women could not go up to the pulpit to speak or hold the Torah. Wasn't the Torah intended for all of us? Nor did I understand how God's "chosen" people had harmed—no, murdered—thousands of Canaanites. Shlomo, an orthodox, Hasidic rabbi, gently responded, "Wait. Wait until the apple is ripe to fall from the tree."

As long as Shlomo was alive, I waited. His singing brought my soul to places it had not known but craved; his stories and teachings nourished me. But when Shlomo died in 1994, I was forced to find another way into Judaism. I turned to the Torah and began to attend evening classes of commentary on the weekly Bible readings.

Six months later, Arthur Samuelson, an editor at Schocken Books, asked me if I wanted to edit a collection of Jewish stories. I said I was interested in editing a collection of biblical stories connected to the holidays. Through my studies of other religions, I had an intuition that, when viewed as a whole, both the holidays and stories that are read on the holidays would reveal a spiritual and psychological meaning about Judaism that was not readily apparent. However, I knew I would have to study seriously to find out what that might be. I asked for two years to complete the book; the book has taken eight years.

Balance in the Bible

As a child, I remember reading Bible stories in Sunday school and finding them rich, multilayered, and mysterious. More than forty years later when I reread these stories in preparation for writing this book, I found some still thrilling, but others disturbing, confusing—and still others, misogynistic. How could Abraham agree to sacrifice his son? Why did God punish Miriam for asking a question? Why do my people refer to themselves as the children of fathers and not of fathers *and* mothers? Is God a changing character in the stories or the one who created the story?

Reading deeper into the texts, I began to hear chords of varying complexities. The texts were multivoiced and full of protest: protest against images, cults, authority, culture, wealth, even patriarchy. However, I began to see a balance in the stories. In almost every instance where there was a predominance of the patriarchal view, a feminine or opposing vision was also present, although often hidden. Plots and characters that moved with great determination in one direction ended up in the opposite. As a trained storyteller, I looked for repetitions and discovered that in almost every instance in which repetition occurs, it varies. One version of creation (Gn 1) is followed by an entirely different version of creation (Gn 2). Moses' Song of the Sea (Ex 15:1–18) is followed by Miriam's Song of the Sea (Ex 15:21). Psalm 78 gives a different ordering of the plagues than Psalm 105. Almost every time a character relates a conversation or tells a story, the narrator changes the content. Different characters offer different reports of the same event. There is no constant voice, no unalterable hierarchy.

The scope of the Bible is enormous; its literary content includes myth, epic, folk tale, magic tale, wisdom tale, legend, satire, poetry, proverb, and praise-song. Although there is a narrator, the narrator's voice changes. Time expands and collapses. The stories are ambiguous, contradictory, paradoxical. Their meanings are elusive and for good reason: there is no reliable, fixed ground in the Bible. If there is one constant, it is that there is no unalterable hierarchy or doctrine. Whatever can be seen is an idol and as such is not dependable. The only constant is the Mystery, the Void.

The Feminine and Masculine in the Bible

As I began to understand the variety and balance of viewpoints in the Bible, I also began to see the balance of the feminine and masculine.

While God, the chief character in the Bible, is referred to as "He," the powerful feminine, or the Goddess, is also present.

For all my adult life, I have been writing, exploring, and telling sacred stories from world mythology. One that is particularly important to me is the story of the Mesopotamian goddess Inanna. Perhaps because my grandmothers died when I was young, I have always been curious to know about my family history: where did my people come from? Who were the parents of Abraham and Sarah? In my late twenties I studied the civilization of Sumer, the land where Abraham and Sarah were born and raised and most likely celebrated new-moon festivals to honor Inanna. Known by her people, the Sumerians, as the queen of heaven, Inanna was the great goddess of love, war, and fertility.

Researching and retelling the four-thousand-year-old story of Inanna, with Professor Samuel Noah Kramer (*Inanna, Queen of Heaven and Earth*), gave me a larger vision of a woman's potential than any I had experienced in Judaism. From the cuneiform texts (which were preserved in clay tablets), we read that the goddess of love, Inanna, joyously celebrated her sexuality in the mystical marriage (*hieros gamos*) known as the wedding of heaven and earth. As spiritual adventurer and goddess of fertility, she wrestled with the god of wisdom and brought back the attributes of civilization to her city. As spiritual warrior, she dared to walk through the gates of the underworld and opened communications with heaven, earth, and the underworld.

In Sumer, she was Inanna; in Babylon, Assyria, and Canaan her goddess qualities appeared as Ishtar, Asherah, and Astarte. Yet, this very same powerful, sexual, spiritual goddess was cursed and rejected by the Hebrew prophets. Jeremiah inveighed against the people for lighting incense for her, baking cakes as offerings to her, and celebrating orgiastic harvest rituals to call forth their own fertility and that of the land (Jer 7:16–20, 44:15–19, 25). Faithfulness to Yahweh, the formless infinite, eternal Spirit of Change meant rejecting the Goddess, the feminine, spontaneous, intuitive connection to nature and matter. I did not know how I could reconcile these opposing views.

But just because the prophets railed against the queen of heaven did not mean that they succeeded in stopping the people from worshiping her. They were able to take her out of the Hebrew Bible, but to my surprise, I found traits of the great queen of heaven in almost all the women portrayed in the Jewish holiday stories. At Passover, Shulamith, the sensuous goddess of love and physical fertility, enchants the king, exudes fruit and spices, and wears the necklace of warriors. At Shavuot, Ruth, the veiled goddess of fertility, lies down on the threshing floor and soon conceives. At Rosh Hashanah, Hannah, the goddess of spiritual fertility, prays for and brings forth a child of wisdom and devotion. At Hanukkah, Judith (whose texts are from the Apocrypha), the fearless warrior goddess, seduces and vanquishes the enemy. At Purim, Esther, the goddess of love and war, wins over the Persian king and rescues her people.

The Feminine and Masculine in God

The worship of the feminine aspect of God existed throughout Jewish history, sometimes hidden, at other times visible and even glorified. Despite the railings of the prophets, the need for the feminine in God was so strong—people wanted an immediate caring divinity to speak with—that from the time of the First Temple (1000 B.C.E.) to the destruction of the Second Temple (70 C.E.), the masses of Jews worshiped not only Yahweh, but also Asherah and Astarte, as is evident from the statues of these goddesses that were found in the Temples side by side with statues of Yahweh.

In the Targum Onkelos, the Aramaic translation of the Hebrew Bible, which has been read continually since its compilation in the first to fourth centuries, the physical presence of God is often referred to as the feminine "Shechinah." This was done to avoid referring to God in human terms. The Hebrew Bible says, "Let them make me a sanctuary where I may dwell." The Targum says, "Let them make a sanctuary that my Shekhina may dwell among them." The Talmud continued this tradition of referring to the physical manifestations of God—the burning bush, the pillar of clouds, the ark of the covenant—as the Shechinah. The word Shechinah comes from the verb *shakhan*, meaning "to dwell," and refers to God's "dwelling" or appearing on earth. According to Raphael Patai in the Hebrew Goddess, "The Shekhina is a frequently used Talmudic term denoting the visible and audible manifestation of God's presence on earth."

The worship of the feminine presence of God went underground for the next thousand years and erupted in the thirteenth century nearly full blown with the Zohar. Its rich, feminine, erotic imagery held to the concept that God is one and omnipresent but developed God's aspects as wife and daughter in the form of the Matronit and the Shechinah. Popular Jewish culture from the thirteenth to seventeenth century adapted Kabalistic beliefs, and worship of the Shechinah flourished. Hasidic beliefs have taken on Kabbalistic customs: the Sabbath bride is welcomed in as the queen of heaven. And in twenty-first century Judaism, another flourishing of the feminine aspect of God is taking place as people refashion the divinity to include the feminine.

The Jewish Holiday Stories

A story is history and mystery. It often begins with an "historical" event. As the Hebrews were about to flee from Egypt—as they were creating story—God insisted that the people remember and reenact the story in which they were participating and tell it to their children. However, for the story to be told and retold it must contain a core of many levels that puts both the teller and the listener into a deeper place of contemplation and transformation. Whether the stories retold in this book happened "literally" or not, they have such power that they shaped the life story of the Jewish people and became foundation stories for Western civilization.

The stories that are associated with the holidays are usually excerpts from the Torah (the first five books of the Bible), the Prophets (Nevi'im), and the Writings (Ketuvim: the literary books—the poetry, proverbs, wisdom literature, and historical books of the Hebrew Bible). The rabbis divided the first five books of the Bible into fifty-four weekly portions (they are doubled when necessary). Each week on the Sabbath, one portion is read aloud. During the time of Judah Maccabee (165 B.C.E.), when the Seleucid king Antiochus forbade the practice of reading from the Torah, the rabbis replaced these readings from the Torah with other sections from the Bible that captured the same meaning. These passages, from the Prophets, were called the haftorot and were later added to the weekly readings as well as to the holidays.

In time, Jews added other books from the Bible to be read during the holidays. In the eighth century C.E., the reading of the sensuous Song of Songs was added to the springtime Passover holiday. Similarly, the Book of Ruth which describes the barley harvest was added to Shavuot, a holiday when grain offerings are given. In the twelfth century C.E., the French rabbis suggested reading Ecclesiastes on Sukkot. In total, five books (or scrolls) from the Bible were added to the readings on the holidays. Each book is known in Hebrew as a megillah. The five megillot are The Song of Songs, the book of Ruth, Lamentations, Ecclesiastes, and Esther.

On each holiday, specific sections from the Torah and Prophets are read in the synagogue, and on certain holidays one megillah as well.

Foreword

When the readings are stories or portions of stories, I have included them in *Treasures of the Heart*. When they are recitations of laws or nonnarrative sections, I have not included them but have chosen other biblical or midrashic stories that are associated with the holidays.

Written and Oral (Midrashic) Teachings

According to Jewish tradition, when God gave Moses the written Torah on Mount Sinai, he also gave him the midrash, or oral teachings, which consisted of two parts: the halakhah, the law, and the haggadah, the stories. The rabbis did not intend for the Bible to be read without the explanation of the oral teachings. The teachings were never meant merely to be read, but rather to be given over from teacher to student—face-to-face and heart-to-heart. In rabbinic tradition, the oral teachings were passed from Moses to Aaron to Joshua and then from one leader of a generation to another. After Moses transmitted God's teachings to his brother, Aaron, Aaron remained seated on Moses' right hand while Moses transmitted the teachings to Aaron's sons, Eleazar and Ithamar. Then when Moses transmitted the teachings to the seventy elders, Aaron remained on Moses' right and Aaron's sons on his left. In this way, the student listened to the teachings many times, each time grasping another aspect of the teaching as the teacher modified its content for the new recipient.

Each generation passed down and created and continues to create its own midrash. The midrash retell, explain, challenge, explore, and open the content of the biblical text. Oral and written stories have always been considered of equal importance, like the right and the left hands. The oral teachings of Moses were passed down from teacher to disciple for forty generations and were written down in the second century in the Mishnah. Further discussions of the Mishnah were written down in the Gemara. These two books of oral teachings were combined into the Talmud during the Jews' captivity in Babylon.

To present a more comprehensible, fuller view of the stories, I have chosen to interweave ancient and modern midrash with biblical text, and have also added my own midrash joining the tradition begun thousands of years ago of recounting oral legends. Whenever the narration diverges from the biblical text, notes in the back of the book provide the specific sources.

Shaping the Stories

On each holiday, small portions or chapters of the larger biblical story are read. For example, on the first day of Passover the entire story of Exodus is not told; only three short portions are read during the synagogue service. I have enlarged almost all the portions of the stories in order to give the full context of the story. I have tried to hold on to the transcendent core of the story and to bring forward and balance the role of women and men. In addition, I've tried to balance the masculine perception of Yahweh by using Jewish tradition as my precedent so that when God is speaking to humans (especially in the case of Moses), God is referred to as the Shechinah, God's feminine presence on earth. I have also downplayed violence and aggression in both God and the Hebrew people. Neither war nor violence can be wished away; they existed, they continue to exist. Telling such stories of our past hopefully encourages us to explore their circumstances and consequences. Just as our views of women in the twentieth and twenty-first centuries have changed from biblical times, we also no longer consider war or violence as the only alternatives to disagreement or aggression.

Each story has been shaped in a different way. For example, on Rosh Hashanah, Genesis chapter 21 is read on the first day and Genesis chapter 22 on the second day. If I presented just the chapters or portions that are read in the synagogue on the holiday, the context of the narrative would be missing. The miracle of Isaac's birth cannot be appreciated without knowing how long Abraham and Sarah had been waiting for a child. And so I began the story of Isaac's birth with the birth of his father, Abraham. In a similar fashion, for Passover and Shavuot, rather than give the passage that is read at the holiday, I have told the full stories from which the small portion appears.

Another factor that affected my choice of lengthening or shortening a story has to do with the particular stories that are in this book. I wanted to form connections between stories so the reader can come to know more about the characters in the Bible, their relationships, and the fabric that binds them together. With that intention, I put Solomon, Ruth's grandson's grandson, into the story of Ruth, and Ruth herself into the story of *Solomon and the Demon King*. I connected Nahshon, a descendant of Judah, who was the first to leap into the Reed Sea in the story of Moses, to his grandson, Boaz, who appears in the story of Ruth, and Boaz to his ancestor Judah whose full story is told in the story of Joseph. Writing as a storyteller, I tried whenever possible to complete each story so it can be read or told on its own.

Ordering the Holidays

As I worked with the stories, I began to sense that the Jewish calendar year begins with Passover, not Rosh Hashanah. In fact, since the time of the Talmud, rabbis have debated whether Rosh Hashanah or Passover was the New Year. They settled the discussion by proclaiming four new years in each year: the first month of the year for people, the sixth month for animals, the seventh month for the creation of the world, and the eleventh month for trees. Rosh Hashanah was chosen as the spiritual birthday, and after the destruction of the Second Temple began to take on as much importance as Passover, the physical birthday of the people.

If I had begun *Treasures of the Heart* with Rosh Hashanah, we would be following the instructions of the rabbis of the first century who with great insight restarted the cycle of the Jewish holidays with the rebirth of the soul that takes place during the autumn harvest and ended it with the very real grief of the exile in the summer at the holiday of Tisha B'Av (a time in the Near East of great heat and dearth). But my instincts were to begin the Jewish calendar year with spring and to follow the biblical instructions that state that the first month of the Jewish calendar is to be celebrated in the spring when the Hebrew people were born as a nation ("This month shall stand at the head of your calendar; it shall be the first month of the year for you" Ex 12:1–2).

The Jewish people have followed this calendar of grief for two thousand years. We have become a people who are expert in grief, repentance, and guilt. But a living religion is continually being fashioned and refashioned—historically, psychologically, geographically, legally, and spiritually. What if we returned to the original calendar with a deeper understanding of its meanings and transformations—a calendar that begins with freedom and the renewal of life in the spring and culminates at the end of winter with the rejoicing that God is with and within us and that the arrival of spring is imminent?

The Vision of *Treasures of the Heart*

By reordering the Jewish holidays so that they begin in the spring with Passover and follow the cycle that was originally ordained in the Bible, we find that a new story emerges. As we journey from spring to winter, from Passover to Purim, we follow the path from youth to maturity. In the first half of this calendar cycle, God, the Parent/Protector, rescues the people from slavery, offers them a covenant to live by, and exiles them for breaking the covenant. In the second half of the year, the people take responsibility. They ask for forgiveness. They build homes and protect and defend themselves and their faith. By the last holiday (Purim), when God dwells within (God is not mentioned at Purim), man, woman, and the community work together to bring about their own redemption.

The new story is the changing historical relationship between God and the Jewish people. As this transformation takes place, there is a parallel development of the soul. As the people mature, the masculine and feminine complement and strengthen each other. At the same time as the feminine and masculine become integrated, the physical manifestation of God moves inside. God/the Shechinah is no longer separate from the individual; the two are one. The maturation of both the Jewish people and the individual begin at Passover and develop with each holiday.

Each story in *Treasures of the Heart* can thus be read as relevant to a particular holiday as well as to a larger story. The variety of stories with their complexity of character and plot, shifting points of view, and protest against spiritual hubris offers each of us a different path toward God and oneness. To some, it is study and wisdom: the immersion in the Torah, whether in its legalistic, aggadic, or esoteric forms; to others, it is action and relationship: the carrying out of God's teachings through acts of kindness; and to others, it is devotion and love of God: hours spent in prayer and the soul's visionary journey to Spirit.

The stories encourage us to develop our own spiritual understanding and faith. They are treasures that grow richer and deeper with time. They teach us the wisdom and life force of Judaism. They invite us to return each year to renew our connection with ourselves and with the ineffable mystery our ancestors called the Silence That Speaks.

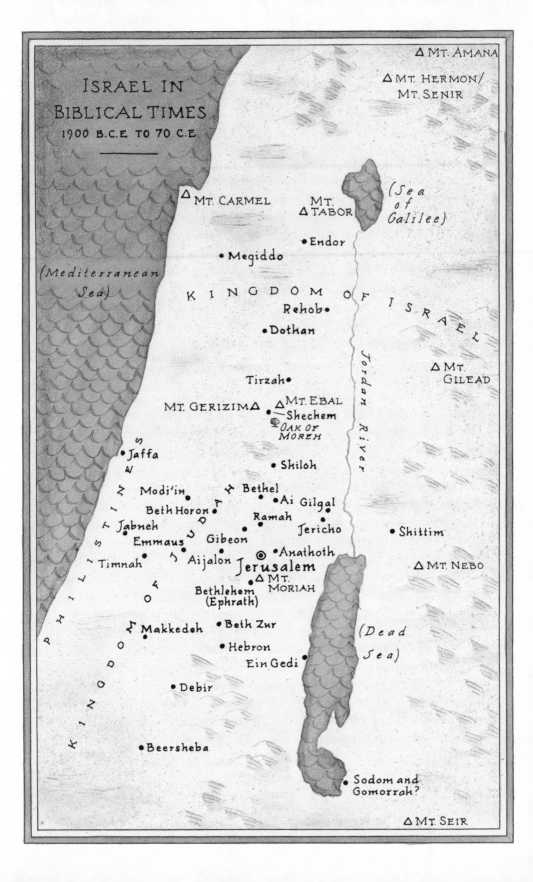

ISRAEL IN
BIBLICAL TIMES
1900 B.C.E. TO 70 C.E.

△ MT. AMANA

△ MT. HERMON/
MT. SENIR

(Sea
of
Galilee)

△ MT. CARMEL

MT.
△ TABOR

• Endor

(Mediterranean
Sea)

• Megiddo

K I N G D O M   O F   I S R A E L

Rehob •

• Dothan

Jordan River

△ MT.
GILEAD

Tirzah •

MT. GERIZIM △

△ MT. EBAL
Shechem
OAK OF
MOREH

• Jaffa

• Shiloh

Modi'in •

• Bethel

Beth Horon •

• Ai   Gilgal •

Ramah •

Jabneh •

Jericho •

• Shittim

Emmaus •

Gibeon •

Timnah •

Aijalon •

• Anathoth

Jerusalem

△ MT. NEBO

△ MT.
MORIAH

Bethlehem
(Ephrath)

Makkedeh •

• Beth Zur

• Hebron

Ein Gedi •

(Dead
Sea)

• Debir

P H I L I S T I A

K I N G D O M   O F

• Beersheba

Sodom and
Gomorrah?

△ MT. SEIR

PASSOVER

About Passover

Passover (in Hebrew *Pesach*) is celebrated in the spring on the full moon of the first month of the Jewish calendar (March or April). The first of the three Jewish pilgrimage festivals, it commemorates God's redemption of the Hebrew people from slavery and their birth as a nation.

Birth is a terrifying and joyous event. The Hebrews were slaves, yet they were afraid to leave Egypt—which is called in Hebrew Mitzraim meaning "narrow place"—to follow their leader Moses into the wilderness. God had to create plagues—great, horrific signs and wonders—to convince them to leave slavery. It was the last and tenth plague that gave Passover its name, for God "passed over" the Hebrews and struck down the firstborn throughout Egypt. God commanded: "You shall tell this story to your children," and since then, as we tell the story, we continue to give birth to ourselves and to freedom, both physical and spiritual. The act of reliving the desert experience continues throughout the eight days of the holiday (seven days in Israel).

During Passover, tradition requires that Jews refrain from eating *chametz* (leavened foods), which means that all grain products that can rise—bread, cake, even pasta—are replaced by matzah (unleavened bread). In a wish to eat the same food that our ancestors took with them in their rush from Egypt, we make matzah from grain that is prepared and baked too quickly to rise. Matzah, the simplest and humblest of food, is known as the bread of poverty and also as the bread of freedom.

Wanting to live in a new way, as the Hebrews did in the desert, many Jews use Passover preparations as a time for a thorough spring-cleaning. In a traditional household, as the holiday approaches, a sense of urgency builds. All *chametz* food is eaten, given away, or sold to Gentile neighbors. New food is bought for Passover. Pots and dishes used throughout the year are put away or purified with boiling water to take away all traces of the old. The night before the eve of Passover, a search for the smallest breadcrumbs is conducted throughout the house by candlelight and all crumbs that are found are swept away by a feather. This intensive and thorough search is the culmination of an interior spring-cleaning. We look for and expel those inflated, puffed-up parts of ourselves that enslave us and take up space that might be made available for experiencing a new freedom.

On the eve of the first day of Passover, family and friends gather in their homes to retell the Passover story with a ritual meal called the Seder. On the table is a large Seder plate on which are arranged examples of ritual food as well as other symbolic objects to be used during the evening. The exact choices vary according to the family tradition. They include a lamb shank or a beet to symbolize the blood of the Passover sacrificial lamb that was placed before each door so that God would "pass over it," a green vegetable representing spring, bitter herbs for the bitterness of slavery, an egg for rebirth, matzah for the unleavened bread, *haroset* (walnuts, wine, apples, cinnamon, and honey) for the mortar used in making the bricks, and a cup to welcome the prophet Elijah. Two recent additions are a cup to represent the well of Miriam, Moses' sister, which supplied the people with water in the desert, and an orange as a response to the rabbi who declared that it was as unlikely for there to be a woman rabbi on the pulpit as an orange on a Seder plate. As the wine is sipped and the ritual food is eaten, each person at the table reads, in turn, a part of the story of the exodus from Egypt.

The story of Passover has roots that go back to God's warning to Abraham that his descendants would be enslaved in a foreign land for four hundred years. It involves hundreds of stories, legends, and traditions. From as early as the second century C.E., the rabbis debated how to bring order to the story of the formation of the Jewish people. An anthology of stories and traditions was agreed upon and written down in the eighth century in a specific order in a book called the Haggadah, meaning "story." Each generation has revised the Passover Haggadah according to its own understanding of liberation.

The story and the ritual of the Seder invite the participation of all generations. In many ways, it is a children's holiday. Often, the holiday takes place in the home where the grandparents, rather than the rabbis, are in charge. There is a lot of singing and eating ritual food with the fingers. The children are allowed to stay up late and encouraged to ask questions. The youngest child's asking of "The Four Questions" starts off the Seder.

About Passover

Passover is fun! I was taken to my first Seder before I could speak. My earliest memories are of a table that stretched into two rooms, candles, delicious smells, many languages, many children, laughter, and singing. The white tablecloths always got dirty. Drinks spilled and no one worried. My grandfather spoke in Yiddish and read in Hebrew. I didn't understand his words. But from watching my older cousins, I knew that one day when I was grown up (five or six years old), it would be my turn to ask "The Four Questions."

At the Seder, "hide and seek" is played by the leader and the children. At the beginning of the meal, the leader holds up a piece of matzah called the *afikoman* (meaning "dessert"), and says, "I'm going to break the *afikoman* into two halves and hide one of the halves. Whoever finds it can claim a prize, but we cannot finish the meal until the missing half is found."

"Prize" is a magic word for the children. Its promise draws them to stay close to the table even though the Passover meal with its readings, songs, and discussions may go on for three, four, even five hours. At the end of the meal, when the long-awaited moment arrives, the leader fusses over the child who has found the *afikoman*, thus making it clear that the children are essential and that the ceremonial meal cannot be completed without them. The *afikoman* is then broken into small pieces and all the generations "eat" part of the story.

At one Passover Seder, my rabbi, Shlomo Carlebach, said, "Knowledge doesn't come from the head. It must be tasted. We need teeth to cut the infinite and make it finite."

Exodus

I Will Become Who I Will Become

At the Passover festival the rabbis remind us that "in every generation each of us should see ourselves as if we had come out of Egypt." If we imagine that at the very moment that we are leaving Egypt (three thousand years ago) God is commanding us to tell the story of what is happening to us to our children when we arrive in the Promised Land, we realize that through stories and storytelling God is linking us to our ancestors and to our descendants. Let there be memory and awareness, God is telling us. Let there be stories!

What follows is the full story of Passover, beginning with Jacob and his family going to Egypt because of the famine in Canaan (around 1450 B.C.E.) and ending with Moses leading the Hebrew people out of Egypt (around 1250 B.C.E.).

This is a story of birth and transformation. An entire people moves from slavery to freedom. The everyday world splits apart, and raw energy pours out in unexpected forms—visions, snakes, parting of the seas.

In the story, I refer to the Red Sea as the Reed Sea, which is the translation of its Hebrew name. And from the moment God appears as the burning bush, I follow the tradition of the rabbis of the first century by often using the name Shechinah for God's feminine presence on earth. As for the sources of the story, the elaborations on Moses' sister, Miriam, are mine; the other legends that I've woven into the biblical text are the rabbis'.

*B*efore the Hebrews were slaves in Egypt, their ancestor Joseph had been governor of Egypt. He had advised Pharaoh to store grain when it was in abundance so there would be food in times of famine. Pharaoh had followed Joseph's advice and when the famine came, and spread to Canaan, Joseph asked Pharaoh to allow his father, Jacob, to settle in Egypt. Pharaoh agreed.

Jacob and his seventy relatives went down from Canaan to Goshen. There, they tended their flocks, lived peacefully, and had children—and more children. But after Joseph's death, a new pharaoh ruled Egypt who was afraid of Joseph's relatives who were becoming numerous and powerful. He spoke to his advisor Balaam who offered the Hebrew men large wages to give up shepherding and build pyramids.

Within months, Balaam reduced their wages and then took away their land. Every morning the men mixed water, sand, and straw to make bricks. All day they carried, loaded, and set bricks. At night they were so tired they nearly fell asleep in the fields. Their wives brought their husbands dinner. And after the men ate, the women held mirrors in front of their husbands and whispered, "Look into the mirror. Oh, who is that beautiful woman next to you?" The men turned to their wives, and the Hebrews continued to have children.

When Pharaoh saw that the number of Hebrew children was increasing, he summoned the two most powerful Hebrew midwives, Shifrah and Puah, and said to them, "When your women give birth, let the girls live. Throw the boys into the Nile." The midwives feared their God more than Pharaoh and let all the children live. Pharaoh summoned the midwives again and said, "Your people are continuing to multiply."

"What can we do?" they protested. "The women are so lively they give birth before we arrive." Pharaoh then ordered any Egyptian who found a newborn Hebrew boy to throw that child into the Nile.

During this time, a young Hebrew midwife named Miriam went to her father, Amram. After Pharaoh's decree, Amram, a righteous man and the great-grandson of Jacob, separated from his wife, for he did not want to cause the death of a newborn child.

Miriam challenged her father, saying, "In this dark time, our midwives have held on to their faith and courage, but you, by separating from our mother, are encouraging other families to separate and are preventing the births of sons and daughters.

"Father, listen to me. The other night I had a vision. I was standing by the sea and saw a white stone. I lifted it. Light entered the stone, causing a bright path to spread across the waters. On the other side of the water an angel beckoned to me. I leapt into the water with my brother, Aaron, and we started to swim. When we arrived at the other side, the angel said, 'You and your brother will lead your people out of slavery to a new way of life.' But when I turned to my brother, it was not Aaron, it was a brother who has not yet been born. Father, come home to our mother."

Amram listened to his daughter's prophecy. He returned to his wife, Yocheved, and they remarried. Miriam and her brother, Aaron, danced at their parents' wedding, while playing their tambourines and singing.

Six months later, Yocheved, who did not show signs of being pregnant, gave birth to a child whose light filled the house. Miriam, her brother, Aaron, and their father could not resist this little boy whose eyes were filled with love and curiosity. But before the child was nine months old, rather than risk the Egyptians discovering and killing him, Yocheved and Miriam took the boy to the Nile. There, Yocheved wove a cradle from the long reeds growing by the river. She sealed it with pitch and covered it with bulrushes. With great tenderness, she slipped her child into the ark and pushed it off into the water. She watched it drift with the current until it was out of sight. Then she went home. But Miriam did not leave the child. She followed the ark as it drifted in the currents of the Nile.

The day was hot. Pharaoh's daughter, the princess Bithiah went to bathe in the Nile. She noticed a little boat in the river and reached out and pulled it to her. Lifting the bulrushes, she saw a child whose face was shining with light. "What a beautiful child," she said. "It must be a Hebrew infant."

A moment later, when the baby started to cry, Miriam, who had been watching by the shore, quickly waded into the water and said to the princess, "I know a mother who is nursing. Shall I bring her?"

"Go," the princess answered.

Miriam ran home and returned with Yocheved, who brought the crying baby to her breast. Immediately, he nursed and was quiet. "Take the child," the princess said. "Nurse him and bring him back to me when he is weaned."

Yocheved brought the boy home. Everyone loved him. Each one called him by a favorite name. His mother called him Jekuthiel, meaning "God returned him," his sister called him Jered, meaning "I descended into the river," and his father called him Heber, meaning "unite," for the child had reunited the family. Two years later, when they brought him to the princess, she took him in her arms and called him Moses, explaining, "I drew him out of the water." And of all the names that had been given to him, the name the princess gave him became his name, for though she was not his blood mother, she cared for him and loved him like a mother.

When Moses was three years old, he was sitting on his mother Bithiah's lap at the royal table next to Pharaoh. Suddenly, he reached out, grabbed his grandfather's crown, and put it on his own head. Surprised, Pharaoh asked, "What is the boy doing?" His advisor Balaam answered, "Your majesty, the boy intends to steal your power. He must be killed at once—"

"Nonsense!" interrupted Jethro, another advisor at the table. "He's just a child. He likes what is bright and glittering. Let's make a test. Put an onyx and a red-hot coal in front of him. If he takes the bright coal, he is clearly innocent. If he reaches for the precious onyx, we will know his intentions are evil and we will kill him."

A burning bright coal and a black onyx were set before the child. As Moses stretched out his hand toward the precious stone, the angel Gabriel, the guardian angel of children, guided his hand to the fiery coal. Moses brought the coal to his mouth and burned his lips and part of his tongue. From that moment on he stuttered, but he lived.

The princess wanted Moses to be the next pharaoh, so she hired the best teachers from foreign lands to instruct her son in philosophy, arts, sciences, and magic. Remembering only what was true, Moses learned quickly. As the adopted son of the princess Bithiah, he was called the young king, and people expected he would be the next pharaoh.

When he was forty, Moses was given a small crown to wear and was sent to travel around Egypt. One day when he was visiting Goshen, a woman came up to him and started to speak. "I am your sister, Miriam," she said. "When you were a child our father called you Heber because you reunited our family. Now we need your courage to unite our people." Miriam invited Moses to come home with her, and Moses stayed with his family in Goshen. At night, he listened to the stories Miriam told him about their ancestors. During the day, he watched the Hebrews toiling in the fields being whipped, beaten, and tortured.

One day, Moses saw an Egyptian taskmaster brutally whip a Hebrew man. Moses looked around. When he saw no one was watching, he struck the Egyptian and hid his body in the sand. The next day Moses returned to the same place and saw two men fighting. One of them, Dathan, was the same man who had been whipped by the Egyptian taskmaster. "Why are you fighting your kinsman?" Moses asked him.

Dathan answered in a voice loud enough for those at a distance to hear, "Who made you a judge? Do you mean to kill me as you killed the Egyptian? You pretend to be the son of the princess, but we know you're the son of a Hebrew midwife!"

As word arrived that Pharaoh wanted Moses to return to the palace, a messenger also came from Bithiah. He whispered in Moses' ear, "Flee! Flee so you might live." The prince who had been preparing for years to be the next king fled from Egypt not knowing where he was going.

For days and months, Moses wandered in the wilderness until he came to the land of Midian. As he approached a well, he saw seven sisters drawing water for their sheep. Rough shepherds tried to push them aside, but Moses protected the young women. One of the sisters brought Moses water. She told him her name was Zipporah and placed her necklace around his neck and pulled him gently, encouraging him to accompany her and her sisters to their home.

When Moses told his story to Zipporah's father, Jethro recognized the stuttering Egyptian from Pharaoh's court. After Moses had eaten, he said to him, "When you were a child, I was an advisor to Pharaoh, but I left and wandered through many lands, studying with many holy people until I found my own gods to serve. I have seven daughters. If you agree to tend my sheep and raise your first child in my tradition, you may choose one of my daughters to marry and live here safely." Moses agreed. He chose Zipporah, and when their first child was born, he named him Gershom, meaning "I am a stranger in a foreign land." Moses studied with Jethro and served him faithfully.

For forty years Moses tended Jethro's sheep and never lost a single one. During this time Pharaoh had died. The Hebrews who were slaves in Egypt hoped that the next pharaoh would lighten their burdens, but the new pharaoh was even more cruel. He forced the Hebrew fathers who could not meet their daily quota of bricks to throw their own infants into the mortar. At last, the Hebrews cried out to God in anguish, "Have you forgotten your people? Have you forgotten the land you promised us?"

One day Moses was wandering on Mount Horeb, God's mountain. From the corner of his eye he saw flames flying out of the top of a thorn bush while the lower part was filled with blossoms. As he started in the direction of the fire, a voice called, "Moses! Moses!"

"*Hineni.* Here I am," Moses answered.

"Do not come closer," the voice said, "for the place on which you are standing is sacred ground. Take off your sandals. I am the Shechinah, the presence of God who appears on earth."

Moses took off his sandals.

"I am the God of your ancestors. I have heard the cries of your people in Egypt and have seen their suffering. You are to return to Egypt and go to Pharaoh and tell him to release the Hebrews."

"Me? Who am I to tell Pharaoh to free his slaves?"

"I will go with you."

"And if the people ask your name, what name shall I say?"

"*Ehyeh Asher Ehyeh*—I will become who I will become," the Shechinah answered. "Tell them that they may know me by the name Yahweh. They will listen to you. Then tell Pharaoh, 'Our God Yahweh wishes us to journey three days into the wilderness to make an offering.' Pharaoh will not agree to free his slaves so I must strike Egypt with signs and wonders until Egypt knows I am God, and Pharaoh frees you. Then you will leave Egypt with gold and silver."

"My sister told me how you spoke with our ancestors. But I am not like Abraham. I am slow of tongue and speech. I do not have much to say. I—I cannot—"

"Who created mouths and tongues? Who created ears and eyes? How was it that you escaped from Egypt and no guard saw you? I will be with you, and your brother, Aaron, will speak for you. Return. Your sister and brother are on their way to meet you."

When Moses went down from God's mountain, his wife, Zipporah, greeted him with their second son. Moses named him Eliezer, meaning "God is my help." He went to Jethro and said, "Release me from my vow so I may return to Egypt to see if my family is alive."

"Go in peace," Jethro said. He blessed Moses and gave him the staff that he had brought out of Egypt that had once belonged to Joseph.

That evening as they were about to set up camp, Moses fell from his donkey. A great snake arose out of the earth. Before Zipporah could cry out, the snake swallowed Moses' legs up to his genitals. Zipporah, who was a priestess, understood that Moses' God was testing them.

She grabbed their second son, Eliezer. Quickly, she cut off his foreskin with a flint stone and said to Moses, "My father made you promise that our first child would be raised in his tradition; but when our second child was born, you were on the mountain, and I did not circumcise him." Zipporah wiped Eliezer's blood on the snake and continued, "My husband, my bridegroom of blood, now your covenant with your God is complete. Our son Eliezer will be as you are." With these words, the snake released Moses and slid back into the earth.

The family continued on their way. Outside Goshen, they met Miriam and Aaron who rejoiced to see their brother. Moses told them what Yahweh had commanded him, and Aaron said, "We will speak with the elders tonight, but let Zipporah and your sons go back to Midian where they will be safe." Despite Zipporah's protests, Moses persuaded her to return to Midian.

Miriam ran to tell the people that her brother had returned.

Serach, the oldest woman among the elders, quietly said, "Yahweh is the name my grandfather Jacob spoke of. He said our God, Yahweh, would lead us out of Egypt."

Moses was eighty years old and Aaron was eighty-three when they entered the great Egyptian palace. They went to Pharaoh, and Aaron said, "Our God, Yahweh, has commanded us to journey three days into the wilderness to give an offering and make a festival."

"*Yahweh?*" repeated Pharaoh. "I have never heard of Yahweh. Who is Yahweh that I should listen to his voice?"

Moses answered, "My God, Yahweh, is the place whose name is mystery."

"Whoever Yahweh is, whatever he wants, the Hebrews are my slaves. If they don't have enough work, let them bring their own straw to make the bricks."

The people complained to Miriam, "Your brother is increasing our suffering."

Moses asked God, "Why are you causing the people more suffering?"

God answered, "Tell the people I will be their God and lead them out of slavery, but Pharaoh will need to see a great show of force to agree. Even then, he will not agree. So I will create signs and wonders until not only Pharaoh but every Hebrew and every Egyptian knows I am Yahweh. Go to Pharaoh, and when he asks for a marvel, let Aaron throw down his staff."

They returned to the palace. Aaron threw down his shepherd's staff and it became a snake. Pharaoh's magicians threw down their staffs and they became snakes. Aaron's snake swallowed their snakes, but Pharaoh hardened his heart and would not let the Hebrews go.

Now God said to Moses, "Go to Pharaoh in the morning before he washes in the lake and say, 'So that you know who Yahweh is, Yahweh will change the water of Egypt to blood.' "

Aaron, at God's command, struck the Nile with his staff. The river and all the water in Egypt transformed into blood. But when Pharaoh's magicians also changed the water to blood, Pharaoh hardened his heart and would not let the Hebrews go.

At God's command, Aaron stretched his staff over the Nile. Frogs jumped out of the river, entering the palace, the houses, the bedrooms, the cups, the bowls, the food. Pharaoh summoned Moses and Aaron and said, "Plead with your God to remove the frogs, and I will let your people go."

Moses went to Miriam and said, "The moment you prophesied is here. Pharaoh has agreed to let us go. The people know you; they trust you. Speak with them and ask them to prepare to leave Egypt."

Miriam had visited almost every Hebrew household in Goshen to help the women give birth. Now she went from house to house and said, "God has listened to our pleas. Pharaoh has told Moses that we may leave Egypt." The people began to prepare, but as soon as Yahweh removed the frogs, Pharaoh hardened his heart and would not let them go.

Aaron, at God's command, struck the earth with his staff. The dust changed into lice, tiny creatures who attacked the bodies of every person and every animal. Pharaoh's magicians struck the earth with their staffs but they could not create life. "This God is powerful," they said.

Then God sent buzzing insects, which for seven days bit the Egyptians and buzzed incessantly until Pharaoh sent for Moses and Aaron and said, "Serve your God here."

Moses said, "We cannot. If we offer an animal sacred to the Egyptians, they will stone us. We must go into the wilderness to serve our God."

"Go then, but do not go far, and ask your God to take away these insects!"

Moses said to Miriam, "Pharaoh has agreed to our leaving. Tell the people to prepare." Again, Miriam did as Moses asked, but as soon as God removed the insects, Pharaoh hardened his heart and would not let the Hebrews go.

God then sent an illness that killed the horses, donkeys, camels, cows, and sheep. When Pharaoh heard that no animals had been killed in Goshen, he hardened his heart and would not let the Hebrews go.

Moses, at God's command, threw fistfuls of soot toward the sky. The soot erupted as boils and blisters on every person and every animal. Then God said to Moses and Aaron, "Go to Pharaoh in the morning and say, 'Our God Yahweh says, "I have let you and your people live so you will know my power. But if you do not let my people leave to serve me, I will send a hailstorm to destroy every animal and every person who remains in the fields." ' " Many Egyptians feared Yahweh and brought their servants and animals inside.

At God's command, Moses lifted his staff to the heavens. Hail filled with fire pounded the land. It shattered the trees, smashed the plants, and killed every person and animal that was not inside. But there was no hail in Goshen. Pharaoh summoned Moses and Aaron and said, "My people and I are guilty. Plead with your God to stop the thunder and hail and you may leave." Moses spread his arms in prayer. But when God stopped the hail, Pharaoh and his courtiers again hardened their hearts.

God then said to Moses and Aaron, "I have hardened Pharaoh's heart so that you can tell your children and grandchildren how I was forced to play with Pharaoh and the Egyptians. At first, your children will not understand. But if they consider how difficult it is to change, they will understand how many signs and wonders are needed before saying, 'It is enough.' Now go to Pharaoh and tell him, 'How long will you not listen? Our God Yahweh says, "If you do not let my people leave to serve me, locusts will eat every living thing not destroyed by the hail." ' "

Pharaoh's courtiers pleaded with him, "Let these people serve their God or Egypt will perish."

Pharaoh summoned Moses and Aaron and asked, "Who will you take with you?"

"Our parents, our children—"

"Your *children*? Children don't give offerings. You are intending to escape. Go, but only the men!"

At God's command, Moses stretched his staff over the land and God sent an east wind that brought locusts. Swarms of locusts spread across the earth. The land was dark with locusts. Not one green leaf was left growing in Egypt. Pharaoh summoned Moses and Aaron and said, "I have wronged you and your God. Forgive me. Plead with Yahweh to remove this death!"

With their crops destroyed and the dead bodies of the locusts covering the land, the Hebrews wanted to leave Egypt. But after sending a west wind that lifted the locusts from the land, God hardened Pharaoh's heart, for the Hebrews were not yet eager enough to leave.

Moses raised his hand to the heavens at God's command. A darkness, so dense and deep and thick it could be touched, moved across the earth. For three days and three nights, if anyone tried to light a fire, the darkness swallowed the light. Pharaoh sent for Moses and said, "Go! Take your parents and your children, only leave your flocks so that I know you intend to return."

Moses protested, "But we must take our flocks. We do not know which animals Yahweh wishes us to give as an offering until we are in the wilderness. You must give us animals for burnt offerings."

"Out of my sight, slave!" Pharaoh shouted. "If I see your face again, you will die!"

After Pharaoh's threat, God warned Moses of the last plague. Then Moses said to Pharaoh, "You will not see me again, for Yahweh will bring a last and terrible plague. At midnight, Yahweh will enter Egypt and every firstborn will die. There will be such grief that your people will offer us gold and silver and beg us to leave." Moses walked out of the palace, burning with anger.

God spoke again to Moses, and Moses spoke to Miriam. Miriam alerted every household, saying, "For more than two hundred years we have been slaves in Egypt. Each year that we have been slaves we have lost a part of our souls. Now God has commanded each household to roast a lamb over a fire and eat the lamb with bitter herbs and unleavened bread while wearing our clothes and sandals, ready to leave. This meal will be called a Passover offering. We are to take the blood of a lamb and brush it on our doorposts with a hyssop branch so that God will see the blood and pass over our houses.

"When we come into the land God promised, we are to continue each year on the full moon of the first month of the year to make a Passover offering to remember this night. At the Passover meal, when our children ask us, 'Why are we eating bread that has not risen?' we are to answer, 'We are eating matzah because when we were slaves, we rushed from Egypt to escape from slavery and did not wait for the bread to rise.' Prepare yourselves to leave. We have been waiting for this moment."

At midnight, one by one, God struck the firstborn. A horrific wail traveled through the land from one end of Egypt to the other. Pharaoh had thought that the firstborn meant the firstborn sons. But the firstborn meant every creature that had come out first—male, female, child, parent, grandparent. Thousands died.

Pharaoh and Bithiah went to Moses' house. Bithiah cried out, "My son, why did you harm those who loved and nourished you?"

Moses answered, "My mother, did any harm come to you?"

"Not me, but the family, the servants—Pharaoh is ill."

"Mother, nine times God showed wonders to the household, the servants, to Pharaoh. Each time Pharaoh refused to allow our people to leave."

Suddenly, the voice of Pharaoh cried out: "I release you. Children of Israel, take your flocks and herds, your children, parents and grandparents. You are your own masters. Take what you wish and serve your God."

Pharaoh's voice was heard throughout Egypt so that every Egyptian knew that he had released the Hebrews. When the Hebrews asked for their wages, the Egyptians seeing death all around them gave the Hebrews gold and silver and pleaded with them to leave.

Miriam went from house to house and encouraged the women, saying, "We do not know where we are going, but the Shechinah will lead us and provide what we need. Bring your tambourines so we can sing to her in moments of joy or sorrow or fear."

Moses wanted to find the grave of Joseph, who had made his brothers promise to take his bones when they left Egypt. He asked his mother where Joseph had been buried. Yocheved said, "Speak with Serach. She is Joseph's niece and was alive when Joseph was living." Serach said, "Joseph was embalmed and his coffin was buried in the valley with the dead pharaohs." But there were many dead pharaohs. Moses returned to Yocheved, and she said, "Look with your nose until you smell a fragrance rising from the earth." Moses soon found the place, but the coffin was deep in the ground. So he shouted, "Joseph, son of Jacob! You saved our lives when we came to Egypt, but we are leaving now. The people are waiting. The Shechinah is waiting. Show yourself!" There was a rumbling in the ground, and the coffin of Joseph rose from the earth.

Joseph's father, Jacob, had arrived in Egypt with seventy relatives. Now six hundred thousand Hebrews as well as Egyptians including Bithiah, the mother of Moses, set out for the wilderness. The descendants of Jacob carried Joseph's coffin. The Shechinah led them by day with a pillar of cloud and by night with a pillar of fire.

When three days passed and the Hebrews did not return, Pharaoh and the Egyptians realized that not only had they lost their slaves but their precious gold, silver, and jewelry. Pharaoh ordered his army to pursue the Hebrews.

At the Reed Sea, the Hebrews heard the thundering of Pharaoh's chariots in the distance. They cried to Moses in fear, "What are we to do? Shall we jump into the water and drown? Shall we go into the wilderness and die of thirst? Shall we fight?" But Moses was praying to God and did not answer. So the people turned to Miriam for help. She lifted her voice and cried, "Beat your tambourines. Sing! Praise God! Your prayers are your greatest weapon."

As the people sang, Miriam saw a white stone lying by the sea. She lifted it. Light flashed through the stone into the water. The waters started to rise—higher and higher—forming a transparent ark sixteen hundred feet in the air.

"Moses," God said, "long prayers are good, but not now. As soon as the first person enters the sea, strike the waters with your staff so they separate."

That moment a descendant of Jacob, Nahshon, leapt into the sea, crying to the others, "Follow me!" Moses struck the waters, and they separated. The Hebrews walked into the sea between the two walls of water. A pillar of cloud moved behind them, protecting them from the sight of the Egyptians. When the last Hebrew crossed to the other shore, the Shechinah called to Moses, "Strike the waters."

Uzza, the guardian angel of the Egyptians, cried out, "*Stop!* Why should my people be killed? They enslaved the Hebrews, but they repaid them well with gold and silver." Gabriel, the guardian angel of children, flew off and returned with a brick with a tiny Hebrew infant embedded in the mortar. At the sight of the child, the Shechinah caused Moses' staff to strike the sea, and the vault of waters crashed down on the Egyptians, drowning them. The angels went before God and said, "This is our hour to sing."

"No," God grieved, "I do not wish to listen to singing when the work of my creation is drowning in the sea."

The next morning when the sky cleared, the Egyptians lay dead in the sand. The Hebrews looked at one another.

Suddenly, Moses began to sing. The men joined him in song. Then, Miriam, the prophetess, took up her tambourine and led the women in song. They danced and sang and praised God:

> *O God, our God,*
> *horse and rider you hurled into the sea.*
> *Down into the depths, they fell like a stone.*
> *With the blast of your nostrils,*
> *the waters stood upright like a wall.*
> *Our strength, our song, our salvation,*
> *who in all the world can compare to you?*
> *Glorious, fearful, wondrous,*
> *the mighty of Moab, the tribes of Canaan tremble before you.*
> *In love you lead your people to your mountain,*
> *to your holy dwelling.*
> *You are our God.*
> *We are your people.*

The Hebrews were no longer slaves. They no longer had to carry, load, and set bricks. They no longer belonged to Pharaoh. They were free.

The Song of Songs

Take Us with You!

Your breath is as fragrant as apples,
and your kiss like spiced wine,
flowing smoothly,
stirring the sleeper's lips to speak.

    An incantation, a whisper—the intoxicating lines of The Song of Songs linger long after they are read or spoken. They reveal the yearning in our souls for intimacy whether for another human or for the divine.

    The rabbis chose what they consider to be the love songs between the Hebrew people and God to be read on the Sabbath during Passover. According to the rabbis, the people call to God to come close, and God calls to them "to come away" with him. In terms of human love and passion, the young bold Shulamith runs after King Solomon, and he returns again and again to her mountain of spices.

    If you hear echoes of ancient Egyptian or Mesopotamian love poetry, remember that the Hebrews originated in Mesopotamia and Sumer and spent many years in Egypt before returning again to Babylon.

    This translation closely follows the biblical text.

This is The Song of Songs, which is Solomon's:

She: Let him kiss me with the kisses of his mouth,
     for your love is more wonderful than wine.
     The oils of your body are fragrant.

The sound of your name is perfume.
No wonder the young women love you.
Take me with you and we will run!

I am black and beautiful, O women of Jerusalem,
like the goat hair tents of Kedar
and the silk pavilions of Solomon.
Do not stare at me because I am so dark.
The sun shone on me, burning me.
My mother's sons became angry with me
and set me to work guarding their vineyards,
but my own vineyard, I did not keep.

While the king rests on his bed,
my perfume gives off its fragrance.
My lover is a bag of myrrh between my breasts,
a cluster of henna, plucked from the vineyards of Ein Gedi.

He: You are beautiful, my love.
Your eyes are doves.

She: O love, it is you who are beautiful,
you who are radiant.
Our bed is fresh and green.
The beams of our house are cedar
and the rafters cypress.

I am a crocus growing on the plains;
a lily growing in the valleys.

He: My love among the young women
is like a lily among the thistles.

She: My love among the young men
is like an apple tree among the trees of the forest.

I long to sit in his shade and to taste his sweet fruit.
He brings me into his vineyard.
His banner of love flies over me.
O, my beloved, feed me with raisin cakes,
comfort me with apples, for I am faint with love.

Let his left hand lie under my head
and his right hand caress me.
Young women of Jerusalem, swear to me,
by the gazelles and does of the field,
that you will not arouse or stir love
until love is ready to awake.

Listen! Do you hear?
It is the voice of my love.
Here he comes, leaping over the mountains,
bounding over the hills.
My love is like a buck, like a young stag.
He is here, standing behind our wall.
He looks through the window,
peers through the lattices,
raises his voice and calls to me.

He: Rise, my love, my lovely one, and come away
     with me.
The winter is past,
the rains are gone and
the buds appear on the earth.
The time for singing has come.
The voice of the turtle dove is heard in the land.
The fig trees form their first fruits.
The blossoming vines give off their fragrance.
Rise, my love, my lovely one, and come away with me!

O, my dove in the clefts of the cliff,
in the secret places of the rock,
let me see your face.

Let me hear your voice, for your voice is clear
and your face is beautiful.

She: Young women of Jerusalem, catch the foxes,
the little foxes who spoil the vineyard;
for our vineyard has just come into blossom.
My love is mine and I am his.
He feeds among the lilies.

When the evening winds arise
and the shadows flee,
return, my love,
and be like a buck or a young stag
on the mountain of spices.

At night on my bed,
I sought the one my soul loves.
I looked for him, but I did not find him.
I shall get up now and go about the city,
into the streets and open places,
searching for the one my soul loves.
I asked for him, but I did not find him.
The watchmen who go about the city found me.
"Have you seen him? Have you seen my love?" I asked them.
A moment after they passed, I found him,
and when I found him I seized him and would not let him go
until I brought him into my mother's house
and into the bedroom of the one who conceived me.
Young women of Jerusalem, swear to me,
by the gazelles and does of the field,
that you will not arouse or stir love
until love is ready to awake.

The Women: Who is she who comes up from the wilderness
surrounded by pillars of smoke,
perfumed with myrrh and frankincense

and all the powders of the peddlers?
Look! Look well!
It is the bed of Solomon escorted by sixty warriors.
Each one is skilled in battle,
yet each one carries a sword on his thigh
to protect him from the terrors of the night.
From the trees of Lebanon,
King Solomon had a palanquin made.
Its posts are silver, its headboard gold,
its cushions purple wool; and the insides paved
with the love of the young women of Jerusalem.

Young women of Jerusalem, come out!
Come out and look at King Solomon!
He is wearing the crown his mother crowned him with
on his wedding day,
the day of the great joy of his heart.

He: My love, you are beautiful,
Your eyes are doves behind your veil.
Your hair is like a flock of goats,
streaming down the side of Mount Gilead.
Your teeth are like two rows of sheep coming up from the
    washing;
each one has a twin and not one is alone.
Your lips are a thread of scarlet wool.
Your mouth is lovely.
Your neck is like David's tower.
The strands of your necklaces are placed one upon another.
From the beads of your necklaces hang a thousand shields
belonging to the mighty warriors.
Your breasts are two fawns,
twins of a gazelle, browsing among the lilies.

When the evening winds arise
and the shadows flee,
I will return to the mountain of myrrh

and the hill of frankincense.
My love, you are beautiful, there is no blemish in you.

My bride, come with me from Lebanon.
We will gaze at the peaks of Amana, of Senir and Hermon.
We will pass dens of lions and mountains of panthers.
You have ravished my heart.
My sister, my bride you have ravished my soul
with one glance of your eye,
with one bead of your necklace.
Your lips drip honey, my bride,
honey and milk lie under your tongue,
and the fragrance of your dress
is the fragrance of Lebanon.

A closed garden is my sister, my bride,
a closed well, a sealed fountain.
Your plants form an orchard of pomegranates,
laden with ripe fruit and sweet spices—
henna, nard, saffron, calamus, cinnamon—
branches of incense, myrrh, aloes—all the sweetest spices.
The well in your garden is a fountain of living waters,
rushing down from Lebanon.

She: O north wind, awake! South wind, rise up!
Blow on my garden and let my spices flow.
Let my love enter his garden and eat his sweet fruit.

He: My sister, my bride, I have entered my garden.
I have gathered my myrrh with my spices.
I have eaten my honeycomb with my honey.
I have drunk my wine with my milk.
Eat, friends, drink! Drink and become drunk with love!

She: I was sleeping, but my heart was awake.
Listen, my love is knocking at the door.

He: Let me in, my friend, my dove, my perfect one.
Let me in, for my head is drenched with dew
and my hair is damp with the night mist.

She: I have taken off my dress.
Shall I put it on again?
I have washed my feet.
Shall I soil them again?

My love thrust his hand
into the opening in the door
and my insides quivered.
I got up to open for my love
but he had turned and gone away.
My soul fainted when I remembered the words he had spoken.
I searched for him, but I did not find him.
I called to him, but he did not answer me.
The watchmen who go about the city found me.
They struck me; they bruised me.
The guardians of the wall took my shawl from me.
Young women of Jerusalem, swear to me,
that if you find my beloved,
you will tell him that I am faint with love.

The Women: Most beautiful of women, how is your lover
so different that you would make us swear like this?

She: My love is shining and ruddy;
the tallest one in a crowd of ten thousand men.
His face is like burnished gold.
His hair is black and curled like a raven's.
His eyes are doves.
His cheeks beds of spices,
banks of sweet-smelling herbs.

His lips are lilies, dripping fragrant myrrh.
His loins are the smoothest ivory,
adorned with bright sapphires.
His legs are pillars of marble on foundations of gold.
He is as wondrous to look at as the cedars of Lebanon.
His mouth is full of sweetness.
All of him is a delight.
He is my friend; he is my love.

The Women: Most beautiful of women,
Where did your beloved go?
Tell us, so we can help you find him.

She: My love has gone down to his garden,
to the beds of spices.
He has gone to feed in his garden and to gather lilies.
I am his and he is mine.
He feeds among the lilies.

He: Beloved, you are as lovely as the green fields of Tirzah,
as radiant as Jerusalem,
as awesome as an army with great banners.
Turn your eyes away from me,
for they overwhelm me.

Sixty are the queens.
Eighty are the concubines.
There are young women without number,
but one is my dove.
She is perfect—
as bright as the morning star
as lovely as the moon,
as radiant as the sun,
as awesome as an army with great banners.

She: I went down to the walnut garden
   to look at the first fruits of the valley,
   to see if the grapevine was in blossom
   and if the pomegranates were in flower.
   And I do not know how it was but my soul swooned,
   and I found myself in a chariot next to my prince.

The Women: Turn! Turn, O Shulamith!
   Dance for us so we can gaze at you!

She: And what will you see when you gaze at Shulamith
   as she dances the Dance of the Two Armies?

The Women: O prince's daughter, how graceful are your feet in san-
      dals.
   The curves of your thighs are like ornaments
   crafted by artists' hands.
   Your womb is a moon-shaped goblet never wanting for wine.
   Your belly is a heap of wheat, surrounded by lilies.
   Your breasts are two fawns, twins of a gazelle.
   Your flowing hair is crimson.
   The king is held captive in its tresses.

He: How beautiful you are! How lovely you are!
   You are love in all its delights!
   Your figure is like a palm tree,
   and your breasts are like clusters of dates.
   I am thinking of climbing that palm tree
   and taking hold of the branches.
   Then your breasts will be soft as grapes.
   your breath as fragrant as apples,
   and your kiss like spiced wine,
   flowing smoothly,
   stirring the sleeper's lips to speak.

She: I belong to my beloved and his longing is for me.
Come, my love, to the fields.
We will go to the vineyards.
We will see if the grapevines are in blossom,
if the first buds of the grapes have formed,
and if the pomegranates are in flower.
There, I will give you my love.
Precious fruit, new and old, wait at our door;
precious fruit, that I have been storing for you.

If only you were my brother
who had nursed at the breasts of my mother,
I could kiss you when we met on the street
and no one would scorn me.
I could bring you into my mother's house
and you would teach me.
You would drink the spiced wine
from the juice of my pomegranates.

O let his left hand lie under my head
and his right hand caress me.
Young women of Jerusalem, swear to me
that you will not arouse or stir love
until love is ready to awake.

The Women: Who is she who comes up from the wilderness
leaning on her lover's arm?

She: I woke you with love under the apple tree,
there where she who gave birth to you conceived you.

Set me as a seal on your heart
and as a seal on your arm,
for love is as strong as death.
Its passions are as cruel as the grave
and its fire is the very flame of God.

Many waters cannot quench love,
nor can the floods sweep it away.
If a man were to give all his wealth to buy love
he would be laughed at and scorned.

The brothers: We have a little sister,
and her breasts are not yet formed.
What shall we do for our sister
on the day her suitors arrive?
If she were a wall,
we would build turrets of silver around her.
If she were a door,
we would enclose her in planks of cedar.

She: I am a wall, and my breasts are like towers.
I have found favor in my lover's eyes,
and I am at peace.
Solomon, you gave your vineyard at Baal Hamon
to your caretakers. Each man had to pay
one thousand pieces of silver for the fruit.
O Solomon, I take care of my own vineyard.
Here are one thousand pieces of silver for you,
and two hundred pieces of silver for those who guard your fruit.

He: My love, you sit in your garden,
and your friends hear your voice.
Let me too hear your voice.

She: Then make haste, my beloved,
and be like a buck or a young stag
on the mountain of spices.

Josiah

Falling Out of God's Embrace

With one battle we can gain physical freedom. Spiritual freedom is a longer route. From the time they arrived in the Promised Land (about 1150 B.C.E.) to the time of King Josiah (640–609 B.C.E.) generations of Israelites did not keep the Passover celebration as God had commanded. A portion of the story of Josiah (II Kgs 23:1–9) is read on the second day of Passover as a reminder that each generation must bring about its own liberation. I've combined biblical texts, legends, and academic sources in the retelling of Josiah.

Josiah, the son of the queen mother, Adidah, was eight years old when he became king. In the eighteenth year of his reign, he said to his scribe, Shaphan, "The Temple is in disrepair. Tell the high priest, Hilkiah, to weigh the silver that's been collected from the people and give it to the overseers to pay the workers so they can buy wood and stones to repair the Temple. Do not check on the silver you give the workmen, for they will surely be honest when they repair the Temple."

The scribe delivered the king's message. A few days later, the high priest sent for the scribe and said, "One of the workmen found an old scroll in the Temple that may be the teachings of Moses." Shaphan

30

opened the scroll, read it, and went immediately to the king. He pointed to the scroll and said with great excitement, "These are Moses' words."

"Let us hear them," Josiah said.

Shaphan opened the scroll and read, "Children of Israel, do not forget what you saw with your own eyes. Do not let it fade from your mind. Speak to your children and your children's children and tell them of the day you stood before God on Mount Sinai when the entire mountain was in flames and God spoke to you from the fire and commanded you to observe the teachings on the tablets."

"The tablets are here," Josiah said, "both those that are broken and those that are whole are in the holy of holies. Continue."

Shaphan went on: "You heard God's voice speaking from the fire but saw no form. God loves you and brought you out of Egypt. For your own sake, remember that since you saw no shape when God spoke to you, do not make sculpted images of any kind for worship. When you look at the sun, the moon, and the planets in the heavens, do not bow down or serve them—"

"Stop!" Josiah cried out, "Woe! Woe! Our land and Temple are full of statues—statues to Asherah, Astarte, and Baal are everywhere. We have not kept the festivals, the commandments, or the teachings. Woe! Woe to all of us!"

Shaphan rolled up the scroll. Josiah ordered the high priest, the scribe, and his ministers to speak with God. The prophet Jeremiah was not in Jerusalem at that time, so they went to Huldah, the prophetess, and asked her what God intended.

She answered, "Elohim, the God of Israel, says, 'I will bring disaster on this place and on all its inhabitants. Rather than keep the covenant, the people have made offerings to other gods, but I will not destroy the Temple until the death of Josiah who will die in peace.' "

Josiah hid the ark with the tablets so they would not fall into the hands of the enemy. Then he summoned the priests, the prophets, and all the people, young and old. When they had gathered before the

Temple, Josiah stood on a platform and said, "Our high priest, Hilkiah, found a scroll in the Temple. I want all of you to listen and tremble, for these are the words that Moses spoke that were written in the scroll: 'You are a people consecrated to God. If you faithfully observe God's teachings and open your heart and soul to God, you will thrive and dwell on the land. When you have eaten your fill and built fine houses, when your herds and flocks have multiplied, when your silver and gold have increased, and everything you have has prospered, beware that you do not become arrogant and forget the One who led you out of slavery through a wilderness of serpents and scorpions and a parched land with no water. Should you begin to believe that you yourself created your own wealth, remember that God gives you the power to be wealthy in relation to your living harmoniously with the covenant. But if you turn your heart away from God and follow the allure of other gods, bowing down to them, you will fall out of God's embrace.' "

Fearing Moses' words and God's anger, Josiah said, "This covenant was made with us, the living, all of us who are here, today. God is speaking to us. I want every statue in Judah to be destroyed."

Josiah ordered the high priest, the Temple priests, and the guards to tear down the shelters in the Temple where the women put on garments to worship the goddess Asherah. After removing every statue and object belonging to Baal and Asherah from the Temple, they were to burn them in the fields and bring the ashes to Bethel, in the kingdom of Israel.

Throughout Judah, Josiah closed the shrines the former kings of Judah had built and stopped the priests from making offerings to the sun, the moon, the planets, and Baal. He desecrated the altar at Topheth in the valley of Hinnom so that parents would no longer offer their children to the fire of Moloch as sacrifices. He destroyed the horses and burned the chariots that the kings of Judah had dedicated to the sun. He destroyed the shrines to Ashtoreth, Chemosh, and Milcom that King Solomon had built. He continued his campaign in the north. In Bethel, he burned Jeroboam's altar. He abolished every cult place that the kings of Israel had built. He killed the priests who worshiped idols and burned their bones.

Josiah returned to Jerusalem and said to the people, "In the scroll that has been found, Moses reminds us that when our children ask what the teachings of God mean, we are to answer, 'We were slaves in Egypt, and God showed us signs and wonders. God freed us and gave us this land that had been promised to our ancestors, commanding us to keep the festivals and follow the teachings.' Now we will offer the Passover sacrifice to God according to the teachings of Moses."

Since the time of the prophet Samuel, such great feasting had not taken place on Passover in either Israel or Judah. Josiah offered thirty thousand sheep and three thousand oxen. The chiefs of each tribe gave the people and the priests thousands of cattle. The priests offered God sacrifices, by sprinkling blood on the altar. As the people stood together in their tribes waiting to receive their portions, hundreds of musicians from the tribe of Levi played and sang. For seven days all of Israel and Judah ate unleavened bread and celebrated Passover.

Each year, Josiah's fervor increased. He wanted to see the country return to the glory of the time of King Solomon. When Babylon attacked Assyria, the Egyptian king informed Josiah that he intended to march through Israel on his way to help Egypt's ally Assyria. The Egyptian King assured Josiah that no harm would come to Israel. But Josiah knew that if Assyria regained its power, Israel would remain their vassal, so he assembled an army and went to attack Pharaoh on the plains of Megiddo.

The prophet Jeremiah urged Josiah to allow Pharaoh to pass through the land. Josiah disregarded Jeremiah's warning. He was certain that Israel had repented, and God would support him. He sent word back to Jeremiah, saying, "Our teacher, Moses, told us that no sword shall enter Israel when she is living in peace and harmony." Caught up in his own fervor, Josiah did not know that although he had torn down their shrines, the people were secretly worshiping foreign gods.

Josiah imagined that he would not be recognized and entered the battle in disguise. Pharaoh's archers shot at him. Josiah was carried back to Jerusalem with three hundred arrow wounds. Although he died in great pain, he died praising God, "Yahweh is righteous. I am the one who rebelled by not listening to his messenger, Jeremiah."

Jeremiah composed a lament for him. All of Judah and Israel mourned for the first king after Solomon to unite the Hebrew people. Josiah tried to reform Judah and Israel, but within months of Josiah's death, his son, Jehoiakim, brought idols back into the Temple and replaced the worship of Yahweh with the worship of gold statues.

About the Stories

Exodus

I did not dare to approach the story of Moses until I was fifty. Prophet, mystic, revolutionary, murderer, fugitive, judge, diplomat, shaman, general; humble, arrogant, patient, impetuous, compassionate, loving justice—what complexity of character and soul. Moses speaks with God and carries out a revolution, leading half a million people out of the great Egyptian empire into the wilderness. And if Moses didn't exist, as many scholars contend because of the lack of historical proof for such an exodus, the biblical story nevertheless creates a believable fiction about the beginnings of a new nation with a protagonist as complex as beginnings are.

The complexity of Moses' soul and the greatness of his accomplishment eluded my understanding. And there was something more. It was the gaps and changes. In the biblical account, he is an infant; in the next account of him, he is grown and kills an Egyptian. He flees to Midian, returns, and confronts Pharaoh. Later, he flees with the Hebrew people, climbs Mount Sinai, and speaks with the supernatural for days on end. Who is this protean man who keeps changing roles and characters? Pharaoh's daughter named him Moses, meaning "I drew you out of the water." Perhaps the man who leads his people from one land to another and from one spiritual state to another is himself to be understood as embodying water and the quality and ability to change.

Moses is educated for forty years in the sophisticated Egyptian religion, culture, and law. For another forty years, his father-in-law, Jethro, trains him in living in the wilderness as well as in the tenets of other religions. Loved and protected by his mothers, sister, and wife, Moses is uniquely prepared to confront the ruler of Egypt and lead his own people into an unknown wilderness to freedom. But each time Moses is absorbed into one way of life, he is catapulted into change. Forced to separate from his parents, his siblings, his family, his culture, his land, and then his wife and children, he undergoes one initiation after another. It may be that because he is forced to separate so many times from a secure, quotidian existence, Moses is open to and seeks a larger understanding of life.

From the moment God calls to him from the burning bush, Moses hears God's voice and chooses to enter God's service. At the burning bush, God commands Moses to do what he fears—to return to Egypt, where he is wanted for murder, and to speak in public. Moses must confront his fears directly. On his way back to Egypt, a snake rises up and attacks him. The same God also tested Moses' forefathers. Abraham was asked to give up both his sons; Isaac was set on the altar; Jacob wrestled all night with God's messenger; and Joseph was sent into the pit of his brothers' anger. Yahweh sets tests to strengthen his leaders' mettle and to raise their spiritual level.

In Egypt the Hebrews undergo a series of initiations even more frightening than those Moses experienced. God's plagues start their destruction of the world at the lowest level, the sea, and rise vertically in reverse order to the creation (as described in Genesis), ending with the disappearance of light. Each of the ten plagues, like life, varies not only in substance but in delivery and reception. Through the signs and wonders of the plagues, God lets the Hebrews understand that there is a force greater than Pharaoh or the priests or the Egyptian gods. This God, called "I will become who I will become," takes away all that the Hebrews have so they will know that what remains is the naked spirit—the spirit of becoming. And Moses, who has learned again and again to give up everything and give himself over to becoming, leads this vulnerable multitude out of Egypt.

Unlike the plagues, the elevation and parting of the waters celebrates rather than contaminates the elements, recalling the creation of the world and the waters that pour out of the birth canal at the time of birth. As the Hebrews go out of the narrow land and cross over into a new land and a new life, the waters push them out. The fluid, moving, changing waters of the sea remind us of a God who has taken on the new name Yahweh, "I will Become who I will Become."

Miriam acts as a midwife for the nation at the time of their birthing. She prophesies the birth of Moses and a new way of life for her people before Moses is even born. She then protects Moses, educates him, and encourages her people to trust the Egyptian-Midianite stranger. She rallies her people and knows the words to sing to commemorate and celebrate their new freedom.

The Song of Songs

The experience of falling in love transforms our consciousness. The literal meaning of *The Song of Songs* is the love of one woman for one man, one man for one woman. Our reality changes as we awake to another world, another life, an *other*. The other is the lure. Our yearning to join the other is the yearning for wholeness and peace.

Although the awakening is invited, it is also feared. Throughout *The Song of Songs*, the woman urges the daughters of Jerusalem, "Do not wake or stir love until love is ready to awake." The people are to be prepared, for this new state of consciousness will change everything. Nevertheless, although there is still the threat from the watchmen, at the end of *The Song of Songs*, Shulamith is ready for love. She has stored for her lover "all kinds of precious fruit." She has confidence in the strength and beauty of her body ("My breasts are like towers and I have found peace in my lover's eyes") as well as in her own spiritual powers ("O Solomon, I take care of my own vineyard"). Not only is her body young, it is powerful. From her neck hang "a thousand shields belonging to the mighty warriors." She "dances the Dance of Two Armies" and is prepared to defend herself. The lovers court, separate, seek each other and find each other again. Larger than the sum of its parts—the tasting, smelling, touching, hearing, seeing—love leads the lovers to the peace that comes from the experience of oneness.

Traditional rabbis allegorize the relationship between the lovers to represent the relationship between God and the Jewish people. Esoteric allegory from the Zohar describes the first line of the poem, "Let him kiss me with the kisses of his mouth," as the people's yearning to once again be kissed by the Shechinah. On Mount Sinai, when the people had said yes and had accepted God's teachings, the Shechinah had, in the form of the Voice, kissed them on the mouth. The Christian church compares the lovers to Christ and the church. Scholars have traced the love poems in The Song of Songs to the songs that were a part of the Sumerian marriage rite between the Sumerian goddess Inanna and her consort Dumuzi. "Radiant as the sun," "laden with ripe fruits and spices," dancing the dance of the two armies, the beautiful, fecund, and powerful Shulamith clearly resembles the great goddess of love, war, and fertility.

The rabbis' chose this springtime story of budding love to be read at Passover, for it parallels the people's radically new consciousness of moving from slavery to freedom. As Shulamith longs to be with her beloved, the Hebrew people yearn to be with their beloved, Yahweh. "Take me with you and we will run," Shulamith implores her beloved. And the Beloved responds, "Rise, my love, my lovely one, and come away with me." The people move eagerly toward their Beloved and begin the slow, arduous path toward freedom and independence.

Josiah

Achieving physical freedom, which allows us to wander freely from the city to the country as the lovers do in *The Song of Songs*, is the first step. Attaining spiritual freedom is a longer process that can only be known through the experience of failure. In *Josiah*, we read that the people have failed to remember their commitment to their Beloved. When Josiah recovers the book of Moses, he weeps and then destroys the images the people have made.

The Hebrew prophets continually decry the people for breaking their marriage vows and worshiping other gods. The prophet Jeremiah laments: "The children are gathering sticks, the fathers building fires, the mothers kneading dough to make cakes for the Queen of Heaven, and they pour libations to other gods" (Jer 7:17–18). But the people protest against Jeremiah, saying, "We will not listen to you. On the contrary, we will keep our vows and make offerings to the Queen of Heaven to pour out libations for her, as we used to do, we and our fathers, our kings and our princes, in the towns of Judah and the streets of Jerusalem" (Jer 44:16–17).

Archeologists excavating in Israel and Sinai have discovered inscriptions in sanctuaries and on votive materials, dating from the tenth to the sixth centuries B.C.E., that seem to confirm that Asherah, a Canaanite goddess of love and fertility similar to Inanna, was worshiped both alone and in consort with Yahweh. It was not that the people abandoned Yahweh, it was that they worshiped other gods, including female deities, in addition to Yahweh.

Josiah, the youthful king of Judah, insists that the people renew their commitment to Yahweh and the worship of one god. He does more than insist. He zealously removes the cultic objects of the foreign gods and goddesses from the Temple and the sanctuaries throughout Judah and kills those priests who had performed or allowed such rituals to take place. Like Moses, who killed those who made the golden calf (Ex 32:27–28), and both Asa, the king of Judah (I Kgs 15:12–14), and Hezekiah, the king of Israel

(II Kgs 18:3–5), who brought about similar reforms, Josiah is successful. But only temporarily, for in the next generation Jeremiah rails again at the people for going against their covenant. Josiah's willful, impatient methods are effective immediately, but a more mature, more inclusive approach might have led to a more permanent, profound understanding among all the people.

The Bible commands the people to love God with all their heart, all their soul, and all their being. To love God, they are asked by God to study the divine laws and teachings and to care for and honor their neighbor's dignity, property, and reputation. But if a person is killed, where is his or her possibility for change, for learning, for redemption? Is it necessary to sacrifice some so that the others will not be led astray? And yet killing God's creations does not seem to guarantee that the next generation will be any more righteous than the previous one. Forcing spirituality on others does not hasten spiritual freedom. Josiah tries to replace the people's freedom of choice with a king's dictates. Like the leaders before him, the imposition of his will barely lasts a generation. Kings cannot provide spiritual freedom. Spiritual freedom is to know that whatever we do will have consequences.

In the three stories we read at Passover, we see a young nation emerging, a young love blossom, and a youthful idealism leading to zealotry. This is the beginning of the calendar cycle: Both God and the people seek a relationship. But it is God who is in charge. God directs and protects (*Exodus*), writes the rules (*Josiah*), and comes and goes at will (The Beloved in *The Song of Songs*).

Who is this Protector/God whom the new Hebrew nation takes refuge in? There are no names that can define God. God is larger than names or conceptions. In an attempt to speak of God, mystical rabbis of the thirteenth century known as Kabbalists call God "Ein Sof," meaning "the Infinite One," "Emptiness," "Without Limit." In the Kabbalah, there are at least seventy names for God, including the Shechinah—the God who manifests as the burning bush and the pillar of clouds. In the Bible, there are ten names for God.

In *Exodus*, Elohim, the God of justice, sends plagues. Yahweh, the God of mercy, grieves when the Egyptians perish in the Reed Sea. God's name, Yahweh, is a verb that means "to be." The name that God gives to Moses in Exodus at the burning bush, "Ehyeh Asher Ehyeh," can be translated as "I am who I am," "I will Become who I will Become," or

"I was, I am, I will be." The midrashic name that Moses offers Pharaoh when Pharaoh asks where his God came from is "the place whose name is mystery."

Each generation chooses a different name according to their perceptions and needs. The generation who was in the process of birth, who needed to grow and change, understood God's name as "I will become who I will become." Moses, the leader of that generation, accepts the challenge to change. His life reflects his God, "I will become who I will become." Moses moves from one transformation to another. Although the Hebrews initially resist, they accept the new vision he and his God offer and set out with them toward the path of transformation—a path that is offered to all of us.

SHAVUOT

About Shavuot

The holiday of Shavuot celebrates the marriage of God and the Jewish people. The second of the three Jewish pilgrimage festivals, Shavuot, which means "weeks" in Hebrew, takes place seven weeks after Passover. It is observed in the third month of the Jewish calendar (May or June)—the season of new life—on the sixth day in Israel and on the sixth and seventh days outside Israel. Known as the Festival of Weeks, its other names are the Festival of the Harvest and the Day of the First Fruits, referring to the first fruits of the summer harvest brought to the altar in Jerusalem.

During the time of the First and Second Temples (from about 1000 B.C.E. to 70 C.E.), pilgrims walked to the Temple in Jerusalem on Passover to be present when the priests made an offering of barley, the first grain to ripen during the yearly cycle. Fifty days, or seven weeks later, the pilgrims returned with offerings of the first fruits—grapes, pomegranates, figs, and dates. On that fiftieth day, the priests made an offering of two loaves of wheat bread.

After the destruction of the Temples, the rabbis linked the fifty days of the slowly ripening wheat to the first fifty days that the Hebrews wandered in the desert so that the day when the people stood on Mount Sinai and became engaged to God corresponded to the offering of the bread and the first fruits. Shavuot became known as the day Israel received the Torah at Mount Sinai. After the synagogue replaced the Temple, the custom arose for homes and synagogues to be decorated with foliage, flowers, and spices on Shavuot in remembrance of the offering of the first fruits. Traditionally, on Shavuot, dairy foods are eaten to commemorate the youthful commitment on Mount Sinai and the first taste of Torah that nourishes like mother's milk.

Today, observant Jews call the seven weeks between the second day of Passover and Shavuot, the Omer, after the barley offering. (An omer is a measure of barley.) During these seven weeks, they prepare for "the engagement" by studying many texts, including *The Ethics of the Fathers*, which contains the teachings of the rabbis: "Who is wise? The one who learns from everyone. Who is strong? The one who subdues the impulse toward evil. Who is rich? The one who is content. Who is honorable? Whoever honors all that is created." On the evening before the holiday, devout Jews stay up all night studying small sections of each of the books of the Bible in remembrance of the day on Mount Sinai when the nation of Israel heard God's words. On the day of Shavuot, Jews gather in a House of Prayer for the holiday service.

I first tasted Torah as a child of four or five when on Yom Kippur my parents took me to the small shul where my grandfather Chaim Barenbaum prayed. Men were singing with great emotion as they held Torahs. Others shouted and sang and fell to the ground at unexpected moments. I loved the wildness and the fervor. The men called out as if offering themselves to an unknown presence. I did not know what they were saying or singing, but I understood their yearning for the unknowable.

Twenty-five years later, when I entered Shlomo Carlebach's small synagogue on Seventy-ninth Street in New York City, I experienced the same passion and joy and outpouring of love for God. From the beginning of the seventies, I studied Torah with Shlomo. Shlomo often spoke of the heavenly dew that arises when people gather together to learn. Before beginning to study, Shlomo would make jokes (he wanted people to be happy and relaxed) and play his guitar to open our hearts and to summon the Presence. Once people had let go of their everyday minds and concerns and there was a sense of joy in the group, he would quote from the Bible reading of the week and then read from the writings of a Hasidic master, often Rabbi Nachman of Bratslav, which related to the Bible reading. Interweaving his own ideas, Shlomo asked for our thoughts.

During those times of intense learning, no one wanted to be more than the other or to profit from the other. Each of us wanted to draw out the other, to listen, to share, to enlarge our understanding of the text. And there were moments when there was no difference between our love and respect for one another and our love and awe for that which we were seeking to serve.

It is said that when two people study the Torah, the Shechinah is present. The unexpected reward for giving over all that we know to each other is that we become empty vessels, allowing new light to enter. Per-

43

haps God also yearns for such an exchange, for after speaking with Moses, God asks him to create a dwelling place for the conversations to continue on earth.

For the past fifty years, Reform Jews have chosen Shavuot, the time of receiving the Torah, for young men and women to be confirmed at the age of sixteen. When I was a teenager, I had the paradoxical experience of being confirmed in the Reform Temple Israel in South Orange, New Jersey, where its newly affluent members preferred the social and cultural aspects of Judaism to its spiritual core. They insisted on a formal atmosphere during services, yet they chose the young intellectual Herbert Weiner for their rabbi. During the time I studied with him for my confirmation, he was writing *Nine and a Half Mystics*, one of the first books to introduce Americans to Kabbalah; and, whether our parents knew it or not, in preparing us for our confirmations, he was imbuing his young students with a Kabbalistic approach to God and Torah.

Kabbalists believe that each section of the Bible that is studied on the evening of Shavuot adds a jewel or ornament to the bride, the people of Israel who will meet their bridegroom, God, the following day. During the service, before the Torah reading, Sephardic Jews read from a *ketubah* (a marriage contract) between God and the people, written in the sixteenth century by the mystic poet from Safed, Israel Najara:

On the sixth day of the third month, the Invisible One came forth from Sinai. The bridegroom, ruler of rulers, prince of princes, said to his beloved (the people of Israel), who is beautiful as the moon, as radiant as the sun, as awesome as an army with great banners, "Many days you will be mine and I will be your redeemer. I will honor, support, and maintain you. I will be your shelter and refuge in eternal mercy. I will give you the Torah by which you and your children will live in health and peace and harmony."

The bridegroom delivered the Torah that is bigger than the earth and broader than the seas. The bride consented to the covenant and an everlasting agreement was made. As a dowry, the bride brought a heart that understands, ears that listen, and eyes that see.

"May the Bridegroom rejoice with the Bride and the bride rejoice with the husband of her youth, while uttering words of praise."

The Covenant

Clouds by Day, Fire by Night

The pivotal moment in Jewish history is the receiving of the covenant on Mount Sinai (1250 B.C.E.). At this overwhelming moment, a theophany occurs. The Shechinah, God's feminine presence on earth, appears both to Moses and to all the people of Israel. In an attempt to describe the indescribable, the people see the Voice and hear the letters.

The covenant is the agreement made between God and the Hebrew people. God gives the children of Israel a set of laws and teachings to follow which will bring them life and well-being. When the people do not follow the covenant, Moses brings the people a second covenant. According to legend, Moses climbs Mount Sinai three times to discuss, argue, and understand God's teachings. The process of understanding God's teachings as revealed in the covenant continues today in every place that Jews gather to study.

I begin the story after the crossing of the Reed Sea and continue to the completion of the tabernacle. In the story, which is a weaving of midrash with biblical text, when God manifests on earth in physical form I use the word "Shechinah" for God's presence on earth.

*I*n every direction all that could be seen was wilderness. After crossing the Reed Sea, the people asked each other, "How will we survive? What will we eat? Will the nations on this side of the sea attack us?" Some clamored to return to the safety of Egypt. Others eagerly

45

searched the bodies of the dead Egyptians for gold and silver. Moses and Miriam reminded them, "God brought us out of Egypt not to give us gold but to take us to a new land and to give us a new way to live."

From the heavens, a pillar of cloud descended, and the people knew it was the Shechinah, who had promised to lead them through the wilderness. By day, the Shechinah, the presence of God on earth, led them with a pillar of cloud and by night with a pillar of fire. Six hundred thousand people, Hebrews as well as Egyptians, watched the sky day and night. When the Egyptians had witnessed the wonders Yahweh had performed in Egypt, many chose to take this new God as theirs. But now wandering through the treacherous wilderness of Shur, filled with poisonous snakes and scorpions, they began to long for the security of their old lives.

Then someone spotted a shimmering light in the distance, and the people rushed toward a pool of water, scooped it up in their hands only to spit it out, for it was bitter. Moses pleaded with the Shechinah, "The people need water. What good are the waters of Marah if they are bitter?"

The Shechinah answered, "Everything created has a purpose. Pluck the bitter leaves of the oleander tree at the edge of the spring and throw them into the water." Moses did this, and when the people tasted the waters, they were sweet.

From Shur, they traveled to Elim, and from Elim, to the wilderness of Tzin where they ate the last of the food they had brought from Egypt. Then the people, even the most righteous, murmured loudly against Moses and Miriam, saying, "Why did you take us from a place where we had food in abundance—cucumbers, watermelons, fish, meat, bread—to a wilderness? We are six hundred thousand people. How will we survive?"

God heard their complaints. That evening, God sent quail that flew up from the sea and hovered a few feet from the ground. Later that night, a wind swept the desert clean. At dawn, dew fell, and then, manna. In the morning, the people looked up and asked, "What? What is falling from the sky?"

Moses answered, "It is manna, food that God is sending to nourish us. For six days of the week, we are to gather as much manna as we need and not more. On the seventh day we are not to gather manna, for on the sixth day a double portion will be waiting for us so we can rest on the Sabbath."

Each person gathered a different amount, but when it was brought back, each portion weighed the same. For every person the manna had a different taste and texture. To the children, it tasted like milk; to the young people, like bread; to the adults, like coriander seed; and to the sick like sweetened barley. Still even though God had warned the people not to gather manna on the Sabbath, when a few people secretly left their tents to look for extra manna, they found nothing. Those who hoarded manna on other days found that it rotted immediately.

From the wilderness of Tzin the Hebrews went to Rephidim, where there was no water. Again, the people protested loudly. Moses called to God, "These ungrateful people are close to stoning me." God comforted Moses. "Forty days ago, they were slaves. All they know is their stomachs. Do not be angry with them. Lead them as a shepherd leads his flock. With your staff strike the rock at Mount Horeb that I will show you." Moses struck the rock, and clear, sweet water poured out for the people to drink.

Every morning for two hours, warm manna fell from heaven. After the sun shone, it melted into a stream that flowed to other nations who found the water tasted bitter. But when wild animals drank from the stream and were eaten, their meat tasted so delicious that the hunters from other nations envied the Hebrews whose God fed them with manna.

Eight hundred miles to the south, a great hunter named Amalek tasted the tender meat of a wild deer and asked his father, Eliphaz, "Why does the God of the Hebrews perform miracles for them?"

Eliphaz answered, "Their ancestor Abraham took Yahweh as his only God. His son Isaac trusted Yahweh with his life. Isaac's son Jacob wrestled with God all night until God blessed him. God will bless you too if you welcome these weary people. Dig wells for them. Offer them bread and water." But at the sound of Jacob's name, bile rose in Amalek's stomach. Not only had Jacob tricked Amalek's grandfather

Esau out of his birthright, he had spurned Amalek's mother, Timna, who had fallen in love with him. Although Timna had become Amalek's father's concubine, she continued to resent Jacob and Jacob's children.

Amalek sent messages alerting the other nations: "The Hebrew tribes have crossed the Reed Sea. Join me so we can attack them before they conquer the earth." The other nations laughed at him. "Conquer the earth! Their God may have performed wonders for them, but they're ragged, crippled, and maimed from slavery, with hardly any weapons to defend themselves." Amalek ignored them. He gathered his army and set out to destroy the unsuspecting Hebrews.

When Moses saw Amalek's great army approaching, he called to his disciple Joshua, "Sound the ram's horn. Gather the descendants of Rachel to prepare for battle!" Moses climbed to the top of the hill with his brother, Aaron, and Miriam's son Hur. Joshua offered to bring Moses a cushion, but Moses said, "Amalek is already attacking our children, women, cripples, and old people. I cannot be comforted when the weak are being slaughtered. Bring me a stone to sit on." When Moses raised his hands in prayer, the Hebrews remembered to pray and they prevailed. But when Moses' arms grew heavy as if jars of water were pulling them down, Amalek prevailed. Aaron then supported Moses' right hand and Hur his left until Joshua defeated the Amalekites at sunset.

To commemorate their victory Moses built an altar, and the Shechinah said to him, "Write these words on the altar and speak them in the ear of your disciple, Joshua, so he will remember: 'The Amalekites are the only nation who did not know awe when the children of Jacob walked through the waters of the sea unharmed. They rejoice in anguish and destruction. I will be at war for all time with those who do not rejoice in creation.' "

Moses' father-in-law, Jethro, heard of the miracle at the Reed Sea and sent word to Moses, saying, "I am coming to meet you in the wilderness. If I am not worthy, at least come out to meet your wife, Zipporah, and her sons who will be with me."

The Shechinah said to Moses, "I want you to love strangers as I do. Honor your father-in-law and treat him with kindness. You were once a stranger in his land."

Moses and the elders went to greet Jethro. Moses bowed to his father-in-law and kissed him, but there was such happiness it could not be told who kissed the other first. Moses brought his family into his tent and recounted to his wife and father-in-law all that had happened since he had returned to Egypt: his visits to Pharaoh, the plagues, Pharaoh's stubbornness, their departure from Egypt, the parting of the waters, the rejoicing at the Reed Sea. Zipporah listened and wished that she had witnessed God's wonders and been present to celebrate with the women. Moses comforted her, saying, "Every day, God creates wonders."

Jethro spoke to the men, "Until now there has been a magical charm around Egypt and no slaves have been able to escape. Your God is greater than all the other gods. I wish to take your God as my God." Jethro gave a burnt offering and when it ascended, he gave a peace offering for the people. That day an extra portion of manna fell from heaven for Jethro, and he sat and ate with the seventy elders.

The next day, Jethro watched as a never-ending line of people passed in front of Moses' tent. From morning to evening, Moses settled disputes, patiently explaining to each person God's teachings and intentions. After several days, Jethro said to Moses, "If you continue to speak with each person, you will lose your strength. Choose people who love truth and hate injustice and appoint them as leaders over groups of a thousand, a hundred, fifty, and ten. Let them regularly judge the small matters and bring you the difficult questions. This way you will have strength, and the people will have peace, for their disputes will be quickly settled."

Moses followed his father-in-law's advice and a new tranquility and well-being spread through the camp. Seeing that all was well with Moses and Zipporah, Jethro returned to his people, and Moses accompanied his father-in-law for a part of the way on his journey.

For the first time since leaving Egypt, the children of Jacob as well as the other people were at peace with one other. From Rephidim, they went to the wilderness of Sinai. The next day, Moses went up on God's mountain, and God said to Moses, "When you speak to the people, speak first to the women. I made a mistake when I did not speak with Eve. She was justified when she said, 'God commanded Adam, not me, not to eat of the Tree of Knowledge.' Tell the people how I carried them to this place, protecting them as if they were on wings of eagles. If they will act as a nation of priests, caring for each other, and agree to carry out my teachings, they will be a special treasure to me."

Moses relayed God's words to the women and then to the men. The people did not question God's wishes but answered, "We will do and we will obey." Moses returned to God and said, "In their love, the people are willing to do even that which they do not know."

God said, "They are ready. They have been purified by the wonders they have seen and by the manna they have eaten. But first I want to ask the other nations if they wish to join you and receive my covenant."

God asked the descendants of Cain, Ishmael, and Esau to accept the covenant. No nation was willing to change its way of living to accept the covenant. But when the mountains heard that God was about to give the covenant, three mountains—Mount Hermon, Mount Tabor, and Mount Carmel—leapt across the seas and quarreled as to which was the most worthy to receive God's presence, until God interrupted them, saying, "I do not wish to dwell on a mountain that disdains others. When I needed a messenger, Moses humbly asked, 'Who am I to speak?' I am not looking for a mighty mountain. I will give the covenant on the lowly Mount Sinai."

Moses returned to God and said, "The people are eager to see your glory and to hear your voice."

"No other nation wishes to accept the covenant," God answered. "Therefore, you are to be joined to each other and responsible for each other. Before, I spoke with you directly as if through a clear glass; now I will come to you in a thick cloud. Tell the people to prepare by washing their bodies and clothes. Place borders around the mountain beyond which no creature shall pass or it will die. In three days, at the sound of the ram's horn, I will descend the mountain." Moses sanctified the people, giving each one a place to see the revelation.

At dawn, on the fiftieth day since they had left Egypt, there was a long, loud blast of the ram's horn. The people came out of their tents and saw that every part of Mount Sinai was smoking. God had descended into the mountain. Thunder crashed over their heads. Lightning ripped through the air before their eyes. The ram's horn grew louder and louder. The people trembled. The mountain shook. Moses said, "It is time to lead the bride to the bridegroom." As Moses led the people to meet the Shechinah, Mount Sinai in exaltation lifted off the earth and hovered over the people like a wedding canopy.

Suddenly, it was silent. There was no sound in the world—not even a bird singing. Then the Shechinah spoke one word, the word Anochi, meaning "I." The Voice was like seventy voices. Each person saw the Voice according to his or her understanding and power. Sacred words flew through the air and the people heard each letter of every word.

"I am the Lord your God, the Eternal Light, who brought you out of Egypt and out of the house of bondage. You shall serve no other gods."

Each time the Shechinah spoke, a wave of perfume washed over the people.

"You shall not make or bow down to sculpted images or other gods."

The Shechinah's voice burned with such power that after hearing only two teachings the people fell backward in fright. Their souls left their bodies, and two angels were needed to restore each person's soul. The people cried to Moses, "The voice of the Shechinah is too powerful. We will die. Let God speak with you and you repeat the words to us."

So the people stayed at a distance and Moses approached the thick cloud and repeated God's teachings to the people:

> *I am the Lord, your God, the Eternal Light, who brought you out of Egypt and out of the house of bondage. Do not place other gods before me.*
>
> *Do not make or bow down to sculpted images or other gods; it is living waters not stagnant ones that will sustain you.*

Do not swear false oaths using my name; a cracked vessel will not hold water.

Remember the Sabbath day and keep it holy; in resting you will be given life.

Honor your mother and father who, like the sun and the moon, are a part of your creation.

Do not murder.

Do not commit adultery so your children will not commit adultery.

Do not steal so your children will not steal.

Do not testify falsely against your neighbor, for your neighbor is created also in the image of God.

Do not covet what belongs to your neighbor or you will begin to break all the commandments.

Each time the people accepted a teaching, the letters flew back to heaven and were engraved on stone tablets. The Shechinah then said to Moses, "Ascend to the summit so that I can give you the tablets, and you can teach the people."

Before Moses went up the mountain, he built an altar. Each of the tribal chiefs brought a burnt offering. Moses dashed some of the blood on the altar; the rest he put in a basin. He read a part of the covenant to the people, and they said, "All that God has spoken we will do." Moses took the blood from the basin and scattered it over the people, saying, "This is the blood of the covenant. Now you will take on Jacob's name, Israel, that means to wrestle. You will be called Israelites, for you have agreed to wrestle with God. I will return in forty days. Aaron and Hur will act as judges in my place, and whoever has a grievance can consult them."

The people went back to the camp. A pillar of fire covered the summit. Aaron, his sons, the seventy elders, and Joshua accompanied Moses partway up the mountain. There they saw a likeness of God, and under God's feet a pavement of blue sapphires. The seventy elders sat and feasted and then returned to the camp.

Moses waited on the mountain for six days. On the seventh day, a voice from the fire said, "Enter." Moses walked to the summit of God's mountain. The clouds parted and Moses entered the fiery midst.

God said to Moses, "I have made a covenant with the people. They are mine, and I am theirs. I wish to dwell among them. Ask them to prepare a place for my presence. On the first day, I created light. Let the people make an ark of acacia wood to hold the tablets that will be their eternal light. Cover the ark with gold. Carve one end of the ark with a male cherub and the other end with a female cherub. Let the cherubim face each other with their wings touching. My presence, the Shechinah, will descend between the embracing cherubim, and from there I will speak.

"On the second day, I separated the waters. Let them weave a purple, gold, crimson, and blue veil to separate the ark from the rest of the tabernacle.

"On the third day, I created plants and grass. Each day, let them place frankincense and twelve freshly baked loaves of bread on a gold table.

"On the fourth day, I created the sun and the moon. Let them make a seven-branched gold menorah and place it opposite the table. The high priest will light the menorah morning and evening.

"On the fifth day, I created animals. Outside the tabernacle, let them make an altar on which they offer two lambs as sacrifices morning and afternoon. Then let them make a second altar for fragrant incense that is lit morning and evening. Place it inside the tabernacle between the table and the menorah. This will be my favorite altar, for the offerings will be expressions of joy.

"On the sixth day, I created man and woman. Let people of wisdom and understanding make the eight garments to be worn by the high priest. Aaron, your brother, who is devoted to the people's peace and happiness, will be the high priest."

Moses listened as God spoke, but when Moses did not return on the morning of the fortieth day, a frightened crowd confronted Miriam's son Hur. They said: "We're alone in the wilderness. Moses has not returned. We need gods to lead us. We must make an oracle."

Hur addressed them with disdain. "A month ago, you made a covenant with God, agreeing not to make graven images. Now you compete with one another to break your promise. You are no better than slaves!" The frightened crowd killed the nephew of Moses. They carried banners like an army and went to Aaron and shouted, "Moses has abandoned us. We are alone. We need a leader. Make us gods who will advise us what to do."

Certain the women would not agree, Aaron said, "Ask your wives to give you their gold earrings."

The women were in council with Miriam. She spoke to them as a teacher, a mother, a midwife. "Moses will return bringing a new vision. We will all change. Change is part of our lives. When we give birth, we do not know what will happen. Each month we pass through days of change. Is not our God called Ehyeh Asher Ehyeh, 'I will become who I will become'? We dwell in change and often in darkness, yet we know that the Shechinah is guiding us."

The men went to the women and said, "God has abandoned us. Moses has not returned. We are alone. Give us your earrings so we can make a new god to tell us what to do." The women refused. They said, "God has not abandoned us. Look up! Every day God is sustaining us, feeding us with manna."

The men turned from the women and took off their own earrings and nose rings and gave them to Aaron. He cast them in a mold and then placed the mold in the fire. A golden calf emerged. In the morning they brought offerings for the calf and cried, "This is our God who brought us out of Egypt!"

Their wild revels rose to heaven, and God said to Moses, "Go! Your people are prostrating themselves before a golden calf. I will annihilate them. Then I will make another nation for you."

Moses grasped the throne of God and said, "My people? Are they not your people as well? What will the other nations think if you took your people out of Egypt and annihilated them in the mountains?"

"My people accepted my teachings. Your people broke them."

"You told me in the wilderness of Shur that everything created has a purpose. If the people are bitter, take the bitterness out of them and make them sweet. If they are stiff-necked, take the fear out of them and make them courageous. You are the one who made a covenant with our ancestors and swore by your name that their descendants would be as numerous as the stars in the sky and the sands in the sea—"

"Go!" God answered. "Take the tablets!"

Moses went down the fiery mountain, carrying two tablets that were written with God's hand. Joshua was waiting at the foot of the mountain. As they approached the camp, the tablets became heavier. Moses saw men dancing around a golden calf, singing loudly and playing musical instruments. Couples were embracing on the ground in a drunken revelry. Moses looked down at the tablets. The last letters flew from the stone and returned to heaven. He could scarcely hold the weight of the stones. Moses dropped the tablets and they shattered.

In a rage, Moses threw the golden calf into the fire. He ground the gold into powder. He mixed it with water and commanded everyone in the camp to drink. Many died. Moses cried out, "Whoever had nothing to do with the calf, stand beside me." Most of the women and the tribe of Levi joined him.

Moses said, "Those who could not resist making idols must be killed." The Levites killed three thousand men. The next day, Moses said, "In the days of our father Abraham, the firstborn in each family were priests. The descendants of the tribe of Levi who held on to their faith and took action to preserve God's name will now be the priests."

Miriam said, "The women who waited and held on to their faith will be rewarded. The gold they kept for God will be returned to them each month as light. Each month, they will hold a new-moon ceremony and sing and dance to honor the Shechinah who gives us strength to dwell in darkness."

Then the people begged Moses, "Return to God. Ask God to forgive us."

A second time, Moses climbed to the summit of the mountain. Miriam saw his grief as well as his exhilaration. She saw that Zipporah no longer adorned herself as the married women did and understood that Moses no longer visited her. Miriam said to the women, "When Moses returns, he will not go to Zipporah's tent. He will prepare the people to enter the Promised Land."

Moses said to God, "The people ask your forgiveness. They know they have committed a dreadful sin. But if you cannot forgive them, then do not include me in the book you are writing. I do not want to be separated from the people."

God answered, "I will send a plague only on those who sinned against me."

Moses stayed on the mountain another forty days and forty nights. During the days, God and Moses spoke. During the nights, Moses reflected on God's teachings and woke with new visions. After forty days, God said, "It is time for you to lead the people to the land I promised your ancestors, a land flowing with milk and honey. But I will not go with you. The constant rebelliousness of the people enrages me and I might annihilate them. I will send an angel to lead you."

When the people heard that God no longer chose to be with them, they wept and stripped themselves of the gold and silver they had so eagerly sought to possess. Moses withdrew to the outskirts of the camp. The Shechinah hovered over Moses' tent and when the people saw her radiance, they knelt at the entrance to their tents and prayed. Only Joshua was permitted to be near Moses when the Shechinah descended.

Day and night, the Shechinah dwelt near Moses. Moses sensed God's love and said, "If I am to lead the people, I need your help. I need to know when is the moment for justice and when is the moment for compassion."

The Shechinah answered, "My presence will be with you."

"But if you do not go with all the people, how will we be different from any other nation?"

The Shechinah said, "I will go with you and with the people."

Then Moses spoke with great longing. "I want to be closer to you. I want to see your glory."

"You cannot see my face and live, but if you go to the summit of the mountain and stand in a cleft in a rock, I will reveal my back to you. Carve two tablets of stone. Leave early in the morning and tell the people that no one is to go near the mountain or they will die."

For a third time Moses climbed to the summit of the mountain. Each day he was gone, the priests blew a loud, poignant cry on the ram's horn. The people repented and prayed that the Shechinah would return to dwell among them.

On the mountain, the Shechinah passed in front of Moses, revealing, one by one, God's thirteen names of mercy. Moses bowed his head in awe at God's infinite goodness and called on God's attributes: "Compassionate, gracious, slow to anger, abounding in kindness and faithfulness, extending your kindness to the thousandth generation, forgiving transgression yet not remitting all punishment but visiting the iniquity of the parents on the third and fourth generations— Source of All Life, take us again as your people."

The Shechinah answered, "I will go with you and drive out the tribes who have not kept the minimum commandments. But if you do not destroy the altars of those tribes, your children will worship their gods."

After forty days and forty nights, Moses descended the mountain, carrying the tablets God had dictated. As he entered the camp, his face was shining with such brightness that the people withdrew in fear. The next day, Moses covered his face with a veil so the people would not be afraid to approach him. He said to them: "Children of Israel, and those who have chosen to become children of Israel, God has given us a second set of tablets. The first were created with perfect justice. These are fashioned with justice and compassion. God wishes to dwell among us and wishes us to create a dwelling place. God has chosen Miriam's grandson, Bezalel, as the master craftsman. He is filled with wisdom and understanding. He knows the crafts needed to build the tabernacle and how to teach others. Anyone who wishes may bring offerings— goatskins, oil, wood, metal, precious stones, incense. But listen carefully: When you create the tabernacle, you are to work six days, not seven. Just as God rested after creating the world, you are to rest on the Sabbath, for a work of holiness cannot be created without rest."

As the people eagerly began to build the tabernacle, Moses transmitted God's teachings. First he spoke with Aaron, then Aaron's sons, then the seventy elders, and then the people. Moses taught so that every person was able to understand according to his or her own understanding. Four times, the people learned the teachings—from Moses, from Aaron, from Aaron's sons, and then, from the seventy elders. Miriam watched over the building of the tabernacle.

Creating a dwelling place for the Shechinah, and at the same time learning God's teachings, filled the people with joy. They brought so many gifts that Moses had to tell them that no more offerings were needed. In three months, the tabernacle was completed. When Moses saw that the tabernacle had been made exactly as God had asked, even to washbasins made from the mirrors that the women had brought from Egypt, he blessed all the workers. But God wanted them to wait three months so the tabernacle would be dedicated on the first month of the year.

On the first day of the first month of the year, Moses assembled the tabernacle. He placed the stone tablets inside the gold ark. He hung the woven veil. He set the gold table in the north, the gold menorah in the south, and the two altars in their places. Aaron dressed in the eight garments of the high priest. Moses anointed Aaron and Aaron's sons with oil. He took blood from a sacrificed ram and placed it on the right earlobes, right thumbs, and right big toes of Aaron and Aaron's sons so that all their actions in the world might be holy and dedicated to God. Aaron offered a sacrifice, and a fire came down from heaven and consumed it.

Then the Shechinah surrounded and filled the tabernacle, and Moses had to go out of the tabernacle. The people rejoiced that the Shechinah had returned. In heaven, too, there was rejoicing. The Shechinah hovered over the tabernacle in the form of a cloud by day and a pillar by night. The people came to understand that when the cloud descended over the tabernacle, they were to rest; and when the cloud lifted, they were to move on.

For forty years, the Shechinah stayed with the tabernacle and was visible to the Israelites in all their journeys.

Ruth

Where You Go, I Will Go

I love Ruth. I love her passion, her courage, her devotion. She risks her life to follow her mother-in-law into enemy territory. Ruth is a Moabite, her mother-in-law, Naomi, is a Hebrew. The Hebrews refuse to allow Moabites to live with them. But Ruth does not want to be separated from the woman she loves, so on the road between Moab and Bethlehem (around 1100 B.C.E.) she declares her devotion: "Where you go, I will go. Where you live, I will live. Your people will be my people, and your God, my God. Where you die, there, too, I will die, and be buried. . . ."

The book of Ruth is read on Shavuot as an example of commitment. I've interwoven oral legends and my own musings with the biblical text.

When the judges ruled Israel, there was chaos and terrible corruption in the land. There was no king and the people did as they wished. During this time, there was a famine, and a wealthy man belonging to the tribe of Judah left Bethlehem with his wife and two sons. They might have stayed to help their own people, but the husband, Elimelech, chose to go to the land of Moab, even though the Moabites had been enemies of Israel.

Soon after they settled in Moab, Elimelech died, and his wife, Naomi, was left alone with her two sons, Mahlon and Kilyon. The sons married Ruth and Orpah, daughters of Eglon, the king of Moab. Naomi welcomed her daughters-in-law. She rejoiced and danced at their weddings, but then misfortune struck the family—ten years of misfortune. Their horses died; their donkeys died; their camels died. They had no children. Then Naomi's sons both died, and she was left poor and bereft, a widow in a foreign land.

One day, when Naomi was working in the fields, she overheard a wandering peddler say: "God has remembered Judah. There is bread again in Bethlehem. The famine is over." At once, Naomi left the fields where she had been working and the place where she had been living and set out barefoot for Judah. Her two daughters-in-law accompanied her.

After they had gone a short distance, Naomi stopped. She turned to her daughters-in-law, Ruth and Orpah. She embraced them and said, "Thank you for accompanying me on my way, but now, each of you return to your own mother's house. How can I thank you? When your husbands died, you might have run after other men, but you stayed and comforted me, you fed and supported me. May God care for you with as much *hesed*, kindness, as you have shown to me. And may you be blessed with comfort and peace in the homes of new husbands."

Again Naomi kissed them. Standing on the road, the three women raised their voices and wept loudly, realizing that if Naomi went on to Judah and the younger women went back to Moab, they would never see one another again. Suddenly, the two younger women protested, saying, "No. We will go with you to your people."

"Go with *me*?" Naomi exclaimed. "My daughters, why would you go with me? Have I more sons in my womb for you to marry? Return—go home. I'm too old to attract a man, and even if tonight, this very night, I were to marry and bear sons, would you wait until they were grown? Would you wait fifteen years, depriving yourselves of marriage and children? No, no, my daughters, you don't want to be with me. I'm too bitter. God has taken all that is dear to me."

Again, the women raised their voices and wept loudly. Then Orpah kissed her mother-in-law and turned back toward Moab. But Ruth clung to this woman who had been a mother to her. She would not leave her. Naomi said to her, "Look at your sister-in-law. She's going back to her people and her gods. Go! Follow her. Return with her."

Ruth did not move. Naomi said to her, "After our people wandered forty years in the desert and crossed the Reed Sea and were hungry and thirsty and asked your people for bread and water, your people refused. Because of this we do not allow the Moabites to live with us. But even if my people allowed you to stay with me, I do not know if any man would marry you. Then how would you live?"

Ruth heard Naomi's concern. Naomi was willing to risk her own life by walking alone to Judah rather than allow her or Orpah to sacrifice their future. Ruth loved this old woman—her kindness, her fearlessness, her devotion to her God. She wanted to be with her. She did not want to be separated from her. She said to Naomi, "Do not force me to leave you, to turn back and not follow you. Where you go, I will go. Where you live, I will live. Your people will be my people, and your God, my God. Where you die, there, too, I will die, and be buried. May El Shaddai grant me this and more. Only death shall separate you from me." When Naomi saw the firmness of Ruth's decision, she said nothing more.

As the two women walked toward Bethlehem, Orpah walked toward Moab. On the way, a band of wild men attacked her. The child born from the rape, Goliath, was the greatest giant of all time. Orpah had three other children, all giants, and never saw Naomi again.

Near Bethlehem, Naomi and Ruth heard the sound of a milling crowd. They entered the city gates and were told that a funeral for a righteous woman had just taken place. Immediately, the women began to buzz around them, whispering, "Naomi? Is this Naomi? Who is the woman with her? Can this really be the beautiful Naomi who went away so many years ago?"

Naomi answered, "Women of Bethlehem, do not call me Naomi. Naomi means 'sweet,' 'pleasant.' Call me Marah. Marah is bitter! I went away from here full and God has returned me empty. Why would you call me pleasant when El Shaddai, the Nourishing One, has afflicted me with grief and sorrow?"

The two women returned to Bethlehem in May at the beginning of the barley harvest, the first full harvest after many years of famine.

The next day, when Ruth saw the harvesters going to the fields, she said to Naomi, "Let me go and find a field to glean so we can eat."

"Go, my daughter," Naomi said.

Ruth set out, not knowing how she would be treated or received in a foreign land. She walked in one direction and then another, looking for a field to glean where she might be safe. It was her good fortune to choose a field belonging to a wealthy landowner named Boaz, who was a relative of Naomi's husband, Elimelech. That morning, Boaz returned from Bethlehem to inspect his fields.

"God be with you," he greeted his harvesters.

"And may God bless you," they answered him.

Boaz watched his workers and noticed one woman bending from her knees as she gleaned while the other women bent from their hips. She was modest and beautiful. He didn't recognize her, but he was drawn to her. He lowered his voice and asked his foreman, "Who's the new gleaner? Who are her people? Who does she belong to?"

The foreman answered loudly, "She's the Moabite who returned with Naomi from Moab—came early this morning—asked permission to glean. She's been working ever since."

Boaz walked toward Ruth and said, "My daughter, listen to me. Do not glean in any other field. I want you to stay here close to my girls. God has told us, 'When you reap the harvest, do not completely reap the corners of your field or go back for the sheaves you have forgotten. Leave these for the orphan, the widow, and the stranger so they can gather food.' My daughter, keep your eyes on the field which the men are harvesting and follow behind them. I will order my men not to harm you. And if you're thirsty, go over to the jugs and drink the water the men have drawn from the well."

Ruth fell to her knees, put her face on the earth, and asked Boaz, "How is it that you are so kind to me when I am a stranger?"

Boaz answered, "I heard what you did for your mother-in-law after the death of your husband, how you left your mother and your father and the land of your birth to go to a people you did not know. Even our father Abraham did not have your courage, for God gave Abraham assurances—blessings and promises—whereas you, your only assurance is your love. May the Shechinah, under whose wings you have asked for protection, reward you fully."

At mealtime, Boaz called to her, "Come, eat with us. Dip your bread in the vinegar so you will be protected from the heat of the day."

Ruth walked modestly toward the harvesters and sat down. Immediately, Boaz handed her a large helping of roasted kernels. She ate and was satisfied and had some left over. As soon as she returned to the fields, Boaz said to his harvesters, "Don't embarrass or criticize her. Pull out some of the stalks and leave them so she can gather them."

All day, Ruth gleaned in the fields. At the end of the day, she beat out what she had gleaned. It was an astonishing amount. An ephah of barley—almost thirty pounds—enough food for ten days! She carried the grain in her shawl to the city and gave it to her mother-in-law as well as the portion she had saved from the meal she had eaten.

Naomi was amazed. "O my daughter, look at how much barley you've brought us! Where did you glean today? Wherever you worked, may your benefactor be blessed."

"I worked in the field of Boaz," Ruth answered.

"Boaz!" Naomi echoed the name with joy. "Praise God who has not forgotten the living or the dead. Praise God who is full of *hesed*. Do you know who Boaz is? He's the grandson of Nahshon, the first one to leap into the Reed Sea even before the waters parted. He's Elimelech's nephew, also from the tribe of Judah. My daughter, he's a relative. He could marry you and redeem you!"

"And that's not all. There's more," Ruth added. "He told me I should stay until the end of the harvest and work with his young harvesters."

"Good, that's good," Naomi agreed. "It's better for you to stay with the young women in his field than to go to another field where you might be harmed."

So Ruth gleaned with Boaz's young women. All day, she gathered the fallen barley, and at night she slept in the fields. After three months when the harvest was over, Ruth returned to the city and stayed with her mother-in-law.

One morning Naomi said to her, "My daughter, I am not at peace. How can I be at peace if you don't have a home of your own? Let's consider together. Our relative, Boaz—you know him from working with his girls. He's not young, but he's a man of integrity and courage. Tonight there will be a celebration at the threshing floor, and he'll be winnowing barley.

"Go to the threshing floor. First bathe and anoint yourself with sweet-smelling oil. Dress in your best clothes. Enter the room quietly. Don't let him see you, but be sure you know where he sleeps so that when it's dark, you can find him. After he lies down, go and uncover his robe. Lie down beside him, and he'll tell you what to do next."

Ruth thought of the first time Boaz had spoken to her. Before Boaz had arrived in the fields, the other workers had avoided her, but after Boaz had treated her kindly, the others welcomed her. Every few days during the harvest he would stop to ask if she was well and bring her a small gift—figs, pomegranates, honey. Ruth followed her mother-in-law's instructions. She bathed and carefully anointed herself with sweet-smelling oil. She slowly combed her thick hair. She put on her best dress and placed a veil over her head.

At the threshing floor, Ruth saw harvesters celebrating and couples embracing in the corners. Boaz was eating and drinking, speaking to this and that person. From time to time he stopped, lifted his arms to heaven, and sang a joyous song of praise, thanking El Shaddai for removing the famine from the land. Then, he moved away from the others and walked to the end of a pile of grain and lay down in the corner. As quietly as a mist, Ruth moved toward him. She uncovered his robe and lay down beside him.

In the middle of the night, Boaz woke up startled as if he'd been caught. He turned and trembled, reached out his hand, and felt the softness of a woman.

"Who? Who are you?" he asked in surprise.

She whispered, "I am Ruth. Cover me with your robe. Bless me, for you are a redeemer."

"I bless you, my daughter," Boaz said, still holding her. "Your latest act of loyalty is even greater than your first. You left your people and went to the land of your enemy because of your love for your mother-in-law; and now when you, a beautiful woman, could ask any young man to marry and redeem you, you ask me, an old man. My people know that you are a loyal, devoted woman. I want to redeem you—do not think I do not want to—but there is a relative more closely related to you. Tomorrow I'll ask him if he will redeem you. If he refuses, I swear I will do so. Stay here tonight. Stay with me until morning."

After a time, Boaz whispered to her, "You are a brave woman to seek your own destiny."

Ruth answered quietly, "My ancestor, the mother of the Moabites, was also brave. Two angels led her and her family from her city, Sodom. The sky caught on fire. Ashes fell everywhere. Her mother, Irit, turned to look back at their home, and was turned into a pillar of salt. My ancestor followed the angels with her sister and father. For days they saw no one. Then they settled in a cave. She was afraid there was no other living man in the world but her father Lot. She wanted the world to continue, so she gave her father wine to drink and slept with him. She named their child Moab, meaning "from father.""

Boaz was silent. Then he said, "I too have a holy ancestor who yearned for a child, but her husband died before she conceived. She married his brother. His brother died. Her father-in-law promised she could marry his third son. When he did not keep his promise, like you, she chose her own journey. She disguised herself as a prostitute and waited for her father-in-law by the roadside. She seduced him and conceived twins. Tamar—her name was Tamar. His name was Judah. Their son, Perez, is my relative."

In the morning, Ruth woke when there was not enough light for one friend to recognize another. Boaz whispered to her, "Come here. Don't let anyone know that you came to the threshing floor. Open your shawl for me so I may fill it." Ruth opened her shawl, and Boaz poured in six portions of barley seed. Then he accompanied her to the town gates.

Ruth returned to Naomi, who was eagerly waiting for her. Naomi looked at her closely and asked, "Tell me, my daughter, who are you?"

Ruth could still feel the warmth of Boaz' hand in the night and his eyes burning into her in the morning as the barley seed flowed into her shawl. She sat down. Naomi sat next to her. Ruth found her voice and said, "He gave me this large amount of barley, saying, 'Do not return to your mother-in-law empty-handed.' "

"Daughter, stay home with me. I know this man. Boaz will not rest until he settles the matter today."

At the town gates, the moment Boaz saw the relative pass by, he called to him, "Plony Almony, come and sit down!" The man sat down, and Boaz gathered ten elders and asked them to be witnesses.

Then Boaz said to the relative, "Naomi has returned from Moab. She has decided to sell a piece of property belonging to our relative, Elimelech. As you know, the land that was apportioned to each tribe is to remain within the tribe. Since you are the closest relative to Elimelech's sons, I am announcing this to you before the elders, so that if you wish to buy the field, you can do so. But if you do not wish to, then say so, for I will buy the field."

Plony said, "I'm willing to be the redeemer."

"Then know," Boaz continued, "that if you buy the field from Naomi, you must also marry Ruth, the Moabite, the widow of Mahlon, so that his name will not be cut off from his community and his inheritance can continue."

"The Moabite!" protested Plony. "No! I don't want trouble. I don't want to risk dividing up my children's inheritance. You redeem the family. You buy the land." And he took off his sandal and gave it to Boaz, which was a sign in ancient times that a transaction had been completed.

Boaz turned to the others and said, "All of you are witnesses. Naomi's husband and two sons died in Moab. Today, I am acquiring from Naomi all that belonged to Elimelech and his sons to perpetuate their name and estate. And, I am inviting Ruth, the Moabite, a woman of integrity, to join our community and be my wife. You are witnesses."

The people at the gate and the elders answered, "We are witnesses. Your ancestors, Judah and Nahshon, blessed you with courage. May you prosper and your name be known. May your wife's new ancestors, Rachel and Leah, who also left the homes of their birth to go to a new land, bless her with courage and children. And may Ruth bear you a child as righteous as Perez, the child Tamar bore to Judah."

Boaz married Ruth and brought her to his home. "My beautiful wife," he said to her, "last night I gave you barley seed. Tonight, I will give you my own seed." He delighted in her all night, and she in him.

The next morning when Ruth awoke, Boaz was still sleeping. Ruth prepared breakfast for him and returned. He was still sleeping. She tried to wake him. He did not stir. She had wanted to live with this good man who had honored, protected and loved her. She shook him. She shook him again and again. He was dead. Ruth wept. Before their life together could begin, it had ended.

God remembered Ruth. Nine months later she gave birth to a little boy. The women of Bethlehem held up the child and said to Naomi: "What good fortune you have. God has given you a child who will renew your life and care for you in your old age. He's the child of your daughter-in-law, and you are blessed, for she loves you and is better to you than seven sons!"

Ruth watched Naomi joyfully bring the child to her breast. Naomi was radiant. The women of Bethlehem said, "A child is born to Naomi." They named him Obed, meaning "service." Together, Naomi and Ruth brought up Obed, who served God faithfully all his life.

Ruth helped to raise Obed's son Jesse, Jesse's son David, and David's son Solomon. Boaz had died, but his strength and kindness remained with her. Ruth's grandchildren and grandchildren's grandchildren sought her company and advice. She lived long enough to watch Solomon rule Israel with wisdom and justice.

Ezekiel

The Silence That Speaks

What does the Creator look like? Twenty-five hundred years ago in Babylon, Ezekiel, one of the Temple priests who was exiled from Jerusalem, enters a meditative trance. The heavens open and in his vision, Ezekiel sees God place his left hand, the hand of power, on him, giving Ezekiel's soul strength to set out on its journey.

This portion of Ezekiel's vision is read on the first day of Shavuot, recalling that on Mount Sinai—in the midst of smoke and fire, with trembling, roaring, senses flying—six hundred thousand people witnessed the Shechinah directly. Kabbalists have created metaphysical maps of ascent based on Ezekiel's journey; yet, whoever ventures toward the Creator is blessed with a unique vision.

*I*n the fifth year of the exile of King Jehoiachin, in the fifth month, on the fifth day of the month, I, Ezekiel, the priest, was standing among the captives by the Chebar River, and the heavens opened and I saw visions of God.

God's word came to me. God's left hand touched me, and I looked and a stormy wind swept out of the north, followed by a huge cloud and a flashing fire that had a glow around it. And in the midst of the fire, there was the Silence That Speaks. In the midst of this silence, I saw four *chayot*, four living creatures.

They had human form, and each had four faces and four wings. Their legs were straight with hooves like calves and were shining like polished copper. Human hands showed under their wings. All four had faces and wings.

The front face was human. The right face was a lion. The left face an ox, and the back face an eagle. Their wings were spread upward with two wings touching the other and two wings covering their bodies. Each moved in the direction of its face. They went wherever the spirit impelled them without turning when they moved. The form of the creatures was a radiant fire, like burning coals. The fire moved among the creatures. Traveling between the creatures was a vision of torches from which sparks of lightning were thrown off. The *chayot* ran and returned like a vision of lightning.

I looked at the creatures and saw four wheels on the ground next to each of the creatures. The wheels gleamed like topaz. Each seemed to be two wheels cutting through each other, moving but not turning. Their large rims were covered with fearsome eyes. When the spirit impelled the creatures to move, the spirit of the wheels moved with them. When the creatures lifted up, the wheels lifted up next to them. And when the creatures were still, they were still, and the spirit of the creatures was in the wheels.

Above the heads of the creatures was a gleaming expanse, a firmament of icelike crystal. Under the firmament, the wings of the creatures were extended straight out toward each other. When the creatures moved, their wings sounded like rushing waters, like the voice of El Shaddai or a mighty army. When they stood still, their wings folded.

Above the expanse over their heads was something like lapis in the shape of a throne, and on this throne was the form of a human being. I saw the Silence That Speaks shining like fire, flaring from the loins upward and from the loins downward. The being was surrounded by a glow like a rainbow that shines in the clouds on a rainy day. This was the vision of God's glory. I saw it and fell on my face. Then I heard a voice speak.

The voice said, 'Mortal, stand on your feet and I will speak to you.' A spirit entered me and spoke to me. It stood me on my feet and I heard what it said. Then a spirit carried me away, and behind me I heard a great roaring sound: "Blessed is the Shechinah, the presence of God on earth."

About the Stories

The Covenant

You were still naked when
I . . . saw that your time for love had come.
I spread my wings over you and covered your nakedness
and entered into a covenant with you . . . so you became mine.

EZEKIEL 16:8

The prophet Ezekiel poignantly expresses the vulnerability of the youthful Hebrew nation at the time of their wanderings and their reliance on God for their well-being. During this time, they follow a path of purification. They eat only manna, food from the Spirit, and journey by the guidance of the presence of the Shechinah—clouds by day and fire by night. Then, on Mount Sinai, the Spirit descends and appears to all the people. They witness God's fiery descent into the mountain and hear God's voice. This is a moment beyond logic, beyond mental understanding. To grasp God's formless presence, which is larger than the logical mind, the senses are thrown awry. But it is too much for the people to contain. They are not ready. Only the elders of the tribe are permitted a partial view of the Spirit.

The one who is prepared, who has been continuously thrown into turmoil in his life, is asked by the people to represent them and confront the Spirit. Like a medicine man or shaman, Moses withdraws from the tribe. He climbs the mountain, walks into the fire, and fasts in order to meet the Great Spirit. After his encounter with God, he brings back a stone engraved with a vision and offers it to his tribe. But the tribe is full of fear. As often happens in a new relationship, they do exactly what they have agreed not to do. When God withdraws in anger from the relationship, the tribe mourns. The golden calf no longer matters. The people who had craved material riches realize that what is most precious to them is their connection to Spirit, and they eagerly strip themselves of their gold and silver.

Moses visits God a second time. The closeness the two share and Moses' commitment to the people touch God. Descending to earth, the Shechinah now pursues Moses, hovering over his tent. Moses spends more time with the Shechinah, and God dictates a second set of tablets that are to be given to the people directly, accompanied by the oral teachings. The relationship grows. The education of the people and the integration of this new vision into everyday life create a process of study and exploration.

Just as the people sought to be close to Spirit, God too wants to be in the midst of the tribe. The building of God's home parallels the creation of the world, thus giving the tribes the opportunity to participate in the mysteries of creation. God then specifically asks that the Torah be placed between the male and female cherubim in the energy field where the feminine and masculine are face-to-face. The Shechinah's specific place of dwelling is above the ark, which contains the teachings.

It is a wondrous, and tragic, event when Moses ascends Mount Sinai. He brings back the teachings but in his wrestling with God he withdraws from his wife and his immediate family. It is with this action that the irony of the name Miriam that means both "bitter" and "beloved of Ammon" is revealed. In a later book of the Bible, Num 13, Miriam is concerned for the rights and needs of Zipporah, but God rejects Miriam's concerns (the new vision must be zealously guarded), and punishes Miriam with leprosy for contesting the leadership of Moses. Not only does Miriam lose her authority in the tribe but for generations the women lose their power. Yet the world cannot exist in harmony without a balance of the masculine and the feminine, and although Miriam nearly disappears from the texts of Exodus, her legacy continues.

Ruth

Generations after Mount Sinai, when it came to celebrating the receiving of the covenant, in addition to reading short sections from the Five Books of Moses, the rabbis also chose for the people to read an entire book about a woman of vision: Ruth, the Moabite.

The feminine energy of the Shavuot relationship is embodied in Ruth, a woman of humility and pride, obedience and independence, loyalty and daring. For me, she is the most fearless and compassionate character in the Bible. Her story of conversion parallels the Hebrew people's acceptance of the extraordinary challenge of taking on a new and unknown way of living. The commitment of the entire people at Mount Sinai is echoed in a personal way when on the road between Moab and Judah, Ruth, a Moabite, says to her Hebrew mother-in-law, "Where you go, I will go. Where you live, I will live. Your people will be my people, and your God, my God. Where you die, I will die, and there I will be buried." This is a heart relationship. It is emotional and unconditional. It transcends borders and preconceived notions. Ruth's quest for relationship is as passionate as Moses' love for the people. On behalf of the people, Moses climbs a fiery and unexplored mountain; on behalf of her beloved, Ruth ventures into the land of the enemy.

With no guarantee for her economic, social, political, or emotional future, Ruth commits herself to Naomi, who is from another tribe, religion, and generation. Ruth understands that Naomi has lost everything that is dear to her—husband, children, security. Ruth's heart is so large that she accepts Naomi's grief. Rather than be affronted that her mother-in-law does not rejoice in her presence and commitment, Ruth accepts Naomi in her suffering and finds a way to provide for both of them. In choosing a husband, Ruth does not select a lusty young man. Instead she follows a spiritual vision and chooses a man of inner strength and virtue; a man of equal daring and commitment, one whose grandfather leapt into the Reed Sea before Moses parted the waters.

Ruth's character is like the strong pure sparks of the first fruits. Her spirit is so expansive, her faith so constant, that she will not allow any obstacle to defeat her. Ruth's love and constancy so touch the embittered Naomi that she searches for a way to help her daughter-in-law. Ruth's continued devotion and attention to Naomi slowly nourishes her so that she is able to return from the empty underworld she has been inhabiting to reach out to another person and so bring about her own joy and fulfillment.

The (very) end of Ruth's story, nearly two hundred years later, is like a fairy tale. At that distant time, the corrupt kingdom of Judges is ruled once again by justice, the justice of King Solomon, who is Ruth's grandson's grandson. The agent of this change is Ruth, who dares the unknown, holds on to her own convictions, follows her intuition, and raises her grandchildren, great-grandchildren, and great-great-grandchildren with the fruits of her experience.

About the Stories

Ezekiel

In *Ezekiel,* we perceive a spiritual vision of moving closer to God. Immediately preceding the destruction of the First Temple, Ezekiel, a priest who was exiled from Jerusalem, enters a meditative state. He sees a fiery chariot upon which he perceives God's glory. His prophetic vision describes an ascent to reach God.

From Mount Sinai, Moses brought his people a blueprint for the social interaction of the people with themselves and with God. After the destruction of the Temples, centuries of rabbis enlarged the blueprint with commentary that became the Talmud. Standing by the river, Ezekiel envisioned a blueprint of the internal worlds of the spirit. Based on Ezekiel's vision, third-century scholars created a metaphorical world to which the soul ascends. Later, mystical scholars called Kabbalists further developed these meditations into complex allegories for reaching God. Without looking through the lens of the Kabbalists' meditations, it is nearly impossible to understand Ezekiel's vision. Kabbalistic metaphors are also helpful in understanding other texts in *Treasures of the Heart,* so I want to introduce a few of their basic concepts.

According to the Kabbalists, below the highest realm of Infinite Being or Emptiness (Ein Sof), there are four heavenly realms that correspond to the four letters of God's name (Y<small>HWH</small>). The highest realm, Closeness (*Atzilut*), holds God's attributes, which are the ten sephirot. Below the realm of Closeness is God's Throne, Creation (*Beriyah*). By sitting, God moves closer to the earth. In this realm, God is concerned with human destiny. The human soul, called *neshumah,* can reach this realm and experience the breath of God. Below Creation is the Realm of Formation (*Yetzirah*) that is inhabited by the Shechinah and the angels, God's messengers, who are the *chayot* that Ezekiel perceives. The soul of Ezekiel arrives in the realm of Yetzirah.

We dwell in the fourth or lowest realm called Making (*Asiyah*) where the spiritual and the physical intertwine. This is the realm of the wheel. Part of its significance is the concept of travel, for the intention of the Kabbalists is to journey through the realms to reach the Silence That Speaks (*chashmal*) where the word of God can be heard.

In his book *Meditation and the Bible,* Aryeh Kaplan asserts that the Hebrew word *chashmal* that begins with the Hebrew letter *chet* is also the number eight and represents the spiritual realm. In order to enter the spiritual realm and begin the spiritual journey, the physical must be transformed. For that reason, the spiritual formation of all male boys begins eight days after their birth, when they are circumcised. This act is intended both to raise the physical to the spiritual and to bring the spiritual, in the form of holy souls, down from heaven.

Heaven is the root. It is the source of light and of souls. Like a branch from a root, the soul descends from heaven and clothes itself in a physical body. The soul always remains connected to the root. The idea of prophecy is to create a hollow container through which the divine light is able to flow and speak. When a person goes against God's teachings, a small cut is made in the divine flow and the spiritual sustenance is stopped until reparations are made. Heaven's root is very long with many branches in each realm. The work of a prophet is to carefully prepare for the journey through years of intensive purification, trance, and meditation in order to ascend the spiritual ladder that Kabbalists often call the Tree of Life. The closer the prophet is to God the more he can become God's instrument and transmit God's teachings to the people.

In his vision, Ezekiel describes the tumultuous ascent into the second realm. He passes through the spiritual confusion of the storm wind, the agitation of the soul; the cloud, the opaqueness of the soul; and the fire, the burning of the soul. He then experiences the glow, a transcendent light. Cleansed of outside interference and desires, he enters the realm of the Silence That Speaks, where God's voice is heard and the reflections of God's glory are seen. When he comes near the highest level, he can only gaze for short moments so that he will not die.

Like Moses, Ezekiel intercedes for the people. In his first vision of the chariot, he perceives four faces on each creature: the human, the lion, the ox, and the eagle. In his later vision of the chariot, Ezekiel replaces the face of the ox, who brought about the sin of the golden calf, with the face of the cherub (Ez 10:14), who guards the presence of the Shechinah and represents the child or the new spirit.

On Shavuot, the Hebrews accept a binding relationship with their new Protector God, and the Lover aspect of the relationship flourishes. The holiday that takes place in the spring displays a bouquet of fragrant images: bitter water turns sweet; indescribable manna falls from heaven; sweet water gushes out of a rock; mountains leap in eagerness to be near their Lover; waves of perfume waft through the air as the Shechinah speaks; Mount Sinai lifts off the ground in ecstasy. God chooses a dwelling place close to the people, and the people seek to please their Parent/Protector/Lover.

The stories read at Shavuot express different aspects of relationship and commitment. In *The Covenant*, after God establishes a relationship with the people, God changes the tablets of justice to tablets of compassion. In *Ruth*, because of her love for her mother-in-law, the Moabite risks her life to follow Naomi to Judah. In return, Boaz, one of the leaders of the Judean community, protects Ruth, and she is accepted and honored in the community. The law is reinterpreted, and a new midrash is given: Moabite women may marry into the Judean community. The very act of accepting and welcoming "the enemy" elevates the spiritual level and vision of the society. In *Ezekiel*, the prophet's soul, in its courage and desire to be close to God, ascends to the second realm of God's kingdom and perceives God's glory; God responds by speaking to him, allowing him to feel the presence of the Shechinah.

The laws given on Mount Sinai set the groundwork for a caring, effective community. A shift begins from a hierarchical conception of society in which one human king controls both power and justice, to a divine power that guides the people through the teachings outlined in the Torah. Following the teachings can lead the people not to wealth or power but to closeness to the One and to the kingdom within.

We may disagree with some of the laws and view others as harsh and needing to be changed, but at that time (about 1250 B.C.E.), the laws or teachings were revolutionary. The intent of the new teachings was for the community to be ruled not by dictators but by laws and teachings which protected the unprotected and provided for the welfare of each of its members. The stranger, the orphan, and the widow were to be fed and cared for. Women were entitled to be sexually satisfied. The rights of slaves were to be protected. Each member of the community was to look out for his neighbor's welfare and property. Each one was to be responsible for the whole.

Something extraordinary happened on Mount Sinai. The Shechinah, the palpable presence of God, descended to earth and was witnessed by all the people. Although the people found such closeness to God overpowering and asked Moses to represent them directly, the experience was never forgotten. To this day, Jews might say to someone they consider a soul mate, "I feel a bond to you. I don't know what it is. Could it be that we were standing next to each other on Mount Sinai?"

TISHA B'AV

About Tisha B'Av

On the day of Tisha B'Av, Jews grieve for the loss of their close relationship to God. In biblical times (1200 B.C.E.), the Hebrew people and God took vows and became engaged at Shavuot, which takes place during the third month of the calendar year. In the fourth month, Tammuz, they broke their covenant by worshiping the golden calf. The people continued to break their commitment; and centuries later in 587 B.C.E., during the fifth month, Av (July or August), God reacted in anger, and the Temple was destroyed. The Second Temple was destroyed in 70 C.E. also in the fifth month, and since then Jews have set aside three weeks of mourning, beginning with a daylong fast on the seventeenth of Tammuz, the time of the golden calf, and culminating in a fast on Tisha B'Av, the ninth day of the month of Av. (Tisha means "nine," and Av means "father.")

There is a disparity in the actual dates of Tisha B'Av. Second Kings states that the destruction of the First Temple occurred on the seventh of Av, although Jeremiah states it was the tenth of Av. The destruction of the Second Temple is generally agreed to have taken place on the tenth of Av. But because people need to acknowledge failure and grief and to set aside time to mourn, the rabbis chose one date, the ninth of Av as the date on which all the disasters would be said to have occurred.

In addition to the destruction of the Temples, tradition also says that on this day the spies that Moses sent to reconnoiter the Promised Land were filled with fear and lost faith in God's promise. On this day in 1492, the Jews who had lived peacefully in Spain for more than five hundred years were banished, and the Inquisition began. And although Yom HaShoah has been added to the calendar as a separate memorial date to commemorate the Holocaust, people also speak of the inexplicable Holocaust on Tisha B'Av.

During the three weeks of mourning, which are also called Between the Straits, there are no weddings or joyous occasions planned, no haircuts, swimming, planting, undertaking of new activities, dangerous journeys, or holding of court cases. The prohibition against undertaking new activities or "planting seeds" corresponds with the geographical place and season. In late July and early August in the Near East, the sun is raging, the ground is dry, and the people are weak from the heat; better to mourn and cleanse than to plant at this time. In fact, in Babylon, the ninth day of the month of Av was a day of sorrow and mourning.

Before Tisha B'av begins, a meal of mourning, consisting of uncooked vegetables, lentils and hard-boiled eggs dipped in ashes, is eaten sitting on low chairs. From sundown (the appearance of the first stars) to sundown, there is a fast. Jews are commanded *not* to study, for study brings joy. The Torah is draped for the day in a black cloth or sometimes removed from sight. Jews give themselves over to grieving. They chant dirges and psalms, sit on low seats, read from the Book of Job, tell stories of grief, and recite from the Book of Lamentations, which is read in full.

Grief and loss bring emptiness. When a person or belief system dies, a void exists. But with this void is created a space for hope, for growth. While working on this book, I lost my home of twenty-seven years and my job of twenty-five years, broke my ankle, and had a cancer scare. But layers below my fear (of how I would survive) and my anger (that this had happened to me) huddled hope and faith, even joy. In the worst moments, I drank a lot of water, prayed, and remembered that life was more than what I was able to perceive. Life is full of change and God's grace, and if I could let go of my sense of loss and fear for the future, I could reconnect to the fullness of life and God's presence.

The moment of epiphany came in Utah, when I decided not to tell the story I had planned to tell at a storytelling performance, but to offer the audience the metaphorical story that I was living. I told the story by Rabbi Nachman of Bratslav, "The Diamond," in which a poor clay digger loses a valuable diamond, with which he had intended to make his fortune, only to realize that it was never meant for him. What we take to be so important at the moment may be of no importance in the future. The story of "The Diamond" ends with these words: "The clay digger thought the diamond was meant for him, but it wasn't. The proof was that he lost it, but if he had given up hope, he could never have had what was meant for him. Without hope, Rabbi Nachman says, we are completely lost. With hope, there is always a chance for life."

What is important is to hold on to our faith. When I realized that I could not presume to know what was meant for me, I let go of fear. I had lost my home and nearly all my material possessions, but I hadn't lost my belief that I was a part of something grander: a pulse, a force; an energy that brings about life and death and is beyond life and death. The "I am" that sustains all life and belongs to each of us; that was here before us and will be here after us.

A parable tells of a father who advised his son, "Do not travel at this time on a ship. It is a season of storms." The son does not listen. So the father says, "If the ship sinks and you lose everything, don't be ashamed and imagine I will not accept you. Return, come back to me, I will always accept you." Despite the horrific stories that are told on Tisha B'Av, Jews believe that God will redeem them and that they can be redeemed. In the late afternoon on Tisha B'Av, hope begins to return, and in some Sephardic synagogues women put on perfume for the afternoon service. As a symbol of the possibility of return, according to legend, it is on Tisha B'Av that the Messiah will return.

To some Jews, the loss of the Temple and the ensuing exile was irreparable. The Sadducees, who had centered their worship on the Temple service, lost both their power base and their faith with the destruction of the Temple. Other Jews, such as the Pharisees, who believed that study and mitzvot (the carrying out of God's commandments) were as important as offering sacrifices, grieved at the loss of the Temple, but they held on to their faith and found a new way of worship. Study flourished, and the thoughts and actions of each individual became as valued as the purity of the priests. The Jewish kingdom was forced to move inward. It was a painful transformation and continues to this day.

What all the disasters have in common is this exile, not only from the land, from the Temple, but from the Shechinah, the presence of God on earth. In grieving, we separate ourselves from others and thus from God. But as we mourn, we can choose to remember that by turning to Spirit and by believing in the oneness and connectedness of all living beings, we can move from isolation to resting in the Spirit. Lamentations ends, "Turn us around, O God. Turn us to you, and we will return."

At the end of Tisha B'Av with the appearance of the first stars, after the fast is broken, people go out to greet and bless the crescent moon. During the seven Sabbaths that follow Tisha B'Av, people continue the process of reconciliation with one another and with God in preparation for the New Year.

The Spies

The Land of Milk and Honey

During Tisha B'Av, we tell the story of the spies and remember how easy it is to lose faith. Even though God created amazing signs and wonders for the Hebrews in Egypt and lifted the waters of the Reed Sea so that they might escape the thundering chariots of Pharaoh's army, and even though in the wilderness, God appeared to the people in the fire and smoke and promised them a land of milk and honey, flowing with streams and rivers, filled with grapes, figs, and pomegranates, within two years of making a covenant with God, when the spies return from the Promised Land (around 1250 B.C.E.) with a frightening report, the people are filled with fear and want to go back to Egypt and slavery. This rendition combines biblical text and midrash.

*W*hen the children of Israel wandered in the desert, God gave them manna to eat. The Shechinah, God's presence on earth, guided them with a pillar of cloud by day and a pillar of fire by night. After two years, the Shechinah said to Moses, "Send the leaders from each of the tribes to scout the land of Canaan."

Moses chose Hoshea from the tribe of Ephraim. In order to give him strength as well as honor, he added the letter *yod*—the first letter of God's name—to the beginning of Hoshea's name, thus changing his name from Hosea to Joshua. Then he said to the leaders of the tribes,

"Go to the Negev and the hill country to see what kind of land it is. Are the people strong or weak? Are the towns fortified? Is the soil poor or fertile? Do not cut down trees sacred to the inhabitants. Walk on small paths, rather than highways. Be courageous and bring us back fruit from the land. The grapes will be ripening."

Twelve chieftains, including Joshua and Caleb, scouted the land. They traveled from south to north, from Tzin to Rehob, and found the land very beautiful. It was filled with olive groves and vineyards, cypress trees and willows. But when the Hebrew chieftains saw the size of the giant Anakites who lived near Hebron, they refused to take back any fruit, for they didn't want the people to see the land's abundance. Caleb drew his sword, forcing the men to bring back figs, pomegranates and grapes. The fruit was so large eight men were needed to carry one branch of grapes. After forty days, they returned to Kadesh in the wilderness of Paran.

"Tell us about the land," Moses asked them, and the people crowded around them and examined the fruit.

The spies reported, "As God said, it is a land flowing with milk and honey, but their cities are fortified and their people are huge. In Hebron, we saw giants. In the hill country, there are Hittites, Amorites, and Jebusites; and by the Jordan and the sea, there are Canaanites."

The people cried in fear. They were afraid to enter a fortified land protected by giants. When Joshua tried to speak, the people shouted him down, saying he had no children of his own to worry about. Then Caleb tried to reassure them. "Why are you afraid? God has promised to lead us through the land like a devouring fire."

"But the people are giants!" the chieftains protested. "The walls of their cities reach up to the sky. Their five-year-old children are larger than grown men. We look like grasshoppers compared to them."

The people broke into loud wails. All night they wept, and in the morning the men turned on Moses and Aaron and said, "Why is God taking us to a land where we will die and our wives and children will be carried off? No! Let us go back to Egypt. It is better to be slaves and live!"

Moses and Aaron fell to the ground, horrified that their people who had witnessed God's great signs and wonders could lose their faith so quickly. Joshua and Caleb tore their clothes and pleaded with the people, "The land we saw was very beautiful. If God is pleased with us, surely God will bring us to this land that flows with milk and honey and give it to us. Do not fear the people in the land. They have lost their protection, for they do not follow God's minimum commandments."

"We will all die!" the men shouted and were about to pelt Joshua and Caleb with stones when the air began to shimmer and then a cloud appeared over the tabernacle that became visible to all the Israelites. The Shechinah said to Moses, "How long will your people ignore me? Despite all the signs and wonders that they saw with their own eyes, why do they have so little faith? I will strike them with illness and destroy them and make you a new nation."

Moses argued with the Shechinah, saying, "If the Egyptians hear that you have destroyed your people, they will say that you were powerless to keep your oath. Everyone knows that you are living in the midst of your people, leading them forward by day with a pillar of cloud and by night with a pillar of fire. I beg you, remember that you are slow to anger and abounding in kindness and forgive the people as you have done since they left Egypt."

The Shechinah answered, "I will pardon them as you ask. But none of the men who failed to remember the signs and wonders in Egypt and my presence on Mount Sinai will see the land I promised their ancestors. Caleb and Joshua, who remained loyal to me, and the women who have always believed in me, will cross the Jordan. The children will see the land their fathers rejected, but the men over twenty will die in the wilderness. Today, they are weeping for no reason. In the future, I will give them reason to weep."

On the day these words were spoken, on the ninth day of the month of Av, Moses said to the people, "Dig your graves and sleep in them tonight." The people dug ditches and lay down and slept in them, not knowing whether they would wake up. The next morning, Moses said, "Rise up and separate the dead from the living." The people woke up and found that fifteen thousand men had died in the night.

For the next thirty-eight years that they wandered in the desert, each year on the ninth day of the month of Av, the Hebrews dug their own graves and slept in them. An entire generation died.

Then, in the fortieth year, when they woke up, no one had died. They thought that they might not have chosen the proper day in the calendar, so they dug their graves for another six days. But when the full moon rose on the fifteenth night of Av, they knew that they had not made an error. They celebrated that day, knowing that those who were still living would enter the Promised Land.

Rachel and the Shechinah

Wailing, Bitter Weeping

The words of the Hebrew prophets grip our hearts. They never stop loving their people even though their people do not listen to them. In the ninth and eighth centuries B.C.E., the prophets denounced the Hebrew people for worshiping other gods and for carrying out God's rituals superficially. They urged the kings of Israel and Judah not to go to war with other nations, since God might use those peoples to destroy them.

The prophets were ignored, and in the ninth century, Assyria invaded the northern kingdom of Israel and deported ten of the twelve tribes of Jacob. One hundred years later, the southern kingdom, Judah, became a vassal of Assyria and then Babylon. This story begins at the time that Judah is a vassal of Babylon.

I've interwoven portions of Jeremiah with biblical passages, history texts, and oral legends. The destruction of the First Temple took place in 587 B.C.E.

Of Jacob's four wives the one he loved the most was Rachel. For fourteen years he worked for her father so he could marry her. After many years of being barren, Rachel gave birth to Joseph. When Joseph was still young, Rachel died on the roadside, near Ramah, giving birth to their second son. Leah, Jacob's first wife, was buried with him in the cave of Machpelah. But Rachel, who was torn from her loved ones, was buried in a roadside grave, so she might comfort her descendants. . . .

Moses had urged the people to live according to God's teachings so they would not be banished from the land. But when the Hebrews returned from Egypt to the Promised Land, they did just what Moses had urged them not to do. They saw the altars of the land filled with statues of gods and goddesses and they prayed to them.

The prophets who followed Moses reminded the people of the vows they had made: "Under the wedding canopy on Mount Sinai, you sang, 'Yahweh is our God, only Yahweh. We promise to love you with our entire heart and soul. We will follow your teachings and to care for one another. We will not serve other gods.' Those were your words."

The kings of Judah ignored their prophets. They ignored God's wishes to care for the needy and the poor, and they brought the statues of other gods into the Temple and placed them in the holy of holies, the very room where the Shechinah, God's presence, dwelt.

The prophet Jeremiah felt the anguish of the Shechinah at the betrayal by her people. He stood by the gate of the Temple and cried out to the people, "Entering the Temple does not take away your lack of justice or your meanness toward the poor. If you place statues of gods in the Temple and on the hillside shrines, and do not keep God's teachings, the grapes and figs will wither and all God has given you will be taken away.

"When our people turned to other gods, the Assyrians came from Babylon in the north and devastated our holy shrine in Shiloh and carried off ten of our tribes to Babylon. The tribe of Ephraim has been cast away. Even the stork in the sky knows her seasons, and the turtledove, swallow, and crane return at their proper times. But you kill, steal, and indulge in adultery and all kinds of immorality. Instead of love, your hearts are filled with greed—greed and deceit. You oppress the poor. You do not release the debtor or free your slaves after seven years. These are God's laws and you do not obey them. 'All is well,' your priest and prophet tell you, when nothing is well.

"I beg you, do not be arrogant and provoke the Babylonians.

Although we pay tribute to them, they are not our enemy. God may use them to destroy you. God has told me that if you do not heed my words, Jerusalem will be destroyed."

Jeremiah was thrown into prison and threatened with death if he prophesied again against the ways of the king and the priests. After he was released, he went into hiding where he dictated God's words to his faithful disciple, Baruch. Baruch read Jeremiah's prophecies to the elders. God's spirit was in Jeremiah's words and the elders insisted Baruch read the scroll to the king, Josiah's son, Jehoiakin. But Josiah's son had other interests. He was forcing the poor to build without pay a huge cedarwood palace with upper stories and windows. He threw Jeremiah's scroll into the fire. He made an alliance with Egypt and rebelled against Babylon.

As Jeremiah predicted, the king of Babylon, Nebuchadnezzar, arrived in Judah with his vast armies to wipe out Jerusalem. The Hebrew prophet who was known to be a friend of Babylon was brought before him. Fearlessly, Jeremiah implored Nebuchadnezzar to consider the result of his actions, "You may wipe out Judah, but the Lord has said that the one who wipes out Jerusalem will also be destroyed."

Nebuchadnezzar took the king and thousands of the most educated citizens captive. He plundered the Temple's treasury, but he heeded Jeremiah's words and left the holy of holies intact. He appointed Josiah's brother, Zedekiah, as his regent and ordered him not to engage in relations with Egypt. But after Nebuchadnezzar left Judah, false prophets in Jerusalem predicted the fall of Babylon. Zedekiah surrounded himself with ambitious young men who despised the gloomy Jeremiah. Within a year after being appointed regent, Zedekiah made an alliance with six neighboring countries to fight Babylon.

When the emissaries met in Jerusalem to discuss their treaty against Babylon, Jeremiah put a yoke around his neck and walked through the city, crying out, "The Lord has said to me, 'I will bring disaster to the kings of Judah who have sacrificed to other gods, built shrines to other gods, and offered their children to Baal. This city will become a ruin, a den for jackals, a desolation; its inhabitants will eat the flesh of their children.' Do not break your covenant with Babylon. Put your neck under the yoke of the king of Babylon; serve him and live."

Jeremiah was thrown into a mud pit. Fortunately, the king's Ethiopian slave had compassion for him and freed him. Jeremiah went into hiding in his native village of Anathoth, but even in hiding, he did not give up hope that Jerusalem and its people might be saved. He sent word to Zedekiah, saying, "If you surrender to the Babylonians, your life will be spared. If you do not, the city and the Temple will be burned." Zedekiah ignored him.

When Nebuchadnezzar heard that his regent had betrayed him, he ordered his generals to destroy Jerusalem. After a two-year siege, the famine was so severe that Zedekiah and his sons fled through an underground water tunnel that led to the plains of Jericho. While they were in the tunnel, a wild deer walked on top of it, attracting the attention of the Babylonian soldiers who tracked it. Just as they were about to shoot the deer, Zedekiah emerged from the tunnel. The soldiers captured him, and his family and brought them before Nebuchadnezzar in Riblah. Zedekiah was forced to watch the slaughter of his own sons before he was blinded and led to exile in Babylon.

The Babylonian soldiers set fire to the cedarwood palace. They tore down the walls of Jerusalem. They burned the Temple and surrounding houses. When the high priest tried to flee, the soldiers captured and slaughtered him. His daughter cried out in horror, and they killed her as well, mixing the father's and daughter's blood together on the altar.

As the Temple was burning, the Shechinah kissed the walls and fled. Each day she appeared at a different place on the Mount of Olives. Weeping, she cried out to the people, "Have the wood and stone statues given birth to you that you call them your beloved? Did they bring you out of Egypt and care for you in the wilderness? Do you not remember the vows you made?"

But the people ignored her tears. They had turned to other gods. Their hearts remained closed.

Jeremiah returned to Jerusalem. As he walked up the hill and entered the city, he saw smoke rising from the Temple and hoped the people had renewed their relationship with God and were offering sacrifices once again. But when he came to the Temple gate, there was no Temple. There was only a pile of stones. All the treasures in the Temple were gone. The nobles, the warriors, the craftsmen were gone. The poorest farmers remained.

Jeremiah wept and cried out, "Which way did my people go? I will perish with them." He walked through the city and heard cries of anguish and saw dead and wounded on the streets. The Babylonian soldiers were relentlessly forcing the people out of Jerusalem. He saw nursing mothers, small children, and old people rushing to catch up to the young men who were being marched away in chains. Jeremiah accompanied them, and then he kissed the little ones and turned back to comfort those who were left in Jerusalem. The soldiers did not stop him, for Nebuchadnezzar had given orders not to harm the Hebrew prophet. When the exiles saw Jeremiah leaving them, they ran to him and cried, "Are you forsaking us?"

Jeremiah answered, "I call heaven and earth as witnesses. If you had only wept when you were in Zion, you would not have gone into exile. Woe! Woe for all of us!"

The Babylonians were afraid that the Hebrews might cry out to their God and ask for forgiveness, so they would not let them rest until they reached the Euphrates River. When they rested, their hearts cracked open and they wept:

> *By the waters of Babylon,*
> *we sat down.*
> *There we sat,*
> *sat and wept,*
> *as we thought of Zion.*
> *There on the poplars,*
> *we hung our lyres.*
> *"Sing us a song of Zion,"*
> *our captors demanded.*
> *"A song of Zion?" we asked.*
> *"How can we sing of Zion*
> *when we are in exile in Babylon?"*

On the road to Jerusalem, Jeremiah saw severed fingers, hands, and legs. He kissed them and put them in his sack. From a distance he heard wailing. God had decreed the destruction of the Temple and the exile of the people, but now the Shechinah was wandering in the empty streets, bereft. Her people, her beloved children, were gone. She had loved and protected and carried them through the wilderness. They had promised to carry out God's teachings. The great journey they had taken together was over. Smoke rose from the ruins of the Temple. In every direction there were shadows, death, blood.

A horrific wail came from the Shechinah:

> *"Woe! I built a wedding canopy,*
> *and the bride is dead.*
> *Woe for my house, my priests, my children!*
> *Where are you, my children?*
> *Did I not plead with you to remember your vows?*
> *Woe! Jeremiah! Go!*
> *Call Moses. Call Abraham.*
> *Wake Isaac and Jacob from their graves so they may console me."*

"Where shall I find Moses?" Jeremiah asked.

The Shechinah answered Jeremiah, saying, "On the other side of the Jordan. Call out, 'Son of Amram, come and see how the sheep you loved so dearly have been devoured.' "

Jeremiah called Moses. Then he went to Hebron, to the cave of Machpelah, and called Abraham, Isaac, and Jacob. Moses asked the angels why he had been called, and they told him that the Temple had been destroyed and the children of Israel had been sent into exile. Moses tore the clothes of glory that the Shechinah had given him; and when he saw Abraham, Isaac, and Jacob, he said, "Fathers of my fathers, the Temple has been destroyed. Our children are in exile."

Together, Moses and the three patriarchs walked toward Jerusalem. One by one, they spoke to the Shechinah.

Moses said, "Creator of the Covenant, at your command, I brought the children of Israel out of Egypt. They accepted your covenant in the wilderness. Why have you forsaken your promise?"

The Shechinah did not answer.

Abraham said, "Invisible Guide, all my life I remained faithful to you. I offered you my son Isaac. Why have you broken your promise?"

The Shechinah did not answer.

Isaac said, "Merciful One, I never disobeyed you. I never went against your wishes. Will you not have mercy on my children who disobeyed you?"

The Shechinah did not answer.

Jacob said, "Protector of the Universe, what has happened to my children?"

"What has happened to my children?" The Shechinah echoed Jacob's words. She wept. She mourned. She could not be consoled.

Then Rachel, who had been buried by the side of the road so that she might comfort her children, rose from her grave near Ramah. She went to the Shechinah and said, "Beloved Mother, I understand your grief. Your people have betrayed you. You have lost your beloved. I too had a beloved and I was betrayed. I loved Jacob, and he loved me. We waited with eagerness to be married. We shared secret gestures and words of love.

"Jacob tended my father's sheep for seven years so he could marry me; but when I was about to put on my wedding veil, my father said, 'Give your wedding veil to your sister. You will not marry Jacob. Because of Jacob's love for you, he will work another seven years for me in order to marry you. Give your older sister, Leah, your wedding dress and veil so that Jacob will think she is you.'

"I felt betrayed by my father, by Leah, and even by Jacob. But when I looked at my sister and saw she was trembling because she was afraid of being humiliated, I did not want her to suffer. I taught her the secret words and gestures that Jacob and I shared, so Jacob would think she was me, and she would not be shamed when they slept together. O God, I am flesh and blood. If I could let go of my jealousy so as not to cause suffering, can you not let go of your anger and forgive your children so they do not suffer?"

Rachel's cry was heard in Ramah. Wailing, bitter weeping. Rachel wept for her children. She refused to be comforted, for her children were gone.

The Shechinah trembled at the depths of Rachel's love. She said to Rachel, "Restrain your voice from weeping. Do not let your eyes shed more tears. For your sake, Rachel, because of your compassion, in seventy years, the children of Israel will return to their land."

Lamentations

A Wound As Great As the Sea

My people are shattered and I am shattered.
Is there no balm in Gilead?
Is there no physician there?
Is there no healing for my people?

On Tisha B'Av, the entire book of Lamentations is read. In 597
B.C.E., the people were sent into exile. In 586 B.C.E., the First Temple
and the city of Jerusalem, the symbols of Jewish faith, were destroyed.

When the sorrow is too great, what is there to do but to weep? On
Tisha B'av, people give public vent to grief. This is a freely rendered,
condensed version of the book of Lamentations.

How solitary she is; our city which was once full of people. She
has become like a widow. She, the great lady among nations,
the princess among provinces, now she gives tribute to others. At
night, she cries wretchedly. Her cheeks are wet with tears. All her companions have betrayed her. They have become her enemies.

In exile she dwells among the nations with no resting place. No
pilgrims approach her Temple. The roads of Zion cry out in grief. The
gates of the Temple are desolate. The priests mourn. Judah's princes
are like deer without pasture; they have no strength before the pursuer.

Her adversaries mock her grief. Those who honored her jeer at her nakedness. There is no comfort from her former lovers. Since her fortune turned, she is alone.

You! Look at me! Is there anyone who has known pain like the pain God has inflicted on me? The assembly is destroyed. The Temple is in ruins. There are no festivals, celebrations, or Sabbaths. Zion's king and princes are in exile. The prophets have no vision from God. The elders sit silently on the earth and grieve. They wear sackcloth and throw dust on their heads. There is no Torah. My eyes fail because of tears. My insides groan. The young women strike their foreheads on the earth. The infants, who have nothing to suck, faint in the open places. They cry to their mothers, 'Food?' 'Water?' They faint from hunger. Their life force pours out onto their mothers' breasts.

O Zion, how can I comfort you? Your wound is as great as the sea. Who can heal you? The visions of your prophets were vanity. They did not reveal your iniquity. They did not bring you salvation. They seduced you with messages of delusion. All who pass by mock you. They hiss and shake their heads at the daughters of Jerusalem, saying, "Can this be the city about which people said, 'Her perfect beauty brings joy to all the world'? Your enemies speak against you. They say, 'This is the day we've been waiting for. We have swallowed up Jerusalem!' " But it is not our enemies, it is God who has allowed our enemies to rejoice.

O people of Zion, let your tears flow day and night like a river. Do not rest. Do not keep still one second! Rise up at each watch and howl in the night! Pour out your hearts like water in front of God.

Elohim! Look at us. Look at the ones you are harming! Mothers are fainting from famine on every street corner. Will you allow women to eat their own fruit—the children they have nursed? Will you allow your priests and prophets to be slaughtered? Your virgins to be raped? Your young men to be killed by the sword? Young and old fall dead on the street. You have slaughtered without mercy. You have set up a roll call, as if it were a festival, but it is for slaughter. Your wrath has kindled a fire in Zion and devoured Zion's foundations. No one who I cradled in my arms remains. My enemies have taken them all.

Remember us! Look at our shame! Our inheritance is given to

strangers, our houses to foreigners. We have no fathers. Our mothers are widows. We pay silver for water. Our enemies pursue us, breathing down our necks. We work without rest. We beg Egypt and Assyria for bread. Our ancestors have turned away from you and died. We bear their wickedness. Servants rule over us. There is no one to deliver us. We venture fearfully into the wilderness to search for our food. Our skin is as hot as an oven. Our dance is transformed into a slow fasting. The crown has fallen from our heads.

All around me is misery and hardship. I see such affliction. You brought me into the dark where there is no light. You wore away my flesh and skin—shattered my bones. When I cry and shout out, you strangle my prayers. My path is a maze. You wait for me in secret places like a bear or lion and strike, breaking me into pieces, forcing me to change my ways. My teeth are broken on the gravel. I have no peace.

Elohim, you have placed your arrow in your quiver and chosen me as your mark. Your arrow is in my insides. The people mock me with word and song. I am filled with bitterness, drunk with wormwood. I no longer know what happiness is. But I have hope. Your mercy has no end. Every morning, you give us life. With all my heart, I cry to you. You are my life. I wait patiently for you to rescue us. I know you will not reject us forever. You cause us grief, yet you are compassionate and merciful. Let us search and examine our ways and turn again to God. Let us lift our hands and hearts to God.

Adonai! I am calling your name from the depths of the pit. Do not shut your ear to my cry. You have seen the wrong done to me, heard the taunts of my enemies. At every street corner, our precious children, once valued as gold, are worth no more than broken pottery.

You have uncovered our sins. Our actions were as dreadful as the wickedness of Sodom that was overthrown in a moment. You have vented your fury on us. Our doom has come. Our pursuers, swifter than the eagles in the sky, chase us and wait for us in the wilderness. Mount Zion is desolate. Jackals walk freely along the streets. But you, O Lord, you live forever. Your throne is for every generation. Why do you forget us? Why have you forsaken us for so long? Return to us. Turn us around, O God. Turn us to you, and we will return.

The Destruction
of the Second Temple

Hardening of the Heart

After the destruction of the First Temple (586 B.C.E.), the Jewish people once again forgot the source of their blessings and the covenant they had made with God. They closed their hearts to the Shechinah and to one another. According to this legend, one small act of meanness led to the destruction of the Second Temple (70 C.E.), the ruin of Jerusalem, and the disappearance of an entire way of life. I've based this story on oral legends and historical accounts.

*W*hen Nero was emperor in Rome, there was great prosperity in Judea. The people were blessed with all they needed. The wells were overflowing; the harvests were abundant; the flocks and herds were numerous. The coffers in the Temple were full. Hardening of the heart seemed a small matter. But it was because of the hardening of the heart that the Second Temple was destroyed and Jerusalem fell.

During the reign of Nero, there lived a man of great wealth and power in Jerusalem. He had many friends and colleagues. In his community there were two men with similar names. The one called Kamtza was his friend; the other, Bar Kamtza, was his enemy. The wealthy man was planning a large party and told his servant to invite Kamtza; but in the turmoil of the preparations the servant misunderstood and, by mistake, invited Bar Kamtza to the house. Bar Kamtza happily arrived at the banquet, thinking that his host wanted to be friends again.

The guests had already gathered when the host walked in. A merry hum of talking, drinking, and eating greeted him. He looked about him. There were great piles of food. Everyone seemed to be enjoying themselves. He gazed proudly at his successful circle of friends: rabbis, scholars, merchants, artists; and then to his amazement, he saw his enemy, Bar Kamtza, was sitting on his couch talking to his friends. Clenching his teeth, he went up to him and said, "Bar Kamtza, what are you doing here? You are my enemy. Leave my house!"

The nearby guests stopped drinking and eating. In a barely audible voice, Bar Kamtza said, "Excuse me, it must have been a mistake. I thought you had invited me because you had wanted to resume our friendship, but since I'm already here, let me pay for whatever I eat or drink."

"No!" the host answered sharply. A hush spread through the room. The guests turned to Bar Kamtza. In a whisper, he pleaded, "Please, don't humiliate me. I'll pay for half the cost of the party."

"No!" the host raised his voice.

"Please. If you allow me to stay, I'll pay for the entire party."

"*No!*" the host shouted, and pulled Bar Kamtza by the arm, walked him to the door, and threw him out.

When Bar Kamtza got home, he was shaking. He thought of all the people who had been at the party. No one had said anything. No one had defended him. Even the rabbis had allowed him to be humiliated. He decided to take revenge.

Bar Kamtza sailed to Rome and asked for an audience with the emperor. Before Nero and his attendants, he said, "I've come to inform you of a plot. The arrogant Jews in Jerusalem are planning a revolt."

"What proof can you give me?" Caesar asked.

"Send them an offering to sacrifice in their Temple. They will surely refuse. Their rejection will be proof that they are planning a rebellion."

Nero agreed and sent a three-year-old calf to be offered as a sacrifice. On the ship, Bar Kamtza, knowing that a blemished animal would not be accepted for a sacrifice, slit the calf's eyelid and lips. The Romans would not regard these markings as blemishes, for they did not affect the functions of the animal, but he knew that any priest in Jerusalem would notice them.

Bar Kamtza brought Nero's gift to the Temple. The rabbis immediately noticed the blemishes and began to debate among themselves. One said, "These are precarious times. It's essential for the survival of our people that we maintain harmonious relations with Rome. Let's sacrifice the calf as it is." Another said, "If the animal is sacrificed, it will set a precedent, and people will think blemished animals may be sacrificed on the altar." A third suggested, "Let's kill Bar Kamtza; then he will not be able to give a report to the emperor." The second rabbi replied, "Is murder now acceptable?"

In the end, the calf was not sacrificed. Bar Kamtza returned to Rome. He reported on the disloyalty of the Jews; and the Roman emperor sent his general, Vespasian, to put down the supposed rebellion in Judea. The Roman soldiers surrounded Jerusalem. War began.

During the siege, the three wealthiest men in Jerusalem went to the rabbis and pledged everything they had in their storehouses—wheat, barley, wine, salt, oil, and wood—for as long as the siege lasted. Although the city had provisions to last for years, many of the rabbis preferred to negotiate a peaceful settlement with the Romans rather than fight; but the Zealots, who controlled the gates to the city, refused. Committed to freeing Judea from foreign rule, the Zealots took the law into their own hands and murdered any person who tried to negotiate with the Romans. They would not allow the rabbis to leave the city, and out of hatred for those who wanted to negotiate, they hardened their hearts against their own people and did the unthinkable: They burned their own warehouses of wheat, barley, and firewood.

A famine began from which there was no escape. The marketplaces emptied. There was no food for rich or poor. The tongues of children stuck to their palates from thirst. Mothers did the unimaginable: They boiled and ate their own children.

In the third year of the siege, Rabbi Yochanan ben Zakkai, who was a disciple of Rabbi Hillel, went in secret to see his sister's son, the leader of the Zealots. He said to his nephew, "Sikra, the people are dying of famine. We do not have strength to fight the Romans. Let me out of the city so I can speak with them."

Sikra answered, "The others would kill me for helping you negotiate with the Romans."

Ben Zakkai persisted. "Sikra, you wanted to retake the Temple so we could pray to God as we once did, but soon there will be no one alive to pray. You are sharp as a dagger. Devise a plan so that I can escape from the city undetected."

Sikra thought of a plan. "Pretend you are very ill. Place something foul-smelling next to you so that people will think you are dead. Tell your disciples to carry you out of the city in a coffin, but do not let anyone else help. People know the difference between the weight of the living and the weight of the dead."

The plan was successful.

Ben Zakkai arrived in the Roman camp and greeted the commander of the Roman troops, by saying, "*Vive Imperator!* Long live Caesar!"

Vespasian, the Roman general, replied, "You're liable to be killed twice. You have called me Caesar when I am not an emperor. And if I am an emperor, why have you not come before to see me to offer peace?"

Ben Zakkai answered, "You are an emperor. Were you not an emperor, Jerusalem would not be given into your hands. Only a king can destroy Jerusalem. I could not come to see you because the Zealots in Jerusalem would not let us leave the city."

Vespasian considered ben Zakkai's reply. In the silence, a messenger arrived from Rome and declared, "Arise! Caesar has died, the Roman Senate has appointed Vespasian the next emperor."

Vespasian tried to stand up, but he had slid off one shoe. When he tried to put it on, he could not, for his foot had become swollen. In confusion, he asked aloud, "What has happened to my foot that my shoe does not fit?"

Rabbi ben Zakkai answered, "Good news has made your foot swell.

Let someone you dislike pass in front of you and your foot will slip into the shoe."

Vespasian followed ben Zakkai's advice and was soon standing in both of his shoes. He said to ben Zakkai, "You are a wise man; you have knowledge of large and small matters. I want to reward you, for you have brought me the news that I was destined to become Caesar. Ask me for what you wish."

"Spare Jerusalem," ben Zakkai replied. "Do not kill any of her inhabitants."

"That is impossible. The Romans have made me general to subdue Jerusalem. Make another request."

Rabbi Yochanan made three requests. "Leave the western gate open so all who leave by the fourth hour may be spared. Let your doctors cure my teacher, the holy Rabbi Tzadok. He has been fasting for forty years so that Jerusalem might be saved. And spare the town of Jabneh so my disciples and I may study and keep God's commandments."

When the dying Rabbi Tzadok was carried to them in a litter, ben Zakkai quickly stood up. Vespasian asked him, "Why do you stand with such reverence before a bag of bones?"

Ben Zakkai answered, "If we had had another holy man like him we could have defeated your armies."

"Where is his power?" Vespasian asked.

"In his love—his love for God and his love for the people."

Vespasian's doctors cared for Rabbi Tzadok. They fed him small amounts of food and water until his shrunken stomach expanded and his strength was restored. Vespasian returned to Rome and sent his son Titus to Judea.

Titus offered to spare Jerusalem, but the Zealots refused to negotiate. Three weeks before Tisha B'Av, the Roman soldiers scaled the walls of the city. The Zealots placed themselves on the Temple steps, certain that God would protect them. The soldiers set fire to the Temple gates. The eyes of the Zealots stung with smoke, but they refused to surrender. When at last they tried to put out the fire, it was too late. The entire Temple burned to the ground. Before it burned, the Roman soldiers ran into the Temple and took out its treasures. When they saw that the Temple was lost, the Zealots withdrew.

Rabbi Tzadok entered the ruins. He wandered about the abandoned Temple and then cried out, "Adonai, why did they not listen?" He leaned against a pillar and fell asleep. In his sleep, God comforted him, saying, "The grief of the faithful is great, but do not separate yourself from the ones who are lost."

Hundreds of thousands of people in Jerusalem were killed or sold as slaves. It began with a seemingly small incident—Kamtza, Bar Kamtza, and the hardening of the heart. It ended with the destruction of the Temple and Jerusalem.

Vespasian kept his agreement. In the small town of Jabneh, scholars gathered with their families. When they heard that the Temple was in flames, they tore their clothes. They wept. They prayed. They grieved.

Rabbi ben Zakkai counseled them, saying, "Listen to one another, respect one another, pursue peace, serve God." The community was at a loss. How could they serve God if there was no Temple where they could bring sacrifices?

Rabbi ben Zakkai said to them, "Prayers will replace sacrifice. We will honor God by doing God's will. God causes the winds to blow, the clouds to bring rain, the plants to grow so we can eat. God serves us. It is good to serve God. We will serve God with study and good deeds."

With no Temple and priesthood, the rabbis intensified their studies. They tried to follow Rabbi ben Zakkai's teacher, Hillel, who when asked to explain the Torah replied, "What is hateful to you do not do to others. That is the whole Torah. The rest is commentary. Now go and study."

Job

Who Feeds the Desolate Places?

Job is good. His heart is open to others. And yet he suffers. In his suffering, his heart discovers a place beyond goodness and evil, a place before the seas are born.

I have followed the gorgeous poetry of Job, condensing many sections, and have added a small amount of midrash, at the beginning and the end.

There was a man in the land of Uz. His name was Job. He was sincere, forthright, God-fearing, and kept away from evil. He had seven sons and three daughters, seven thousand sheep, three thousand cattle, five hundred oxen, and five hundred donkeys. He was one of the most important men in the East; yet he often went himself to visit orphans and widows to help them.

Job's sons held feasts in one another's houses and invited their three sisters to eat and drink with them. Job feared that his children might be arrogant in their hearts because of their wealth so he offered burnt sacrifices for each of them and asked the needy to pray for them. After eating, Job always sang praises to God. He hired musicians to play for him; and when they tired, he would take up the harp and play for them.

Now one day when the angels of God were praising God, Satan

the Accuser was in the midst of them, and God said to Satan, "Where are you coming from?"

Satan answered, "I was walking about, wandering the earth."

"Then have you noticed my servant Job?" God asked. "There is no one like him on earth. He is sincere, forthright, God-fearing, and keeps away from evil."

"Well, of course, Job fears you," Satan answered. "Have you not protected him and his household? You bless his work and multiply his possessions; but if you were to stretch out your hand and destroy what is his, he would curse you in your face."

God said to Satan, "We shall test him. All that is his is yours, only do not kill him."

Satan left the presence of God.

One day, a messenger arrived at Job's home and said, "Your cattle were plowing and your donkeys were grazing near them when the tribe of Sheva appeared. They took your livestock and killed your servants. I was the only one to escape." The messenger was still speaking when a second messenger arrived and said, "A bolt of lightning fell from heaven, burning your sheep and shepherds. I was the only one to escape." As he was speaking, a third messenger arrived and said, "Three troops of Chaldean soldiers took your camels and killed your shepherds. I was the only one to escape." He was still speaking when a fourth messenger arrived and said, "Your sons and daughters were eating and drinking wine in the house of your oldest son when a great wind from the desert struck every side of the house and all your children died. I was the only one to escape."

Job stood up. He ripped his clothes and tore out his hair. "Disaster! *Disaster!*" he shrieked, and fell to the ground and prayed, "From my mother's womb, I came out naked. Naked I will return. The Lord gives and the Lord takes away. Blessed is the name of the Lord." Job did not curse God.

Again the angels gathered before God. Satan also stood before God, and God said to him, "Where are you coming from?"

Satan answered, "From wandering the earth and walking about."

"Then you have noticed my servant Job?" God asked. "There is no one like him on earth—sincere, forthright, God-fearing, keeping away from evil. Despite your trials he held on to his faith."

Satan answered, "A man will comply in order to protect his own life. But if you were to put your hand on his flesh and bones, he will curse your face."

God said, "He's in your hands. Do what you wish with him, but keep him alive."

Satan left God's presence.

Satan struck Job with boils from the soles of his feet to his head. Job scratched himself with a potsherd and sat down in the midst of the ashes. To support them, Job's wife, Zitidos, became a water carrier. But when she lost her job and was forced to cut her hair to buy bread and Satan cursed her, she said to Job, "Will you still hold on to your faith? Curse God and die!"

"Do not utter such profanity! Shall we accept the good from God and not the bad?" Job's lips spoke no curses.

Job's three friends, Eliphaz, Bildad, and Zophar, heard what had happened to him. They came from their homes to grieve and comfort Job. When they did not recognize him, they cried loudly and wept. Each one tore his coat and threw dust on his head. They sat with Job for seven days and seven nights. No one said a word, for they could see how deeply Job was suffering.

Then Job broke the silence, cursing the day and night he was born. "Why didn't I die in the womb? Why was I laid on my mother's knees and offered her breasts to suckle? If I had been a stillborn child, who was hidden and had never seen the light, I would be resting in a quiet grave where the unimportant and the important dwell together, where the servant is free from his master.

"Why does God give life to those who suffer? They wait for death, and it does not come. They dig for death with greater eagerness than for hidden treasures. Before eating, I sigh. My groans pour out like water. That which I feared has happened, that which I dreaded is upon me.

"God tears me, gnashes me, shames me, hedges me in. If only I could find God and present my case. Surely if God knew the path I have taken, I would emerge from God's test as pure as gold, for I have treasured God's teachings more than food and walked steadfastly in all God's ways. Yet who can control God's wishes? Look at the others: the thief, the murderer, the adulterer. The wicked grow rich and powerful. They steal the orphan's donkey. They take the widow's ox. They make the poor go naked and steal their food. Look at the children of the wicked. They are singing. They play the tambourine and harp and rejoice. They turn from God and end their days in prosperity! Is this not so? Who will say I am a liar? I have no peace of mind. I live in torment without rest."

Eliphaz the Yemenite spoke, "May I answer you or will you become more anguished? When you were the one to preach, your words lifted the stumbling and strengthened the faltering. But now when trouble reaches you, you lose patience. Doesn't your innocence reassure you? Is your religion of no comfort to you? Do you know of any innocent person who perished or truly righteous person who was destroyed? Those who plough mischief reap what they have sown. God's breath destroys them. God's anger consumes them.

"A word was whispered to me, and my ear grasped a bit of it. In the thoughts and visions of the night when slumber falls on people, fear and trembling fell on me and my bones were disturbed. A wind passed my face, the hair of my flesh stood up, but I did not recognize its appearance or the image before my eyes. I heard a faint voice say, 'Can a person be more righteous than God or more pure than the Creator? How can God trust those who live in houses whose walls are clay and whose foundations are dust and who will die without ever having known their own fate?'

"Why are your eyes flashing like that? The person whom God tests is fortunate. Do not reject the reproaches of El Shaddai. God does not benefit from you. Even if you were perfect, you would be of no benefit to God. You ask, 'What does God know? Can God see through the clouds?' You speak deviously because you are guilty. God has reproved you because your wickedness is great. You stripped the naked of their clothing, kept water from the thirsty, withheld bread from the hungry, sent widows away empty.

"Were you born before Adam and heard God's plans? What do you know that is not the wisdom of all of us? Listen to us. The three of us are men of maturity who are older than your father. God gives pain but heals the wound. God can judge through a dark cloud. Instead of keeping your old ways, pray to God. God will be your treasure and listen to you and what you wish for will be accomplished."

Job answered, "If my anguish and rage were placed together on a scale, they would outweigh the sands of the seas. Therefore, I am stammering as I answer you. My spirit drinks the poison of God's arrows. Would that God would grant my request and crush me. That would bring relief. Is my strength granite, my flesh brass? Is there no help? Your answer shrivels my soul. If I were in your place, I would encourage you. Instead you invent lies, dig a pit for me, and turn my day to night. Did I ask you for anything? Money, rescue, ransom? Just tell me what I have done, and I will listen in silence. Look at me! Am I lying to you?

"My life is a mere breath of wind. In the same way as a cloud disappears, the one who goes down to the grave will not rise up, return to his house, or be recognized again. My days are spent without hope. They pass as swiftly as a weaver's shuttle.

"I am strangling. My God, I ask you: Why don't you forgive whatever transgression I may have done, for I am lying on the dust? Am I a dragon or a sea serpent that you keep constant watch over me? You terrify me with dreams and frighten me with visions. Why do you concern yourself so with man, punishing him every morning, testing him every hour? Can you not turn away for a moment so I can swallow my own spit? The moment I lie down, I toss in anguish until dawn. My flesh is infested with worms. My skin is covered with scabs. As a slave longs for shade and a servant hopes for wages, I have endured months of toil and nights of exhaustion. My soul cries out to you in bitterness."

Job's friend Bildad the Shuhite answered, "Your words create a great wind, but you need to bridle your tongue and consider before you speak. You tear yourself apart in anger. Do you imagine that God is not just? If your children have sinned, God has sent them away with their transgressions. If you seek God and are pure and upright, God will reward you and your end will be great. Ask your ancestors what they have learned. We know little, for our days on earth pass as quickly as a shadow. Can papyrus grow without a marsh? Can reeds grow without water? Those who forget God will wither and other plants will take their place.

"If you are blameless, God will not harm you, but the light of the wicked man will be extinguished. He will be paralyzed with fear. Terror will eat his skin. Death's oldest child will devour his strength. His memory will vanish from the earth. He will be driven from light to darkness and chased out of the world. He will leave no survivors, neither child nor grandchild, in his dwelling. The world will shudder in horror at his story. Such is the fate of those who do not know God."

Job answered, "How long will you continue to reproach and humiliate me? You should be ashamed to judge me, acting as my superiors! But if you insist on adding to my misery, at least realize God has not acted justly with me. As long as I have breath, I will speak what is true and not give up my integrity. I have been crying 'Outrage!' but no one answers me. God has fenced my way so I cannot pass.

"I have no dignity. I am broken, uprooted like a tree, separated from my friends and family. My relatives have failed me and my good friends have forgotten me. Those who live in my house look at me as if I am a stranger. I call my servant, and she does not answer. My wife abhors my breath. The children find me loathsome. Everyone I loved has turned against me. You three, have pity! Why do you persecute me as if you are God? Look at my peeling flesh. If only my words could be written, inscribed in a book, graven on a rock. But I know that my Redeemer lives and when my flesh falls away, I will see God.

"I am powerless and overcome with desire for God, and what help do you offer me? Do I not know God's wisdom and power? The underworld trembles naked before God. God stretches the world over empty space and binds the water into clouds. God moves mountains that do not even know they have been overturned. God causes the earth to quake, the sun to withhold its rays, the stars to dim. God stretches out the heavens and earth and performs deeds and wonders without number.

"Yet when God passes near me, I do not know the moment. Suddenly, God may strike, and who am I to say to God, 'What are you doing? Let us come together to debate'? If God slew Rahab and the twisting Sea Serpent, how then will God listen to my words? If it is a trial of strength, God's might is beyond mine. If it is a trial of judgment, who will summon me to court? I am blameless, but I cannot find rest. There is no arbiter between us who will place her hand on both of ours.

"My soul quarrels with life. I say to God, 'Tell me why you have condemned me. Why are you quarreling with me? Why do you reject me and praise the wicked? You know I have done no wrong, but no one can save me from your hands. You made me from clay and will return me to clay. You poured your spirit into me, covered me with bones and sinews, clothed me with flesh and skin, granted me life and kindness and watched over my spirit. I know you gave me everything, yet if I did sin, you saw me and chose not to cleanse me of my sin. Instead, you hunt me like a lion, continually forcing a verdict on me. You increase your anger against me. Why then did you take me from the womb? I wish I had not existed. Stop! Withdraw from me so I can strengthen myself a little before I go to the land of darkness, the land of no return where light is darkness."

Job's third friend, Zophar spoke, "You go on and on and boast in such a way that others are afraid to answer you. I wish God would speak and reveal the mysteries to you so you would know you are being punished less than you deserve. Can you know God's purpose? Have you scaled the heights of the heavens or the depths of Sheol? Put away your wickedness so you can lift your face to God. Then all this will be as waters that have flowed past you. Since the beginning of time, the triumph of the wicked is short and the joy of the flatterer, one moment."

Job answered, "What great wisdom you offer me! I could just as well ask the animals, birds, or fish for advice. We all know God's hand controls every living being. I know it is God who makes the waters flow and dry up, who gives counsel to judges and priests and turns them into fools, who causes nations to rise and fall. But I want to reason with God. If you would be silent, maybe then you would know wisdom.

"I beg you, listen to my heart. You are speaking deceitfully in order to curry God's favor. What if you were the ones to be questioned? What if God's terror fell on you? You would panic, and your proverbs would disintegrate like ashes. Be silent so I may speak. Whatever happens, let it happen. I am holding my flesh by my teeth. If God kills me, I will still have trust. My defense shall be my salvation.

"All who are here, listen! Let my words flow into your ears. I am presenting my case. Who will argue with me? Shaddai! I ask only two things: Do not withdraw from me, and do not let your terror overwhelm me. Speak! I will answer you. Or let me speak and answer me. What are my transgressions? Tell me my sins! Why do you hide from me and take me for your enemy? Why pursue a driven leaf? Why torment a dry stalk of grass?

"We are born from mortals. We open like a flower and then wither. We last as long as a shadow and vanish. A tree that is cut down may sprout again when it scents water, but when we lie down, we do not rise again. Until the heavens fade away, we will not awake from our sleep. If you hide me in the underworld until your wrath is over and I die and revive, I would eagerly serve you again, but you have sealed my transgression in a bag. The mountains are crumbling, the stones wearing away, my flesh clings to me, my soul cries out in anguish.

"Where can wisdom be found? Where is the place of understanding? No one can set a value to it. It is not found in the land of the living. The deep says, 'It is not in me.' The sea says, 'I do not have it.' We cannot buy it for gold. Its price is above rubies. God alone knows its ways and places. God sees the world, weighs the winds, measures the waters, sets a course for the rains and thunderstorms, and says to us, 'Wisdom is the fear of God. To run from evil is understanding.'

"How I wish I were still young when God's light watched over me and God's counsel was with me and my young men were around me. Then, I washed my feet with butter, and oil poured out from the rocks. I went to the city gate and took my seat in the public square. The young people who saw me hid, and the old men stood up respectfully. Princes and nobles refrained from speaking when they saw me. The people waited for my words as if for rain, and after I spoke, there was silence. Whoever knew of my deeds praised me; whoever saw my acts bore witness.

"I helped the poor, the orphan, and whoever had no one to help them. I brought joy to the widow's heart. I was the eyes for the blind and the feet for the lame. I knocked the teeth out of the greedy and plucked the victim from their jaws. I thought that I would live as long as the phoenix and die with my household, and that my offspring would continue. But now the young laugh at me. I am their gossip, their conversation. They spit in front of me. Out of hatred, they provoke me and under darkness they attack me. Terrors pursue me. My salvation flees from me like vanishing clouds.

"At night, my bones and sinews ache. With great effort I change my clothes. Because of my boils, I sit in the mud. I cry out to you, but you do not answer me. You give me to the demons. My substance dissolves. I have become dust and ashes. Could it be that I did not have sufficient compassion for those in despair? I had set my path for good and received evil. I stand up in the assembly and cry out for help. My companions are the jackal and the ostrich. My skin falls from me. My harp grieves and the song of my flute is a lament.

"But you must know: I have done no wrong! I made an agreement with my eyes never to gaze at an unmarried woman or lurk in my neighbor's doorway. I know such actions lead to destruction. I honored every case brought by my slaves or bondwomen, for one creator formed all of us. I never put hope in gold or confidence in jewelry or rejoiced in wealth. I did not rejoice in the misfortune of my enemies or allow a stranger to lodge outside my tent. As for my sins, I did not hide them. Let God bear witness for me. If my enemy wishes to write a book, I will gladly tell him my secrets. I will speak no more. My words are ended."

The three men did not have any more to say, for it was clear that Job considered himself to be righteous.

Elihu, from the family of Abram, became angry. He was angry with Job because Job thought he was more righteous than God. But he had waited to answer Job because he was younger than the others. Now when the others were silent, he spoke, "I am young and was in awe of you and afraid to speak. I thought, 'Days speak and years teach wisdom.' But it is our spirit and the breath of God that gives us understanding. Since you could not convince Job or answer him, I must speak, for I cannot hold my tongue anymore.

"Job, listen to my words. I speak to you with knowledge and sincerity, for the spirit of God created me and the breath of God gave me life. I stand before God as you do, a human, formed from clay. You do not need to fear me or be overawed by me. You have said, 'I am innocent without transgression. Yet God has found pretenses to consider me an enemy.'

"You are wrong to speak like this. God is greater than we are. Why do you fight God because God refuses you an accounting? Once God speaks, God does not speak a second time. God answers in different ways, in a dream or a vision of the night. When deep sleep falls upon us, God opens our ears. If we do not respond to the message, God checks our pride and strikes us with physical suffering so we might repent.

"Yet if an angel, one angel among a thousand, acts as a mediator on our behalf, our actions and speaking in our favor: 'Give her a reprieve. Deliver him from the pit. I will pay the ransom,' then God will restore us so that we are even stronger than in our youth. If we then pray to God to bless us so we can joyfully see God's face, we will be full again of righteousness. If we can say, 'I have sinned. I turned right into wrong and did not know my error,' then we can save ourselves from going down to the pit and instead live in God's light. Job, if you would answer, do so. If not, listen, and I will teach you wisdom."

Elihu went on, "Wise men, listen to me. The ear tastes words as the palate tastes food. Let us examine together what is right and know what is good. Who is this man who says he is innocent and accuses God of being wrong and adds rebellion to his sins? Look up at the sky, at the clouds that are higher than you. Can you imagine that what you do affects God? What does God gain from your goodness or your transgressions? Your actions affect mortals, not God.

"You say you cannot see God. Wait, Job. Wait for God. God is our teacher. God does not withhold reward from anyone who merits it.

God gathers our spirit and returns us to dust. In a moment, at midnight, God causes a nation to pass away and removes its strength. God shatters the mighty and puts others in their place. We cannot understand God's ways.

"Do you hear the rumblings, the sound of God's voice? Lightning spreads across the earth and then a great roar. It is God's voice but we cannot trace it. God commands the snow and rain to descend to the earth. The people go inside; the animals run to their lairs for shelter. A whirlwind approaches from heaven. The clouds fill with moisture.

"Listen, Job. Stand still and consider God's wonders. The clouds are covering the bright light in the heavens. Golden rays emerge. God's glory is awesome. Whatever we might try to say would hide God's secrets. We cannot find God. The power and judgment and goodness of Shaddai is great. The wise know they cannot perceive God. . . ."

From the whirlwind, God spoke to Job and said, "Who are you who darkens my design by speaking words without knowledge? Stand and prepare yourself. I will ask and you will answer. Where were you when I laid the foundations of the earth? Who decided its measurements? Who stretched out the measuring line across the earth? Were you there when the morning stars sang and the angels rejoiced? Did you watch over the birth of the sea when I wrapped her in a blanket of cloud and swaddled her in a fog? Who shut the doors of the sea when the waters poured out of the womb and I said, 'To here your surging waters may come, but no farther?'

"Did you ever wake the morning and let the sun know its place so it might travel to the corners of the earth, shaking the wicked from the darkness? Have you descended to the depths of the sea and walked in the abyss? Have the gates of death been revealed to you? Have you seen the doorkeepers at the place of darkness? Do you know the width of the earth? Tell me if you know: The path to light? Where darkness dwells—so you may take it to its home? Do you know where I stored the treasures of snow and hail for a time of trouble and battle? Surely, you know all this! You were born long ago and have counted many years.

"Who causes the rain to fall in the wilderness where no human lives? Who feeds the desolate places with tender sprouts? Does the rain have a father? Who gives birth to the drops of dew? Who brings forth frost from the heavens? Can you shape the Pleiades with chains or open the clasps of Orion? Can you bring forth the constellations in their time? Do you know the laws of the heavens that influence the earth? If you lift your voice to the clouds, will a flood of water pour over you? Can you send out the lightning so that it says, '*Hineni!* I am ready!' Who placed wisdom in the body's inner parts and gave the mind understanding?

"Will you hunt for the lioness to satisfy the appetite of the young lions when they crouch in their dens waiting to eat? Who prepares the prey for the raven when his children wander about without food? The mountain goats and hinds give birth. The months pass and when their time comes, they endure their agony. Their children grow strong in the wild; they go away and do not return. Who gives the wild donkey the wilderness for his home? The wild donkey mocks the city's noise and refuses the urgings of the driver. The hills are his pasture and he seeks for every green sprout. Does the wild ox want to serve you, to sleep in your barn? Can you tie him to a furrow with a rope? Will he plow the valleys behind you? Can you rely on him to bring in your harvest?

"The stork leaves her eggs on the earth, warming them in the ground. She forgets they can be trampled on and cracked. She hardens herself against her own children as if they are not hers. She does not fear for them, for I gave her neither wisdom nor understanding, so she spreads her wings and laughs at horse and rider. Who gives the horse strength and power to leap like a locust? The horse has no fear and does not flinch at swords or javelins. He sniffs war from afar, and to the sound of the ram's horn, he responds, 'Hurrah!'

"Is it your wisdom that allows the hawk to soar? Does the eagle fly and build his nest in the mountain summits because of your command? The eagle lodges on the crags and searches for his food. His eaglets gulp down blood. Where there are corpses, you will find the vulture. You have reprimanded God, what do you have to say now?"

Job answered, "I am of so little weight. How can I answer? I put my hand to my mouth. I spoke once. I will not say more. I spoke twice. I will not continue."

God spoke from the whirlwind: "Prepare yourself. I will question you and you will answer. Will you challenge my judgment and condemn me so you are justified? Can your voice thunder like God's? Dress yourself in beauty, splendor, and majesty. Scatter your rage and see that every cruel, haughty person is crushed and humbled. When you can do this, I will admit that you have some strength.

"Look at the behemoth whom I made with you. He eats grass as cattle do. His strength is in his loins and his power in the navel of his belly. He makes his tail stand up like a cedar. He is the first of my works. Only his Creator can draw a sword against him. The mountains where the wild animals play give him food. The lotus trees give him shade, and the willows of the brook surround him. Can you or anyone else capture him?

"As for the leviathan, can you bring him out of the water with your fishhook? Can you catch him with a rope? Will he speak softly to you and ask you to kindly make a covenant with him? He turns iron into straw, bronze into a rotting tree. His teeth strike terror. His breath ignites coals. When he rears, the angels withdraw. No arrow can stop him. Will you play with him like a bird?"

Job said, "I know you can do everything. You can carry out any plan you choose. You ask me, 'Who gave counsel without understanding?' I realize I was speaking about your ways, but I did not really understand them. They were beyond what I knew. You said, 'Listen now, I will speak. I will question you and you will answer.' Before, I knew you from what the others had said, but now that I have seen you, I have no words. I am merely dust and ashes."

After speaking to Job, God turned to Eliphaz and said, "I am angry with you and your two friends because you did not speak in a forthright way as did my servant Job. Now take seven bullocks and seven rams and go to my servant Job and bring an offering so that he prays for you. Even though you did not speak honestly as Job did, for his sake, I will not harm you." The three men obeyed.

At the moment that Job prayed for his friends, God restored his fortune. God doubled all that Job had had in the past. His brothers and sisters and all his former acquaintances came and ate with him in his house. They comforted him for all the misery that God had brought on him, and each one gave him money and a gold ring.

God blessed the end of Job's life more than the beginning. Job acquired fourteen thousand sheep, six thousand camels, one thousand cattle, and one thousand donkeys. After the death of his wife, he married Jacob's daughter, Dinah, and had seven sons and three daughters. He named his daughters Jemimah (dove), Keziah (cinnamon), and Keren-Happuch (horn of eye paint). In all the land of Uz there were no women as beautiful as Job's daughters. Job gave them an inheritance together with their brothers. He lived another one hundred and forty years and had the good fortune to hold four generations of children on his knees.

When he knew he was dying, he gathered his ten children to him and said, "When I am gone, you must care for the poor, be generous to them, and treat the needy with respect." For three days he was ill and his daughters remained by his side.

On the fourth day, Job saw angels descending from heaven. He got out of bed and gave a harp to his oldest daughter, an incense burner to the second, and cymbals to the third and said, "Play and welcome the angels." They played and sang and praised God. They were the only ones to witness the Shechinah enter the room, kiss their father, and take his soul to heaven.

There was great grief after Job died, especially among the poor, the widows, and the orphans. For seven days they did not bury him, for they did not want to be separated from his body. They feared that no one else would care for them as Job had done.

About the Stories

Woe is me that two mysteries have been revealed to me—the mystery of calamity and the mystery of salvation.

RASHI

All the stories told at Tisha B'Av involve calamity. An entire generation of men who left Egypt is killed. Jerusalem and the Temple are destroyed. On their path to spiritual freedom, the people walk into the wall of their own limitations and fail in their commitment to God. Yet, within calamity lie the seeds of salvation. In *The Spies*, the women and the children, who remained devoted to God, enter the Promised Land. In *Rachel and the Shechinah*, God's heart changes because of Rachel's compassion. In *Lamentations*, the people realize the extent to which they are bereft when they lose their connection to God. In *The Destruction of the Second Temple*, Rabbi Yochanan ben Zakkai advises the rabbis that serving others is the way to serve God.

Calamity and grief are the result of the people's betrayal of their covenant with God. Implicit in the stories is the message that a change of conduct will bring about salvation. These and other stories told on Tisha B'Av suggest that good is rewarded and evil is punished. They balance the story of Job in which suffering is seemingly not a consequence of bad deeds or betrayal. Suffering seems arbitrary, yet in the story of Job it is the "living experience" of suffering that brings wisdom and compassion. Job loses everything and is hurled into the void, but it is there that he meets the Source.

At the beginning of the Book of Job, Job is self-confident, righteous, and God-fearing. He does everything right, even making offerings for his children *in case* they should sin inadvertently. There is a kind of hubris in the "perfect" Job who tries to tend not only to his own spiritual life but to that of his children. Yet, God loves Job and proudly points him out to Satan, who challenges Job's inner marrow by taking from him his wealth, family, name, friends, and health. Despite his three friends' contention that God is always just and their insistence that he confess his sins, Job refuses to admit any wrongdoing. He extols his own goodness and asks only that God answer him. He defends himself, insisting on two things: the truth of his own experience and an answer to God's actions.

Elihu, a young observer, suggests that communication is possible with God, but not necessarily in the particular manner that Job seeks. Job does not reply. When he stops speaking, when he stops defending himself and is silent; when at last he listens, he hears God speak.

God's speech in the whirlwind, which could be perceived as a divine song, cracks open Job's carefully controlled and planned moralistic vision of the world. God reveals creation, darkness, evil, death, chaos, terror, primal energy, the behemoth, the leviathan—the underbelly of the world.

In Job's new vision of the vastness of the universe, he comes to understand that he, as part of the universe, is a combination of its fullness—good and bad, perfect and imperfect, craving righteousness while standing in awe at the wildness and indifference of the behemoth or leviathan. Metaphorically shrunk to the size of a mote ("dust and ashes"), Job glimpses God's inexhaustible splendor, which is beyond a human being's concept of time or ethics. In accepting God's mystery and the ambiguity of the soul, he does not succumb to Satan's wager by cursing a moralistic God. Instead, he answers God: "Before, I knew you from what the others had said. Now that I have seen you, I have no words. I am a mortal, dust and ashes." Job now perceives reality without blinders or constructs. He has no words. He has experienced a part of God that is beyond the world of words.

Job's trials are similar to those of a medicine man being tested. Shamans rarely choose to be healers. On the contrary, they are visited with overwhelming adversity, often involving loss of property, relationships, and physical strength, as well as journeys to "other worlds." They are tested to the point of extinction (or enlightenment) until they agree to take on the calling that they have been asked to accept. Having touched death, darkness, and the mysteries, the shamanic healer learns to accept what suffering brings and transforms the suffering into helping others.

God's testing does not end with Job's reply. God tests him one final time by asking him to forgive those friends who have belittled him. Job's acceptance of his friends' betrayals reflects how deep is his understanding and acceptance of the immensity and oneness of the universe as well as his awe and love of God. In understanding that everything is a part of God, Job understands that his friends are also a part of God. Job forgives them and God rewards him with double his former prosperity. Previously, he had seven thousand cattle, now he has fourteen thousand. Animals in fairy tales can be viewed as energy, and once Job accepts his wild and evil as well as his righteous instincts, he is blessed with twice the energy he previously had.

God also rewards Job by giving him as many children as he had before. This time Job does not attempt to control his children's spiritual lives. The daughters, whether new or "restored," are no longer the same women who are being "entertained" by their brothers. These are women who have work of their own. Job honors them with names that indicate that they are skilled in the shaman's craft: Jemimah or "dove" indicating the spirit; Keziah or "cinnamon," an herb which calls forth the spirit; Keren-Happuch or "eye paint" which evokes the spirit in the ceremony created to bring about transformation. When we are told that "in all the land of Uz there are no women as beautiful as Job's daughters," we know that their beauty is their souls shining.

God's revelation of the fullness of the universe is as unexpected as Job offering women independence. There is no other instance in the Bible when a father willingly offers his daughter an inheritance. Having passed through the darkest suffering, Job rejoices in life and does not choose to "keep control," for as a mature adult, he understands that is impossible. Rather, he chooses to give away his control by offering his daughters their own inheritances so they might flourish in their own way. Job previously was the wealthiest man in material goods: he owned cattle, donkeys, mules—earthly possessions. Now his daughters, who are engaged in spiritual matters, carry on Job's true inheritance, the work of the spirit.

On Tisha B'Av, the engagement between God and the Jewish people fails. The adolescent nation rebels against the teachings and loses faith in their Protector. After constant betrayals, God, the Parent/Protector, kicks the people out of the Promised Land. In exile, the people begin to mature. They appreciate God's teachings and the home God had given them. They repent and return to God. But once again, they turn their hearts against one another; and the Temple and Jerusalem are destroyed a second time.

Part of the wisdom of the stories told on Tisha B'Av is the appreciation that more than scholarly knowledge or intellectual intention is needed. When offering the people the Covenant, God declares that if we give up all other worship—idols, possessions, physical cravings, as well as our fears, insecurities, pettiness, and desire for control—we will receive every blessing imaginable.

How then do we serve God? Rabbi Yochanan ben Zakkai advises us that in serving others, we are serving God. He says, "If you have a sapling in your hand, and you are told, 'there is the Messiah,' go on with your planting, and afterward receive him." Love God, study God's teachings, care for others! The everyday life and the open heart become the new teaching.

From failure, a larger vision is revealed. The tears shed on Tisha B'Av moisten the ground for the seeds of redemption to be planted.

ROSH HASHANAH

About Rosh Hashanah

The holiday that is now celebrated as Rosh Hashanah changed greatly over three thousand years. The Bible assigned the first day of the seventh month during the dark of the moon as a time of rest, contemplation, and celebration while the harvest was gathered in. In the time of the First Temple, this day was called the Day of the Sounding of the Shofar, for the only biblical commandment of the holiday was to listen to the shofar. The shofar, or ram's horn, serves as a reminder for the people to implore God for forgiveness. According to legend, it sounded on earth for the forty days Moses pleaded with God on Mount Sinai before receiving the second set of commandments.

After the Jews returned to Jerusalem from the Babylonian captivity in 485 B.C.E., Ezra, the prophet and high priest, chose the first day of the seventh month to assemble the people before the Water Gate. He read the Torah aloud and explained it to them in such a way that they could understand it without having to consult the priests. The people wept when they realized how far they had strayed from the teachings. Ezra urged them not to grieve but to open their hearts to God and to celebrate their return to the land and to God. He advised them to go home, to eat and drink, and to share what they had with those who were in need.

The Jews returning from Babylon brought back Babylonian traditions. In captivity, the Jews witnessed the Babylonians celebrate a festival called Akitu. In the seventh month of the year, the gods assembled in the capital city for seven to twelve days to decide who would live and who would die. The king was put through a period of trial and testing, and if he survived, he was crowned and honored. Two hundred years after Ezra, prayers extolling the kingship and majesty of God were added to the holiday service. God became "the king of kings" who rendered judgment as to who would live and who would die, and in 300 C.E., the name of the holiday was changed from the biblical name, Day of the Sounding of the Shofar, to Rosh Hashanah.

About Rosh Hashanah

According to the Talmud, which was written five hundred years after Ezra, on Rosh Hashanah each person's fate is determined in a metaphorical Book of Life, but each person is able to change his or her fate through four paths of transformation: charity, prayer, change of conduct, and change of name.

This time of transformation and transition when our fates are changing and we pass from the old to the new is precarious, for past customs and beliefs are abandoned before new ones are tried and established. Throughout the centuries, tribal people created ceremonies at liminal moments by wearing masks, beating drums, and blowing horns to reinforce the spirit of the community and frighten away negative forces. Jews continue to keep the commandment of blowing the shofar as an integral part of the New Year holiday.

A rabbinic midrash connects the blowing of the ram's horn to repentance and God's mercy: In heaven, Abraham asked God, "One day you told me Isaac would be my seed and the next day you told me to offer him as a sacrifice. I did not understand, but I did not question you. Now I ask you to do the same with Isaac's children. When they go against your teachings, remember that they do not always know what they are doing and remind yourself of the willingness of Isaac to do whatever you asked and forgive them."

God answered, "If the children of Isaac wish to be forgiven, let them pray and blow the ram's horn on Rosh Hashanah. The sound of the ram's horn will remind me of the binding of Isaac, and I will forgive them. Each time the shofar blows on Rosh Hashanah, your merit and Isaac's merit will rise to heaven."

On the seven Sabbaths before Rosh Hashanah, Jews now read the portions of the Prophets that focus on consoling the Hebrew people in their exile. During the last four weeks before Rosh Hashanah, the shofar blows every day, to remind Jews of the necessity of active repentance and reconciliation with their family and neighbors so they will be ready to stand before God.

Other traditions have arisen around the holiday. The custom began of visiting the graves of relatives the day before Rosh Hashanah to say the Kaddish, the prayer for the dead in which God the creator of life is praised. According to Kabbalistic belief, the soul is eternal, and so there is always the possibility of communication between worlds. We are blessed with the challenge of continual renewal, for just as the good deeds of our ancestors can cause God to be more lenient in judging us, we believe that by praying for our departed, relatives can help to elevate their souls.

Today, observant Jews spend Rosh Hashanah in prayer and at celebratory family meals and often buy new clothes for the New Year. Some Jews wear white clothes to symbolize purity. They dip bread and apples into honey hoping for a sweet year and wish one another Shanah Tovah, meaning "a good year." On the afternoon of the first day of Rosh Hashanah, Jews go to a flowing body of water, a river, or sea, and in a ceremony called Tashlich, meaning "to cast away," throw bread crumbs, or other offerings which are meant to represent sins, into the water.

During the ten days between Rosh Hashanah and Yom Kippur, prayers and psalms are recited intensively. It is a time not only of quiet introspection and prayer but of active fixing, of seeking out any person we may have harmed to ask his or her forgiveness, and of extending our forgiveness to those who have harmed us so there can be a mutual reconciliation.

The ten days between the two holidays are called the Days of Awe. Asking forgiveness is an awesome event. Only when there is reconciliation in the community, which is sought on Rosh Hashanah, is it possible to pray to God on a deeper level on Yom Kippur.

Every year at the conclusion of the Rosh Hashanah service, my rabbi, Shlomo Carlebach, would say to our congregation, "One thing, I beg you, during these next days before Yom Kippur, do not say anything bad about anyone. You never want to say anything that might harm another, but on Yom Kippur whatever you say against others is taken in heaven against you." What a simple request—not to say a word against another person. And yet what a profound and challenging statement: to truly realize that the other is ourself and in harming the other we harm ourselves. I have yet to go ten days.

Moses had used the shofar as a call to battle. Today the piercing sound of the shofar in a house of prayer is a call to inner battle. Its piercing blast wakes the soul. *Who have I harmed? How can I make amends? Who can I help? How can I dance with the Shechinah? What is separating me from living a life of joy?* The shofar sounds one hundred times throughout Rosh Hashanah. It pours through every vertebra in the spine. It is the loudest alarm clock I know: *Wake up!*

Abraham and Sarah

The Birth of Isaac

Since I was a child I wondered about my ancestors Abraham and Sarah. Where did they come from? Who were they?

Abraham and Sarah lived four thousand years ago (in 1900 B.C.E.) among people who worshiped many gods and goddesses in the city of Ur in the land of Sumer (called Shinar in the Bible). In Ur, Abraham had a vision of a different divinity, one with no physical manifestations. This God whom he called El Shaddai told him to leave his father's land to go to an unknown place and promised him numerous descendants. His wife, Sarah, accompanied him. Like Abraham, Sarah had great spiritual power and may well have been a priestess of the Goddess, for wherever they traveled, the kings of the ancient world coveted her presence.

Their spirituality drew them to one another and also separated them. The story of the birth of their long-awaited son, Isaac, is read in synagogue on the first day of Rosh Hashanah.

I've combined many oral legends and my own musings about Sarah with the biblical text to tell the story of Isaac's birth.

In Sumer, people worshiped many gods—the sun, the moon, the morning and evening star—as well as their king, Nimrod. When Nimrod's advisors warned him that a boy would be born who would steal his power, he ordered a birth-house to be built and the women to give birth there. Thousands of infant boys were slaughtered. Despite

Nimrod's decree, one evening at dusk, one of the pregnant women, Emtelai, instead of going to the birth-house, left the city of Ur to go alone into the wilderness. In a cave, she gave birth to a child she named Abram.

As a young child, Abram lifted his hands to praise the sun god. The sun set. He lifted his hands to praise the moon god. A cloud covered the moon. He held out his hands to the goddess of the morning star; she disappeared into the morning light. Then he understood that there was one force who had created and was creating life for all that was. Abram called this invisible force El Shaddai, the Nourishing One.

When he grew up and worked in his father Terah's shop, Abram spoke about the invisible force, El Shaddai, who was creating life. Many people came to listen. But when Nimrod's advisors informed the king that Abram was praising an invisible force called El Shaddai rather than the king, Nimrod ordered his guards to seize Abram and throw him into a fiery furnace. He then commanded every citizen in Sumer to bring branches to feed the fire and watch El Shaddai's favorite child burn. Three days later when the furnace was opened, the logs had burst into blossom and Abram was sitting in a garden of blossoming fruit trees, joyously singing praises to El Shaddai.

Sarai was a priestess in the temple, where the moon god as well as Inanna, the goddess of the morning and evening star, were worshiped, but she had never seen a protective force as powerful as the one Abram was singing to. She watched Abram intently. Then she turned to her mother and whispered, "El Shaddai loves Abram." Sensing her daughter's interest, Sarai's mother asked, "And you?" Sarai kept her eyes on Abram and answered, "He sings well."

A few days later, the mothers spoke. Abram's mother said, "My son speaks your daughter's name as if he's praying. Who can blame him? Everyone sees her radiance." Sarai's mother nodded. "Since she was a child, the gods have been drawn to her. Wherever she goes, clouds follow and protect her."

"Abram may need her protection." Emtelai said. "It would be best if he leaves Ur before Nimrod invents another test for him."

"Sarai may also need to leave Ur. The high priestess is jealous of her powers."

The mothers arranged a wedding. A few weeks later, a caravan left Ur. Terah, Abram, Sarai, Abram's brother Nahor, Nahor's wife Milcah, and Terah's grandson, Lot, set out for Canaan. But when they reached the city of Haran, where the moon god was worshiped, they learned that the high priestess was ill. Even though Sarai no longer served as a temple priestess, the people of Haran asked her to help to prepare the crescent-moon ceremony. Sarai arranged the procession according to the customs in Ur. The procession went on until dawn and the people begged Sarai to stay.

Every day Abram went into the fields to sing praises to El Shaddai. One day, El Shaddai spoke to Abram and said, "*Lech l'cha*, go! Leave this land and your father's house, and go to a place I will show you. You will be a great nation. Your name will be great. You will be a blessing for all people and all those who bless you will be blessed."

Abram's father and brother chose to remain in Haran, but Sarai was eager to leave. She told Abram that the night before she had dreamt of sacred oak trees and longed to listen to the sound of the wind in the oaks, not to the many temple jealousies. Abram was seventy-five and Sarai was sixty-five when they left Haran with their nephew Lot, their followers, and all the wealth they had acquired.

As they entered Canaan, Sarai said, "Let us stop at this grove of oak trees near Shechem." At the oak tree called Moreh, meaning "teacher," God appeared to Abram and said, "I will give this land to your descendants." Abram built an altar of stones in Shechem to mark God's words. Then he traveled south and set up his tent near Bethel. He looked about at the beauty of the land and called out God's name. Then he built another altar to El Shaddai.

When a famine spread across Canaan, rather than return to Haran, Abram, Sarai, and Lot set out for Egypt. As they traveled, Abram watched the clouds dancing over Sarai's head and said to her, "The Egyptians love beauty. I am afraid they may kill me because of your powers and your beauty. Say that you are my sister so I will not be harmed."

As soon as they entered Egypt and the Egyptians saw how beautiful Sarai was, she was brought to Pharaoh's palace. Pharaoh had lost his strength and was unable to stand up. At Pharaoh's insistence, Sarai restored his waning powers. In gratitude, Pharaoh offered her precious jewels and brought her to live in his palace as his wife. But God soon afflicted Pharaoh and his household with plagues.

The palace priests made inquiries. When they found out that Abram was Sarai's husband, not her brother, they informed Pharaoh. Immediately, he summoned Abram and asked, "Why did you not say, 'She is my wife'? Why did you say 'she is my sister' so I took her as my wife. Go, take your wife and leave Egypt." But because she had cured him, Pharaoh gave Sarai silver and gold and his daughter Hagar as a servant, and he gave Abram camels, donkeys, sheep, and servants.

Abram traveled from Egypt until they came to Bethel where he had built an altar to God. His herds and flocks had increased. Eager to share his wealth, he offered his nephew, Lot, sheep and oxen. But when arguments broke out between their servants, Abram said to Lot, "I do not want to quarrel. We are kinsmen. Choose whatever part of the land you wish, and I will take the rest." Lot chose the plains of Jordan, which were as fertile as the land of Egypt, and Abram and Lot parted peacefully.

Abram and Sarai continued to travel north. As they were approaching Hebron, Sarai cried out, "Look! There are the sacred oaks I dreamt of!" She sprinkled flour and poured beer before each oak. Under the sacred trees, she set up a large tent with its doors open to all directions so people would come to be healed. At last, Sarai was content. No temple priest or priestess would direct her life. She could live directly with Spirit. Abram too was content. He built an altar where he welcomed travelers, gave offerings to El Shaddai, and sang songs of praise.

Ten years passed and El Shaddai appeared to Abram in a vision, saying, "Your reward will be great."

"Who shall I give my reward to if I have no children?" Abram asked. "Shall I make my servant, Eliezer, my heir?"

"Go out into the night," El Shaddai answered. "Look up at the heavens and count the stars. I brought you from Ur to give you this land. Your descendants will be from your own blood and as numerous as the stars in the heavens and the sands of the sea. They will be so many they will not be able to be counted or measured."

When Abram asked God how he was to know that the land would truly be his, God asked him to give an offering of a heifer, a goat, a ram, a turtledove, and a bird. The next day, after Abram made this sacrifice to El Shaddai, as the sun was setting, he fell into a trance. Then a dark dread descended on him, and God foretold the future of Abram's children: "Your descendants will be strangers in a foreign land. For more than four hundred years they will be enslaved and oppressed. In the end, I will punish their oppressors, and in the fourth generation your descendants will return here with great wealth but not until the Amorites force me to drive them from the land."

On his way back to his tent, Abram heard Sarai cry out in her sleep. He went into her tent. Sarai awoke shaking and said, "I was dreaming. The sky was burning. Smoke and ashes were everywhere. Trees were dying. One tree took root. I will bring you my loyal servant, Hagar. Go to her so I may have an heir."

Abram went willingly to Hagar, believing he would have the heir El Shaddai had promised. But as soon as Hagar became pregnant, she looked at her mistress with disdain. Sarai heard how tenderly Abram spoke to Hagar and said to him, "I gave you my servant. Now because of how you speak with her, she acts as if the child she's carrying is hers. The fault is yours. Let your God decide between Hagar and me."

Abram said, "Hagar is your servant. Do with her as you wish."

Wrapped in hurt, Sarai spoke so harshly to Hagar that she fled into the wilderness. God's messenger found her weeping by a well on the road to Shur and called her by her name, "Hagar, slave of Sarai, where are you coming from? Where are you going?"

"I am running away from my mistress, Sarai."

"Do not run away," another angel said. "Return to your mistress. Agree to her demands. You will have a son who will be a wild ass of a man, with his hand against everyone, and everyone's hand against him. But he will live with his brothers, and his descendants will be too numerous to count."

"El-Roi," Hagar called to God. "You are the God of seeing. You have seen into my heart." Hagar returned and served Sarai. Nine months later, she gave birth to a boy and named him Ishmael, for God had heard her suffering.

When Ishmael was thirteen and Abram was ninety-nine, God appeared before Abram and said, "I am El Shaddai. I will make a covenant with you and give you many descendants." Abram fell to the ground and placed his forehead on the earth.

El Shaddai continued, "Your name will no longer be Abram but Abraham, for you will be the father of nations. Your descendants will be kings, and I will be a god to your descendants and give you and them this land of Canaan where you are living. As for your part of our covenant, you must circumcise every male living in your household, and in the future, at the age of eight days, each male child must be circumcised. Your wife's name will change from Sarai, meaning 'crescent moon,' to Sarah, meaning 'leader,' for she holds the understanding to guide the people. I will bless her, and she will give birth to a son."

"Sarai?" Abram laughed. "Can a child be born to a man one hundred years old? Shall Sarah give birth at ninety? And Ishmael—will you consider him as well?"

"I will bless Ishmael. His descendants will be numerous, but my covenant will be with Sarah's son, Isaac."

Abraham carried out God's commands. As he was dozing in the heat of the day, he heard a sound. He looked up and saw El Shaddai approaching. Then he saw three messengers.

Quickly, he ran from his tent to greet them. "Please stay," he said. "Rest under the oak trees and I will bring you food to eat." Abraham brought water to bathe his guests' feet and then ran to Sarah's tent and asked her to quickly knead flour and make cakes. Next he hurried to find meat and milk. When the calf was prepared, he set the food before the messengers and waited on them as they ate under the oak trees.

One of the messengers asked, "Where is your wife, Sarah?"

"There—in the tent," Abraham motioned.

"I have come to bless her," the messenger said. "When I return next year your wife will have a child."

Sarah, who was sitting at the entrance of her tent, overheard and laughed. She thought to herself, I am past childbearing. Now that we are old shall we renew our pleasure?

"Why is Sarah laughing?" El Shaddai asked. "Is anything too difficult for me?"

Sarah said, "I did not laugh."

"But you did laugh," God insisted.

Sarah admitted, "Not only am I past childbearing, but in Ur I was a priestess. If a priestess has a child, the child is thrown into the river, given to others to raise, sacrificed—"

"You will keep your child," Abraham's God promised.

"I will sing your praises," Sarah said.

The messengers stood up and Abraham escorted them on their way. When they came to the hills overlooking the plains where Abraham's nephew, Lot, lived, God confided in Abraham that the cities and plains of Jordan would be destroyed, for instead of caring for strangers, the people living there had committed crimes against them. The only man who honored and welcomed strangers was Abraham's nephew Lot.

Abraham urged God to spare the cities if ten innocent people could be found. But the next day, orange flames shot up into the sky. Smoke filled the air. Ashes fell. The thriving cities of Sodom and Gomorrah and the fertile plains of Jordan were burnt to cinders.

Day turned into night. In the darkness, with ashes falling on the sacred oaks, Abraham and Sarah left Hebron. They walked for days. As the sky cleared, they came to Gerar, the region between Kadesh and Shur. Abraham again called Sarah his sister. The king of the Philistines, Abimelech, heard of Sarah and summoned her. But God spoke to Abimelech in a dream and said, "If you do not return this woman to her husband, you will die."

"Will you kill me if I am innocent?" Abimelech protested.

God answered, "I knew you were blameless so I did not let you touch her. But Sarah's husband is a prophet. Restore Sarah to him so you may live."

The next morning Abimelech said to Abraham, "What wrong did I do to you that you brought such guilt upon me? For what purpose did you say that Sarah was your sister instead of your wife?"

"I did not know if your people respected strangers and honored the gods. In truth, she is my sister, my half-sister, my father's daughter, who became my wife. When we left my father's house I asked her to say of me, 'He's my brother.' "

Abimelech offered Sarah a thousand shekels of silver and gave Abraham sheep and cattle and servants and said, "My land is yours. Settle where you choose." Abraham and Sarah settled in the land of the Philistines.

One night Sarah came out of her tent. Abraham's arms were raised in prayer. Sarah remembered the moment in Ur when he was sitting in the garden of blossoming fruit trees joyously singing. Softly, she began to sing the songs to El Shaddai that Abraham had taught her. Abraham turned. She was standing in the moonlight, fresh and radiant. He met her in song, and Sarah laughed joyously.

Nine months later, Sarah gave birth to a little boy and brought him to Abraham, saying, "This child is a gift of El Shaddai. What will you name him?"

Abraham took the child in his arms and said, "I will call our son Isaac, meaning 'he will laugh.' Let Isaac laugh as we did the night you called out El Shaddai's name."

When Isaac was weaned, Abraham gave a great feast. His teachers, Shem and Eber, came from Hebron; his father and brother came from Haran. The women surrounded Sarah and Isaac, and Sarah happily offered to feed their infants, for her breasts were overflowing with milk.

Isaac grew up with his older brother, Ishmael. He adored Ishmael and wanted to do everything his older brother did. Ishmael liked to hunt, so Isaac liked to hunt. As Isaac found other interests, Ishmael teased him and shot arrows at him to provoke him. Ishmael's jeering, rough ways made Sarah afraid for Isaac and she went to Abraham and said, "I do not want Isaac to share his inheritance with Ishmael. Send Hagar away with her son."

Abraham did not want to be separated from his firstborn son, but that night God said to Abraham, "In all that Sarah says, listen to her voice." The next morning Abraham prepared water and bread. Without looking at her, he told the mother of his older son, "You must leave and take your child."

Hagar was stunned. Abraham placed a waterskin on Hagar's shoulder. Furious, Hagar turned on Sarah and said, "Now that you have your son, you send mine away. You take away his father, his home, his inheritance so your son might inherit his father's blessings!"

"Get out!" Sarah shouted.

Hagar and Ishmael walked into the wilderness. From a distance, Sarah could hear Hagar sobbing "My son, my son." When the waterskin was empty, Hagar thrust Ishmael under some bushes. She sat at a distance, a bow's shot away, and said, "I cannot bear to watch him die of thirst." Then she burst into tears. Ishmael also wept.

God heard Ishmael weeping, and an angel said, "Hagar, do not be afraid. God has heard Ishmael's voice. Go over to him. He will be the father of a great nation." God opened Hagar's eyes, and in front of her she saw a well. Quickly, she filled the waterskin and gave water to Ishmael to drink. They stayed in the wilderness until it was time for Ishmael to marry. Then they went to Egypt where Hagar chose an Egyptian wife for her son. After Ishmael had four sons and a daughter, they returned to the wilderness of Paran and settled not far from Abraham.

The years passed and Abraham wanted to see the face of his son. One day, he said to Sarah, "I've heard that Ishmael's tents are near here. I will go to see him."

Sarah said, "If you must go, promise me you will not descend from your camel."

At noon, Abraham reached Ishmael's tents. Ishmael was gone, but Abraham saw a woman in the tent. The woman did not ask who the visitor was. Abraham called out, "My daughter, I am weary from my journey. Can you bring me water to drink?"

She called back, "We have no water or bread."

Abraham called to her again, "My daughter, come out of the tent so I may see you."

Ishmael's wife came out and they stared at each other. Then Abraham said, "When your husband returns, tell him that a very old man from the land of the Philistines spoke to you and told you to tell him to put away his tent pin and to find another one."

When Ishmael returned and heard his wife's words, he knew that the old man was his father and that his wife had not honored him. He divorced his wife and married a Canaanite woman.

Three years later, Abraham went again into the wilderness hoping to see his son. Ishmael was hunting, but his new wife came out of the tent at once and said, "Please, come into the tent and rest and eat for you must be weary."

"No, I will not stop," Abraham said, "but I would be glad for some water to drink." She ran into the tent and returned with bread and water. Abraham's heart was glad. When he finished eating, he blessed God and said, "My daughter, when your husband returns, tell him a very old man from the land of the Philistines ate the water and bread you gave him. The old man was glad and said to tell your husband that he has a very good tent pin and must take good care of it." Ishmael settled his family close to Abraham.

Twenty-six years passed. Then word reached Sarah and Abraham that new oaks were growing in Hebron. Sarah wanted to live in Hebron near the sacred oak groves. Abraham traveled south to Beersheba with Ishmael. There, he planted a tamarisk tree and a vineyard surrounded by four gates that were always open. Every traveler who came was fed and welcomed. After a traveler had eaten and wanted to thank Abraham, he would answer, "Do not thank me, thank El Shaddai, the Nourishing One, who gives the breath of life to all things." Abraham's tent became a resting place for all travelers, but during this time, he made no sacrifice to El Shaddai.

The Binding of Isaac

God Will Provide

On the first day of Rosh Hashanah we read the story about an old couple, Abraham and Sarah, who receive the fulfillment of their dearest wish: a child. On the second day of Rosh Hashanah we read that their miraculous gift is to be taken away. So we consider: What is our relationship with God when we are asked to give up what we love the most?

I've interwoven midrash with biblical text in telling The Binding of Isaac.

Satan the Adversary was speaking with God and said, "You are so proud of your servant Abraham. You speak of him all the time. But have you considered that twenty-six years have passed since the birth of Isaac and in all this time he has not made one sacrifice to you? Why should he bother? He has everything he needs—land, wealth, an heir."

God answered, "If I were to ask him to sacrifice his son, he would do so immediately."

So God tested Abraham, saying, "Abraham."

And Abraham answered, "*Hineni.* Here I am."

God said, "*Lech l'cha*, go! Take your son whom you love. Take Isaac and go to the land of Moriah and offer him as a burnt offering in the place I will show you."

135

Abraham left Beersheba with his servant Eliezer and Isaac. As he approached the sacred oaks at Hebron, he saw golden clouds dancing over Sarah's tent. He went inside and said, "Isaac is grown. I want to take him to the city of Hebron to learn with Noah's son, Shem."

Sarah said, "Take the boy, but do not keep him long, for my soul is bound within his soul."

Early the next morning, before Sarah awoke, Abraham saddled his donkey. He split wood to provide fire for the burnt offering. He himself took a knife and a firestone, and with Isaac, Ishmael, and Eliezer, he started off toward the place that God had told him. As they were walking, Ishmael said to Abraham's servant, Eliezer, "My father will give Isaac as a burnt offering to God, and when we return, he will give me his inheritance, for I am his firstborn."

"You were sent into the wilderness with your mother," Eliezer said, "you'll receive no inheritance. I am his servant who has served him faithfully day and night."

On the second day, as they were walking, Abraham thought of the conversation he had overheard the day before. If Isaac died, who would have his inheritance? Did he dare to take the life of the child he loved? Isaac was not even a man. He had no children. Had he heard correctly? Hadn't God promised him descendants? Abraham hadn't asked for anything, yet God had given him everything he needed.

At that moment, Satan, disguised as a handsome young man, appeared on the road. "Where are you going, old man?" he asked Abraham. "Have you lost your wits? Are you intending to harm your own child? Would God ask you to do such a deed? Everyone will think you're crazy. Go home, old man!" But Abraham knew the voice of God, and this was not God's voice.

On the third day, Abraham saw a cloud over a distant mountain and in the cloud was a pillar of fire. Abraham said to Isaac, "What do you see on that distant mountain?"

Isaac answered, "A cloud, a pillar of fire, and the glory of God in the cloud."

"What do you see on the mountain?" Abraham asked Ishmael and Eliezer.

"Mountains," they answered, "mountains and more mountains."

"Wait here with the donkey," Abraham said to them. "The boy and I will go up on the mountain and pray. Then we will return."

Abraham gave Isaac the wood to carry, and he took the firestone and the knife. The two of them started up the mountain together. As they were walking, Isaac opened his mouth to speak but no words came out. Then he said, "*Abba*, my father."

Abraham answered, "*Hineni*. Here I am, my son."

"*Abba*," Isaac asked, "we have the fire, the knife, the wood, but where is the lamb to be burned for the offering?"

Abraham answered, "God will provide the lamb for the burnt offering, my son."

They walked up the mountain together. At the place God had spoken of, Isaac helped Abraham to build an altar. Then Abraham lifted Isaac up onto the wood. When Isaac knew that he was to be the offering, he said, "Father, take off your sandals and with your straps bind my hands and feet. I wish to be as brave as my brother Ishmael; but my soul is trembling, and when I see the knife, I may shake and the sacrifice will be blemished. And father, promise me you will not speak of this to Mother if she is standing on a roof or near a well. I am afraid for her."

Abraham's eyes were swimming in tears. His hand trembled as he picked up the knife. Abraham looked at the fire in the cloud and said, "I lift my eyes to the mountains. Where will my help come from?"

At that moment, the heavens opened, and Abraham and Isaac saw the angels weeping. One was saying, "Look! A child is about to be killed." Another said, "His own father is about to kill him." Tears poured from the eyes of the Angel of Mercy into Isaac's eyes. For a moment, Isaac was blinded and his soul left him.

"Creator of the Universe," the Angel of Mercy cried, "What has become of your promise to Abraham?"

God saw that the hearts of Abraham and Isaac were one and said, "Stop them."

The Angel of Mercy cried out, "Abraham! Abraham!"

"*Hineni*," Abraham answered.

The angel said, "Do not put your hand on the boy."

"Who are you?" Abraham asked.

"I am a messenger of God. Do not harm the boy. I know now that you fear me, for you did not withhold what is most precious to you. Your descendants will be as numerous as the stars in the sky and the sands of the sea. Through your descendants, the other nations will be blessed. Lift your eyes."

Abraham lifted his eyes and saw a wild ram caught by his horns in the thicket. He offered the ram to God as a sacrifice. He called the place On God's Mountain There Is Vision.

At that moment, Satan, disguised as an old man, appeared outside Sarah's tent and said, "Sarah, El Shaddai has asked for Isaac. Your husband, Abraham, has just delivered him, his hands and feet bound, to be sacrificed."

"No!" Sarah screamed. She ran to the city of Hebron. Isaac was not in the house of Shem. Sarah could scarcely breathe. She'd lost her son, her faith in her husband, her faith in El Shaddai. Just then, Satan appeared on the roadside and said, "Sarah, I lied. Abraham did not kill your son. Your son, Isaac, is alive."

"*Ahhhhhh.*" Nine wails roared through Sarah's body, and as the last one left her, her soul ascended. It did not return. Sarah was one hundred and twenty-seven years old when she died.

Isaac returned to Hebron. No clouds danced over Sarah's tent. Isaac called, "Eema? *Eema?* Mother, where have you gone?" Then he wept. Abraham wept. Abraham's servants tried to comfort Abraham. Neither Isaac nor Abraham could be comforted. Not only Abraham's family grieved, but all the country grieved, for Sarah was a great healer, and after her death there was confusion.

Memories of his life with Sarah sifted through Abraham. He remembered the day he chased a calf through a field to feed the three messengers who had come to announce the birth of Isaac. The calf had entered a cave, the cave of Machpelah. A wonderful fragrance scented the air. Inside were Adam and Eve.

He decided he wanted to bury Sarah in the cave of Machpelah.

When he spoke to the Hittites and asked to buy the cave, they answered, "You are a prince. We will not refuse you land for burial."

"I wish to buy the land as a burial place," Abraham said.

Then Ephron who owned the land said, "Because it is for a holy woman, I will give you the land."

But Abraham insisted, "Let me pay for the cave and the land and all the surrounding trees. I will pay whatever price you ask."

"What is four hundred shekels of silver?" Ephron said. Four hundred shekels was a great sum of money, but Abraham gladly weighed out the silver so that Sarah would be buried in the cave of Machpelah by the oak trees she loved.

Sarah was buried in her fine clothes. Noah's son, Shem, Shem's great-grandson, Eber, Abimelech, and many great kings followed Sarah's coffin to the cave of Machpelah. For seven days the people mourned and consoled Abraham and Isaac. Then Abraham returned to Beersheba. Soon after Sarah's funeral, he received news from his brother, Nahor, in Haran that the wife of his youngest son had just given birth to a daughter. Her name was Rebekah.

At the very moment that Abraham was offering Isaac to God, God was preparing Isaac's soul mate to enter the world.

Hannah

I Asked for Him from God

In the Hebrew Bible the last words of the story preceding the book of Samuel (Judges 21:25) are: "In the days when there was no king in Israel there was corruption and chaos in the land." If we consider the baseness of the people and the lack of any righteous leaders at the time (1250–1100 B.C.E.) that Hannah is living, her request of God for a righteous child takes on an entirely different dimension. She wants a child not only for herself but for all the world.

Two stories of birth, the birth of Samuel and the birth of Isaac, are read on the first day of Rosh Hashanah in celebration of the New Year. I've interwoven oral legends with the book of Samuel.

*I*n the days when there was no king in Israel, there was corruption and chaos in the land. In those days, there lived a woman named Hannah, whose name means "grace." She lived with her husband, Elkanah, in Ramah on a mountain called Twin Hills Visible to Each Other.

Every year at the festivals they went together to the shrine at Shiloh and often stopped to invite others to go with them. The old priest Eli would offer their sacrifices on the altar; but when he was too busy, Eli's sons who were also priests took the offerings. After sprinkling the animal's blood on the altar and burning its fat, the priests were permitted to take a small part of the meal offering for themselves; but even before a sacrifice was put into the fire, Eli's sons would plunge their forks into the offering, and whatever their forks picked up, they would take. If anyone protested, they would answer, "Give it to us, or we'll take it by force." Hannah noticed the greedy manner in which Eli's sons kept the best parts of the offerings. When she saw that Eli did not reprimand them, she asked her husband to avoid Eli's sons and to wait for Eli, to give their offerings.

The years passed. Hannah and Elkanah were happy, but they had no children. Two, three, four—ten years passed. Still Hannah remained barren. Hannah suggested to Elkanah that he take another wife so that he might have children. Elkanah married Peninah and built a house for her on the hill facing Hannah's house. Within a year, Peninah gave birth to a child. The next year, she had a second child. The third year, she had a third child.

On each of the festivals, Peninah and her children went with Elkanah and Hannah to Shiloh. Each year, Elkanah made an offering that he divided among Peninah and her children. But even though Hannah had remained barren, he always gave her the best part of the meat, for he loved her. When Peninah saw this, her heart was jealous and she taunted Hannah, "Did you get an extra piece for your son? Oh, oh, what am I saying? Your son? You don't have a son. I'm the one with so many children I can hardly remember their names!"

After nine years of being tormented, one year at Shiloh when Elkanah offered Hannah a particularly choice portion of meat, she burst into tears and refused to eat. "Hannah," Elkanah asked, "why are you crying? Why don't you eat? Don't I mean more to you than ten sons?"

Hannah did not answer. She walked past Eli, the priest who was sitting near the shrine. Closing her eyes, she prayed, "Creator of the World, for nineteen years I have been silent. Can you not see my grief? My heart is calling to you. Can you not in all your creation find one child for me to love? I want there to be a righteous leader in our land.

I beg you, give me a righteous child to nourish and raise, and I will bring him to the sanctuary to serve you faithfully, and no razor will touch his head." As she spoke, she struck her heart with her fists, imploring God to listen to her.

Eli noticed a woman flailing her arms. He stood up and walked closer to her. Her lips were moving, but he heard no voice. He cried, "Stop, woman! Stop drinking! You've drunk enough already!"

Hannah turned to him and said, "No, I haven't drunk wine, new or old. I've been pouring out my heart to God, praying for a child. If God gives me a child, I promise to bring him here to serve God faithfully."

Eli had not seen such devotion in many years. He blessed Hannah, saying, "May God give you the child you've asked for."

"May your blessing be fulfilled," Hannah answered. Her face free of sorrow, she left the shrine and went and ate her portion of the offering. When the family returned to their home, Elkanah went into Hannah's tent. God remembered Hannah's prayers, and she conceived. Six months and a few days later, she gave birth to a little boy. She named him Samuel, meaning "I asked for him from God."

Soon after Samuel was born, the household prepared to leave for Shiloh, but Hannah stayed home. She said, "I promised the boy will serve God. When I bring him to Shiloh, he will appear in the presence of God and remain in God's house forever. Until then, I want to keep him close to me." Knowing the child would be hers for only a short time, she spoke to him day and night. She sang to him and taught him everything she knew.

The years passed. When Samuel was four and had stopped nursing, Hannah set out with him for the shrine. She brought a young bull as a meal offering, flour for a gift offering, and wine for the libation. In the courtyard, many people waited in line. Full of confidence, Samuel asked the man in front of them, "Why is everyone waiting?"

The man replied, "We're waiting for the priests to sacrifice our animals."

"But the law does not say that we cannot sacrifice our animals ourselves," Samuel protested.

"That's true," the man agreed with the boy. "Since the priest sprinkles the blood on the altar, we've become accustomed to also letting him do the sacrifice, but we can do our own sacrifices." And one by one, following the words of the little boy, the people began to sacrifice their own animals.

When Eli heard what was being done, he asked for the person to be brought to him who had changed the tradition. In surprise, Eli looked down at a four-year-old child. Samuel looked up at the priest and spoke fearlessly. "The teachings do not say that we cannot sacrifice our animals ourselves."

"Yes," Eli answered sternly, "but the teachings tell us that a student who challenges a teacher without permission shall be severely punished."

"No!" Hannah cried, rushing between them. "I'm his teacher," she said. "Don't you remember me? I'm the woman you thought was drunk, and this is the little child I prayed for."

"I will pray that you should have another child, but this child has acted in such a way that he may not live."

"No. *No!*" Hannah cried. "Listen, listen to me! I'm the woman who came to the shrine to pray for this child, this very child. He's the child I promised to God. You blessed me, saying, 'May God give you the child you've asked for.' God gave me this child. I raised him and dedicated him to God. I named him Samuel."

"Samuel!" Eli repeated the name in astonishment. At that moment, he remembered the prophecy that a child named Samuel would lead Israel and that the woman kneeling before him, who had tears in her eyes, had asked for such a child. Eli stretched out his arms and announced, "Let everyone hear me! The Samuel who has been prophesied is among us. Let us rejoice."

Hannah realized that everything she had asked for had come into being. She had asked for a child, a righteous child who would serve God in the sanctuary. Samuel was righteous, wise, and fearless and had been accepted as a priest. Not able to contain herself, the words of a song poured forth from her lips:

My heart leaps with joy.
You have made me triumphant.
Because of you,
I can open my mouth and defy my enemies.
My rock, my redeemer, my salvation,
who can compare to you?
I do not wish to set myself above others,
for it is you who weigh all deeds.

All peoples, all nations, listen to my voice.
There will be a time of change:
Those who are stumbling will become strong.
The rich will become servants to earn their bread.
The hungry will be fed.
The barren women will give birth.
The mother of many will be forlorn.

Creator, Destroyer, you create the world; you bring about death.
You take us down to the grave; you lift us up.
You make us poor or rich, humble or proud.
You raise the needy from the dunghill
and set them beside princes on seats of honor.
You search every part of the world until you find the king;
then you give power to the anointed one.

Speak, Hannah, do not be silent!
Sing of the wonders God created with you.
Samuel will serve in the temple.
His wisdom will be a light for all people.

What Hannah prayed for came to pass. Samuel became a priest and a prophet, and he anointed the first kings of Israel.

Soon after Hannah returned to Ramah, she gave birth to a second child. The following year she bore a third child. Hannah gave birth to three sons and two daughters, but each time Hannah gave birth, two of Peninah's children died. When Hannah conceived her fifth child, Peninah begged her, "Pray for me, Hannah, be merciful. Be more compassionate than I was. The song you sang at Shiloh has become an unfolding prophecy. I have lost eight children. I beg you, ask the Merciful One to let me keep the ones who remain."

That year when Hannah went to Shiloh, she prayed, "Lord of Hosts, I never wished any of Peninah's children to die. I wanted only to serve you myself. Let Peninah's children live. She is overcome with grief."

The Shechinah answered, "You were destined to have seven children. Since you prayed for Peninah, she will keep her children, and you will have only six children."

Each year when Hannah went to Shiloh, she brought Samuel a coat that she had spun and sewn with her own hands. Whenever Hannah saw Samuel wearing her coat and serving God faithfully, her heart overflowed with joy. Eli too was pleased with Samuel's goodness. He was a righteous man. He was the great-grandson of Aaron, the first high priest, but his own sons did not serve God in their hearts.

When Eli learned that his sons were polluting the sacrifices and seducing the women who gathered at the entrance of the sanctuary, he called them to him and said, "If you harm another man, you can be judged. But if you sin against God, who can intercede?" Eli's sons heard their father's words and disregarded them. Eli did not stop them.

Rumors spread. One day a stranger entered the sanctuary and went to the gate where Eli sat. The man said to Eli, "God has sent me to say to you, 'Your family are descendants of Aaron. When they were slaves in Egypt, I chose your family from all the tribes to be priests—to burn incense, to light the menorah, to wear the priest's coat, to make offerings on the altar. Why have you honored your sons more than me by allowing them to fatten themselves on the choice parts of the offerings? I wanted you and your sons to serve me forever, but your sons have destroyed the purity of the people's offerings by polluting the sacrifices. Not one of your descendants will live long enough to become an elder. I will choose another priest to serve me faithfully.' These are God's words. I have no more to say."

The messenger stopped speaking and disappeared.

That night, Eli could not sleep. He had devoted himself to serving God, yet he had not watched over his own sons. His vision had been poor, and now he could scarcely see.

The menorah near the holy of holies was still burning. Samuel was meditating on the cherubim when the Shechinah called out, "Samuel."

"*Hineni*, here I am," Samuel answered, and he ran to Eli and said, "Here I am. You called me."

"No, I did not call you," Eli said. "Return to your bed and lie down."

Samuel went and lay down. Again, the Shechinah called to him in Eli's voice so as not to frighten him. And again Samuel got up and went to Eli and said, "Here I am. You called me."

"No, no, I did not call you, my son. Go back and lie down."

Samuel did not know it was God, for God's word had not yet been revealed to him. A third time the Shechinah called, "Samuel."

"*Hineni*, here I am," Samuel answered, and he got up and went to Eli and said, "Here I am because you called me."

Eli then knew it was God who was calling the boy and he said to Samuel, "Go, lie down, and if you hear a voice again, say, 'Adonai, your servant is listening.' "

Samuel went and lay down.

The Shechinah came and stood there and called as before, "Samuel, Samuel."

And Samuel answered, "Speak, your servant is listening."

The Shechinah said to Samuel, "I have told Eli that his house will be punished because he knew that his sons were disgracing themselves and polluting the sacrifices, and still he did not stop them."

The next morning, Samuel opened the doors of the house of God. He was afraid to speak of his vision to Eli, but Eli called Samuel and said, "Samuel, my son."

"*Hineni*. Here I am."

Eli asked, "What did the Shechinah say to you? Do not conceal anything from me, for God will curse you worse than me if you conceal anything."

Samuel told Eli what God had said. Eli listened. Then he nodded and said, "What God does is good."

From then on, whatever Samuel spoke came to pass. In every part of Israel, from Dan to Beersheba, from north to south, the people knew that Samuel had become God's prophet. And as the time passed, the song that Hannah had sung before God began to unfold. . . .

The people saw that the surrounding nations had kings and begged Samuel to give them a king. At first, Samuel protested, saying that there is only one true king. But the people persisted, and so God told Samuel to choose Saul, a simple, ordinary man, a descendant of Benjamin, to be the first king.

Samuel anointed Saul king, and there was a great celebration in Gilgal. But Saul was not worthy of being king. When the Philistines were about to attack, he did not wait for Samuel to prepare the proper sacrifices, and when God ordered him to wipe out the Amalekites, he spared their king, Agag. God withdrew his support from Saul and ordered Samuel to go to Bethlehem to anoint David king of Israel.

For the rest of Samuel's life, war raged between Saul and David. After Samuel died, the Philistines gathered a great army with David as their leader and were about to attack Saul. Saul asked God for guidance. God was silent. The urim and thummin, the divining beads in the high priest's breastplate, did not communicate with him, nor did his dreams, nor the prophets. In desperation, Saul disguised himself and went with two of his servants to a woman from Endor who was known to conjure spirits.

"Bring me the spirit of the person I shall tell you," he said to her.

"I cannot," the woman replied, "King Saul has forbidden such magic."

"I promise you, you will not be punished. Call up the spirit of Samuel."

The woman spoke words that could not be understood. A vapor rose from the earth. Then a form appeared. It was the form of an old man. It was Samuel, wearing the coat that Hannah had made for him.

"Why have you disturbed me?" he asked Saul.

"I'm in great trouble. The Philistines are attacking and God no longer answers me."

"Why do you ask me? God has given the kingship to David because you did not wipe out evil as you had been told. If you had waited one more day, you would have seen me. You and your sons will be with me tomorrow."

Saul flung himself on the ground, crying, "Samuel, Samuel."

Vapor covered Samuel's face, and all that Saul could see was the coat that had been woven by a woman who had burned with desire to bring into the world a righteous servant of God.

About the Stories

Abraham and Sarah

> *Although your desire tastes sweet,*
> *doesn't the Beloved desire you*
> *to be desireless?*
> *The life of lovers is in death:*
> *You will not win the Beloved's heart*
> *unless you lose your own.*
>
> RUMI, "Drowned in God"

Abraham, the "father" of the Jewish people, is a man of great vision and depth: he is courageous, hospitable, generous, compassionate. He is also a mystic who is consumed by his God. But as Rumi, a descendant of Abraham and an Islamic mystic, tells us, in order to be with "the Beloved," we must give up everything. Abraham's tragic greatness arises from the conflict between his desire to satisfy the wishes of his God and the needs of his family.

In his youth, Abraham follows his inner vision: to worship a different god and to leave his father and civilization to follow the commands of that god. He shares what he has with others and struggles with God to spare the lives of innocent people. Yet, he does not know how to say no. He does not know how to deal with jealousy. He loves his son Ishmael but does not protect him. When his wife tells him to send Hagar and his child away, he does not secure another place where they would be protected. Instead, he abandons his child and so helps to bring about the enmity between the descendants of his sons, Ishmael and Isaac.

God tests Abraham by asking him at the age of ninety-nine to cut off a portion of his most tender, most potent physical possession, the foreskin of his phallus. In commanding Abraham to circumcise himself, Ishmael, and the men of his household, God wants Abraham to elevate the physical to the spiritual so that the most mundane act of urinating, as well as the

149

most sacred act of love-making, will be done with consciousness of God. And he wishes Abraham, the parent, to teach his sons to do likewise—to link all of life to the holy.

God then sets an even more challenging test than sexuality before Abraham. Although God had led Abraham to believe that he would be a father to generations, God seemingly reverses this promise by demanding that Abraham offer Isaac as a sacrifice. Why does Abraham, who challenged God to spare the innocent lives of the citizens of Sodom and Gomorrah, not challenge God to spare the life of his and Sarah's son?

Abraham cannot say no to God. Having taken on God's name with his decision to elevate his physical body, he understands that since the gift of Isaac came from God (he was one hundred when Isaac was conceived, Sarah was ninety), the gift of Isaac also belongs to God. In letting go of Isaac, Abraham cancels the future, disavows the past, and enters the realm of mystery, God's realm of "I am," the present.

Although Abraham surrenders himself to God, he is agreeing to take the life of another human being. Despite the fact that it is God's command, he avoids telling the mother of their child that he is taking their son to be sacrificed and never has the chance to speak with her again. Nor do Abraham and Isaac speak again in the biblical texts. Abraham offers his essence to God, and that essence is returned with manifold blessings; but in the exchange, he loses his wife and the closeness to his son Isaac. Abraham is a father to many new disciples of El Shaddai, but he cannot find a satisfactory solution to the problems within his own home.

Sarah, like Abraham, has great spiritual status. From the biblical text, we know that clouds (a sign of the Shechinah) hover over her tent. The great kings of the world offer her large, extravagant gifts; Abraham pays an exorbitant amount for a burial place befitting her status; kings and wise men attend her funeral; and God chooses her to be the mother of the Hebrew people.

Sarah chooses to follow Abraham to unknown lands where by herself she negotiates successfully with kings, bringing wealth to Abraham. Her understanding is such that God advises Abraham to heed Sarah's advice; she is clearly of equal stature to him. But despite Sarah's wisdom and power, with the birth of children, she is not able to find a way to live with and help Hagar and Ishmael. Afraid of Ishmael's influence over her son, Isaac, Sarah insists that her slave Hagar who has become a cowife to Abraham leave their home and take Abraham's child Ishmael with her. Sarah negotiates with kings but cannot find a way to cohabit with a difficult stepson.

Abraham and Sarah, the parents of the Jewish people, in their good-ness of intention, give their descendants life, hope, and difficulties to unravel for generations.

The Binding of Isaac

The binding of Isaac is Isaac's story as well as Abraham's and Sarah's. It is the story of a son being initiated into the spiritual realm by his father. Initiation involves a direct confrontation with fear, death, and the numi-nous. Isaac knows that his father admires and loves his older, half-brother, Ishmael. When his father asks him to go with him, Isaac wants to be as strong and as brave as Ishmael. At the moment that Isaac willingly offers himself, his future is provided: Rebekah is born. So it is with the initiation of young tribal men. Once they confront death, they are ready to take on the role of adults. Isaac's willingness to sacrifice brings about both spiri-tual rebirth and actual birth.

Abraham and Isaac emerge with greater faith in God, but what about Sarah? Why does she lose her life? Many possible causes may have led to Sarah's death: grief and anguish over the suffering of her child; anger at Abraham's betrayal; reliving the guilt that she caused Hagar, another mother, to suffer; shock caused by the reversal of her feelings. Yet Sarah has experienced shock before. She left her birthplace in Ur, was held cap-tive by kings, witnessed the destruction of Sodom and Gomorrah, gave birth to a child after menopause.

In all of these tumultuous events and changes, Sarah agrees to follow and support Abraham and his God. To Abraham she says, I'll go where you want, I'll risk my life, I'll agree to your son Ishmael visiting. But the one thing that she insists upon is that no harm come to her child. What we may be willing to endure for ourselves, we are not always willing to allow our child to endure. It is too much for Sarah that Abraham should give their child as a burnt offering. I hear her broken sobs as the sounds of Sarah shutting down her body. She is outraged. Her child, her essence, and her power have been taken from her.

Yelala! Sarah lets out a wail. She cries at Abraham's betrayal. She howls at El Shaddai's seeming betrayal. She weeps for the child's anguish. Her wail is not one note but a many-toned howl that commentators have com-pared to the broken notes of the shofar. Rachel wails in grief for the chil-dren of Israel. Sarah howls in anguish for the child, her child, lying on the altar.

On the altar, Isaac sees God, but Sarah, at the moment of Isaac's death, sees Satan, God's adversary. She sees the disconnection, not the connection. And so, weakened, vulnerable, angry, she loses the thread leading back to life. She could not and would not return from the betrayal.

Another interpretation is to consider Sarah's death as a part of Isaac's initiation. In Exodus, the Hebrew slaves pour out of the narrow womb of Egypt, out of the Reed Sea, to be physically reborn as a people. On Mount Moriah, Isaac's manhood is tested. Male initiation in most tribal societies means the adolescent boys leave their mothers to go with their fathers into the wilderness to face death. They survive ordeals and testing so that they can depend on themselves and not on their mothers. The mother is metaphorically killed so that the boy can become a parent. In fact, in the biblical account, Sarah dies immediately after the birth of Isaac's future wife, Rebekah, is announced.

The two interpretations of Sarah's death do not exclude each other. Sarah has been pushed to her death, and Sarah must die. Although Sarah may have chosen to die, her death is tragic, and I grieve for her. Clearly, Abraham does as well. The biblical text discusses with unusual detail the great lengths to which Abraham went in order to purchase a fitting burial place for Sarah near the oak trees she so loved. In death, Sarah's wishes are granted. She shares a resting place for all time with her husband, her son Isaac and his wife Rebekah, her grandson Jacob and his wife Leah.

Biblical stories with problematic, disquieting endings may not come to an immediate resolution; but more often than not, an unexpected healing may take place in another time, space, or spiritual realm.

Hannah

In juxtaposition to the karmic turmoil and splitting apart of the family in the stories of Abraham, Sarah, and Isaac, reconciliation of the family is at the root of the story of Hannah. Abraham and Sarah give birth to the first Jewish children, resulting in a cacophony of love and hatred, hierarchy and injustice. Hannah attempts to give justice and a new order to the wickedness wrought by Abraham's descendants.

The meanness and perversity of Abraham's descendants reaches its nadir in the narrative in the Hebrew Bible which precedes Hannah. At the end of the book of Judges (Jgs 19–21): A Levite man goes to Bethlehem to bring back his runaway concubine. On their way home, an old man offers them shelter but the men in the town, from the tribe of Benjamin, pound on his door and demand he give them the Levite man. The old man offers them his virgin daughter and the Levite's concubine. They grab the Levite's concubine and rape her until she dies in the morning. The Levite cuts her into twelve pieces and sends the pieces to the tribes of Israel, demanding justice. A civil war begins. Rape, cruelty, horror, and sadism mark the end of the book of Judges. Enter Hannah.

Years ago, I might not have been as inspired by a woman of Hannah's goodness, clarity of purpose, and concern for others—partly because I might not have made the connection in the Hebrew Bible between the end of Judges and the beginning of Samuel, and partly because her story in the Bible is hidden. With the information from midrash, a portrait of a unique, determined, devoted woman emerges. In our first encounter with Hannah, we learn two essential facts: Hannah cares for others, and she is deeply committed to her relationship with God. She encourages others to go with her to the sanctuary. Once there, she insists that her offerings to God be properly sacrificed.

Like her foremother, Sarah, Hannah suggests to her husband that he take another wife. But unlike Sarah, when the wife she suggested for her husband turns against her, Hannah does not retaliate. Instead, she seeks a solution to her problems by turning to the Source of Life. It is not just a child that Hannah wants. If so, she would have asked for children. Hannah wants righteousness. She wants goodness. She wants a world that exists in God's service. From the first time we meet her, we learn that she has the patience to wait for the proper priest rather than risk that her offerings to God may be polluted. Hannah is not asking for herself. If she were, she would have wanted to keep the child. Hannah's desire is for a different world. And Hannah fights for that world. That is what makes Hannah into a prophet.

She faces one challenge after another. She stands up to Eli, the priest, and defends herself. She acknowledges God's gift and includes God's name in the name she gives their child. She goes against custom and stays home to raise her child in her own way. As an artist might give herself over to the creation of a work of art, a businessman to a deeply loved project, a political activist to a mission, Hannah gives herself over to that which she believes in: the raising of the child she will offer to God. When that child's life is threatened, Hannah rushes in and again stands up to the hierarchy persisting until she is heard and acknowledged.

Visionary, prophet, teacher, warrior—Hannah is one of the most extraordinary women in the Bible. Filled with her own love of God and righteousness, she does not allow herself to be diverted from her devotion. She acts with clear and judicious vision. When Peninah attacks her, she does not busy herself with revenge but allows life to work its own design. She offers Peninah mercy and in doing so, her heart opens with even more devotion. Hannah not only brings a prophet into the world, she herself becomes a prophet. Hannah's mothering is of the deepest kind. Her wish is for the spiritual well-being of the world.

On the first day of the New Year, two very different stories of birth, desire, and intention are read. Surely the rabbis chose well to put these stories together, for we learn as much about parenting from the juxtaposition of the stories as from regarding each story separately. Sarah and Hannah are both eager to have children. Sarah wants an heir and is willing to do anything to protect that heir, even if it means sending away another mother's child into the wilderness and separating that child from his father. Hannah wants a righteous child to guide her people. She refuses to react out of jealousy but rather clings to her faith in God, and when the moment comes, she keeps her promise and returns her child to the Source of Life. Her child, Samuel, whose goodness and devotion to God reflect the closeness to God that is sought on this holiday, is the physical and spiritual fruit of her desire. After Samuel is accepted into the priesthood, Hannah joyously bursts into song, for she has an epiphany and foresees God's plan.

On Rosh Hashanah, God is no longer the Parent/Protector. Now the people are the parents and are responsible for their actions. God wishes Abram to teach his sons, Ishmael and Isaac. Hannah chooses to educate her son Samuel and defends the education she gives him. Abram and Sarai assume new names. With the insertion of the letter *hay*, which represents "God," into their names, God-consciousness is now inside them. As the people care for others and become adults, God becomes internalized. The women in these stories also take on more responsibility and leadership. Sarah advises kings. Hannah seeks her own destiny. However, there is not yet a partnership between men and women.

If we overlay the four-thousand-year-old historical relationship of God and the Jewish people upon the cycle of the holidays, we see that Rosh Hashanah occurs midway through the cycle and marks a change in the development of the Jewish soul. After the destruction of the Temples at Tisha B'Av, the role of the priests as intermediaries ends. Since there is no one to connect them to God, the people must make their own sacrifices and decisions.

On the first day of Rosh Hashanah, we make requests of God. On the second day, God does the asking. How strong is our faith in the Source of Life? Are we willing, like Abram and Sarai, to take on the covenant and change our names so God may dwell within us?

YOM KIPPUR

About Yom Kippur

Yom Kippur, the Day of Atonement, is considered by some to be the holiest of days, the Sabbath of Sabbaths. It is observed ten days after Rosh Hashanah in the seventh month of the Jewish calendar (in September or October). To commemorate the importance of the day, many Jews wear white clothes or *kittels* and the Torah scrolls are adorned with white covers.

In biblical times, it was on Yom Kippur, after the people had been asking for forgiveness for forty days for having worshiped the golden calf, that Moses brought the second set of tablets from Mount Sinai. At that time, and in our time also, turning back to God allows God's presence in the form of the Torah to return once again to the people.

In Temple times, and especially during the Second Temple, the Hebrew people solemnly gathered in Jerusalem on Yom Kippur. Eating and drinking, intimate physical contact, wearing leather shoes, washing for pleasure, and anointing were forbidden. People participated in prayers and sacrifices for personal and communal atonement. The high priest entered the holy of holies; he called out God's ineffable name; and two goats were offered for the purification of the Temple and the people. Once the people learned that their offerings had been accepted, there was great celebration. In the afternoon, young people danced joyously in the orchards, and matchmaking often followed.

After the destruction of the Second Temple, the rabbis forbade ecstatic celebration on the afternoon of Yom Kippur, and the entire day became solemn. Since then, atonement for the community no longer depends on the purity of the high priest. Now it is each person's deeds and prayers that affect the entire community's well-being. The rabbis stress that individual repentance is the first step to drawing close to God; giving charity and helping others brings one even closer. Rabbi Eleazar said, "A man who gives charity in secret is even greater than Moses."

About Yom Kippur

On the eve of Yom Kippur the moving prayer of Kol Nidre is sung. The prayer is an absolution of vows and obligations. It is chanted three times, first in a whisper, then louder, and the third time with urgency. Originating between the sixth and tenth centuries c.e., its practice was discouraged by rabbis until the fifteenth century, when it became essential for the Marranos, Jews living in Spain during the Inquisition, who would have been killed if they practiced Judaism publically. In time, Kol Nidre came to fulfill a collective need to be forgiven regardless of particular circumstances. Despite the best of intentions, human perfection is not possible, so we ask in advance for forgiveness.

During the evening, morning, and afternoon services, ten times the community confesses a list of sins aloud. The Hebrew word for sin means "to miss the mark," which leads to a disconnection from God. Yom Kippur is a renewal of the entire community's relationship with God. In crying out our errors in the first person plural, we ask the Divine Source to be merciful toward each of us and the entire community of Israel. If we know that we are innocent of a particular failure, we still confess it, both because we are responsible as a community for one another and because even if we have not consciously committed that error, there is always a possibility that we are responsible for an aspect of it.

The entire day of Yom Kippur, from morning to sunset, is spent in the synagogue. In addition to confessing failures and asking for forgiveness, Jews read stories of their past and praise God. There is often a small break in the afternoon to rest before the afternoon and evening services.

As the hours pass and we have not eaten or drunk anything, we let go of all outer activity and move into an altered state. Now is the moment we seek God face-to-face. It was often at this time in the day that in our synagogue Shlomo Carlebach, who acted as cantor as well as rabbi, would whistle the prayer I remember as the potsherd prayer:

> *Who are we?*
> *What is our life?*
> *A vessel soon to become a potsherd,*
> *grass about to wither,*
> *a fading flower,*
> *a cloud breaking up into the air,*
> *dust flying into space,*
> *a fleeting dream.*

As Shlomo whistled, I would think of my ancestors, many of whom had sacrificed their lives in order to live according to these teachings.

About Yom Kippur

Twenty-five hundred years later, we speak about the Temple sacrifices with reverence, for although slaughtering animals may not befit a twenty-first-century sensibility, the shepherds gave what they had. Their wealth was their animals and they sacrificed them to God. They too understood that if they went against God's teachings, heaven and earth would decay, and if they would reconnect to God, a new year could begin. Thinking of the shepherds who were my ancestors, I imagined we shared the same prayers: *Please God, I am not perfect, but let me be connected to you and your teachings. Forgive the mistakes I have made by turning away from you and your ways. I know everything I have is yours and I am returning a part of it to you. Help me to be closer to you. I want to be yours. I want to belong to the Oneness of the universe.*

In the last service of the day, Neilah, meaning "closing" or "locking," people ask to be sealed in the metaphorical Book of Life, before the gates of heaven which opened at Rosh Hashanah, close at the end of Yom Kippur. There is a spirited call and response, with the prayer leader crying out the Sh'ma, "Hear O Israel, the Lord our God, the Lord is One," and the congregation repeating the cry. The prayer leader then cries out three times, "Blessed is the Creator of the Universe forever and ever." The congregation echoes these words. Lastly, the prayer leader with full strength cries to God seven times, "The Lord is God." Seven times the congregation echoes the affirmation with increasing fervor.

At nightfall, the shofar blows for one last time, and the New Year begins.

The Holy of Holies

God's Awesome Name

From the time of the Exodus, on the tenth day of the seventh month, Jews have devoted themselves to one day of atonement by following God's commandment "You shall practice self-denial and do no work so you will cleanse yourself of your sins" (Lv 16:29–34). In Temple days, as part of the ritual of atonement, the high priest called out God's ineffable name, sent a sacrifice to Azazel (Satan the Adversary), and entered the holy of holies with offerings. With the destruction of the Second Temple and its priesthood, the priest's ritual of expiation is no longer observed. However, it is still read (Lv 16) on the morning of Yom Kippur.

What makes this ancient rite still meaningful? Before he entered the holy of holies, the high priest was warned, "Remember you are coming before the Judge who sits on the throne of justice and destroys evil. You cannot enter the presence of God if the enemy is inside you." The journey the high priest made into the holy of holies was perceived as being too dangerous for an ordinary person to risk because behind the veil was an all-seeing, all-devouring Being. But with the high priest gone, we ordinary beings must each enter the holy of holies and go before the One who sees the enemy inside us.

I've added Kabbalistic interpretation to help explain the high priest's actions in the holy of holies and my own words to the prayers of the congregation to make them more immediate. The reading of this story from the Yom Kippur prayer book is shared between the reader (the leader of the service) and the congregation.

O God, who can do what you have done? You spread the world over empty space. When darkness enveloped the world, you brought forth light. You set a crystal sky to divide the waters and then gathered the earthly waters into the deep. The earth budded and blossomed. You placed glorious lights in the sky next to the constellations. You brought fish and birds from the waters, animals from the dust, man and woman from your image.

Adam and Eve, the first man and woman, lived in a garden filled with fruit trees and streams. You warned Adam: "Do not eat from the Tree of Knowledge." The serpent enticed Eve and Adam to eat the fruit from the Tree of Knowledge. You commanded Adam, Eve, and the serpent to leave the Garden of Paradise. Adam was to work, Eve to suffer in childbirth, and the serpent to crawl on its belly. Eve gave birth to Cain and Abel. Cain and then Abel brought offerings to you. You spurned Cain's offerings and preferred Abel's gifts. Cain murdered his younger brother. You set Cain to wander but marked him so he would not be harmed. Eve had a third child, Seth. The children of Cain and Seth turned to other gods and forgot you.

Ten generations after Adam, Noah was born. He heeded your command and built an ark. Because the people harmed one another, you set the rain upon the earth for forty days and forty nights. When the rains stopped, Noah brought offerings that you accepted. You made a covenant with Noah that you would never again destroy the earth by water. But when the people built a great tower to proclaim their greatness, you scattered them across the earth.

Ten generations after Noah, in the city of Ur of the Chaldees, Abraham heard your voice and followed your words. In his old age, you tested Abraham, and he offered you his son Isaac. To Isaac's son Jacob were born twelve sons and one daughter. One of Jacob's sons was Levi. Levi's great-grandchildren were Aaron, Moses, and Miriam. You chose the children of Aaron to be your priests and to make offerings to you at the appointed times. From the tribe of Levi you consecrated a high priest who wears a breastplate with the urim and thummin and lives in the Temple.

O God, you gave life to our ancestors. You give us life. How can we thank you? We bring you offerings to acknowledge the life you give us. The high priest will bring you our offering. He will call to you, asking you to forgive us. He will enter your Holy Presence in all purity. Forgive us so that we may be close to you again.

Each year, seven days before Yom Kippur the high priest was taken from his home to prepare for the holiday. Another priest also prepared in the event that the high priest was not able to carry out his responsibilities. During these seven days, the high priest studied his duties for the Day of Atonement and was continuously sprinkled with purifying water by the elders. If he was knowledgeable, he discussed the teachings with the elders. If not, they would teach him. If he could read the Scriptures, he would read the books of Job, Ezra, and Chronicles. If he could not, the elders read to him and urged him not to do anything differently than he had been instructed. He knew that Aaron's older sons, Nadav and Avihu, had approached the holy of holies without being properly prepared and that flames had leapt out and killed them. Nevertheless, the high priest turned aside and wept because the elders did not trust him, and the elders also turned aside and wept because they did not trust him.

"Prepare for this day!" they urged him. "You will enter the holy of holies and call out God's name! If you are not completely pure in thought and body, fire will shoot out and consume you. All the people are depending on you. You are the one who will bring us forgiveness."

At dawn, on Yom Kippur, the high priest went to the place of immersion. A curtain was placed between him and the people. He removed his clothes. Naked, he lowered himself into the cold water so that every part of his body, including his head, was completely covered. When he emerged, the elders gave him gold clothes to put on, and he sanctified his hands and feet with water from a gold pitcher. Five times during the day he immersed himself in water, sanctified his hands, and changed his clothes.

In his gold clothes, he performed the first part of the morning ritual—slaughtering a bull and seven sheep—and sprinkled the blood on the altar. The other priests finished the sacrifice. He entered the Temple and carried out his daily duties. He cleaned the menorah, lit the morning incense, made the daily offerings of fine flour, and placed the twelve baked loaves of bread on the table. Accompanied by the priests playing music on harps and tambourines, he poured the wine libation.

He returned to the place of immersion, bathed, and put on white clothes. Quickly, he went to the bull that was his personal sin offering. He put his hands on the head of the bull, and standing in awe before God, he recited the words of his first confession: "O God, I have gone astray. My family and I have walked in a crooked path. I beg you, forgive my errors, intentional and unintentional. Forgive our errors, intentional and unintentional. You dictated and Moses wrote in the Torah that this is the day you promised you would purify us."

As he pronounced with fear and devotion God's awesome name— Yhwh—the priests and people, who were standing in the courtyard, bowed, fell to their faces, and together cried out, "Blessed is your name forever and ever." The high priest continued intoning, completing God's Name at the same time as the people finished their blessing. Then God's voice entered him, and he said to the people, "You are cleansed."

At the Nicanor Gate, at the east side of the Temple, two white male goats, twins in height and size, were waiting. Going to the lottery box that held the fate of the goats, he reached up and drew two lots without looking at the lottery box. "For God" was written on one lot. "For Azazel" was written on the other. Whichever hand held the lot marked "For God" he placed on the goat in front of that hand and said, "A sin offering for God." Again, upon hearing the awesome name of God, the priests and people in the courtyard knelt and gave thanks, saying, "Blessed is your name forever and ever." The high priest then tied a scarlet wool thread on the horns of the goat intended for Azazel, and gave it to its caretaker. He tied another scarlet thread to the doorpost of the Temple. The priests watched the scarlet thread to see if it turned white.

The high priest returned to his own bull and confessed a second time in the name of the priests, "O God, I have gone astray. I have walked in a crooked path. My family, all the priests of Aaron, and I have walked in a crooked path. I beg you, forgive my errors, intentional and unintentional. Forgive our errors, intentional and unintentional." With fear and devotion, he pronounced God's awesome name—Yhwh—and together the priests and people cried out, "Blessed is your name forever and ever." Then filled with God's voice, he said to the people, "You are cleansed."

With a sharp knife, he slaughtered the bull he had blessed and let the blood fall into a basin. He let another priest stir the blood so that it would not congeal. He then went up to the altar with his shovel and took out the innermost fiery coals.

As the high priest was about to enter the holy of holies, the oldest priest stopped him and said, "Know that when you enter the holy of holies if you do not concentrate on what you are about to do, you will fall and die and Israel will not receive atonement. The eyes of all of Israel are on you. Look inside yourself and be certain you are purified. Remember, you are coming before the Judge who sits on the throne of justice and destroys evil. You cannot enter the presence of the One if the enemy is still within you."

The high priest answered, "I have searched my heart and asked for forgiveness for all the ways that I lost my connection to God. May the people do the same." Nevertheless, the priests tied a rope to the leg of the high priest so they could pull him out in case he died.

The moment came for the high priest to enter the holy of holies wearing his white clothes. In his right hand, he carried the shovel of fiery coals. In his left hand he held the ladle with the fragrant incense that had been especially prepared for Yom Kippur. He placed the shovel containing the coals on the floor between the male and female cherubim and piled the fragrant incense on the coals. The room filled with smoke. Then he walked backward out of the holy of holies. He prayed that God would send the amount of rain that was needed for the year, that the people would be provided for, that no woman would miscarry, that the trees would be fruitful, and that Judah would be sovereign in her land.

He went to the priest who was stirring the bull's blood and took the blood. He reentered the holy of holies and with his finger sprinkled the blood one time upward gesturing and then seven times downward in front of the ark where the Shechinah dwelt. As he sprinkled the blood, he counted, "One. One plus one. One plus two. One plus three. One plus four. One plus five. One plus six. One plus seven." Each time he spoke the number one, he concentrated on God's divine aspect of understanding flowing down from heaven and uniting with one of God's seven earthly aspects—loving-kindness, power, beauty, victory, splendor, foundation, and sovereignty. By the last sprinkling, the divine aspect of understanding and the earthly aspect of sovereignty were united. A second time, he quickly walked backward out of the holy of holies.

The high priest then slaughtered the white goat that was the offering to Yahweh and let the blood pour into a basin.

A third time, he entered the holy of holies and sprinkled the goat's blood, which was the people's offering, between the male and female cherubim. Concentrating on God's divine aspect of understanding flowing down and uniting with God's seven earthly aspects, he sprinkled the blood once upward and seven times downward. A third time, he quickly walked backward out of the holy of holies.

He then mixed the blood of the white goat that belonged to the community with the blood of his own bull. He stood before the inner altar and sprinkled the mixed blood between the altar and the menorah. As he sprinkled the blood once upward and seven times downward, he invited God's understanding to unite with God's earthly aspects. Then, he poured the remaining blood on the outer altar.

He went up to the goat that was to be led to Azazel. He placed both his hands on the head of the goat and confessed the intentional and unintentional sins of the people: "Please, God, the people have gone astray. They have walked in a crooked path. Forgive their intentional, unintentional, and perverse sins." With fear and devotion, he pronounced God's awesome name Yhwh. The priests and people bowed, fell to their faces, and together cried out, "Blessed is your name forever and ever." Then, filled with God's voice, the high priest said to the people, "You are cleansed."

Another priest led the goat carrying the transgressions of the people toward the wilderness. There were ten booths stationed from Jerusalem to the precipice in the desolate wilderness. At each booth, another priest waited to lead the goat. At the last booth, the priest led the goat toward the precipice and then watched from a distance.

As the goat was being led toward Azazel, the high priest cut up the bull and goat. He removed their sacrificial parts and put them in a plate to be burned on the outer altar. He returned to the Women's Courtyard and recited portions of the Torah. Both he and the people anxiously waited to see the sign of God's forgiveness: the scarlet thread in the sanctuary turn white.

The high priest bathed and put on gold clothes. He made sacrifices, returned, bathed, and put on white clothes. He entered the holy of holies and removed the ladle and shovel he had brought in the morning. For the fifth and last time, he bathed and put away his white clothes, and put on gold clothes. He entered the sanctuary. He gave the afternoon burnt offering, lit the afternoon incense and the menorah. He gave meal and flour offerings and wine libations to the accompaniment of music.

He was brought his own clothes. His face was radiant. Escorted by the priests and his friends, he went home and celebrated leaving the holy of holies alive and in peace. The people surrounded him, singing and full of happiness—the scarlet thread had turned white and they believed they were once again living in God's embrace. The high priest asked God to bless the people with health and prosperity and the land with abundance.

Those who saw the high priest walk out of the holy of holies say that his face was as dazzling as the heavens, as wondrous as a rainbow, as splendid as the first creatures, as bright as a wreath on a young woman's head, as full of grace as the faces of a bride and groom, as awesome as Moses' face when he returned from speaking with the Shechinah, as glorious as the morning star. Ah, those who saw the high priest's face were happy. They went out into the fields and celebrated. All afternoon, there was singing, dancing, and courting under the apple trees.

Now that the Temple is gone, we can no longer see the face of the high priest, the celebration at the Water-Drawing, the scarlet thread turning white, the singers, the joy of the people. We can no longer make sacrificial offerings to you, asking your forgiveness. But we know you love stories and that you asked to dwell among us, so we tell you this story as part of our offering. We ask for forgiveness and to be united in your embrace.

Jonah

The Sea Stood Still

In the afternoon of Yom Kippur, after more than eighteen hours of fasting, we read the book of Jonah in synagogue. Although we may have been running from God all year, each time we hear the story of Jonah, we are taken aback. Jonah is a prophet! How can he imagine that he can escape from God? Listening to this story of surprises in which the prophet rebels, a fish swallows a man, an entire city repents—where anything and everything seems possible—emboldens us to imagine that we too might transform and be close to God.

On Yom Kippur, we each enter the holy of holies, the belly of the whale—a confining, isolated place. There, we confront ourselves and pray that God will see our goodness and forgive our failings and that we too will look at others and see their goodness and forgive them.

In retelling Jonah, I've added oral legends to the biblical texts.

Jonah was the son of a poor widow. He and his mother were so poor that they hardly had enough to eat. God spoke to the prophet Elijah and told him to go to the city of Zarephath in Sidon where a widow would feed him. Elijah arrived in Zarephath. He saw a widow gathering wood and called to her, saying, "Bring me some bread."

She answered, "I have nothing but a handful of flour and a little oil in a flask. With these two pieces of wood, I will make a fire to cook

169

a small cake for my son and myself. We will eat it and after that we will die."

"Do not be afraid," Elijah persuaded her. "Do what I ask. Make two small cakes—one for me, and one for you and your son. The God of Israel has promised that you will not lack flour or oil."

The widow did as Elijah asked, and she and her young son had enough to eat. Elijah stayed in the widow's upstairs room, but soon after this, the little boy became ill, so ill that his soul left his body.

The mother rushed to Elijah and said, "Until you came, I was considered a righteous woman. But because of your extreme righteousness, all my faults are in front of me. You found rest in my house, but now my son is no longer breathing."

"Bring me your son," Elijah said.

The mother quickly carried her son upstairs to Elijah's room and laid him on the bed. Elijah leaned over him. He put his hands on the child's hands. He brought his mouth close to the boy's mouth. Three times he did this, each time intensively praying, "Dear God, I beg you, restore the child's soul."

God listened to Elijah, and the boy's soul returned to him. When Elijah gave the child back to his mother, she held her son to her heart and said, "Now I know you are a man of God. You have given my son back his life. The words you speak are true. I will now call him Jonah, son of Amittai, after you."

Elijah trained Jonah to be a prophet. When Elijah died, Elisha took over Jonah's training. Elisha sent Jonah to anoint Jehu, who was from the tribe of Manasseh, to be king of Israel.

For sixty years, Jonah pleaded with Jehu, his sons, his grandsons, and the people of Israel to change their ways so that God would not destroy them. At times, they listened, but when they turned away from God and no harm came to them, the people called Jonah a false prophet. Still, Jonah continued to plead with his people.

Then, God spoke to Jonah, saying, "Jonah, son of Amittai, rise up! Go to the great city of Nineveh, and tell them that their wickedness has come before me."

Jonah rose up, but he did not go to Nineveh. The people of Nineveh were the enemies of the Hebrews. Nineveh was east of Jerusalem. Jonah did not want the people of Nineveh to repent, so he went west. He walked until he came to Jaffa, the western-most city in Judah. He went down to the harbor and found a Phoenician ship about to sail for Tarshish, the western-most port in the world. Eagerly, Jonah paid for his passage, boarded the boat, and went down into the hold, away from God's sight. He drew his cloak over his head and fell asleep.

A day after the ship set sail, God hurled a mighty wind across the sea. The wind grew into a fierce, raging storm, tossing the ship in every direction so that it was in danger of being broken into pieces. Yet when the sailors looked about them, they saw in the distance that the sea was calm. In fear, each sailor cried out to his own god, "Save us!" Then they threw the cargo into the sea to lighten the ship's weight, but the storm continued to rage.

The captain searched the ship looking for a way to save it and heard someone snoring in the hold. "Sleeper, why are you sleeping at a time like this?" he cried, and pulled Jonah's cloak from his head. "Wake up, go up on deck, and pray to your God so we do not all perish!"

On deck, the storm had grown fiercer. The sailors had gathered and were about to throw stones to find out who was responsible for the storm. When they saw Jonah, they insisted that he join their circle. One sailor twirled a stone. Everyone watched as the marked stone went around and around until it slowed down and the narrow part pointed to Jonah. A second sailor twirled the marked stone. Again it pointed to Jonah. A third time, the stone was twirled and pointed to Jonah.

The sailors pounced on him with questions. "Who are your people? Where do you come from? What is your work? Why has this evil come to us?"

Jonah answered, "I am a Hebrew. I fear Elohim, the God of heaven, who created the seas and the dry land."

"What have you done to provoke the wrath of your God?" the men cried.

Jonah explained, "My God, Elohim, told me I was to go to the city of Nineveh to tell the people to repent, but I tried to run away."

"How shall we calm the sea?" the sailors asked.

"Throw me into the waters. The storm is attacking you because of me."

Not wanting to throw a holy man into the raging waters, the sailors went to their oars and tried to bring him to dry land. But the waves became higher and the sea wilder. Then the sailors, who were each of different faiths, called in one voice, "Elohim, Jonah's God, we beg you, please do not let us perish on the account of your servant's soul. Do not accuse us of having taken an innocent life. We know the choice is yours."

Still praying, they threw Jonah into the raging sea. To the sailors' amazement, in minutes the crashing waves quieted into gentle ripples and the fierce wind into a silent breeze. The dark clouds vanished. Light appeared. The sea stood still. The sailors gave offerings to Elohim and vowed to go to Yahweh's Temple when they returned to land.

God had prepared a great fish for Jonah. The fish swallowed Jonah, and for three days and three nights Jonah was inside the fish. At first, he was lodged in the upper, male part of the fish; but when the fish opened his mouth and swallowed again, Jonah was forced down into the lower, female part among the embryos. In terror, he prayed:

Adonai, from the belly of the underworld
I am calling you.
I am calling to you from Sheol.
Do you not hear my voice?
You hurled me into the deep,
into the heart of the sea.
Billows sweep over me.
Waves crash above me.
Adonai! Shall I not see you again?
Shall I never again look at your holy Temple?

The deep enfolds me,
the waters engulf me.

Seaweed entangles my head;
I am falling, falling
down
to the bottom of the mountains.
The earth shuts her gates on me forever,
but you pull me up from the grave.

Adonai, as my life was leaving me,
I remembered you;
I prayed to you and my prayer
entered your holy Temple.
Those who refuse to abandon vanity
will not know mercy.
In gratitude, I will bring you sacrifices.
I will keep my vow to you,
for you, Adonai, are my salvation.

God spoke to the great fish, and the fish opened his mouth and spewed Jonah out onto dry land.

Then, God spoke to Jonah a second time, saying, "Rise up! Go to the great city of Nineveh and cry out the words I tell you." Jonah set out at once for Nineveh.

As he approached the great city and saw its high towers gleaming in the sun, Jonah trembled because of the extreme wickedness of the people who lived there. Nineveh was so vast it took three days to walk through it. After walking one day, Jonah stopped and loudly called out, "In forty days, Nineveh will be overthrown."

Immediately, the words of Elohim passed through the city, and every person there heard and changed their clothes and put on sackcloth. The king came down from his golden throne, put on sackcloth, and sat in ashes. He sent out a proclamation: "No person or animal, herd or flock, shall eat, graze, or drink water. People and animals are to wear sackcloth and call out loudly to God. All people must turn from their evil ways and let go of anything that does not belong to them.

Anyone who knows must repent! We must pray that Yahweh will be forgiving and turn away his wrath so we do not perish."

The king and all the people returned what they had stolen to their rightful owners. The king's palace was torn down to return stolen bricks. Treasures that were buried in ruins were returned. And not only objects but plants and trees that had been stolen as saplings were uprooted and returned to their owners.

When God saw the people of Nineveh had turned away from evil, God's anger turned to compassion.

Jonah did not rejoice. He was exceedingly angry.

"Adonai," Jonah said, "when I was in my own land, I fled because I knew that you are merciful and slow to anger. I knew that you are full of kindness and willing to renounce stern decrees. I knew you would not destroy the people of Nineveh. But now that they have repented, they may become stronger than the Hebrews who refuse to repent. I do not wish to see this. Take my life. It is better I die than live."

God said to him, "Are you so exceedingly angry because of my goodness?"

Jonah did not answer. He left the city and went to the east of Nineveh and made a booth. He sat in its shade and waited to see what would happen to the city.

God then caused a *kikayon* tree to grow over Jonah's head. Jonah rejoiced in the tree that gave him shade and protection.

The next morning, God prepared a tiny worm that inched its way toward the plant, opened its mouth, and attacked the roots. Jonah watched the beautiful tree wither.

Then God caused a stifling east wind to rise up and still the other winds. The sun beat down on Jonah's head and he became faint. In his anger, he said to God, "It is better I die than live."

God said, "Jonah, are you so exceedingly angry because of the tree?"

Jonah answered, "I am angry to the point of death."

"Jonah, Jonah," God said. "You took pity on a tree that you did not create. You did not tend it or help it to grow. It was created and perished in one night. Shall I not have compassion for Nineveh, a great city with thousands of animals and one hundred and twenty thousand people who, like small children, do not know the difference between their right hand and their left? Would you not wish these people, who are the work of my hand, to choose life and live?"

About the Stories

The Holy of Holies

Korban, the Hebrew word for sacrifice, literally means "to draw close." The intent of sacrifices or offerings is to draw close to God, which is the special intent of Yom Kippur. Every day throughout the year, morning and afternoon, during the time of the Temple, the priests made offerings to God on the outer altar. There were burnt offerings for God and meal offerings that were shared between God and the people and priests. Once a year, on Yom Kippur, an additional offering was made to Azazel, or Satan, who is the Adversary.

Part of our humanity lies not only in our desire to act righteously, but in our understanding and acknowledgment of our dark hidden wounds that push us to harm others and ourselves. We do not praise these destructive parts but we acknowledge that they are a part of us and life. God fills the world, surrounds the world, and is greater than the world. But when God contracts and manifests in these particular biblical narratives, a "historical" God is presented who releases a terrifying fury on humanity. Yet, according to midrash, after each disaster, this God is also full of regrets. The offerings to God were made in response to conscious mistakes as well as gratitude. The offering of a goat to Azazel acknowledges the darkness that we perceive in both God and ourselves.

When asking for forgiveness on Yom Kippur, the high priest called out the divine name of God, the tetragrammaton Yhwh, channeling God's grace from heaven to earth.

Y—Yod, represents God's fatherly mind aspect of wisdom.

H—Hay, represents God's motherly, intuitive heart aspect of compassion and understanding.

W—Vav (whose numerical value is six), holds the next six of God's attributes: loving-kindness, power, beauty, victory, splendor, and foundation.

About the Stories

H—Hay, the fourth letter, represents God's sovereignty on earth, the Shechinah.

As the high priest called out God's four-letter name, the people joined him, creating a love duet to God that finished at the same moment. The high priest entered the holy of holies, bringing God's preferred offering of incense, which was made up of ten parts sweet-smelling fragrances and one part foul-smelling fragrance. The inner chamber filled with smoke.

After the fall of the Temple, when the rabbis were debating whether to allow The Song of Songs to enter the canon, Rabbi Akiva compared the passion of love to the passion for God when he said, "All the books of the Bible are holy, but The Song of Songs is the holy of holies." The lovers in The Song of Songs yearn for union. Likewise, there is something erotic and sexual about the actions of the high priest. He walks *into* the dark inner sanctum that is clouded with smoke and perfume. His intention is to be with God—to enter the *between* place—the place between male and female, the place of creation where one becomes two and two becomes one, the place of being where the Shechinah dwells. He sprinkles blood on the fiery incense that is set between the male and female cherubim and asks to be entirely filled with God's presence. In the deepest moment of sexual intimacy, there is oneness, the self disappears, and there is no difference between giving and receiving.

Earlier in the day, the high priest calls out God's awesome name. Now he is calling out the numbers corresponding to God's aspects to further draw out God into the earthly domain. In the same moment that the high priest is asking God to descend to earth, he is physically joining himself to God's presence with his offerings. In likening The Song of Songs to the holy of holies, Akiva is suggesting that human and divine love are the source of creation and the inspiration for the people's well-being.

The Hebrews lived among Sumerians, Babylonians, and Canaanites who worshiped the goddess and celebrated her powers in a yearly ritual act, called the sacred marriage rite, in which the king climbed the ziggurat to enter the goddess's holy of holies. Their act of consummation was intended to bring fertility so that the people and the land would have new life. The other nations asked for rebirth in terms of physical fertility. The high priest asked for rebirth in terms of forgiveness and renewal. Both rituals needed the presence and union of the masculine and feminine.

During the Yom Kippur ritual, forgiveness was achieved through fatherly wisdom (*chochmah*) and motherly compassion (*binah*). With wisdom, the people acknowledge and give up their sins; with compassion, God forgives them. The desired result of the union or balanced harmony between divine and mortal, masculine and feminine, wisdom and compassion, knowledge and awe, is the continuation of creation—the New Year.

The story of *The Holy of Holies* begins with God's first creation—"You spread the world over empty space." God brought about the first creation—the world. The task of the high priest was to unite heaven and earth, the masculine and feminine, and to create a new soul each year for the Jewish people. The ritual of entering the holy of holies to "commune" with the Shechinah symbolizes a union of the male mortal with a female divinity as well as a conceptual union of God's masculine and feminine aspects. According to Kabbalistic belief the Temple is the place where new souls were incubated.

At Yom Kippur, the unfolding relationship between God and the Hebrew people arrives at the nexus that binds them together: giving and receiving—sacrifice, prayer, and God's ineffable name. The exact pronunciation of the tetragrammaton, God's name, YHWH is no longer known. However, we do know that the name for God is a verb related to the meaning "to be." That is what the high priest called out ten times during the day: *Be!* And the congregation, blessing the name, responded, "Blessed is Being." The high priest asked that the people might be purified so that they could enter a state of oneness with God and be renewed for life for another year. It is the holiness and joy of being in a state of oneness with God that the people and the high priest craved, for in this state exists creation and the potential for every possibility imaginable.

A high priest no longer performs this ancient ritual. Now it is our turn. Let us consider ourselves to be the high priest entering our inner sanctum three times, each time asking God for forgiveness. If we imagine that the third time we enter our inner sanctum we bring the blood of our own transgressions mixed with the blood of the transgressions of the community, we begin to understand why the task of the high priest was so arduous. To present God with our own transgressions and those of our community demands that there is no resentment, no hatred, no separation from any part of ourselves or from the community. In the place where Pure Being dwells, any impurity or deception is immediately noticed. But if we are love, we become the burning field of smoke that rises up between wisdom (the male cherub) and compassion (the female cherub), and dance with joy. Our offering is accepted. We are inscribed in the Book of Life for one more year.

Jonah

Jonah undergoes a trial similar to that of the high priest. For sixty years, he has been a prophet continuously urging his people to repent. Then God asks him to consider the Ninevites, the enemies of the Israelites, and urge them to repent. Jonah runs away. Who would choose to empower their enemy? To overturn Jonah's preconceptions God causes him to be thrust into the waters, the primeval element that existed before the world was formed, the primeval element that cleanses and purifies.

Both the high priest and Jonah enter charged territories. Jonah's is the male/female belly of a fish that is filled with embryos. In this place, there is no bad or good, enemy or friend; there is only being. This state of being reminds Jonah of the state of being that he knew in the Temple, the state of oneness with God. He prays to God and he is reborn. Nevertheless, when God asks him a second time to help his enemy, he is not able to extend his compassion to all of life.

At Yom Kippur, there is a change in the way the people approach God. When they were in their adolescent relationship with God at Shavuot, God's presence on Mount Sinai was so frightening that the people implored Moses to be their intermediary. Having passed through the grief of Tisha B'Av and the reconciliation of Rosh Hashanah, at Yom Kippur, they are strong enough to imagine a personal relationship with God.

In the journey of the calendar from Passover to Purim, in which the soul moves from dependence to independence in approaching God, there is always a sense of hubris. The soul moves forward in eagerness. But when it imagines it is advancing by its own efforts rather than God's grace, it falls back in despair. So at Yom Kippur, we read the story of the high priest in which there is union with God and the story of Jonah in which there is a failure to appreciate God's oneness.

When Jonah enters a place of death and rebirth in the belly of the fish, he experiences God's power and majesty and pleads to be reconnected to God. But once he returns from the awesome place, he is diverted by his emotions and tribal loyalties and allows his preconceptions to separate him from the miracles that are constantly being displayed before him.

If Jonah, a holy prophet, cannot let go of his vanities and prejudices, despite being thrust into the belly of the whale, how much more difficult is it for us non-prophets to cling to Being rather than to doctrines and vanities? Letting go of our pride or fear and acknowledging our continually wounded and wounding self is the first step toward forgiveness and purification.

Our deepening understanding of the complexity of life leads us to appreciate Jonah's struggles and to realize that the enemy is not on the outside. The enemy is within us: The enemy is our own preconceptions and misunderstandings. The time of atonement is a moment of great challenge, for upon experiencing the oneness of life, we are asked to care for all of life.

SUKKOT

About Sukkot

Sukkot, which in Hebrew means "booths" or "tabernacles," commemorates the Israelites' journey through the wilderness when they lived in temporary huts called sukkot. The Israelites believed that the clouds of glory, which had withdrawn when they made the golden calf, returned on Sukkot and hovered over them like a tent or a sukkah. Sukkot begins four days after Yom Kippur on the evening of the full moon of the seventh month of the Jewish calendar (September/October), and continues for seven days.

On the first day of Sukkot, in celebration of their reconciliation with God at Yom Kippur and in gratitude for the bounty of the harvest, pilgrims brought grain and animal offerings to Jerusalem. The Temple priests sacrificed seventy bulls to God and asked for peace and well-being for the seventy nations of the world.

On the second day of Sukkot in a ceremony known as the Joy of the Water-Drawing, pilgrims carried water from wells to the altar, where they prayed and made offerings for rain for the winter season. That night, by torchlight and candlelight, they celebrated until dawn on the steps of the Temple courtyard, singing and dancing to the ecstatic music of flutes, harps, cymbals, and trumpets. The Talmud says, "Whoever has not seen the rejoicing at the place of the Water-Drawing has not seen rejoicing in his life." One legend reports that when Jonah was participating in the Joy of the Water-Drawing, the spirit of God came to him and he became a prophet.

The harvest festival, Sukkot, also called the Season of Our Joy, was the most important and most joyous of the three pilgrimage festivals. Each of the pilgrimage festivals suggested a different aspect of freedom: Passover—physical and legal freedom; Shavuot—spiritual and cultural freedom; and Sukkot—inner freedom.

Sukkot has three commandments. First, to build and dwell in a sukkah as an extension of the home or synagogue. Second, for individuals or synagogues to acquire the four species of plants—the *etrog* (citron), myrtle, palm branch, and willow (all of which come from trees)—for ceremonial use. And third, to rejoice during the holiday.

Today preparations for Sukkot begin immediately after Yom Kippur with the loving construction and decoration of beautiful, small temporary shelters on a balcony or next to a home or synagogue. The roofs are made from materials that grow in the earth. The coverings of the roof are partially open to the heavens so that there is more shade than sunshine in the day and the largest stars can be seen at night. Devout Jews choose to live for one week in the sukkah to be close to God and to experience the joys of inner freedom that we experience without the distraction of material goods.

Before Sukkot, each person, family, or synagogue buys a beautiful lemon-like fruit called an *etrog*. They also buy a cluster of branches that takes its name from the center palm branch, the *lulav*, and includes myrtle and willow. During the morning prayer service, as the psalms are being sung, each person holds a *lulav* in his or her right hand and an *etrog* in the left hand. The people stretch out their arms. They bring the upright *lulav* and oval *etrog* together and shake them in the six directions—the four cardinal directions—east, south, west, and north—plus toward heaven and earth. Each time the *etrog* and *lulav* are offered to one of the six directions, they are shaken three times and then brought back to the heart. The four species of fruit are autumnal offerings, expressions of gratitude, similar to the barley offerings that were made during Temple times at Shavuot.

In fulfilling the third commandment of Sukkot, people visit the sukkah where they eat, drink, pray, study, and tell stories. An essential element of Sukkot is extending hospitality and taking in guests. Since the time of the Kabbalists, observant Jews invite a different *ushpiz*, symbolic guest such as Abraham, Isaac, Jacob, Joseph, Moses, Aaron, and David, to enter their sukkot each night of the holiday. Many of these guests were wanderers, and so when their stories are told, we further experience the temporary quality of living in the sukkah. More recent tradition invites guests such as Sarah, Rebekah, Rachel, Leah, Dinah, Yocheved, Miriam, Deborah, and Esther, as well as prominent male and female figures in Jewish history.

One of my favorite stories our rabbi, Shlomo Carlebach, told in the sukkah was *The Etrog*. A short and seemingly simple story, yet each time Shlomo told it I understood it differently. When I first heard it, I thought it was about the importance of family peace. Now when I think about it, it also suggests that if we hold fast to our connection to God, we cannot but live joyfully and peacefully. . . .

Nahum and Sarah lived in Chernobyl. Nahum owned the prayer straps, the *tefillin*, that were written by Ephraim, the scribe of the Baal Shem Tov. They had the unique quality that no rain or water could harm them. A wealthy man in Chernobyl offered Nahum 10,000 roubles for the *tefillin*, but Nahum refused. Many times when they did not have enough money to buy food to eat or wood to heat the house, his wife, Sarah, had asked him to sell the *tefillin*, but he had always refused. The family could live happily for five years on 10,000 roubles, but the *tefillin* were more important to Nahum than money.

Then, one year Sukkot was approaching and there were no etrogs to be found. The commandment for Sukkot was to pray while holding an etrog. Nahum went from market to market looking for an etrog. The etrogs, which came from Palestine or Turkey, had not arrived that year. Nahum became more and more worried. One evening, just before Sukkot as he was walking out of the synagogue, he saw a man with a box that holds an etrog. He ran up to him and asked, "Is that—do you have an etrog?"

The man answered, "Yes, I bought the etrog several months ago in Turkey when it was green and stored it in a cool place until now. Look!" He opened the box. There was a full, round beautiful etrog.

"Please," Nahum said. "I want to buy it."

"You couldn't possibly afford it," the man said, looking at Nahum in his worn, threadbare clothes.

"How much do you want?" Nahum asked.

"Ten thousand roubles," the man answered.

"Wait here," Nahum said and he ran to the home of the wealthy man and sold him his *tefillin*.

When Nahum opened the door to his home, glowing with happiness, Sarah said, "You have been sad for days, tell me, what has happened?"

"Look!" he said, "look at this beautiful etrog!"

"Nahum, it's a beautiful etrog, but how could you afford to buy such a beautiful etrog?"

"I sold the *tefillin*."

"You? Nahum!" she screamed. "How could you do such a thing? What will happen to us? If we were in need, we could have sold the *tefillin.*" In her anger, she grabbed the etrog from his hand and threw it on the ground, smashing it.

Nahum gasped.

A moment later, Sarah was horrified. They could have returned the etrog. They could have sold it. Now they had nothing. Nahum turned white. He opened his mouth to say something and closed his mouth.

"I'm sorry," Sarah sobbed.

Nahum took his wife in his arms and said, "Sarah, let me tell you a story. Once we had the *tefillin* of the Baal Shem Tov. It is gone. Once we had a beautiful etrog. It is gone. But those two losses are small compared to the loss of my temper. If I had lost my temper, I would have lost my connection to you and to God and to all that is. What we have is our lives and our love for God. Let us be grateful that God revealed our true bounty to us."

During the prayer service on the seventh day of Sukkot, called Hoshanna Rabbah (Great Salvation), each person carries five willow branches and circles the Torah seven times. As the people sing psalms asking for rain, they beat the willow branches on the ground until the leaves fall off. Some Jews stay up all night reciting psalms or special prayers for rain and dew to ensure the continuation not only of human life but of life for all the world.

Watching members of my congregation beating the willows on the ground, I often thought of Hopi ceremonies at the Second Mesa in Arizona and imagined that on this harvest day the Jews most closely resemble the tribal people we once were. Like the Hopis, we ask for rain and peace, not just for ourselves, but for the world. By waving and shaking the oval etrog and the upright palm leaf together, we call our attention to the joyous joining of the masculine and feminine that is a necessity for fullness in life. And we call to God in all the directions to return our love and to sustain the world.

Solomon and the Demon King

A Heart with Skill to Listen

Solomon was one of the wisest men in the ancient world. During the forty years he was king (around 900 B.C.E.), Israel prospered, its borders expanded, and there was no war. People traveled from many kingdoms to seek his wisdom and to see the wonders of his kingdom. Hundreds of fabulous legends are attributed to the man who was said to know the language of the birds, the animals, and the demons and had seven hundred wives and three hundred concubines.

Using the portion read on Sukkot of Solomon consecrating the Temple (1 Kgs 8:2–21), I've interwoven many legends to create the story of this wisest of men discovering his own relationship with the Creator.

Before King David died, he called his son Solomon to him and said, "In my life I've known great joy and great sorrow. I fought many battles and am leaving you a country that is strong and united. Every day, I sang praises to God and wanted to build a home for the Shechinah, God's presence on earth. I was not allowed to do so because of the blood I shed. But God told me in a dream that a son of peace would be born to me who would build the Temple. You, my son, are to build the Temple. Take my ring. It is inscribed with God's name. When you wear it, remember from where your blessings come, and your deeds will be blessed."

After David died, Solomon went to the sanctuary in Gibeon and made an offering to God. That night he slept by the altar and in his dream God said to him, "Tell me your wish. Whatever you wish will be yours."

Solomon answered, "You made me king in my father's place. I have been given power, but I do not know how to rule the people. Give me a heart with skill to listen so I can distinguish between good and evil and can govern with justice."

God answered, "Because you asked for wisdom to serve your people and not long life, riches, or vengeance, I will give you a heart with more understanding than anyone who has ever lived."

Solomon made two offerings and returned to Jerusalem. The next day he sat on the throne of judgment. On his right sat Ruth, the great-grandmother of his father, David. Into the courtroom burst two prostitutes fighting over a child. Each one claimed to be the child's mother. The first woman said, "Give me my child. Your child died."

The second woman, who was holding the child, said, "You killed your child in your sleep. This is my child."

"I'm the mother!" the first one shouted.

"He's mine!" the second one shouted, moving the child away from the other woman.

The people in the court turned to the new king to see what he would do. At last, Solomon said, "One woman says the child is hers. The other woman says the child is hers. Bring me a sword. I will cut the child in two. I will give half the child to the first woman who spoke and the other half to the second woman."

When the guard returned to the courtroom with a sword, the first woman screamed in terror, "*No!* No, don't kill him! Give her the child. Let him live." With her arm raised as if she would strike the child, the second woman shouted, "Yes! The king is right. Cut the child in two."

Solomon said, "The child will not be killed. Give the child to the first woman who spoke. She's the true mother."

The people said to one another, "Our new king listens to the hearts of others; let us pray that he continues to be so humble."

God had given Solomon wisdom and he could understand the language of plants, from the cedars of Lebanon to the tiny hyssop that grows in the cracks of the walls. He could understand the language of the animals, the birds, the serpents, and the demons, but he did not build the Temple his father had asked him to build, for he did not know where to build it.

Then one night in his dream, a voice spoke to him and told him to go to Mount Zion, where two brothers shared a field. One was a bachelor, the other had a large family. The next evening Solomon walked to the field he had seen in his dream. By the light of the harvest moon, he saw the bachelor carrying sheaves of wheat to his married brother's part of the field and worrying aloud, "Will my brother's children have enough to eat?" The next night, Solomon returned and saw the married man carrying sheaves of wheat to his unmarried brother's part of the field and worrying, "My brother lives alone. What if he doesn't have enough to eat?"

Solomon said to himself, "This is the field of brotherly love. Here I will build the Temple." But the Temple still could not be built, for God had decreed that no material of war should harm a stone that was to be part of the temple of peace; and the master builder only knew how to quarry stones by using iron. Solomon and the master builder and the high priest were pondering how the Temple might be built when the high priest suddenly remembered the shamir.

"The shamir?" the others asked.

The high priest went on, "My father told me that in the time of Moses there was a tiny creature, not larger than the first digit of my smallest finger. This tiny creature, who could cut through stone, was the one who engraved the letters on the high priest's breastplate. If we find the shamir, we can build the Temple." But no one knew where the shamir was to be found. Solomon summoned the animals to Jerusalem. Not one had seen the shamir.

Solomon decided to search in other realms. He summoned the demons. He flattered them, saying, "I've heard that your king, Asmodeus, is very wise. Tell me about him."

"Yes, yes," they answered proudly. "Our king knows everything. He is the Demon King. Every morning, he studies secretly in heaven.

Every afternoon, he glides invisibly into earthly houses of study. Every evening, he returns to his home on the Red Mountain, lifts the claw-shaped stone, and drinks pure water from his well. But he will not reveal his secrets to you."

"I will send my trusted servant, Benaiah," Solomon said, and he took off the ring his father had given him that was engraved with the four letters of God's name. He attached it to a chain and gave it to Benaiah, saying, "Bring me back the Demon King."

Benaiah found the Red Mountain and placed a carafe of wine near the claw-shaped stone. At dusk when Asmodeus returned, the intoxicating scent of the wine caused him to open the carafe. He sipped the wine, tasted it, and then drank until he fell asleep drunk. Immediately, Benaiah slid down from the tree where he was hiding and bound the Demon King with chains. On their way home, Asmodeus awoke and tried to shake off the chains. "Be still," Benaiah said, "You are wrapped in God's name. Do you not see the ring that is holding you?"

In Jerusalem, Asmodeus attacked Solomon, saying, "You believe that the world is yours. But when you die, what will become of you? Your measure will be six feet of earth. How dare you summon me in such a way? What do you want?"

Solomon answered, "I want to build a Temple for God and need to find the shamir."

"Ha ha." The Demon King chuckled. "The great Solomon wants the tiny shamir. Of course, I know where the shamir lives. I know all the secrets. The prince of the sea gave the shamir to the wild hen, who keeps the shamir tucked inside her breast feathers. Every morning she flies to the mountain summits and places the shamir on the cliffs. As the shamir crawls across the cliffs, they open just as the earth opens after a rainstorm. Then the hen scatters seeds into the openings. Trees grow and rocky terrains flourish, but the hen would rather die than give up the shamir. You will never get the shamir from the wild hen."

"Benaiah will!" Solomon said.

Benaiah found the nest of the wild hen. He covered it with a transparent stone. When the hen returned and could not reach her children, she set down the shamir so it would pierce through the stone to the chicks. Benaiah, who was hiding in the brush, grabbed the shamir in one hand and pushed the stone off the nest with the other. He brought the shamir to Solomon, who gave it to Hiram, the master builder.

It took seven years to complete the Temple. The outer walls and gates were decorated with gold; the inside walls and ceilings were sweet-smelling cedarwood. In the holy of holies, the inner shrine of the Temple, a male and female cherub stretched their wings toward each other. All was in readiness for the Shechinah, God's presence on earth.

At the harvest festival of Sukkot, the elders of the tribes of Israel gathered in Jerusalem. Solomon commanded them to bring the ark of the covenant from Gibeon in a great procession accompanied by harps, horns, and trumpets. The priests made sacrifices at the altars. But, as they carried the ark of the covenant up the steps of the Temple, the Temple gates shut in their faces. Rather than force the gates open, Solomon began to recite songs of praise.

At the words "O gates, lift up your heads so the Shechinah, the Presence of Glory, may come in," the gates asked, "Who is the Shechinah, the Presence of Glory?" When Solomon answered, "The Lord Mighty in Battle," the gates leapt off their hinges and began to beat him. Solomon ran through the streets of Jerusalem with the gates following and beating him until he turned and said, "Forgive me. It was my father, King David, who wished to build a home for the Shechinah. May David's name be blessed."

Immediately, the gates returned to the Temple and allowed the priests to enter. The priests placed the ark on the floor between the cherubim and they opened their wings to receive the Shechinah. Then they fanned their wings and a great cloud of incense rose up and chased the priests from the room.

Outside the Temple, Solomon stood before the assembly. He lifted his arms to heaven and said, "Creator of the Universe, you kept your promise to my father, David, that his son would build your house, but how can this house contain you? Even heaven cannot contain you. We ask only that you listen to our prayers."

For eight days, Solomon and all of Israel celebrated. The people then returned to their homes, rejoicing in God's blessings and extolling Solomon's praises, "The great Solomon, the mighty Solomon, the wise Solomon—can there be anyone on earth greater than Solomon?"

With the people's praises in his ear, Solomon went to Asmodeus and said, "Demon King, I have one more question for you. If you answer me, I will release you."

Asmodeus flattered his captor. "Great Solomon, wisest man on earth, to answer you would be my great pleasure. Speak your question."

"Tell me the difference between truth and illusion."

"Ah, that is the greatest secret of all, and only the great Solomon is worthy of knowing the difference between truth and illusion. Open my chains, lend me your magic ring, and the secret is yours."

Eager to know the secret, Solomon gave Asmodeus his ring and opened his chains. In a flash, the Demon King threw the ring into the sea, grabbed Solomon, and tossed him sixteen hundred miles away. Then, he put on Solomon's clothes. He put on Solomon's boots. He took on Solomon's appearance. He sat down on Solomon's throne. And no one knew the difference.

Solomon, who had been the wisest, richest, most powerful man on earth, became a wandering beggar. All that remained to him were the clothes he had been wearing and the staff he was holding. When he met people and asked, "Do you see this staff? I am Solomon, king of Israel," they laughed in his face. They jeered him, saying, "Are you mad? King Solomon is sitting on his throne this very minute! Who are you?"

One day, Solomon met a beggar who invited him to share his dinner of berries and greens. As they ate, the poor man said to Solomon, "No one who meets you can doubt your merit. Perhaps you were greedy or arrogant in the past? But the Creator is everywhere. Keep your heart open, for who knows who you are to meet or what you are to learn."

After being tormented in his country, Solomon went to Ammon, the land of his enemy. There he found work as a servant in the palace. In two years, he became the chief cook. The princess Naamah noticed how tasty the food had become and went to the kitchen to see who was preparing the meals. The moment Solomon began to speak, Naamah knew she was where she had always wanted to be. She returned the next day to be in his presence. They spoke again. The next day she returned and the next. One day, she took him into the garden to show him the apple tree under which her mother had given birth to her.

"You have awakened my soul," Solomon said to her, "with one glance of your eye, with one bead of your necklace." Filled with longing, the princess cried to the winds, "Let my spices flow. Let my love enter my garden and eat my sweet fruit."

They became lovers. Each day they met in the garden, the vineyards, or the palace. Each day their love grew until one of the guards spoke to the king and queen. Immediately, they summoned their daughter to the throne room and said, "The chief cook is a Hebrew beggar. He will be banished today from the kingdom."

"If you banish him," Naamah replied, "you separate me from my soul. Banish me as well."

Furious at her defiance, they cried, "Go! Follow your worthless beggar. You too are banished."

"Oh love," Naamah said to Solomon, "set me as a seal on your arm and as a seal on your heart, for we have been banished."

"We can never be banished from God's kingdom," Solomon reassured her, "for love is as strong as death."

The princess left the land of her birth with the beggar. As they wandered across the desert, Solomon used his staff to find water. He discovered streams that led them to oases where they stayed for many months. Then they set out again and traveled until they arrived at the sea. One day as Naamah was preparing to cook a fish, she found a ring in its belly. She examined it and then brought it to Solomon, saying, "This ring has strange writing. Do you know these letters?"

Solomon looked at the ring and threw his arms open in praise. "Blessed is the Lord who created heaven and earth," he cried. "Oh love, you have found the ring my father gave me. And these—these are the letters of God's name. Now we can return home."

In Jerusalem, Solomon showed his ring to his trusted servant, Benaiah. That night they crept into Asmodeus' bedroom. Benaiah lifted the covers to examine the Demon King's feet. They were claws. Demons can transform themselves into any shape they choose, but they can never hide their claws. When Asmodeus awoke and saw Solomon holding the ring, he cried out and disappeared.

Solomon went to the Temple and gave two offerings. One was for meeting his wife, Naamah. The other was for learning the difference between truth and illusion. Illusion was to believe that his measure was in his boots, his clothes, or his staff. Truth was to know that his measure was in his connection to the Creator who was always with him.

After this, Solomon ruled with even greater wisdom, and people came from many lands to ask his advice. One day as Solomon was sitting on his throne, an old man and woman knelt before him. Their faces nearly touched the floor. "Help us, great Solomon. Our daughter fell in love with a Hebrew beggar. In a moment of foolish anger, we banished the two from our kingdom. Now we are searching for both of them."

Solomon asked, "What is the name of your daughter?"

"The name of our blessed daughter is the princess Naamah."

Solomon said, "Many years ago, I too was on a journey, and I met a beggar who advised me to keep my heart open to whatever I was to learn and to whomever I was to meet. On your journey, in looking for a beggar you've learned that every person in your kingdom is precious, including the beggars. The Hebrew beggar you are searching for returned to his own kingdom. I am that beggar."

The king and queen looked up in surprise. Recognizing Solomon, they cried, "Forgive us."

Solomon said, "I am grateful to you, for you are the parents of my wife. Your daughter, Naamah, is here, sitting on the throne at my side."

Naamah came down from her throne to greet her parents; and, as they embraced, Solomon sent the guard to bring their son, Rehoboam. Solomon watched Rehoboam walk into the throne room. One day, he thought to himself, he would give his son the ring his father had given him. He wondered what his son would wish for.

Kohelet

For Everything There Is a Season

"For everything there is a season and a time for every purpose under heaven: A time to be born and a time to die, a time to plant and a time to reap." Most of us know these lines but we may not know that they are from the book of Ecclesiastes that is called Kohelet in Hebrew. Kohelet is read on the Sabbath of the harvest festival of Sukkot. It is in the autumn, when our work is done that we "take stock." If death awaits us all, what is the meaning of our work? What is the meaning of our days on earth? Kohelet struggles with this question.

Who is Kohelet? The name means "the assembler" or "the teacher" and is a pseudonym for Solomon. He was considered one of the wisest men in the ancient world; tradition attributed to him the writing of The Song of Songs in his youth, Proverbs in his middle years, and Ecclesiastes in his "ripe years."

This is a freely rendered version of Ecclesiastes.

I am Kohelet, the son of David, the king in Jerusalem. I have lived so long that some say that I speak with the words of a wise old woman. The experiences of a lifetime I now set into words:

"The breath—the breath; all is the breath! If everything comes and goes like the breath, what benefit is there for us to labor under the sun? A generation comes, a generation goes, and the earth remains. The sun rises, the sun sets, then it hurries to the place from which it has risen. The wind goes to the south and travels around to the north and returns in a circle. All the rivers go to the sea, and the sea is not filled. This is all without end. It is so wearisome that one can hardly begin to form words.

No eye can possibly see everything. No ear can possibly hear everything. What has happened will happen again; what has been done is that which will be done, for there is nothing new under the sun. But wait, can it be said, "Look! That is new!'? No, it is not true! That too has already happened. There is no memory about the earliest times, for the end of times, there also will be no memory."

I, Kohelet, was king over Israel in Jerusalem. I set my heart to seek and acquire wisdom, to understand everything under the sun. But this great gift of curiosity is a torment that God has given us. I have seen all that has happened under the sun and I know now that I was pursuing the wind, for all is fleeting, like the breath that comes and goes. I said to myself, "I gathered more wisdom than any of my ancestors who ruled in Jerusalem. I tasted all experience, madness, and folly, and what did I learn? I've been in search of the wind. In knowledge, there is vexation, and in more knowledge, there is more suffering."

Come now, I said to myself, let me try merriment and enjoy pleasure. But behold, even that was fleeting. Laughter? I said, It is madness. Pleasure? What does it lead to? While seeking wisdom, I indulged my flesh with wine to grasp the secret of folly so that I might know which of the two ways was best for mortals who have only a few days to live.

Are there enough words for all I have done? I built magnificent houses, planted vineyards, designed gardens and parks with every kind of plant and fruit tree. I made ponds to water young forests and acquired singers, servants, herds of cattle, flocks of sheep, until I had more possessions than any of my ancestors who lived in Jerusalem. But it was not enough. I gathered silver, gold, and the treasures of kings and princes. I had everything that gives delight. All of this, I did with wisdom. I did not deny my eyes anything they asked for or refuse my heart any pleasure. I found enjoyment in my labor. But when I looked more deeply at the actions of my hands, at all my work and effort, I saw that all of it was fleeting. It was a pursuit of the wind, like a breath that comes and goes and is of no benefit under the sun.

I pondered wisdom, madness, and folly, and I realized that there is one event that happens to us all. What happens to the fool will also happen to me. The wise person, just as the fool, is forgotten. Why then did I spend so much energy acquiring wisdom? The wise person dies the same as the fool.

So I hated life. Since all is fleeting and a pursuit of the wind, everything done under the sun tasted bitter to me. I despaired as I thought of my work and effort. Everything I have worked and labored for I must leave to the one who follows me. And who knows if my successor, who has not labored as I have, will be wise or foolish? This worry is also passing. What reward do any of us have for our toil and striving under the sun? Our days are filled with pain, and at night there is no peace of mind. But this too changes, like a breath that comes and goes.

There is nothing better for us than to eat and drink and enjoy our work. And this too is God's gift, for who but I can enjoy myself? Whoever pleases God receives wisdom and the ability to enjoy life. But whoever displeases God works without stopping and then is forced to leave his wealth to the next person. And even this changes, like the breath that comes and goes.

For everything there is a season, and a time for every purpose under heaven:

> *A time to be born and a time to die,*
> *A time to plant and a time to reap,*
> *A time to kill and a time to heal,*
> *A time to break down and a time to build up,*
> *A time to weep and a time to laugh,*
> *A time of grieving and a time of dancing,*
> *A time to throw stones and a time to gather stones,*
> *A time to embrace and a time to refrain from embracing,*
> *A time to seek and a time to lose,*
> *A time to keep and a time to throw away,*

A time to tear and a time to mend,
A time to be silent and a time to speak,
A time to love and a time to hate,
A time for war and a time for peace.

I have seen the task that God has given each of us to engage in. Everything happens in its proper time. But, although God has set eternity in our hearts, we cannot fathom what God brings to pass. So I have come to understand that there is nothing better for us than to enjoy ourselves and to do good, for whenever we eat and drink and enjoy our work, we are appreciating God's gift.

God's works will be forever. We cannot add to them or take away from them. We live in awe of God's works. What is has been and that which may come into being has already been. God watches, as one event pursues another.

And I observed that under the sun where there should be justice and righteousness, there is wickedness, and I said to myself, there is a force higher than the highest who is keeping guard, and God will judge the righteous and the wicked, for there is a time for every purpose and every experience. But God would have us know that with all our ponderings and pursuits, we are no more than the animals.

Our fate and the fate of animals are the same. Death comes to the one as to the other. We all have one breath. We are not superior to animals, for we go to the same place. From dust we came and to dust we return. Who knows if the human spirit rises to the heavens and the animal spirit falls down to the earth? Since there is no one to bring us back to see what happens after we are gone, let us rejoice in all that we do, for that is our portion.

When I considered all the suffering under the sun, I saw the tears of the oppressed. They had no comforter. But the oppressors who had power also had no comforter. People work without cease and strive to outdo their neighbor, and to what benefit? The fool does no work; the competitor works day and night. Better to work in a restful way.

Look at the one who is alone, without wife or child. He does not stop his labors. He deprives himself of pleasure and to what end? Two are better than one, for if they fall, the one will lift up the other, but woe to the one who has no one to lift him up. And if two lie together, they will be warm, but how can one be warm alone? If there is danger, two are stronger than one, and three even stronger.

Consider God's creation! Who can do what God has done? Enjoy your good fortune when it is yours, and in the time of misfortune, remember, this is also God's work. I have seen good people die despite their goodness and the lives of the wicked prolonged despite their wickedness. Better not to be too good or too wise. The race is not to the swift, or the battle to the strong, or fortune to the wise, or wealth to the intelligent, but time and chance happens to each of us. Like fish caught in nets or birds trapped in snares, none of us knows our time. What wisdom have I learned?

> *A good name is better than precious oil.*
> *When you make a vow to God, hasten to fulfill it.*
> *A worker's sleep is sweet while a rich man's gold keeps him awake.*
> *Better to have a patient rather than a haughty spirit.*
> *Do not rush to be angry; anger is the province of fools.*
> *Wisdom is better than weapons of war, but one person can destroy*
>   *much good.*
> *There is no person who does not sin.*
> *A live dog is better than a dead lion.*
> *Do not worry about harsh words; you, too, may have cursed others*
>   *in your heart.*
> *Not one of us can prolong the life breath or control the day of our*
>   *death.*
> *Live joyfully with the one you love for that is your portion in life.*
> *Whatever you do, do it with all your heart; there will be no work in*
>   *the grave.*

I claim to be wise; and yet, what have I learned? I had intended to learn the secrets. I went without sleep day and night so I would know all that God brings to pass. But I cannot fathom God's creation. It is beyond my reach. The secrets are deep, very deep; who can discover them?

Listen, my children, listen to me: Rejoice now in your youth. Be guided by the desires of your heart and your eyes. Only remember that whatever you do, you will be accountable before God. Remove anger from your heart and weariness from your flesh, for youth and black hair are as fleeting as the breath that comes and goes. Delight now in the days of your youth, before the sun and moon and stars grow dark and the clouds return with rain and the days of sorrow come and you say, 'I have no pleasure.'

The days will come when the doors to the streets shut and the songbirds are silent, when the old who fear heights and the dangers of the road will set out for the grave and the mourners will fill the streets, when the silver cord snaps and the golden bowl breaks, then the dust will return to the earth from where it came and the breath to its Creator who gave it.

The breath—the breath; all is the breath!

I am Kohelet. I have spoken to you with the words of a wise woman. I have tried to teach by setting my wisdom into proverbs— hopefully, to stir you! But, be careful! There is no end to making books and too much study wearies the flesh. What matters is to fear God and keep God's commandments. In the end, all our actions, all our secrets, good and bad, God will reveal.

About the Stories

Solomon and the Demon King

Solomon seeks wisdom so that he might govern justly. Kohelet seeks wisdom in order to learn everything under the sun. Both Solomon and Kohelet claim that they want wisdom, but initially they want control and order. Solomon attempts to carry out his father's instructions by building the Temple. But the gates of the Temple throw him out. Why? Who is Solomon?

A pretender: Solomon was not building the Temple to praise and honor the Shechinah, as his father desired. Rather, he was building the Temple to carry out his father's wishes. The Temple expects Solomon, at the very least, to acknowledge that his own desire is not for the Shechinah but to do his father's bidding. The Temple gates insist that Solomon acknowledge that he doesn't yet know who he is. Once Solomon executes his father's wishes, a dark side of his ego appears. Who is Solomon?

A seeker: In his arrogance and greed for knowledge, in his hubris, Solomon makes a deal with the Demon King. He trades his father's ring to acquire wisdom. But wisdom cannot be bought. As it is written in Job (28:12–28), "Where can wisdom be found? Where is the place of understanding? No one can set a value to it. It is not found in the land of the living. We cannot buy it for gold. . . . God alone knows its ways and places. God sees the world, weighs the winds, measures the waters, sets a course for the rains and thunderstorms, and says to us, 'Wisdom is the fear of God.' " At the end of Ecclesiastes it is written, "What matters is to fear God and keep God's commandments." It is hard to fear God when one is living in comfort. The Hebrews had to leave the security of Egypt to be offered the covenant. Solomon must leave his kingdom and the great Temple he built to find the well of understanding.

The wisdom that King Solomon seeks is not in the known world. He must give up all pretensions, all borders, all identity. He must experience the loss and emptiness that will allow him to truly know and fear God. The Demon King, as all enemies do, tosses "him" away—the "him" that is represented by his clothes, his boots, and his throne. He separates Solomon from his father by throwing away the father's ring. Who is Solomon now?

A beggar: Solomon takes refuge with a beggar who, unlike Solomon's father, asks nothing of him. Rather, he reassures Solomon of the goodness of his soul and of the value of the journey he is on, encouraging him to stay awake to the presence of the Creator. Who is Solomon now?

A servant: As a cook serving others, Solomon must understand the cycle of the sun, the moon, the earth, the winds, and the waters that will nourish the plants and animals that he will gather. Then he must learn the properties of the plants and animals so that he can combine them in such a way as to create nourishment for others. Previously, Solomon asked for discernment to know the ways of mortals. Now he is learning the ways of the universe. His heart is expanding. Who is Solomon now?

An open heart: The princess of the kingdom responds to the open heart. The souls of Solomon and the princess are drawn together and animate each other. In ancient lands, banishment is death, but their love is stronger than death, Solomon is now living under God's protection and Solomon and Naamah choose love over power and security. Who is Solomon now?

A lover without fear: As he departs a second time from a known kingdom for the unknown, he travels with and honors the feminine. His love of the fearless and compassionate princess Naamah, whose name means "soul," returns Solomon to his roots. Naamah finds David's ring that is engraved with God's name. Previously, Ruth who chose love at great risk to herself sat by his side as he ruled. Now Naamah, also a fearless warrior of love, sits by his side. Who is Solomon now?

A king whose kingdom is within: Solomon gives thanks for receiving the gifts he had not even thought to ask for. In wanting to replace his father, he had asked for a heart with skill to listen so he could govern others. But no man can replace his father. Each person must find his or her own connection to the governing force within and to holiness. In losing his kingship or ego-ruling self, Solomon found his own relationship to the Shechinah's presence and can claim the Temple he built as his work, for now he knows that there is no structure: The Shechinah is within and without. He cannot control either his destiny or his son's. He cannot control his kingdom. He can only acknowledge the fullness of life that one feels when living close to the Shechinah's presence.

Kohelet

Solomon's fall from his position as king and his loss of identity is the place where Kohelet begins: What is the meaning of our position, possessions, and identity if we and all we have will vanish with our death? "The breath—the breath; all is the breath!" *Hebel*, the Hebrew word for "breath," also means mist, vapor, vanity, and that which is ephemeral and transient. *Hebel* holds the clue to the answer. We humans live by breath, but implied in the concept of breath, mist, and vapor is a larger container from which the breath or mist arises and returns. The searcher would know the meaning, yet Kohelet does not succeed. "I cannot fathom God's creation. It is beyond my reach. The secrets are deep, very deep, who can discover them?" (Eccles 8:16–17).

We learn that there is a season for every purpose, that wisdom is preferable to folly, and relationship to being alone. But the door that reveals the mystery of the universe does not open for Kohelet. Instead, according to Kohelet, we must accept and prepare for the day when we and all our possessions will return to dust. We cannot pierce the mystery of the breath; for we are the breath. We can however understand its transient nature. At the end of Kohelet's ruminations, we are advised to move away from the earthly pursuit of knowledge—"Too much study wearies the flesh," and to place ourselves in God's hands—to turn toward the awe of the universe and to live in accordance with the divine laws ("fear God and keep God's commandments").

Like Job, much of the poetry of Kohelet is breathtaking; but unlike Job, the Shechinah does not appear to Kohelet/Solomon. Kohelet tells us *about* God, but never directly experiences God's presence. Perhaps that is why Kohelet is not content. In his excessive curiosity and movement, he never experiences the still small voice and receives a direct transmission. The sum of his wisdom is vast and he indicates a path for us: "I have come to understand that there is nothing better for us than to enjoy ourselves and to do good, for whenever we eat and drink and enjoy our work, we are appreciating God's gift." But he knows enough to know that beyond wisdom lies the Source.

The miracles of Passover and Shavuot create a foundation for the people, physically (Passover) and spiritually (Shavuot). After the soul has been "fixed" at Rosh Hashanah and Yom Kippur, through repentance and reconciliation, the challenge is to realize that God is omnipresent and to appreciate the miracle of everyday life lived in an awakened way: "Our choice is to accept God's gift. To eat and drink and enjoy the pleasure of our work" (Eccles 5:17).

In the twenty-eight events that *Kohelet* lists as being part of everyday life, two are written without the infinitive "to": grieving and dancing, symbolizing death and marriage. At these times, we stop. We give up our studies or mitzvot to attend funerals and weddings. Respect has always been paid to the dead. But at Sukkot, respect is also given to the importance of marriage.

The Solomon who had seven hundred wives and three hundred concubines was the one to whom The Song of Songs was attributed and the one who built the Temple. In building the Temple, Solomon created a home where the feminine and masculine aspects of God might join together. The union between God and mortal that was begun at Yom Kippur continues during the seven days of the Sukkot honeymoon.

In the stories of Sukkot, there is a shared appreciation of man and woman: Solomon and Naamah enrich one another's spiritual lives. Solomon's wisdom stirs Naamah's understanding. Naamah's understanding deepens Solomon's wisdom. Each one awakens the soul of the other. Nahum and Sarah also awaken together to a new level of spiritual understanding and rejoice in one another. In *Kohelet*, Solomon extols the goodness of married life: "Two are better than one, for if they fall, the one will lift up the other" (Eccles 4:9).

Sukkot is a time of completion, harvest, and fullness. It is also a time of paradox. The harvest represents material goods in all their abundance. Yet no matter how much one accumulates or builds, material life is limited. Both *Solomon and the Demon King* and *Kohelet* address the turning from the quest for earthly power to choosing to live intimately with the Shechinah, who provides the only true shelter.

SIMCHAT TORAH

About Simchat Torah

Simchat Torah in Hebrew means "rejoicing with the Torah." Just as the seven weeks of Passover lead to Shavuot and the seven Sabbaths after Tisha B'Av prepare for Rosh Hashanah, the seven days and nights of the Sukkot honeymoon lead to Simchat Torah, and to the bridegroom's rejoicing in the beauties and wonders of his bride, the Torah.

God said, "Tarry with me one more day." Following God's request, the Israelites remained in Jerusalem one more day. This day was called Shemini Atzeret, meaning "eighth day of completion." This was a quiet day, a day of introspection, of completion, of preparation for winter. On Shemini Atzeret, the Israelites recited prayers for rain to renew the earth. On this day, which later became Simchat Torah, they read the passage describing the death of Moses. (Outside of Israel, Simchat Torah was celebrated the next day.)

In Deuteronomy, the last book of the Torah in which Moses reiterates God's teachings, it is decreed that every seventh year all debts are to be canceled and the land be allowed to lie fallow. During that seventh sabbatical year, the people were to gather on the first day of Sukkot to listen to the reading of the entire Torah. By linking the reading of the Torah to the year in which they do not work the land, the people were encouraged to realize that as God sustains them, their work is to sustain others. In the tenth century c.e., the rabbis in Babylon changed the seven-year reading of the Torah to a yearly reading, and thus linked the holiday of Simchat Torah to the completion of the yearly Torah cycle.

In our time, on the evening and day of Simchat Torah, the Torah scrolls are taken from the ark, and people circle the pulpit seven times while holding the Torah scrolls and joyously dancing with them. In some synagogues the singing and celebration continue until late night, even until dawn. On the morning of Simchat Torah, in many congregations, all the members (including children), are called up to the altar, in groups or singly, to read from Deuteronomy.

Then one person is called to read the last words of the Torah (Dt 33:27–34:12). That person is called the Bridegroom of the Torah. Immediately following the last words of Deuteronomy, the scroll is rolled back to the beginning and another person is called to read the first words of the Torah (Gn 1:1–2). That person is called the Bridegroom of Genesis, for the beginning of the Torah is Genesis. The metaphor of the bride and bridegroom echoes the relationship established on Mount Sinai when the Torah was first given, and God was the bridegroom and the children of Israel the bride. Now the people are the bridegroom and the Torah is the bride.

Like all Jewish holidays, Simchat Torah is celebrated differently depending on the branch of Judaism that a person belongs to. In my hasidic synagogue only the men dance with the Torahs. But in some modern orthodox, and all Reconstructionist, Reform, and Conservative synagogues, women also dance with the Torahs. There is no one hierarchal authority for all of Judaism, and each congregation is experimenting with ways of coming closer to the Torah.

Recently, I participated in an innovative Simchat Torah ceremony in Boulder, Colorado, that Rabbi Zalman Schachter-Shalomi initiated. The scroll of the Torah was completely unrolled and made a large circle, about ninety feet. Everyone in the room held a part of the scroll and stood in a large circle. Then Zalman stood inside the circle of the Torah and went around the circle translating from the Hebrew whatever section each person was holding. Zalman advised us, "Study and guard the portion you are holding and see what it reveals to you this year."

Since the destruction of the Temples, Torah has become the land and home of the Jews. Knowledge of the Torah has become the definition of Jewish adulthood. In preparation for the coming-of-age ceremony called bar or bat mitzvah, each young person takes responsibility to learn and read aloud one portion of the Torah. The young people spend months learning the section of the Torah that was read at the time of their birth. Then when their birthday comes (at twelve years old for girls, thirteen for boys), they chant that section and comment on its meaning. Through the preparation for their bar and bat mitzvahs, the young men and women enter one part of the dense land of the Torah and begin to explore its secrets and interrelationships.

About Simchat Torah

The preparation of Jewish children to guard the land of the Torah reminds me of the Australian aboriginal Dreamtime. The native Australians, whose lives are bound to the guardianship of the land, are instructed at birth to return to and care for their birthplace by singing its songs. They are to do this for themselves and for the community. It is their belief that if each person is given a part of the land to look after, the entire land will be cared for. The stories of the land, the place-names, the stones, and the stone formations all reveal their ancestors' exploits on the earth; teach appropriate moral behavior; and help the young people learn about the covenants of living, which concern the interrelationship of the land with the people, the animals, and the plants.

Similarly, as the last and first words of Torah are read at Simchat Torah, all its many stories are also summoned into life. Kabbalists say that Torah existed before the world began. Moving forward and backward in time and space, Torah is a doorway to all the worlds.

The Death of Moses

To Sing God's Praises

Moses brought the Hebrew people out of Egypt, gave them God's teachings, and led them through the wilderness for forty years. But God would not permit him to enter the Promised Land. We do not know why this decision was made. Was it because Moses had hesitated when the Shechinah first asked him to return to Egypt? Was it because he had lost his temper twice, by killing an Egyptian and striking the rock at Meribah? Perhaps it was to prevent the people from worshiping him as a deity? Or maybe he was needed to accompany the souls of those who died in the desert to heaven?

Moses battles desperately with God. He does not want to die. He wants to live and sing God's praises. From the moment that Moses encounters the Shechinah at the burning bush until his death, they engage in a passionate relationship. In this retelling of the death of Moses, oral legends portray the lovers' conversations and give us a glimpse of the depth of their love.

The last two chapters of the Torah (Dt 33, 34), describing Moses blessing the people and his death, are read on Simchat Torah. This telling is mostly oral legend with a small portion of biblical text.

God lets the righteous know the day of their death so they can bless their children. For nearly forty years, Moses, Aaron, and Miriam led the children of Israel through the wilderness. After Aaron and Miriam died, Moses asked the Shechinah, "When I die, who will care for the children of Israel? Who will lead them? Who will replace me?"

The Shechinah answered, "Not your own children, but your disciple, Joshua, will be your successor. The one who cares for the fig tree, who waters and tends it, will eat its fruit. Joshua, who served you morning and evening with devotion, will be your successor. Place your hand on Joshua and bless him."

Moses went to Joshua and said, "My beloved disciple, God wishes you to be the next leader. From now on when I'm teaching, don't sit on the ground with the others, sit next to me on the bench." Moses placed both hands on Joshua and blessed him with insight, understanding, and a face as radiant as the moon. Then he brought Joshua before the high priest, the elders, and the people and said, "God has chosen Joshua to be our next shepherd."

The Shechinah said to Moses, "Prepare the people to fight the Midianites and then to cross the Jordan to enter the Promised Land." But the people resisted. They knew that God had decreed that Moses would die in the desert. Rather than cross the Jordan and go into the Promised Land without him, they refused to fight the Midianites. In their youth, they had wanted to stone their harsh, stern leader; now they wondered who would love and protect them as Moses had? Who would have the endless patience or wisdom to care for their daily problems? But Moses forced them to draw lots. Twelve thousand were to fight, twelve thousand were to guard the supplies, and twelve thousand were to pray for those who were fighting. Moses chose Phinehas, the high priest's son, to lead the troops.

"This will not be an ordinary battle," Moses counseled Phinehas. "You'll be fighting five Midianite kings and Balaam, the greatest sorcerer of all time. Take the ark of the covenant into the battle. Wear the high priest's breastplate and the gold forehead plate with God's name inscribed on it."

On the day of the battle, Balaam walked at the head of the Midianite army. When he saw the army of Israel marching toward him carrying the ark and heard their powerful prayers, he spread his arms and flew into the air.

"Who will catch the sorcerer?" Phinehas cried out.

Zaliah, who knew sorcery, leapt into the air. But Balaam took a path the young sorcerer could not follow. He soared through five levels of air and disappeared. Phinehas shone the forehead plate inscribed with the name of God at the place in the heavens where Balaam had vanished. The clouds broke up. Balaam lost his protection and fell from the heavens. Placing his head on the ground before Phinehas, he cried, "Never, never, never will I harm the people of Israel. You have my word!"

"Your word? What would I do with your word?" Phinehas retorted. "It was your word that convinced Pharaoh to enslave the Hebrews. It was your word that nearly convinced Pharaoh to kill his grandson Moses." He ordered Zaliah to kill Balaam. Zaliah lifted his sword, but it fell from his hands. He took up another sword, but Balaam's magic destroyed whatever weapon he took up. "Evil can only be destroyed by its own element," Phinehas said, and he found a sword with serpents on both sides. With this sword, Zaliah killed Balaam. From Balaam's bones, poisonous snakes crawled in every direction and spread across the earth.

Ten times God had decreed that Moses would not enter the Promised Land. Yet each time that the children of Israel had gone against God's teachings and Moses had pleaded for them, God had been merciful. So Moses believed that God would also be merciful with him. After the Midianites were defeated, he said to God, "My teacher, you taught us the laborer shall receive his wages. I brought the children of Israel out of Egypt. I led them through the desert. Now that they are about to enter the Promised Land, shall I not share their joy?"

God answered, "Moses, before heaven and earth, I vowed you will not enter the Promised Land."

"And I vowed I would not leave my father-in-law, Jethro. But you released me from that vow when you said 'Go, return to Egypt.' Release yourself from your vow, so I may enter the land of Israel."

"I have no master," God replied.

Moses knew power. He put on sackcloth. He drew a circle on the earth and stood in the center of it. He said, "I will not move from here until your judgment is suspended." As he recited fifteen hundred prayers, the heavens and earth started to tremble. The angels asked God, "Is the order of the world changing?"

God answered, "Lock every gate in heaven so Moses' prayers do not enter!" But the prayers of Moses, like slashing swords, ripped open every closure. At last God said, "Moses, even if you pray three thousand prayers, you shall not enter the Promised Land."

"Merciful One, if I cannot enter, let my bones enter."

"Not your bones."

"If I cannot go in this lifetime, let me go after my death."

"Neither in life nor in death shall you cross the Jordan."

"Why are you so angry with me?" Moses asked. "With all your creatures, you show mercy. You forgive their mistakes once, twice, many times. Why do you forgive the transgressions of the children of Israel and refuse to forgive me?"

God answered, "The sins of the people are not the same as the sins of one person. It has been decreed that you shall die. Moses, what was the name of your father?"

"Amram."

"And his father?"

"Izhar."

"And his father?"

"Kohath."

"And his father?"

"Levi."

"And his father?"

"Jacob."

"Did they all not die? If your life was spared, people would make you into a god and worship you."

"Creator of the World, rise up from your throne of judgment and sit down on your throne of mercy. You loved me when I was young. You came to me in my youth, when you appeared in the thorn bush. Do not be like a king who loves his servant when he's young and strong and throws him away when he's old. Let me live and atone for my mistakes and sing your praises. You have the power to do as you wish."

"Moses, what more can I do for you? I changed the natural order of the world for you. I caused food to fall down and water to rise up. I forgave the people when you asked. The book of teachings is not called the Book of God but the Five Books of Moses. I have given you honor. Greater honor is waiting for you. Three hundred and ten worlds of paradise are waiting for you. You will not need the light of the sun, the moon, or the stars. My glory will clothe you. My splendor will shelter you. What more do you wish?"

"I do not wish to die. I wish to live on earth and sing your praises."

Moses spoke with the sun, the moon, the stars, the planets, the rivers, the mountains, the hills, the deserts. He pleaded with them, "Speak to God that I might live."

They answered, "Moses, we are dust. We are without form and void. From dust we came, to dust we will return. How can we plead for you?"

"I was like a king once," Moses moaned. "What I commanded came into being. I struck the sea and the waters separated. Now I am a beggar, begging for my life, and no one will include me in their prayers! Joshua! Where is Joshua?"

Moses went to his beloved disciple and said, "Joshua, if God takes me, I will no longer be able to teach you or the people. Pray for me."

Joshua burst into tears. His only wish was to learn from Moses. He started to pray, but Samael, Satan's angel, said to him, "Are you opposing God's will which is perfect?"

Joshua said to Moses, "Satan's angel will not let me pray."

Moses went to the high priest, Eleazar, Aaron's son, and said, "When God was angry with your father for making the golden calf, I saved him. Pray now that God will allow me to enter the Promised Land." But as soon as Eleazar began to pray, Samael appeared to him and said, "Are you purposely disobeying God's command?"

Moses asked the seventy elders and the people to pray for him. They went to the tabernacle and with tears entreated God to let Moses live, but before their prayers could reach the throne of mercy, the angels snatched them away.

The heavens, the earth, the people could not help. Moses turned to the Shechinah, who said, "Moses, there is a time to live, and a time to die. This is your time to die. I will not listen to your plea."

God was angry with Moses for disrupting the heavens and the earth when his fate had already been decreed. But when Moses began to recite God's thirteen names of mercy, the divine wrath subsided and God asked, "Moses, why are you so afraid to die?"

Moses answered, "I'm afraid of the sword of the Angel of Death."

"I will take you myself," the Shechinah said.

"Then I will prepare. You told me, 'This is your time.' With the time that remains to me, I will serve Joshua."

For the last thirty-six days of his life, Moses served Joshua from morning to evening, as a disciple serves a master. The first night when Joshua saw Moses preparing his clothes, he was ashamed to have his master become his servant and he asked, "What are you doing?"

Moses answered, "Did you not delight in serving me? Now it is my delight to serve you." And he taught Joshua everything he knew, including the secret wisdom that he had received from his master, Zagzagel. Each day Moses wrote God's teachings in a scroll.

On the seventh day of the last month of the year, Moses knew he would die. He called the people together and read to them from the book of teachings. Joshua commented on the meaning of what Moses had read, and there was no disagreement between them. Moses' face shone like the sun and Joshua's like the moon. Then Joshua turned to Moses and said, "My teacher, I know the laws, for I have been with you day and night. But what will happen when we enter the Promised Land and I give one person land on a mountain and he wants land in the valley, or I give another person land in the valley and he wants land on a mountain?"

Moses reassured him, saying, "God has promised that the apportioning of the land shall be done peacefully. But ask me about any of the laws, for soon I will not be able to answer."

Joshua looked at Moses with love, and Moses said, "Even if you have no questions, come here so I may kiss you." Joshua went to Moses and kissed him and wept. Then a voice from heaven said, "Moses, you have four hours to live."

"Merciful One," Moses pleaded, "let me live as Joshua's disciple."

"Moses, I have sworn by my name that you will not cross the Jordan."

"Then, by the power of your name, change me into a tiny fish who can swim across the Jordan."

"Moses, I would be breaking my vow."

"Then lift me up so my eyes can skip across the land."

"That I can do. Walk to Mount Nebo, to the summit of Pisgah opposite Jericho."

When Moses arrived at the summit, God gave Moses the power to see all the land. Moses saw the building of the Temple and the destruction of the Temples. He saw all that had happened and all that would happen from the beginning to the end of time.

Then a voice said, "Moses, you have two hours to live."

"Timeless One, let Joshua lead the people into the Promised Land, and let me stay and live on this side of the Jordan."

"Moses, if you stay on this side of the Jordan, you will not be able to attend the festivals at my sanctuary, and then the people will also not go. Every seven years, the people are to gather to listen to a reading of the Torah. If you are alive, they will choose to go to the teacher rather than the disciple, and there will be a rebellion."

"Greatest of Transformers, let me live and be a beast here in the field who eats grass and drinks water. Let me see the world and sing your praises."

"Moses, you have said enough words."

"I beg you, can I not be a bird, a little bird, who does not cross the Jordan but flies each day to a different place and sings your praises and gathers seed and drinks water and returns each night to its nest?"

"Moses, there is no more time."

Moses knew he could no longer escape his death.

In his last hour, Moses went to the children of Israel and said, "God has told me I may not cross the Jordan. Joshua will lead you across the Jordan. I implore you. I call heaven and earth as witnesses. When you enter the Promised Land, do not be lured by other gods, but follow God's laws and teachings so that you might live. All these years I've rebuked and scolded you. Now I wish to bless each tribe and beg you to forgive me for being harsh and stern."

Moses blessed each of the twelve tribes. Then the people said, "Moses, our teacher, we forgive you, but it is we who provoked you. Forgive our lack of faith, our fear, our anger."

"I forgive you, and when you enter the holy land, remember me and my bones and say, 'Woe. Woe to the son of Amram, who wanted so much to be with us but whose bones are buried in the desert.' "

"Moses, what will become of us? Who will convince God to make miracles?"

"God did not make miracles for me. God created miracles to wake you up. Do not rely on kings or princes. They can do nothing in the face of death. Put your trust in God. Whatever you've done, whatever you do, pour out your heart to God. God is with you every moment."

Moses wrote his last teachings on the scroll for the people. Then he went to Joshua's tent. When they saw Moses, they said, "Moses, we've come to ask you to teach us."

But a voice said, "Learn from Joshua."

Joshua began to read from the book of teachings with Moses seated on his right and Aaron's two sons at his left. Moses listened, but as he listened, his understanding vanished, so that when the people asked him to comment on what Joshua had read, he could not. At that moment, he knew he no longer wished to live. He did not want to live wishing for what he did not have or carrying jealousy.

Moses kissed and embraced his beloved disciple. He said to him, "May you be at peace, and may all of Israel be at peace with you." Moses was one hundred and twenty years old. He went to his tent. He sat and wrote God's name.

In heaven, God knew that Moses was at last ready to die. "Gabriel," God said, "bring me the soul of Moses."

"I cannot," Gabriel answered.

"Michael," God said, "bring me the soul of Moses."

"I dare not," Michael said.

"Zagzagel," God said, "bring me the soul of Moses."

"I would not," Zagzagel answered.

"I would! Let me go!" said Samael, Satan's angel. "I've been waiting for this moment since Moses was born."

"Go!" God said.

In great glee, Samael descended to earth, but as he entered Moses' tent, Moses' eyes burned with such fire that Samael was nearly blinded. He fled back to heaven and pleaded, "Great Master, send me anywhere, but do not send me for Moses' soul."

"You asked to go," God said. "Return and do not come back without Moses' soul!" This time, Samael crept up to Moses' tent. Before he reached it, Moses shouted, "I will cut off your head!"

Samael fled. Moses took his staff and chased and beat him until God said, "Stop, Moses. We need Samael for the others."

Moses returned to his tent. He lay down, put his feet together, and folded his hands across his chest.

No one but God could bring Moses' soul. God went with Gabriel, Michael, and Zagzagel. They surrounded Moses' bed. God said to Moses, "Close your eyes."

Then God said to the soul of Moses, "It was decreed that you would live in this man's body one hundred and twenty years. It is now time for you to return to heaven."

The soul of Moses answered, "Creator of all souls. I know you want me to leave Moses. But I love him. I do not want to leave him."

"Come," God said, "I will take you to the highest heaven. You will dwell with the angels under my throne of glory. We are all waiting for you in heaven."

"I am content here," she answered. "There is no body as pure as the body of Moses. I would rather stay with him than mingle with the angels."

At last, Moses comforted his soul, saying, "Return, my beloved. God is waiting for you, and I am ready."

When the soul heard that Moses was willing, she agreed. Then the Shechinah kissed Moses on the lips and took the soul of Moses to heaven.

The children of Israel mourned for Moses for thirty days. The angels mourned. The sun, moon, and planets mourned. The Shechinah asked, "Who will defend the children of Israel? Who will argue with me? Oh, my beloved, in all of Israel, where will I find another prophet like you?"

Joshua

We Are Witnesses

A first reading of the book of Joshua *might suggest that a divinely appointed tribe is entitled to kill and dispossess the "foreigner." A deeper exploration reveals that one of the story's villains, Achan, is a wealthy Hebrew from the powerful tribe of Judah, while the story's heroine is a poor foreign prostitute named Rahab. Being divinely appointed does not relate to gender or birth but rather to following and living the teachings. We can consider the book of* Joshua *at a literal level as the conquest of land or on a metaphorical level as a conquest of inner land in order to find inner peace.*

The first eighteen lines of the book of Joshua *are read on Simchat Torah to describe Joshua's assumption of leadership after Moses' death. I begin this rendition of the book of* Joshua *with the story of Jacob's daughter Dinah (1400 B.C.E.) which brings about the pollution of the land. If we know that the land has been polluted, we understand the importance of bringing back the bones of Joseph, the most righteous Hebrew, from Egypt to redeem the land (1200 B.C.E.).*

*W*hen Abraham first arrived in Canaan, he came to the city of Shechem. Beside an oak tree called Moreh, which means "teacher," God appeared to him and said, "I will give this land to your descendants." In that place, Abraham built an altar to God.

Two generations later, Abraham's grandson Jacob arrived in

Shechem, with his wives, his sons, and his daughter, Dinah. By the oak tree called Moreh, Jacob purchased a parcel of land for five shekels from Hamor, the chief of the region, and there he too built an altar.

Jacob's daughter Dinah was sixteen. She walked in the fields and met the women of Canaan, who invited her to their new-moon festival. Dinah went with her mother, Leah, to watch the Canaanite women dance and rejoice. Hamor's son Shechem noticed Dinah and asked his friends the name of the young woman. He was told that her name was Dinah and that she was the daughter of Jacob, the Hebrew, who had recently returned from Haran. Shechem gazed at Dinah and his eyes delighted in her.

Several days later when she was walking in the fields, Shechem approached her. They walked together for a time and agreed to meet the next day. The next day they lay in the fields, gazing at the clouds. Passion overcame them. Their bodies sought each other. Then Shechem loved Dinah even more than before. His soul cleaved to hers. He spoke kindly to her, caressed her, and took her home.

From that moment, Shechem could think of nothing but wanting to be close to Dinah. Hamor loved his son dearly. He went to Jacob and said, "My son has lain with your daughter. He loves her and honors her. He is eager to marry her. Our land is open to you. Settle where you wish. Let your men marry our daughters and our men will marry yours so that our tribes become one."

Jacob did not answer. His older sons were in the field tending the sheep. He remembered when he had first met his wife Rachel at the well in Haran. She had been Dinah's age. At the sight of her he had rushed toward her and kissed her. Rachel's father had tricked him into working fourteen years so he could marry her; yet those years had gone by quickly, for each day had brought him closer to the day that Rachel would be his bride.

When Jacob's sons returned from the fields, they were outraged that a man had slept with their sister without asking their consent. Shechem returned with his father and said to Dinah's brothers, "I have come to ask for permission to marry your sister. I love Dinah. I will gladly pay whatever price you ask so that Dinah may be my wife."

Two of Dinah's brothers, Simeon and Levi, answered, "Our great-grandfather Abraham made a covenant with our God, promising that all his descendants would be circumcised. If each man in your tribe agrees to be circumcised, you can marry our sister; and we will dwell among you and be one people. But if you do not agree, we will take Dinah from you."

Shechem spoke with the men of his tribe. The Canaanites saw the love their chief's son had for this foreign woman, and they agreed. On the appointed day, the men from Shechem came out of the gate of the city and were circumcised. Then each one returned to his home and lay in great pain and discomfort. Dinah was in Shechem's house. She nursed him. They eagerly awaited their marriage.

On the third day, Simeon and Levi, Dinah's brothers, entered Shechem's house saying they were bringing wedding gifts. In front of their sister, they opened their packages, took out their swords, and slew her lover. Then they went swiftly from tent to tent, from house to house. Their brothers joined them. They killed every man in the city. No man in Shechem could defend himself. Blood ran through the streets.

Jacob grieved. Rachel grieved. Leah, the mother of Dinah, grieved. The earth keened with grief at the deeds of Jacob's sons.

Ten years passed. When Jacob's older sons saw that their father preferred his wife Rachel's son Joseph to them, they sold their brother into slavery. Joseph was taken to Egypt. The earth could not abide the presence of the brothers. In time, a famine devoured the land. The seeds lay barren in the earth.

Jacob's sons went to buy grain in Egypt where they discovered that their brother Joseph had become governor. Joseph forgave them and invited them to settle in Egypt. Before he died, he made them promise to bury his bones in Canaan. But after Joseph's death, the Hebrews were lured into slavery. For two hundred years, they toiled as slaves until at last they cried out to God in anguish. God sent Moses to lead the Hebrews out of Egypt. They fled carrying Joseph's bones. When they came to the Reed Sea, God lifted the waters sixteen hundred feet in the air. The miracle was witnessed as far away as Canaan.

From Canaan, Joshua saw the waters shimmering in the air. Joshua was born in Canaan with a strange birthmark on his back in the form of a fish. When his parents saw it, they were afraid it meant their child would kill his own father, so they abandoned him at a well. A Canaanite woman who heard the child crying named him Nun after the Egyptian god of the waters. She brought him home and raised him as her son. Joshua was quick and capable and at a young age was given the position of tax collector.

One day when he went to collect taxes, a man refused to pay him. Joshua struck him. The two began to wrestle. Joshua's shirt ripped, and the older man screamed in horror. Frightened, Joshua lashed out and mortally wounded him. When Joshua tried to help him, the older man began to sob. He put his hand on the mark of the fish and said, "My son, forgive me. We cannot run from our fate. Return to our people who are in Egypt. Help them, and we will both be forgiven." After telling Joshua that he was his father and that they were descendants of Joseph's son Ephraim, he died in his son's arms.

Joshua became Moses' disciple, serving him faithfully for years. When Moses appointed him the leader of Israel, Joshua wept. He loved Moses; he wanted to serve him, not replace him. Before Moses died, he blessed Joshua with wisdom and courage and said, "For forty years, we have been carrying Joseph's bones in the wilderness. Promise me you will bury them in Canaan. Joseph's holiness will sanctify the land. May you and the people of Israel find peace."

After Moses died, God said to Joshua: "It is time for the people to cross the Jordan to enter the land I promised to Abraham. I am giving the descendants of Abraham the land because its inhabitants have not observed the basic commandments of kindness and hospitality to their neighbors. Keep my teachings in your heart and on your lips. Recite them day and night. Only if you keep them faithfully, will I not forsake you, and will the Promised Land be yours."

Joshua told the people that God was giving them the land of Canaan and that they were to prepare to cross the Jordan in three days. They responded eagerly, saying, "We will do what you command. We will obey you as we obeyed Moses; let God be with you as God was with Moses."

Joshua then sent Caleb and the high priest's son Phinehas to spy on the land of Canaan. Disguised as pottery merchants, they arrived in Jericho at the house of the harlot Rahab. The next afternoon, there was a pounding on the door. Rahab signaled to the spies to hide on the roof. She opened the door and stood there with her hands on her broad hips. The king's messengers asked, "Where are the men—the Israelites—who came in the night?"

She tossed her long hair from one side to the other side and answered, "Yes, some men came to me, but I don't know from where. They are gone. If you go quickly, you might find them." As soon as the king's messengers went through the city's gates, the gates closed for the night.

Rahab found the spies on the roof hiding under stalks of flax. She spoke to them in a low voice: "From Jericho, we saw the waters of the sea rise in the air. My people are in dread of your God, but they refuse to change their ways. It is time for change. I wish to take your God as my God. I know your God, Yahweh, rules heaven and earth and has given you the land. Swear to me by your God that, because I have been loyal to you, you will be loyal to my family, to my father and mother and sisters and brothers and all the household, and that you will save them from death."

Rahab's house was on the outer side of the city wall. As she prepared a scarlet cord to let them down from her house, the men said, "When we invade the land, tie the scarlet cord to your window, and if you keep our mission a secret and God gives us the land, we will be loyal to you. Keep your family inside your house when we come. Do not venture outside. If anyone harms you or your family, their blood will be on our heads."

Rahab answered, "Let it be as you say. Flee to the mountains and hide there for three days until your pursuers return."

Rahab tied the scarlet cord to her window. The men set off, and after three days, the spies descended from the mountains, went to Joshua, and told him how Rahab had helped them and that the land would be theirs, for the people were afraid of them.

Early the next morning, Joshua and the people walked to the banks of the Jordan. The leaders went through the camp, advising the people, "When you see the ark of the covenant carried by the Levite priests, move forward and follow it, but let there be a distance between you and the ark. The ark will guide you so you will know where to go, for this is a road that you have not traveled before."

Joshua advised the people, "Purify yourselves. Tomorrow, God will perform wonders in your presence."

The next day, carrying the ark of the covenant, the priests walked toward the waters that were full from the spring rains. As the priests stepped into the Jordan, the waters rose in the air and could be seen by all the inhabitants of Jericho. The priests walked with the ark to the middle of the river and stood there until all of Israel had crossed over to the other side of the Jordan.

According to God's instructions, Joshua chose one man from each tribe to take a stone from the exact middle of the Jordan where the priests' feet were standing and to place the stone on the shore for a memorial. Then Joshua said to the people, "When your children ask, 'What is the meaning of these twelve stones by the side of the river?' you can explain to them that it was the ark of the covenant that caused the waters of the Jordan to rise up and allowed the people to enter the land." As his own offering to God, Joshua, son of Nun, set twelve stones under the water, where the priests had been standing, and they are there to this day.

After the people crossed the Jordan and the priests stepped out of the Jordan with the ark, the waters flowed again. God blessed Joshua, and the people revered their new teacher as they had revered Moses. Then God said to Joshua, "The men who left Egypt, with the exception of you and Caleb, have died during the forty years they wandered in the desert, but the children who were born in the wilderness have not yet dedicated themselves to me. If they are to inherit the land, if they are to be guided by the ark of the covenant, their hearts must be open, and they must be circumcised." Each man in the camp agreed. They were eager to revere and love and serve God. The men were circumcised with flintstones, and no one left the camp until the men were healed and restored to life. They called the place where they stayed

Gilgal, meaning "liberty," or "circle," for they had chosen to walk in God's ways.

Four days later, on the full moon of the first month of the year, the Hebrews offered a roasted lamb for the Passover sacrifice. They danced and sang as they celebrated the first Passover in the Promised Land. The next day they ate matzah, and when they ate the food of the land, the manna stopped falling from heaven.

That night, Joshua, the son of Nun, was walking outside of the camp. He looked up and saw a figure approaching with a drawn sword. Joshua went up to the stranger and asked, "Are you from our camp? Or are you an enemy?"

The messenger replied, "I am the captain of God's army. I have come to you. I am the Shechinah."

Joshua threw himself on the ground and asked, "What are your wishes?"

The Shechinah answered, "Remove your sandals, for the place where you are standing is holy."

The sharpness of the stones under his feet reminded Joshua that his task was not only to apportion the land, but to prepare the people to settle in the land by carrying out Moses' instructions. As Moses had asked, Joshua then led the people to Mount Ebal where they built an altar with the round river stones that the men carried from the Jordan River. On the altar the people gave burnt and peace offerings. The people stood on either side of the ark. Half the tribes faced Mount Ebal; the other half faced Mount Gerizim. To all the assembly—men, women, children, and strangers—Joshua read every word from the Book of Teachings and repeated the blessings and curses that Moses had asked him to speak at Mount Ebal. Then he took a round altar stone and wrote the teachings in seventy languages on the stone so that any person who wanted to could learn them.

The Shechinah said to Joshua, "Speak to the people in Canaan and tell them that they have three choices: They may follow the teachings and live in peace. They may leave the land, or they may resist; but if they resist, we will make war." Joshua did as God instructed, and many of the people who were oppressed by their kings chose to join the Israelites. But the king of Jericho ordered his soldiers to shut the gates of the city to prevent the Israelites from entering.

Then the Shechinah said to Joshua, "I will deliver Jericho into your hands. Let the priests, accompanied by soldiers, circle Jericho for six days, walking in front of the ark of the covenant and blowing rams' horns. On the seventh day, let the people walk with the priests and circle the city seven times. Then, at the long sustained sound of the ram's horn, let the people give a great shout. The walls of Jericho will fall. At that moment the men are to go forward." Joshua repeated God's commands to the people, adding that they were to be silent and not open their lips until he commanded them to shout.

For six days, seven priests walked in front of the ark of the covenant and blew rams' horns. The people in Jericho did not respond. On the seventh day, after the priests blew a long, anguished blast on the rams' horns, Joshua cried to the people, "God has given us Jericho. This is the first city we will take and like the first fruits we are to give it back to God. Only Rahab, the harlot, is to be spared and those who are in her house, for she hid the messengers. Do not take anything from Jericho for yourself. If you do, calamity will befall us. Now is the time to shout!"

The people hurled a great loud shout, and the walls of Jericho began to fall into the earth. Rahab, watching from the window, saw the Israelites streaming into the city. The walls of her house were trembling and her father and mother cried, "We must flee!"

"We are witnesses," Rahab protested. "Did we not see the waters of the Reed Sea and the Jordan rise into the air? Yahweh is now destroying the great wall of Jericho." The sound of the rams' horns drew closer. Looking out the window, Rahab saw a tall man, surrounded by soldiers. She ran to the door and opened it.

"Quickly," Joshua said, "bring all your family."

As they ran from the house, the wall of the city where their house had been, moved forward, upward, and then tumbled into the earth. Joshua led Rahab and her family through the shouts of the battle to the

Israelite camp at the outskirts of Jericho. He brought them to the tent of Caleb's daughter, Achsah, and asked her to watch over them.

After the defeat of Jericho, God ordered Joshua to march against the city of Ai. Instead of leading the army himself, Joshua sent three thousand troops to capture Ai and stayed near Rahab's family.

Word arrived the next day that the Israelite troops had been routed in the battle and Joseph's grandson Jair had been killed. Joshua and the elders tore their clothes. They covered their heads with dirt and lay on the ground before the ark of the covenant until evening. Joshua cried to the Shechinah, "Why did you lead us across the Jordan so that we would be destroyed by the Amorites? When the other tribes hear we have fled, they will turn on us and erase our name from the earth."

The Shechinah answered Joshua: "Arise. The people have broken the covenant and taken what is not theirs. If they do not purify themselves, they will continue to run from their enemy, and I will not be with you."

Joshua summoned the high priest and asked him to put on the breastplate. All twelve stones in his breastplate were shining brightly except the stone representing the tribe of Judah. That stone had no luster. The tribe of Judah protested their innocence, but the other tribes attacked them.

"Stop!" a descendant of Judah cried out. "I am responsible. I am Achan, a descendant of Judah's son Zerah. I went against God's word. I do not want the others to die."

"Why did you bring trouble on us?" Joshua asked him.

"I did not need to do it," Achan answered. "I have money. I saw a beautiful shawl woven in Ur—I saw two hundred shekels of silver and fifty shekels of gold—I buried them under my tent. I was greedy."

Joshua sent messengers to Achan's tent. They found everything that he had described buried in the earth. Then Achan and the mantle and the silver and gold, and his sons, daughters, animals, and possessions were taken from the camp; and all of Israel stoned him and put fire to them. They covered his ashes with a huge pile of stones that are still there.

Joshua defeated the city of Ai by means of an ambush and set fire to it. After this, the Shechinah was always with him.

Five kings saw the great gathering on Mount Ebal and banded together to attack the city of Gibeon that had become an ally of the Israelites. The people of Gibeon asked Joshua for help. Joshua asked the Shechinah, "Shall I endanger my own people by defending a foreign city?"

The Shechinah answered, "If you separate yourself from those who are distant from you, you will soon separate yourself from those who are close to you. You yourself are a foreigner—a descendant of Asenath, the daughter of an Egyptian priest."

Joshua set out with all his troops. The Shechinah killed more Amorites with boiling hailstones than the Israelites slew in battle. As the Amorites fled, Joshua cried out, "O sun, stand still at Gibeon. O moon, stand still in the Valley of Aijalon." To show her love for Joshua, the Shechinah caused the sun to halt in the heavens for one day and one night without moving.

The five kings were captured and brought before Joshua, who said to his officers, "Come forward, place your feet on the necks of these kings." The kings' bodies were then hung from five trees to show Yahweh's strength and to inspire fear throughout the land. At sunset, the kings were thrown back into the cave in which they had hidden during the battle. Large stones, which are still there, were placed over the mouth of the cave.

For seven years, the Israelites fought against the Amorites, Hittites, Perizzites, Jebusites, and Hivites. Those tribes who kept God's minimum commandments continued to dwell among them. Those who refused were destroyed. The people fought, but it was God who won the battles.

Then the Israelites returned to Gilgal, and the land had rest from war. Alone and in groups, the people went to Joshua to ask for land. Joshua granted Caleb, who had accompanied him to Canaan forty years before, Hebron and its surrounding land. In turn, Caleb gave his daughter the land of Debir and, at her request, the Upper and Lower Springs that made the land fertile. The five daughters of Zelophedad whose father had no sons asked for land and because they were descendants of Joseph he gave them a portion of land in the north that had been given to the tribe of Joseph's son Manasseh.

Joshua assembled the people at Shiloh. They set up the Tent of Meeting and placed the ark of the covenant in the holy of holies. At the Shechinah's direction, Joshua and the high priest apportioned land to the seven tribes who had not yet taken their land. Eleazar, the high priest, drew the name of a tribe from one basket and the name of its land from another basket. The house of Joseph was apportioned the land in the north; the tribe of Judah the land in the south.

All the tribes were to gather before the ark of the covenant every seven years to listen to the reading of the entire Torah. Each tribe was to care for its own members. A poor family was to receive loans without interest. No land was given to the descendants of Simeon or Levi, for their father, Jacob, wanted them to be scattered because of the harm they had done to the Shechemites. The Levites, who were priests, were given forty-eight towns from the tribes who had already received land, in order to offer sacrifices and to teach the people.

Then the Shechinah said to Joshua, "Tell the Israelites to set aside six cities of refuge which are easily accessible so that any person, Israelite or stranger, who unintentionally kills another person may flee and find refuge. If the fugitive stands at the gate of the city and declares what has happened, the elders shall take him in. They shall give him a place to live and teach him a skill until he has stood trial before the community, for a killer may not be harmed without the testimony of more than one witness. The death of an innocent person pollutes the land, and you shall not pollute or defile the land in which you live."

Joshua remembered Joseph's bones that Moses had entrusted to him. Joseph had never harmed anyone. His brothers had betrayed him and sold him into slavery, yet when he became governor of Egypt, he did not choose to retaliate. Joseph chose instead to reunite his family and end vengeance. Joshua buried Joseph's bones in Shechem near the oak tree where his brothers had massacred the inhabitants.

One by one, the people came forward and placed stones and earth on Joseph's grave. When Rahab placed a stone on Joseph's grave, Joshua looked at this strong, courageous woman who had chosen to become an Israelite. He always felt at ease when he was near her, but there had been many matters he had had to attend to. Now his work was done.

Joshua asked Rahab to walk with him on the land Jacob had purchased from the Shechemites. As they walked, he asked her if she would marry him. She tossed her hair to one side and answered, "It is good that you have taken your time to consider. I have made up my mind. The answer is yes."

Joshua and Rahab were married. They had five daughters who were the ancestors of eight prophets including Huldah, Ezekiel, and Jeremiah; all of whom urged the people to follow God's teachings.

When Joshua was old, he assembled the tribes of Jacob by the Teaching Tree in Shechem. He brought the ark of the covenant from Shiloh and had the elders and the people stand before it. He said to them, "Yahweh, the God of Israel, says to you, 'Your ancestors lived beyond the Euphrates and served other gods. I took Abraham and Sarah across the river and led them through Canaan. Their son Isaac married Rebekah; they had two sons, Jacob and Esau. Esau inherited Mount Senir. Jacob's children went down to Egypt. I sent Moses, Miriam, and Aaron to lead the children of Israel out of Egypt. The Egyptian chariots and riders died in the sea. You dwelt many days in the wilderness. You crossed the Jordan and came into Jericho. I fought for you and the fear of me drove the Amorites and Canaanites out of the land. I gave you land that you did not work, cities that you did not build, and vineyards that you did not plant.

" 'Choose who you will worship—the gods your ancestors served beyond the Euphrates, the gods of the Egyptians, or the gods of the Amorites in whose land you have settled. This land is yours not because of your merit but because the inhabitants needed to be driven from the land. But if you do not follow the teachings, you too will be driven from the land. The choice is yours. Choose which god you will serve and thus how you will live.' "

Joshua said, "Rahab and I and our children have made our choice. The choice is now yours."

The people answered, "We will not abandon Yahweh to serve other gods. The Shechinah brought us out of slavery and watched over us in all our travels. We will not forsake Yahweh or the teachings."

Joshua said, "If you forsake Yahweh and turn to other gods, Yahweh will deal harshly with you, and the land will spew you out as it has spewed out those who acted with cruelty and perversion. You have been given the teachings. You are your own witnesses that you have chosen to serve God."

The people answered, "Yes, we are witnesses."

Joshua made a covenant for the people and recorded it in a book. At the shrine Jacob had built in Shechem, Joshua, the son of Nun, set a great stone and said to the people: "See, this stone, this stone will be a witness against you if you break your faith, for it heard all the words that God spoke to us, and it heard your response." Joshua placed the stone at the foot of the Teaching Tree. The people returned to the land they had been given.

Joshua died at the age of one hundred and ten. They buried him on his own property, a small portion of land in the hill country of Joseph's son Ephraim. During the time that Joshua lived, the children of Israel served God with love. They followed God's teachings and cared for one another.

Genesis

Let There Be Light!

When the rabbis divided the Torah into weekly readings, they wisely arranged it so that its completion, which describes Moses' death, would coincide with Simchat Torah, which occurs in the autumn, at the time of the dying of the earth. On the day of Simchat Torah, the reading of the beginning of Genesis immediately follows the reading of the last words of the Torah, describing the death of Moses. The linking of the death of the man who brought the Torah to the founding of the universe suggests that not only does death lead to life, but despite death, God's creation and presence continue.

God's presence is infinite, beyond our imaginings. The Torah in its infinite wisdom offers us a glimpse of God. If we are to come close to God, we embrace the Torah by reading it again and again. And so the Kabbalists noticed that the last word in the Torah is "Israel" and the last letter of Israel is l. The first word in the Torah is "beginning" (bereshit) and the first letter is b. Once we come to the end of the Torah, we begin again. L, the last letter, and B, the first letter, form the Hebrew word "lev" meaning "heart." The goal of learning the Torah is not merely to study but to bring the Torah's teachings into our hearts to change our actions.

In the beginning, God created the heavens and the earth. The earth was empty and without form. Darkness was on the face of the deep and the spirit of God hovered over the waters.

God said, "Let there be light." And there was light. God saw the light was good, and separated the light from the darkness. God called the light day, and the darkness night. There was evening, then morning. The first day.

God said, "Let there be an ark in the midst of the waters to separate the waters from the waters." God made a dome and separated the waters that were under the dome from the waters that were above the dome. It was so. God called the expanse heaven. There was evening, then morning. The second day.

God said, "Let the waters be gathered together under the heaven into one place and the dry land appear." It was so. God called the dry land earth and the gathered waters seas. And God saw it was good.

God then said, "Let the earth give forth vegetation; plants giving seed and fruit trees bearing fruit, each according to its kind." It was so. The earth then brought forth vegetation, plants with seeds according to their kind, trees with fruit according to their kind. God saw it was good. There was evening, then morning. The third day.

God said, "Let there be lights in the heavens to separate the day from the night. They will be the signs for the festivals, days, and years, and they will give light on earth." It was so. God made two large lights. The greater light ruled the day. The smaller light ruled the night. God also made the stars. God set the lights in the heavens to give light on earth. God saw it was good. There was evening, then morning. The fourth day.

God said, "Let the waters swarm with living creatures, and let flying creatures fly over the earth in the heavens." God created the great sea monsters and every creature who moves in the waters and every creature who flies in the air. God saw it was good and blessed them, saying, "Be fruitful and multiply. Let the sea creatures fill the seas, and let the flying creatures multiply on earth." There was evening. There was morning. The fifth day.

God said, "Let the earth bring forth living creatures according to their kind, the animals of the flock, the crawling creatures, and the wild animals." It was so. God made the wild animals, the animals of the flock, and the crawling creatures of the earth. God saw it was good.

Then God said, "Let us create humans in our image, after our likeness. Let them be guardians of the fish of the sea, the flying creatures of the air, and all the moving and crawling creatures of the earth."

God created humans in God's image, male and female. God blessed them and said, "Be fruitful and multiply. Fill the earth and be responsible for the fish of the sea, the flying creatures of the air, and every living creature that moves on the earth." God said to the people, "I give you every plant yielding seed that is upon the earth and every tree with seed bearing fruit. They are yours for food. I have given to all the creatures of the earth and the flying creatures of the air, and to everything that moves on earth that has the breath of life, green plants for food." It was so. God saw all that had been created. It was very good. There was evening, then morning. The sixth day.

The heavens and earth were finished. Since God finished the work of the creation on the seventh day, God refrained from work. God blessed the seventh day and called it holy, for on this day God rested.

God rested, but the seventh day, the Sabbath, was not content. She complained to God, saying, "All the other days have partners. Day One has Day Two. Day Three has Day Four. Day Five has Day Six, but I am alone."

"You are right," God answered the Sabbath. "Every living creature needs a companion. I will give you the people of Israel as your companion. They will welcome you to earth each week and delight in your company. And in welcoming you, they will remember the creation. You, in turn, will give them a taste of heaven and the oneness of creation."

Centuries later, God remembered the promise, and, on Mount Sinai, said to the children of Israel, "Remember the Sabbath and make her welcome. Prepare for her. Sing to her. Honor her. Delight in her and she will delight in you."

About the Stories

The Death of Moses

In *Exodus*, we meet a child whose eyes are filled with love for others and curiosity about the world. Wherever he goes, as infant, boy, man, slave, or fugitive, his life force is such that he draws others to him; and yet, he remains humble. In *The Covenant*, Moses enters a state of holiness where for long periods he withdraws from humanity, fasts, and gives himself over to the Shechinah. Three times, for forty days each, Moses climbs Mount Sinai. He returns with a living document, a guiding map by which the people might evolve a meaningful way to live together and be in relationship with God.

The boy who lived among the Hebrew, Egyptian, and desert cultures becomes an intermediary between God and humanity. He wrestles with God on the part of the people and he wrestles with the people on the part of God. He complains, but he does not tire. His love for the people and for God does not diminish. After forty years of caring for the myriad demands and troubles of his people, he does not wish to stop serving.

God says to the people, "Tarry with me one more day." Moses begs God to also be allowed to tarry. If only to be a fish or a tiny bird—anything—so long as he can continue to experience God's awe and sing God's praises! How can God allow a man of such vitality, stature, and service—a man who would willingly be a fish—to die? There are no divine avatars in the Bible; there are great people who are mortal.

As with many spiritual leaders, Moses' spiritual heirs are not to be of his own blood. Aaron instinctively knows that after the Shechinah appears to his brother, entrusting him with the task of freeing his people, Moses could not care for his own family. Aaron sends Zipporah back to her people. Before Moses and Zipporah separate, in what appears to be an initiation ritual (the text is ambiguous and corrupt), Moses' wife cuts off the foreskin of their child. This act joins Moses to the covenant of his ancestor Abraham, and from that moment he is entirely bonded to God.

When asked to lead, he leads; when asked to teach, he teaches. When he can no longer lead, Moses serves Joshua; when he can no longer serve, he wants to offer praises, and when his mind can no longer function, when he can no longer remember and can no longer offer praises, not wanting to live in darkness, he is ready to leave the earth. When Moses dies, the Shechinah takes his soul to heaven, and the people are left with his teachings—The Five Books of Moses, or the Torah.

Joshua

Not until after the destruction of the World Trade Center towers did I decide to include Joshua in *Treasures of the Heart*. Previously, I had viewed the book of Joshua as a horrific story of unspeakable genocide that had been used by Bible readers to promote acts of aggression or vengeance. September 11, 2001, brought war to my neighborhood. From Sixth Avenue, I stood in the street and watched the second tower fall. As I walked home, I felt we were now one world. Vengeance would not help, our only hope would be understanding. I wanted to know more about holy war and entitlement, so I reread Joshua.

To my surprise, I discovered a very different message from what I had imagined. The Hebrews cannot decide to "take" the land. The land was a gift, a conditional gift, depending not on their will, but on their deeds. Moses lives the teachings and passes them on to Joshua. In the biblical text, God's first words to Joshua are to remind him to keep the teachings in his heart and on his lips day and night. At the end of Joshua, God asks all the people to make a similar commitment.

God's teachings are at the root of the stories in the Bible, and each story expresses them in a different poetic form. The story of Moses begins and ends with water. The infant Moses is placed in the water and the Hebrews are pushed through the waters of the Reed Sea. Both Moses and the people are in transition; they must move through "amniotic" waters to be born. The book of Joshua begins and ends with stones. Stones are a sign of permanence, marking the new relationship that the people have made with God.

River stone, flint stone, altar stone, teaching stone. The people establish themselves in the land, stone by stone. Abraham builds an altar of stones to commemorate God's appearance and the gift of the land (Gn

12:7). As the people enter the land that God had promised to them, God tells Joshua that they should build an altar with river stones to remember the moment when the ark of the covenant (the teachings) held back the waters. Joshua in turn builds an underwater stone monument for the Invisible. Next, God asks Joshua to take flint stones to circumcise the men so their consciousness might be raised. Then the people, of their own accord, bring stones to create a stone altar to God. Joshua inscribes the teachings on an altar stone so that they will be made available to everyone in the land.

Wall stone, breastplate stone, killing stone, hail stone, grave stone, witness stone. God promises that the wall stones of Jericho will fall. The stones of the high priest's breastplate divine the truth; Joshua commands the people to pelt the transgressor with killing stones. God battles for the people with hail stones; Joshua seals the mouth of the cave where the dead kings are placed with burial stones. In Shechem, the very place that God promised to give land to Abraham's descendants, Joshua sets up a witness stone.

Imagine a stone being a witness! But if the land has become purified, then the earth is alive and holy. The waters of the river rise into the air, the walls tumble down at the sound of voices, the sun halts in the sky, the stone bears witness. More than any other book in the Bible, Joshua is an animistic story in which the elements of the natural world form the story's third protagonist: there is God, the people, *and* the land.

The etymology for Rahab, according to *The Hebrew and Aramaic Lexicon of the Old Testament*, is "broad," "open," "wide," "expanse of land," "to open oneself wide," "to spread." I had sensed the importance of Rahab in the story of Joshua. I saw her as a worldly, courageous, mature woman who, because of her own merit, responds to Joshua, a man of devotion who is selfless, resolute, fearless. But I had not considered her mythological significance. When I think of her mythologically as the broad, open, wide land, I see her as a chthonic being representing the primordial force of nature.

Joshua also has a mythological dimension. In the Bible he is always referred to with the epithet son of Nun. Nun is the name of the Egyptian god of the primordial ocean, the watery abyss, the dark. Joshua has known the abyss. He fell into chaos when he killed his own father. By going through his own darkness and becoming a disciple of Moses and a servant of Yahweh, Joshua, a murderer, has understood that a person can transform. Unlike his namesake, Nun, Joshua emerges from the primordial place and is establishing a new order.

What more powerful partner could Joshua choose to unite with than Rahab? She can be understood to represent both the powerful female and the primordial force of nature. As the strong female, she is giving up the old and choosing a new way of life—Yahweh's teachings. As the primordial land, her acceptance of Yahweh indicates that the earth (which previously pushed out Jacob's children) is willing to receive Yahweh's children. By marrying Rahab, Joshua is aligning himself with a mature woman and the earth's primordial powers. The descendants of a conscious warrior and an open, accepting woman are prophets who will directly transmit God's teachings.

These are times of upheaval. The Hebrew people are leaving the protected wilderness. Joshua has created an alliance with the earth, but he is about to guide the Hebrews into a land whose inhabitants are violent, immoral, and cruel. How will the Hebrews survive? Extreme measures must be taken.

In the stories in Genesis, it was God who took extreme measures. At the apocalyptic moments when the perversion of the people had gone too far, God brought on the Flood. When the people had become too arrogant, God destroyed the Tower of Babel. But in the book of Exodus, God commands the Hebrews to conquer the land and kill its inhabitants. Why is it necessary that they kill the land's inhabitants?

One interpretation is that God's justice is being meted out. Four generations earlier in the Bible, God told Abraham that his descendants would return to the land when the "wickedness of the Amorites is at its height" (Gn 15:16). The horrific crimes of the Amorites are polluting the world. If this pollution is not stopped, the moral fiber of the world will be destroyed. (To grasp the magnitude of the crimes of the Amorites, we can compare them to the crimes of the Sodomites who tortured and killed strangers rather than welcome and help them.) This then is the moment of justice.

But why doesn't God do the killing? Why must the Hebrew people do the killing? Perhaps God is asking the people to be responsible. They must be willing to fight for the land that will be theirs. War is a fact of life. In biblical times it established tribal identity, borders, authority; it brought temporary order and sometimes rest. The biblical writers in Joshua establish a code of behavior for war: Take only your share, defend your allies, keep your promises, do not cut down fruit-bearing trees. The Hebrew people must be willing to fight, just as Abraham must be willing to sacrifice Isaac. But in the wars in the book of Joshua, it is not they but God who brings the victory. "The kings and their lands were conquered by Joshua with a single stroke of his sword, for God fought for Israel" (Jsh 10:42).

Since there seems to be no clear archeological evidence for such a conquest, and since the victories occur because God does the greater part of the fighting, it seems to me that war in Joshua might also be interpreted metaphorically. God is telling the Hebrews what they must be willing to do if they are to live in a new land. To live in the Promised Land, the Hebrews cannot live partially with Yahweh and partially with other gods. They must be willing "to kill": to completely rid *themselves* of their own violence, perversion, and cruelty. They must give themselves over entirely to the teachings. Without the teachings, the people cannot conquer the land. They cannot even enter it, for it is the "ark of the covenant" that lifts the water of the Jordan River.

If we examine Joshua again in the context of the Hebrew Bible, we realize that we are reading it forward and backward. Before the Hebrews entered the land, God prophesied that the Amorites would be forced out of it. And we who read the Bible (as well as those who compiled it in exile in Babylon) know that the descendants of those Hebrews who entered the land will leave it in exile. We know that from the time of Solomon, the kings did exactly what was intolerable to God: They set up shrines to other gods; burned their children; consulted ghosts and diviners; killed innocent people; were arrogant, greedy, immoral, and corrupt.

In Joshua, God urgently advises the people to follow the teachings. The biblical reader, who already knows that the people will fail, must understand that God's wishes are ultimately that the people keep the covenant and turn from the temptations that will lead them away from the teachings. Whether they remain in the Promised Land depends upon their adhering to the teachings that they have agreed to take on.

The external storyline in Joshua is the conquest of wrong actions and the establishment of a new order. There is another message in this story of battles and violence: the covert message of one who lived the teachings. Joseph did not continue his family's violence, jealousy, hatred, and anger. By asking for his bones to be returned to Canaan, Joseph imagined a way, after his death, to bring about his brothers' redemption. Joshua's task was to decide where to bury Joseph's bones.

Joseph had lived the teachings that were intertwined with the land.

Shechem was the first place Joseph's ancestors had come to. Here, by the oak of Moreh, the Teaching Tree, God had made a covenant with Abraham, and here in Shechem, Joseph's brothers had polluted the land by going against the teachings and massacring the inhabitants. Here, too, in Shechem, Joseph's sister, Dinah, was thought to be buried. By placing Joseph's bones near the Teaching Tree, Joseph, a man of purity whose goodness brought fragrance to the land of Egypt, would redeem the land of Canaan for his ancestors, his descendants, and his family.

This covert message of the importance of Joseph's goodness underlines the other three points. A relationship is being built between God and the people (symbolized by the stones). The union of Joshua and Rahab provides a container for this new relationship. To live in the land is to live the teachings, and Joseph is the embodiment of the living teachings that do not die. The Promised Land may be won and lost, but Joseph's goodness, carried out by Joshua, continues with Joshua's descendants, the prophets whose words illumine our lives. As in so many of the Bible stories, the stories take place simultaneously in the past, the future, and the present.

As a coda to the Torah, the book of Joshua is filled with the terror of war and the healing of reconciliation. The silent stone that Abraham placed under the oak tree of Moreh, the Teaching Tree, is now a speaking stone, for it is engraved with the words recording the dialogue between God and the descendants of Abraham and Sarah.

Genesis

In the beginning, there is no form. As God in the form of Ein Sof—the Unknowable Infinity, the formless eternal force—begins to differentiate, the world comes into being. The One becomes two: heaven and earth, light and darkness, day and night, man and woman. The word begins the world. The word is God. God is nothing and everything. Just as on Mount Sinai, God's teachings flew in space as letters, God's words, formed of Hebrew letters that are containers of divine energy, animate existence.

God speaks ten times in the creation story, and with each proclamation, according to the Kabbalists, another attribute of God is revealed. As God moves from oneness to differentiation, at the end of six days God's image is revealed in man and woman. Then on the seventh day, God withdraws and rests. God's dynamic movement, which is glimpsed in Ezekiel's vision of the *chayot* running back and forth (Ez 1:9–12), is portrayed in

Genesis—God moves, rests, expands, contracts: God is. The God Who Is, craving a partner, a relationship, creates the world.

Man and woman, who are created in God's image, are commanded by the Torah to rest like God did, and to return to the oneness of creation. It is on the Sabbath, the day of rest, that humankind becomes a part of God's eternal movement, by resting and cleaving to God. In cleaving to God, in seeking oneness, in recognizing God, there is no death.

Genesis is also a template for the life of the soul. The soul is empty upon formation; then light, or consciousness, arrives. The body is created mostly of water and some dry parts. The process of evolution follows, leading to a male and female self, and then a time of rest and return. The story of Genesis can be viewed as the revelation of God, as well as the revelation of the soul.

The cycle of life and death, round like a stone, circular like the scroll of the teachings, spirals through time. To participate in holiness, we are urged to honor God's work, to serve God, and to rest, rejoining the oneness of creation.

In the stories we read at Simchat Torah, Moses dies, the leadership is passed on, and the world continues. But with Moses' death, the vision he offers the frightened Hebrew slaves of a Parent/Protector God dies. Moses can no longer intervene for them. Each person is to be responsible. Moses' successor, Joshua, offers the people the teachings on Mount Ebal, and this time the people do not faint (as they did in *The Covenant*) but agree to follow God's teachings.

Ending the Simchat Torah readings with the death of Moses might have caused a rupture in the Hebrews' connection to God. Instead, turning to Genesis, the beginning of the Torah, re-weds each person to life and creation. In Genesis "God created humans in God's image, male and female." God's image is masculine and feminine. We are not separate from God, we are in God's image. God's goodness and inexhaustible creativity reside in each of us.

HANUKKAH

About Hanukkah

At the darkest time of the year, when, in the northern hemisphere, the sun barely crosses the sky and the earth is without color, Hanukkah is celebrated. When the outside world is without light, people react by creating "festivals of light." Hanukkah, which means "devotion," "rededication," "initiation," is celebrated on or near the winter solstice, at the time of the waning moon. Known as the Festival of Lights, it begins on the evening of the twenty-fifth day of the tenth month of the year (December) and lasts for eight nights.

Hanukkah is the only major holiday that is not ordained in the Bible. However, it is the only one for which there are historical accounts due to the writings in the Apocrypha that were preserved by the early Christian Church. In the Book of the Maccabees, we read that the Syrian Greeks (the Seleucids) defiled the Temple in Jerusalem in 168 B.C.E. A small band of courageous Jews led by Judah Maccabbee defeated the Greek army, and in 165 B.C.E., Judah Maccabee and his soldiers rededicated the Temple. The people joined the soldiers, rejoicing and singing songs of praise. Some say the celebration went on for eight days to replace the seven days of Sukkot plus Shemini Atzeret that Judah and his soldiers missed when they had been hiding in the mountains. Since that time, the festival has been joyfully observed every year for eight days (I Mc 4:36–59, II Mc 10:1–8).

The account of Hanukkah in the Talmud does not dwell on Judah Maccabee or warfare. Rather, the second-to-fourth-century rabbis who wrote the Talmud speak about God's miracle of lights: "When the Hasmonean dynasty defeated (the Greeks), they found only one cruse of oil with the seal of the high priest which contained sufficient oil for only one day, yet a miracle was wrought and the oil in the lamp burned for eight days" (Shabbat 21b). For the portions of the Torah read on Hanukkah, the rabbis chose readings from Numbers (Num 7–8) having to do with the offerings brought to build the tabernacle. For the Hanukkah haftorah, they specifically chose a reading from the prophet Zechariah: "Not by might and not by power, but by My spirit says the Lord of hosts."

For years, Hanukkah remained a minor holiday with controversy as to its meaning. Does Hanukkah commemorate the miracle of the light lasting eight days? Or the militaristic victory that, despite impossible odds, allowed Judaism to regain its strength and transform itself from a localized, cult-based religion to an international, book-based religion? At the end of the nineteenth century, Hanukkah began to take on a greater importance in the cycle of festivals when the more assimilated Jews wanted a holiday to correspond to Christmas, and the Zionists, eager to reestablish a Jewish state, wanted role models who exhibited courage and self-sacrifice.

The happy, relaxed holiday of Hanukkah is celebrated in the warmth and protection of the home. It has no holiday restrictions. The candles are placed from right to left in the *hanukkiah*, a special menorah that holds eight candles plus a ninth servant candle. Whoever lights the candles does so with the servant candle, moving in the opposite direction, from left to right. In this way, all directions are cared for. Over the eight days of Hanukkah, thirty-six lights are lit, corresponding to the thirty-six *lamed vovniks*, hidden saints, whose secret acts of holiness, according to tradition, hold the earthly world together.

In the first century C.E., there were two differing schools of Jewish philosophy. Their respective leaders, Shammai and Hillel, argued with each other concerning the order in which the lights should be lit. Shammai believed that the soul's work was to begin by defeating evil, and so he contended that eight candles should be lit the first night and one less candle on each of the following nights in order to diminish passion or evil. Hillel, who argued that goodness leads to the eradication of evil, believed that one candle should be lit the first night and on each night another candle added so as to increase light or goodness. Hillel prevailed, and the lights of Hanukkah are lit in ascending order.

On the first night of Hanukkah, children, mothers, fathers, aunts, uncles, grandparents crowd together around the menorah. It is dark outside. There is never a full moon. The lights have not yet been lit in the house. From baby to grandparent, all hush and wait in the darkness for that most simple and amazing event: "Let there be light."

And there is light. Everyone knows the ritual—each night of Hanukkah one more candle is lit—yet watching one empty wick after another in the darkened room burst into life feels like a miracle. There was no light, and then, together, we witness light. Spirit enters the home, filling it with a sweet, meditative peace.

Today in some homes where several generations celebrate together, everyone brings his or her menorah and the entire room is filled with light. People sit near the *hanukkiah*, which is placed in front of a window. They watch the candles burning for as long as they last. They do not work by their light. They relax and enjoy the light. Prayers of praise and thanksgiving are recited and songs follow the candle lighting. Then gifts are exchanged.

In our home, my mother lit the Sabbath and Hanukkah candles. My grandfather always gave each grandchild a silver dollar. At the time I thought that the large, round, shining coin was the greatest treasure imaginable. Our family sat down to eat the traditional Hanukkah supper—heaps of light, crispy, warm potato pancakes (*latkes*). After supper, we made music together: my father on the vibraharp; my brothers, Martin and Gary, on the cello and piano; and I on the violin.

In other families, children play with a dreidel, a top that has a Hebrew letter written on each of four sides: N, *nun*, for *ness* ("miracle"); G, *gimmel*, for *gadol* ("great"); H, *hay*, for *haya* ("happened"); and SH, *shin* for *sham* ("there"). The four letters stand for the words "A great miracle happened there."

Hanukkah continues for eight nights. The number seven is concerned with the completion of earthly matters. Eight is one beyond the earthly and is related to the spiritual realm. Hanukkah brings the weekday into holiness.

Judith

❧

Her Beauty Captured His Soul

Can one woman defeat an army of two hundred thousand mercenary soldiers? An ordinary woman could not. A woman carrying the powers of the Warrior Goddess might possibly accomplish what was not possible.

Ancient readers knew from the start that the story of Judith was a fiction: Its villain, the great Nebuchadnezzar who in the story is said to be the king of Assyria, was actually the king of Babylon, and the location of Bethulia cannot be found. But even if the elements in the story are fictional, the terror that comes from the threat of extermination is real. At the time of Judah Maccabee (second to first century B.C.E.) when many scholars believe the story of Judith was written, Israel was being threatened with annihilation, and the Jews were desperate to be rescued by their Warrior God.

Whether Judith or this story's Nebuchadnezzar did or did not exist, Israel is still being threatened with extinction, and all aspects of life at this time on our planet—animal, mineral, and plant life—are similarly threatened. I've always been drawn to this story because of its message that in an impossible situation one person can and does make a difference. The story of Judith is often told on the last night of Hanukkah. I've condensed the account in the Apocrypha and added a few details of my own to make the story more immediate.

*T*he Assyrian king Nebuchadnezzar, who regarded himself as God, ruled the great city of Nineveh and insisted that all the surrounding countries pay him tribute. When the king of one of the neighboring countries built a wall one hundred and five feet high and seventy feet wide, Nebuchadnezzar was outraged. A neighboring country was daring to defend itself against God! Nebuchadnezzar sent messengers to the west, to the rulers of Damascus, Lebanon, Jerusalem, Egypt, even Ethiopia, demanding that they come to his aid at once.

"*Ne-bu-chad-nez-zar?*" The rulers of the west twisted their lips. "Who is he? We have not heard of him or his generals." They laughed at his arrogance and sent his messengers back in disgrace.

Nebuchadnezzar struck his fist on his throne and swore, "I shall wipe out those who defied me from the face of the earth!" He summoned his general, Holofernes, and ordered him to attack every western country that had defied him. And if they did not surrender, to slaughter their people, plunder their land, and show no mercy.

Holofernes assembled one hundred and twenty thousand soldiers—the largest army ever seen in the east. He brought goats and sheep to provide food, and camels, donkeys, and mules to carry the provisions. The army crossed the Euphrates and headed west. They slaughtered every person who resisted them and destroyed every town that did not open its gates. At harvest time, they descended to the plains of Damascus and set fire to the wheat fields.

Every person living in the seacoast cities of Sidon and Tyre fell into fear and trembling. Messengers were sent to Holofernes. They fell before his feet and said, "Great Holofernes, servant of Nebuchadnezzar, we are your slaves. Our houses, land, and servants are yours. Everything we have is yours. Treat us as you wish. We ask only that you do not kill us."

The people of the seacoast cities welcomed Holofernes' army, showering them with garlands of flowers and dancing before them with tambourines. Holofernes marched into their cities, destroyed their sanctuaries, cut down their sacred trees, and proclaimed, "There is only one god, and he is Nebuchadnezzar! Only he may be worshiped as God." Holofernes then continued south until he came to Dothan, a town opposite Judea. There he waited for thirty days for new supplies.

Terror of Nebuchadnezzar's army struck every Israelite living in Judea. The high priest in Jerusalem alerted Uzziah, the leader of the town of Bethulia, saying, "Nebuchadnezzar's army will enter Judea by way of the mountain passes that surround your town. Since the roads are narrowest there, you must secure your mountain passes. That is where it will be easiest to stop them." All of Judea prepared for war.

When it was reported to Holofernes that the Israelites were closing their mountain passes, he summoned the local generals and asked, "Who are these people living in the hill country? What is their source of power that they alone, of all the people in the west, refuse to surrender?"

Achior, the Ammonite general, stepped forward and said, "Holofernes, Great Lord, I will speak to you truthfully. These people believe in the God of heaven who asked them to leave Mesopotamia. They settled in Canaan, but when there was a famine, they went to Egypt where the king of Egypt turned against them, forced them to make bricks, and later enslaved them. They cried out to their God, who struck Egypt with plagues so that the Egyptian king released them.

"With the help of their God, they crossed the Jordan and returned to this country; but when they abandoned the path of their God, their Temple was razed to the ground and they were taken into captivity. Again, they cried out to their God, who allowed them to return from many different countries to Canaan. They have just reoccupied the hill country and rebuilt their Temple. If at this time they are following the teachings of their God, we must pass them by, for their God will protect them, and the world will laugh at us."

"Laugh at *us*?" the Canaanite generals roared at Achior. "What are you saying? The Israelites have no army, no king, no weapons. Achior is a coward. Thrash him! Go forward, Holofernes! We'll gobble them up!"

Holofernes said to Achior, "Are you advising us not to make war on the Israelites because their God will defend them? Dear prophet, if you think there's any other God than Nebuchadnezzar, we'll send you to your God, and when you next see my face, you'll be praying to your

Hebrew God. Oh, don't look so downcast. We'll take you to him at once! Tie him up!"

As Holofernes' soldiers tied Achior to a tree below Bethulia, the Israelites pelted them with stones, and the soldiers fled. Immediately, the Israelites untied the general and brought him to their town. Uzziah, the town leader, came forward and questioned him.

Achior said, "I am an Ammonite general. I spoke the truth about your people to Holofernes. I told him that if the Israelites follow the commandments of their God, they will be protected." Word spread through Bethulia, and the people, alone or in groups, went to Achior to praise and comfort him. Uzziah took him to his home. That night Achior's story was retold in every household in Bethulia, and each family renewed their prayers to God.

The next day Holofernes moved his army, which had now swelled to one hundred and seventy thousand men, toward Bethulia. When the Israelites saw the soldiers swarming over the land like locusts— thousands, tens of thousands, hundreds of thousands—they were terrified. "The earth will collapse," they said. "The mountains and valleys will not be able to bear their weight." The Canaanites and the Assyrian army encircled Bethulia.

For thirty-four days the Israelites had no access to water. Their water jars were empty. Their wells went dry. Children became sick. Young people collapsed on the streets. Then all of Bethulia went to Uzziah and protested, "We must surrender. We are dying of thirst. Give our town to the Assyrians at once. It is better for us to be slaves so we can live. Go to Holofernes and surrender."

"Courage!" Uzziah answered. "Give God five days. If five days pass and no help comes, I will surrender." The men went back to their posts, and a great depression fell on the town of Bethulia.

In Bethulia there lived a woman named Judith. Her husband, Manasseh, had died of sunstroke during the barley harvest three years and four months before. Judith was beautiful, shapely, and rich, and people thought she would quickly remarry. But no, she had loved her husband, and after his death, she did not look for another man. She wore sackcloth and lived much of the day in a tent on the roof of her house. When her husband was alive, she had worked ceaselessly helping him build up their estate. After God in one moment had taken him, she chose to live quietly and peacefully, appreciating God's gift of life. Her one companion was her servant, Ora.

That afternoon, not long after Uzziah had spoken in the marketplace, Judith was startled by her servant's unusual bustle. She went down into the house. Ora's powerful hands shook and her bracelets rattled as she said, "Uzziah has promised to surrender our town in five days if God does not bring rain."

Judith said to Ora, "Bring Uzziah and the town elders to me."

The elders hastened to honor Judith who was known as a woman of wisdom and integrity. When they were seated, Judith smiled at each of them. Then she opened her hand, spread her fingers and said, "Five! Are you giving God five days to do *your* bidding? If we cannot fathom the human heart, how can we unravel God's design? God draws close to test us. God tested our ancestors, and now we are being tested. We are being asked to defend our town so that our children and women are not killed and the Temple and altar in Jerusalem are not destroyed."

"Yes, what you are saying is true," Uzziah agreed. "Since you were a child everyone has known that you've always spoken with wisdom. But the people are thirsty, very thirsty. You are a pious woman. Pray that God fills the cisterns with rain."

Judith lowered her voice. "I will do more than pray. I will do more than you can imagine. I will do something that our children will speak about for generations. Tonight my servant and I will go out the city gates and before the days are over of which you have spoken, God will rescue Judea by my hand. Do not question me, for I will not say what I will do until it is done."

After the elders left, Judith went up again to the roof and prayed. "Adonai, the Assyrians depend on their horse and rider, their sword and shield. They mean to defile your altar and slaughter your people. But they do not know you. You are the God of heaven and earth, the creator of the waters, the creator of the universe, the protector of the oppressed. Adonai, I beg you, give me lips of guile and a strong hand to show every nation that no one protects the people of Israel but you."

After praying, Judith went down into the house. She took off her sackcloth and bathed. Then she anointed herself with oil and rich perfume. She put on a beautiful dress that had always pleased her husband when she'd worn it for festivals and joyous occasions. She slipped on her gleaming silver anklets, rings, earrings, necklaces—to attract the eyes of any man who would see her. She prepared wine, oil, barley, figs, and bread and gave these to Ora to carry.

The two women went to the gate where Uzziah and the elders were waiting. The men's eyes opened in surprise. They hardly recognized Judith. She was completely transformed. "Open the town gate," she said, "so I may do what I spoke of." The sentries opened the gates and the men watched the two women walk down the mountain toward the enemy.

"Stop!" the soldiers cried at the first outpost. "Who are your people? Where do you come from? Where are you going?"

Judith looked from soldier to soldier and answered in a clear, sweet voice, "I am a daughter of the Israelites. I go to Holofernes, the commander of your army, to tell him how he can conquer all of Judea without losing the life of a single soldier."

"Well spoken, woman," the soldiers said. They had never seen such a beautiful woman. "We'll take you to him. When you stand before him, don't be afraid to tell him just what you've told us." Struck by her grace and beauty, one hundred men pushed and shoved one another eager to be close to her.

Holofernes was resting on his bed under a purple and gold canopy that sparkled with emeralds and precious stones. Judith's arrival was announced. Holofernes came to the front of his tent preceded by slaves with silver lamps. Judith's perfume filled the tent. She knelt on the ground. Holofernes was huge. Towering. He could crush her and all her people. The strong animal odor of his boots swept over her and she trembled.

"Courage, woman," Holofernes said. "Do not be afraid. Why are you here?"

Judith stood, and Holofernes drew in his breath. Here was a

woman of beauty. Judith looked at Holofernes. Then she lowered her eyes and answered in a deep, enticing voice, "Long life to your master, Nebuchadnezzar, the lord of the world! Long life to you! Everyone knows that you are a genius. There is no one in the world as brave, cunning, or skilled in battle as you. But my lord and master, the words that Achior spoke to you are true. Our people cannot be defeated if we live according to God's laws.

"I have come to you because my people have little food or water and are about to break God's laws by eating the first fruits of the harvest rather than offering them to God. I am a pious woman. I fled because I do not want to be in Bethulia to see my people go against God's teachings. I beg you, let me stay in your camp and pray to God every night, and when God tells me that they have broken the law, I will guide you and your army on secret paths to Jerusalem, where you will be crowned king."

"Woman, you are beautiful. You are eloquent. And if you do as you promise, you will sit next to me on the throne. Now come and eat at my table."

Judith smiled at him with appreciation. "My lord and master," she spoke humbly. "I have brought my own food. I wish only to stay in the camp and then go and pray in the valley at night."

"What if your provisions run out? How would we get more?"

"May your soul live. Surely the Lord will let me accomplish his plan before my provisions are no longer needed."

Holofernes had never met such a woman. Eloquent, humble, beautiful, alluring; she was his equal. She was meant to be a queen. He closed his eyes and imagined her without clothes. Then he assigned her a tent and gave permission for her to pray where and when she wished.

For three nights, at midnight, Judith awoke and walked with her servant, Ora, through the Assyrian camp. She washed in the springs and prayed to God to guide her. On the fourth day, Holofernes said to his servant Bagoas, "I have waited long enough. If we let such a woman go without seducing her, everyone will laugh at us. Tonight we will have a banquet for my attendants. Persuade the Hebrew woman to accept our hospitality."

Bagoas went to Judith and said, "Tonight my master wishes you to come to his tent to drink wine and take pleasure like an Assyrian daughter in the palace of Nebuchadnezzar."

Judith answered, "Who am I to resist my Lord? I hasten to serve my Lord. Tell him it will be my greatest joy until my dying day."

Judith anointed herself with spiced perfumes. She put on sparkling jewelry and her most beautiful dress. Ora went first and set down the fleeces in Holofernes' tent. Then Judith entered and reclined on the fleeces in such a way that Holofernes was beside himself with desire.

"Eat! Drink! Enjoy yourself fully!" he cried.

"Oh yes, yes, my Lord, I am delighted to do so, for since the day I was born, I have never felt more worthy than this evening in your presence."

Judith ate and drank what her servant had prepared for her. She toasted Holofernes. She flattered him. Holofernes was in ecstasy.

"More! More!" he urged her.

Judith continued to praise his greatness, his goodness, his genius. He reached out to stroke her and she praised him. She poured wine for him and brought the wine to his lips. Her perfume, her voice, her body surrounded him. He had never been so satisfied in his life. The hour was late. The attendants withdrew to their own tents. Judith said to her servant, "Wait outside the tent. At midnight we will go together to the valley to pray." Bagoas left Holofernes' tent and closed it from the outside.

Judith was alone with Holofernes. He was drunk, lying on his back, sprawled across his bed. She looked at his gleaming sword hanging from the bedpost and listened to his steady breathing. Then she prayed, "Adonai, give me strength to do what must be done." Slowly, she walked across to the bedpost and pulled the sword from its scabbard. With her other hand, she grabbed his hair. Strength flowed through her.

She struck his neck—once, twice! The head fell off. She ripped the silk canopy from the bedpost and wrapped it around Holofernes' head. It was still warm. Ora was waiting outside. Swiftly, she lifted the embroidered flap. Ora took the bundle and thrust it into their food sack.

With quiet dignity, the two women walked through the camp as they had done every evening. They bypassed the valley and quickly climbed the mountain to Bethulia. From a long way off, Judith shouted, "Open the gates. Open the gates!"

"It's Judith!" the sentries shouted as they pushed the gates open. People came running. No one had expected to see her alive. They kindled a fire and eagerly crowded around the two women. Judith pulled the head from the sack, held it up, and said, "Praise God. This is the head of Holofernes, commander of the Assyrian army! Praise God who protected me every moment!"

The people fell to the ground in amazement. Judith looked about her and said, "Put the head on the battlements. When morning comes, appoint leaders and let every man march down to the plains. When the Assyrians see the head, they will flee in panic. Chase them and slaughter them as they retreat. But before you go to your posts, where is Achior? Bring him so he can identify Holofernes."

The Ammonite general looked at Holofernes' head, cried out, "Adonai!" and fainted. When he revived, he fell at Judith's feet and said, "The elders told me there was a woman in Bethulia who was wise and full of faith, but they did not tell me of your courage. In every tent in Judea people will be blessing you. In every nation, people will speak your name with awe. Tell us what happened from the moment you left the gates."

As Judith told the people about her journey, they accompanied her every word, shouting with joy. When Achior realized he was shouting loudest of all and praying in Hebrew, he cried out, "Adonai, let me too serve you as an Israelite." Judith heard him and said, "Achior, your name means 'brother of light.' You brought us light and blessed us by telling our story and reminding us of the source of our strength. We welcome you." Achior was circumcised that night and converted.

The next day at dawn Bagoas called to Holofernes, and there was no answer. He called again. Again, there was no answer. Slowly, he opened the curtain of Holofernes' tent. When he saw Holofernes' body thrown on the ground without his head, he gave a great shout. He tore his clothes. He wept. Then he ran to the tent where Judith had been staying. When he did not find her, he rushed back to the generals and cried, "One! One Hebrew woman defeated the house of Neb-uchadnezzar! Holofernes is lying dead on the ground *without* his head!"

The Assyrian commanders shouted so loudly that fear and trembling fell on every Assyrian soldier. One hundred and seventy thousand soldiers fled by whatever path they could find. The Israelites pursued them, slaughtering them and taking the booty from their camp. There was so much booty that the people looted the camp for thirty days. To Judith they gave Holofernes' embroidered tent, his silver, his drinking bowls, and all his furniture. The high priest in Jerusalem, accompanied by the elders, went to Bethulia to praise Judith, for she had not given up hope that God would protect Judea.

From all over Judea, women, young and old, alone and in groups, made their way to Bethulia. They wanted to meet the woman who had done what no soldier had dared to do. They wanted to meet the woman who had done what no priest could imagine. They wanted to thank her, to praise her, to rejoice with her, to dance for her. To honor the dancing women, Judith made wands of vine leaves and gave one to each woman.

Judith and the women wore wreaths of olive leaves. Judith took her place at the head of the procession and led the women as they danced. Armed and garlanded, the men followed them, singing songs of praise. These are the words that Judith and her people sang:

> *Praise the Lord with song.*
> *Praise the Lord with cymbals.*
> *Praise the Lord with tambourines.*
>
> *The Assyrian came out of the north*
> *with his armies and multitudes.*
> *He said he would burn my land.*
> *He said he would kill my people.*
> *He said he would carry off my virgins.*
> *No champion could topple him.*
> *No giant could destroy him.*

Judith

The Lord stopped him
with the hand of a woman.
Judith disarmed him with words,
soft clothes, and perfume.
Her sandal ravished his eye.
Her beauty captured his soul.
Her sword cut through his neck.

My Lord, you speak and the world comes into being.
You give your breath and the world is formed.
You toss the mountains from their foundations
to mingle with the waves.
You melt rocks like wax,
but to those who fear you,
you are merciful.
A person may offer a sweet-smelling sacrifice,
but those who truly fear you live forever.

Sing to the Lord a new song.
Praise the Lord with song.
Praise the Lord with cymbals.
Praise the Lord with tambourines.

Judith and the people of Bethulia filled their wagons with treasures and went to Jerusalem. Everything that had belonged to Holofernes, Judith offered to God. They stayed in Jerusalem for three months rejoicing. Then Judith returned to Bethulia. She rewarded Ora and gave her her freedom. She continued to spend part of each day in her tent. At the festivals, men and women visited her, sought her advice, and celebrated with her.

Before her death, Judith distributed her property among her relatives. Her fame continued to spread, and when she died at the age of one hundred and five, all of Israel mourned for seven days. For many years, no nation dared to attack Judea because of the name of Judith.

The Maccabees

A Time of Unspeakable Horror

When Mattathias Maccabee stood up before a Greek altar in the small village of Modi'in in Israel (166 B.C.E.) and said, "I refuse to live if I cannot live in a holy way," Israel was a vassal state of the Syrian Greek (Seleucid) empire and ninety percent of the Jews living in Israel had abandoned their faith. Many had assimilated because of the allure of the Greek culture (Greek had almost completely supplanted Hebrew as the common language). Others had adopted Greek customs in fear of the Seleucid emperor's decree that anyone found practicing Jewish customs would be killed. Spiritual practice could no longer be separated from politics.

The Maccabees is a challenging story. Courage, faith, and bloodshed! It poses the question for which there is no easy answer: When—if ever—is war justified? In retelling the story, I've used modern history texts, the Talmud, and Maccabees I and II.

For centuries, Jews traveled to the Temple in Jerusalem to be in God's presence. Three times a year, on the festivals of Passover, Shavuot, and Sukkot, they came from as far away as Egypt and Babylon to worship and pray and give offerings of grain, fruit, and animals. Outside the Temple before two thirty-foot-high altars, priests blew trumpets and offered animal sacrifices morning and afternoon.

The Temple could be seen at a great distance, for its outer walls shone with gold plates. Before entering the Temple, people washed and purified themselves in the tiny cubicles that were dug into the surrounding hillside. Inside the Temple, there were three rooms. The first was a large light-filled room whose sweet-smelling cedar walls were etched with carved palm trees, cherubim, and flowers. In the second, smaller room, the Temple priests performed the daily service. Twice a day they lit the oil in the menorah and the incense on the altar. They offered baked bread and poured libations into the gold cups and bowls.

No one was allowed to enter the third room, which was dark and windowless. It was called the holy of holies. Inside this room, were two fifteen-foot-high cherubim. Under their wings rested the ark of the covenant, containing the teachings God had given the people on Mount Sinai. It was a place of silence, calm and peace, and it was said that the Shechinah, God's presence on earth, dwelt in this room on the wings of the cherubim.

Once a year at Yom Kippur when the Jews crowded into the Temple, the high priest entered the holy of holies to ask the Shechinah to accept the people's offerings and to forgive them. The forgiveness and well-being of the people, the land, and the animals depended on the purity of the high priest at the moment that he entered the holy of holies. The people trusted the high priest who, for centuries, had been a descendant of Moses' brother, Aaron, or had been chosen by God. But the people's faith in the high priest ended at the time of the Greeks.

After Alexander the Great conquered the Near East in 333 B.C.E., Greek became the spoken language. Many Jews became scribes who interpreted their customs and beliefs for the Greeks. Attracted by the allure of Greek culture—its science, arts, and theater—they chose to be educated at Greek gymnasiums, where they studied philosophy and competed naked in sports. When they attended Greek theater and public events, or frequented Greek homes, they sacrificed and prayed to Greek gods. The beauty of Greek culture and its philosophic questioning stirred their minds, and their hearts turned away from the Shechinah. The many laws of the Torah began to seem like cumbersome, irrational cultic practices.

At this time in 168 B.C.E. in Jerusalem, a wealthy Jew, with the Greek name Menelaus, sent a secret message to the Syrian-Greek emperor, Antiochus IV. In his message, he insinuated that the high priest of Jerusalem was about to make a secret treaty with Antiochus' enemy—Egypt. Immediately, Antiochus replaced the high priest with Menelaus' brother, who set up a gymnasium inside the Temple where Jews were allowed to compete naked. In an effort to remake Judaism in a Greek mode, the high priest changed his name from Joshua to Jason and encouraged Jews to shave their beards and not to concern themselves with keeping the Sabbath or studying Torah.

Menelaus followed his brother as high priest and reformed Judaism even more by moving the dwelling place of the Shechinah, from next to the covenant in the holy of holies to outside the Temple. He set a large stone on the outer altar under the open skies, and said, "This is called the Most High." He proclaimed the stone to be the God of the Jews.

The traditional Jews were horrified. Many left Jerusalem for Egypt or moved into the hills so they could continue to live according to the laws of the covenant. Then rumors arrived that Antiochus had been killed fighting in Egypt. The traditional Jews still living in Jerusalem rejoiced and destroyed his statues. But the rumors proved false. Antiochus was alive, and when he heard that the city of Jerusalem had destroyed his statues as well as every statue of the Greek gods, he turned toward Jerusalem intent on wiping out the cult that had dared to oppose him.

Antiochus entered the Temple and took its sacred objects—the gold altar, menorah, table, cups, and bowls. He tore down the embroidered veil that separated the second room from the holy of holies and paraded the embracing cherubim in the streets. He looted the Temple's treasury to pay his troops. He ordered his army to murder those who had destroyed his statues. After his soldiers had murdered forty thousand Jews, he returned to Antioch assured he had forced the Jews to conform to Greek culture. But on the contrary, the Hellenized Jews whose relatives had been murdered lost their sympathy for Greek ways and the traditional Jews became even more observant.

When Antiochus heard that the Jews were continuing their practices, he sent his general Apollonius to Jerusalem. On the twenty-fifth day of the tenth month of the year, Appolonius' troops placed a large statue of Zeus on the high altar outside the Temple. They sacrificed a pig and sprinkled its blood throughout the Temple. They dedicated the Temple as a Greek temple, and prostitutes and soldiers reveled throughout its rooms. Jews were forbidden to celebrate the Sabbath and the new moon, to study Torah, to circumcise their sons, or to eat food different from the Greeks. More Jews fled to Egypt or hid in the hill country.

It was a time of unspeakable horror. Pro-Greek Jews turned against their own relatives and reported them to Antiochus' soldiers who patrolled the streets of Jerusalem. Respected Jews who refused to renounce their God and eat pork were publicly tortured. Mothers with circumcised sons were thrown from the cliffs with their infants clinging to their necks. Jews found studying Jewish texts were tortured and murdered. A woman named Hannah was forced to watch as each of her seven sons was slain for refusing to bow to a Greek statue. Outside of Jerusalem, in every town and village in Judea, altars were built to Greek gods. Ninety percent of the Jews converted.

In Modi'in, a small village in the mountains, a Greek officer assembled the Jews before an altar to Zeus. He called on Mattathias, a village elder, to renounce his faith. Mattathias had left Jerusalem with his wife and five sons when Menelaus had been appointed high priest. The Greek officer said to him, "You are respected by everyone in this village. Come forward. Sacrifice and eat the pig. Then take your place among the emperor's friends and you will be rewarded with gold and silver."

Mattathias walked to the altar and spoke loudly. "The other nations may have forgotten their right to worship their ancestors. My sons and I have not forgotten our God. We will not break our covenant. We do not live in Jerusalem, but we pray every day to our God." As he spoke, another Jew fearing for his life ran to the altar, crying, "Prayers? What do prayers accomplish when anyone who protests is killed? Who cares what we eat or who we worship as long as we survive? Give me the sword. I'll sacrifice the pig!"

Mattathias froze. More important to him than his own life was his love for God and his wish to keep God's laws. He lifted his sword and cried, "I do not want to survive if my family and I cannot live in a holy way." He struck the Jew who had rushed to the altar and then killed the Greek officer. Immediately, his sons leapt to his defense and killed the other officers.

"Anyone who wishes to keep God's covenant, come with me!" Mattathias shouted, and he and his sons fled to the hill country, taking food and the dead soldiers' uniforms and weapons. The Hellenized Jews were horrified that Mattathias had killed a fellow Jew, but other devout Jews who had gone into hiding joined him and his sons. When Antiochus' soldiers realized that the Jews wouldn't fight on the Sabbath, they slaughtered hundreds of Jews until Mattathias claimed a larger interpretation of the law and determined that although Jews could not attack on the Sabbath they could protect their lives and defend themselves from being slaughtered.

In their first year, Mattathias and his sons trained new recruits and harassed the Greek soldiers. At the end of the year, Mattathias knew he was dying and named his son Judah his successor. The family took on Judah's nickname, Maccabee, meaning "hammer." Mattathias urged Judah to remember to pray every day and to ask for guidance in following the laws of the covenant.

The loss of his father intensified Judah's devotion. Believing that their people could be saved only if all the Jews in Judea followed God's commandments, the Maccabees made surprise attacks on isolated villages. They tore down Greek altars. They circumcised Jewish infants. They forced circumcision on adult Jews. They killed those who refused. A civil war began among the Jews. Frightened Hellenized Jews turned to Antiochus for help.

Antiochus ordered Apollonius to return to Jerusalem and wipe out the Maccabees. A solid force of twelve thousand marching soldiers moved into Judea. Judah chose a narrow pass for a battleground. As the Greeks emerged two by two from the narrow mountain pass at Beth

Horon, the Maccabees were waiting and attacked with slingshots and farming implements. The mercenary army fled. Antiochus sent a second force of twenty-four thousand men. Again, Judah's army defeated them by surprising them at a narrow pass.

Antiochus realized that there was a major rebellion in Judea. He opened his treasury and offered his soldiers a year's pay to wipe out the Maccabees and settle foreigners in their land. Three Seleucid generals set out for Judea. Forty thousand professional soldiers camped on the open plain of Emmaus, fifteen miles from Jerusalem. Before the battle began, Nicanor, one of the generals, invited slave traders to bid for Jewish soldiers. A deal was made: ninety Jewish soldiers for one silver talent.

Vastly outnumbered, Judah remembered his father's advice. He prayed to the Shechinah and then assembled the men. Respecting the laws of the covenant, he said to them: "Is there anyone who has recently built a new house and not dedicated it? He must go home, for he may die in battle and another man will dedicate his house. Is there anyone who has planted a vineyard and not harvested it? He must go home, for another person may eat his harvest. Is there any man who is engaged but has not consummated the marriage? He must go home, for another man may take his bride. Is there any man who is afraid to fight? He must return home or he will make others fearful as well."

Many went home. At dawn, when those remaining saw the size of Antiochus' army, they pleaded with Judah to retreat. "We are outnumbered eight to one. Let us flee or we will all perish!"

Judah said to them, "How was it that our ancestors were saved at the Reed Sea? Victory does not depend on numbers but on strength from heaven." The Maccabees prayed. Then they blew trumpets, burst into battle song and attacked with such furor that, to their own surprise, they broke the ranks of the mercenary army, and the slave traders returned to their homes empty-handed.

The commander-in-chief of the Seleucid army, Lysias, set out with an army of sixty thousand soldiers. His plan was to attack Jerusalem from the south, from Beth Zur, because the tribes who lived there were enemies of the Jews. Judah knew he had no chance of defeating sixty thousand soldiers. Prayer was his only recourse. He fell to his knees and prayed to God, "You halted the charge of the great giant Goliath. We are as small as your shepherd David. We depend only on you. Make our enemy fearful. Give us courage so we can live according to your laws and honor your name!"

As Lysias' men moved in columns up the hill to Jerusalem, the Maccabees leapt out of the trees and gullies, shrieking and blowing trumpets. Their wild battle cries sent the advance units crashing back into one another. When Lysias saw that the Maccabees would rather die than surrender, he hesitated. In his moment of hesitation, he was summoned back to Antioch. The treasury was empty.

Judah knew that Antiochus would send another army, yet he sent his troops to fight the soldiers stationed in Jerusalem and to take the Temple back from Menelaus. As fearsome as the advancing Seleucid army had been, the Maccabees had always gone forward, but when they arrived at the Temple, they stopped.

The golden Temple was in ruins. The gates were burned. The once fragrant cedarwood walls were covered with blood. The priests were gone. The treasures were gone. Weeds grew in the holy of holies. The soldiers tore their clothes. They fell to the ground. They buried their faces in the earth and put dirt over their heads and wept.

Then someone blew a triumphant blast on the trumpet. Suddenly they realized that the Temple was theirs again. Everyone wanted to offer a thanksgiving sacrifice. But the Temple and the altar had been defiled, and before offering a sacrifice, they had to restore and purify the Temple. They made new vessels, a new altar, and a table for the twelve loaves of baked bread. They crafted a seven-branched menorah. They made an altar for incense and a veil to protect the holy of holies. But they could not find any oil to burn in the menorah, for the Greeks had used all the containers of oil. They searched the Temple and its grounds until they found one sealed flask with just enough oil to last one night. It would take eight days to make new oil.

The next day was the twenty-fifth day of the tenth month of the year. Once again, the burnt offering was sacrificed and the service began. Sweet incense filled the air. The priest lit the lamps, offered bread, and poured wine. The people sang. They waved palm branches, fell to the ground, and prayed, for the Temple had been purified and Shechinah could return.

The next morning, the priest discovered that the oil was still burning in the menorah. It burned not for one night or two or seven, but for eight nights. The people came to the Temple to celebrate. Once again, they could keep the laws of the covenant. Judah and his brothers and the people said, "Every year, let us celebrate the rededication of the Temple with rejoicing and thanksgiving." In time, the celebration was called Hanukkah, meaning "dedication."

The soldiers ornamented the front of the Temple with golden shields and made doors for the gates and storehouses. They went to the towers and built high walls surrounding Jerusalem to fortify the city. They waited for the return of Antiochus' army.

The Maccabees kept control of the Temple for only a short time before the Seleucids once again defeated the Jews. Decades later, the descendants of the Maccabees, the Hasmoneans, regained control over Jerusalem. Soon after this, they became Hellenized and oppressed their own people.

In 70 C.E., the Romans destroyed the Temple. Only one of its walls, the Western Wall, stands in Jerusalem. Since that time, there continue to be many different communities of Jews, from those who honor each of the Torah's laws to those who never enter a synagogue. Yet, every year in the dark of winter, Jews from almost all communities celebrate Hanukkah. They place a menorah in the windows of their homes. They recite prayers. They sing and light candles. The golden light of the candles recalls the golden Temple where priests once lit the menorah in the room next to the holy of holies. Today, it is our prayers, songs, and candlelight that summon the presence of the Shechinah.

Joseph

The Meaning of Dreams Is with God

Joseph might despair because he has been sold into slavery by his brothers and banished from his land (1450 B.C.E.). But when he has the opportunity, Joseph does not return betrayal with violence. Where does Joseph's inner strength lie? Where does our inner strength lie? How do we find alternative solutions to violence and betrayal? These are questions that we all ask.

During December, a time for turning inward and for dreaming, a portion of Joseph is read on each Sabbath, including the Hanukkah Sabbath. I've retold the biblical text interweaving oral legends.

At seventeen, Joseph went to tend sheep with his older brothers. After several months, he returned to his father, Jacob, and told stories against his brothers. Jacob did not reprimand him, for he loved Joseph. Joseph was the son of his favorite wife, Rachel, who had died near Ephrath, giving birth to their second son, Benjamin. Jacob mourned for Rachel and placed a pillar on her grave. Every time he looked at Joseph, he saw Rachel and his heart softened. Jacob spent many hours with Joseph, giving over to him the teachings he had received from Shem and Shem's great-grandson Eber.

He made Joseph a coat that had many colors. It was of fine linen and strong, yet so delicate it could be held in one fist. When his older brothers saw how much time Jacob spent with Joseph and the coat of many colors that he made for him, they hated Joseph and could not speak peacefully to him.

Then Joseph dreamed a dream and he told his dream to his brothers, "We were all in the fields binding sheaves. My sheaf arose and stood upright. Your sheaves bowed down to mine." The brothers looked at Joseph with his painted eyes and carefully groomed hair and asked, "Shall *you* rule over us?" And they hated him even more.

Joseph dreamed another dream and said to his brothers, "Listen to this dream I have dreamed. The sun, the moon, the eleven stars came down from heaven and bowed to me." His father rebuked him, saying, "What is this dream you have dreamed? Shall I and your mother and your eleven brothers bow to you?" Yet he wrote down Joseph's dream and the time and place he had dreamed it. Soon after this, Joseph's brothers left home and went to pasture their sheep in Shechem.

"Joseph," Jacob called.

"*Hineni!* Here I am, Father," Joseph answered.

"Go and send me word of your brothers and the flocks."

Joseph set out from Hebron. On the way, he met a man who asked him, "What are you looking for?"

Joseph answered, "I am looking for my brothers."

"They have moved their flocks to Dothan," the man said.

When his brothers saw him coming, wearing the brightly colored cloak, Simeon, the second oldest, said, "Here comes the master dreamer. What new dream does he bring us? Let's kill him and say a wild beast devoured him. Then we will see what becomes of his dreams."

Reuben the oldest said, "No, do not kill him. Let's throw him into one of the dry pits our father dug to find water." When Joseph came closer, they seized him, took off his cloak, and threw him into the nearest pit.

"Brothers!" Joseph cried in terror. "What have I done? There are snakes and scorpions in here! Whatever I have done, forgive me. I meant no harm. Answer me! Brothers!"

Not wanting to listen to Joseph's cries, the brothers left the pit and went and sat at a distance. As they were eating, they saw a caravan of Midianite traders with camels carrying perfume and myrrh to Egypt. Judah said, "Let's sell our brother and not have his blood on our hands."

The traders saw birds circling one of the pits. They looked into the pit and saw an incredibly handsome young man shouting for help. They drew him out and started to leave when the brothers ran toward them, shouting, "Where are you going with our slave? He was disobedient and we threw him into the pit."

The merchants drew their swords and said, "Your slave! He's more handsome than any of you. Maybe you're his slaves?"

"YAH!" Judah bared his sword and let out such a horrific cry that the merchants moved back.

"No need to quarrel," they said. "If your slave was rebellious, sell him to us. We will give you twenty pieces of silver."

With the silver, Joseph's brothers bought shoes to show their dominion over the dreamer. Then they killed a small goat, dipped Joseph's cloak in the blood, and brought the coat to their father. "We—we found this," they said. "We do not know if it's your son's coat or not."

Jacob brought the coat to his face. "It is my son's coat. Torn!" he howled. "A wild beast devoured my son. Torn—torn—Joseph is torn to pieces!" Jacob tore his clothes, put on sackcloth, and wept. His children could not comfort him. He said, "I will go down to my grave, grieving for my son."

As the Midianites came to Ephrath where Joseph's mother Rachel was buried, he broke away from the traders and ran to his mother's tomb, crying, "Oh Mother, wake up! Your son has been sold into slavery. We are leaving Canaan. Awake, Father is grieving. Awake, Mother, awake and comfort him."

Joseph fell on the grave, weeping. Then he heard a voice heavy with tears speak to him from the depths. "My son, I hear your groans. I see your grief. Go down to Egypt. Do not be afraid. God is with you." The Midianites pulled him from the grave and sold him in Egypt to Pharaoh's officer, Potiphar, for four hundred pieces of silver.

After Joseph crossed into Egypt, his brother Judah married Ali-yath, a Canaanite woman. They had three sons. When the oldest, Er, was of age, Judah married him to Tamar, a descendant of Shem. Er died and Judah's second son, Onan, married Tamar, but when he too died, Judah said to Tamar, "Stay a widow in your father's house until my youngest son, Shelah, is of age." But Judah was afraid that if Shelah married Tamar he too would die, so he refused to send him.

Then Judah's wife died. After a period of grieving, he set out for Timnah for the sheep shearing. When Tamar heard that her father-in-law was coming up to Timnah, she took off her widow's clothes and sat by the entrance to Twin Wells. Judah saw her and thought she was a cult prostitute, for she had covered her face. He said to her, "Let me come into you."

"What will you give me as payment?" she asked.

"I will send you a goat from my flock."

"Leave me a pledge of your seal and staff until you send the goat," Tamar insisted.

Judah gave her what she asked. He went into her, and she conceived. Then, she took off her veil and put on her widow's clothes.

Judah sent a friend to her with a goat so he could redeem his seal and staff, but the man could not find any cult prostitute near Twin Wells. Three months later, Judah was told, "Your daughter-in-law, Tamar, is pregnant. She has played the harlot."

Outraged, Judah said, "Let her be burned." But as she was being taken to her father-in-law, she gave a seal and staff to Judah's messengers and said, "The father of my child owns this seal and staff. Ask Judah if he recognizes them."

Judah examined the seal and staff. They were his. He closed his eyes, remembering. Then he said, "She is right, more right than I. I did not keep my promise. I did not send her my youngest son."

Tamar was pregnant with twins. As she was giving birth, one of them put out a hand, and the midwife tied a crimson thread to the hand. But when he withdrew his hand and the other twin burst out first, she said, "What a breach you have made," and she called him

Perez, meaning "he bursts forth." Then the second son, who had the crimson thread on his hand, came out, and she called him Zerah, meaning "shining."

Joseph did not know that his brother Judah had suffered, losing his wife and sons. Joseph was alive in Egypt, and God was with him. Whatever he did for his new master, Potiphar, went well. When Potiphar saw Joseph's abilities, he gave him his keys and made him steward of his household. He gave him training in the arts, and Joseph painted his eyes, curled his hair, and began to walk in a mincing fashion like the other Egyptians.

From the moment he came to her house, Potiphar's wife, Zuleika, was drawn to Joseph. At first, she touched him and caressed him as if he were her son. But then her passion grew wilder and she whispered in his ear, "Sleep with me."

Joseph refused.

Day after day she asked him until he said. "How can you suggest such a thing? My master has not withheld anything from me except you, his wife. Would you ask me to harm him and go against God's teachings?"

Zuleika was blind with passion. She waited until the household went to celebrate the overflowing of the Nile. She pretended she was ill and then when everyone was gone, she got out of bed and dressed herself in gold robes, put on perfume, and scattered blossoms on the floor. As Joseph passed on his way to work, she grabbed his cloak, and implored him, "Sleep with me."

In terror, Joseph pulled away from her and fled. But the front part of his cloak remained in her hand, and that evening the scorned Zuleika said to her husband, "Your Hebrew slave tried to grab me, but I screamed. I screamed until he ran away. This is his cloak."

Joseph was whipped and put into a dungeon with Pharaoh's prisoners. Even then God was with Joseph, and the prison keeper made him overseer of the other prisoners.

Ten years passed. One morning, Joseph was bringing water for two prisoners, Pharaoh's butler and baker, who had been accused of trying to kill their master. Joseph noticed how sad their faces were and asked them, "What is troubling you?"

"We have dreamed dreams," they answered, "and there is no one to tell us the meaning of our dreams."

Joseph said, "The meaning of dreams is with God, but tell me your dreams and I will try to help you."

The butler said, "In my dream, I saw a vine with three branches. The branches budded, blossomed, and grapes appeared. I pressed the grapes into a cup and gave Pharaoh a cup of wine."

"The three branches are three days," Joseph said. "In three days Pharaoh will free you and you will place Pharaoh's cup in his hand again. But when all is well with you, remember me, and tell Pharaoh that there is a slave in prison who was kidnapped from the land of Canaan, and here also he has done no wrong."

When the baker heard this, he said, "Listen to my dream. In my dream, I was carrying three baskets on my head. In the top basket were pastries for Pharaoh. Birds were eating the pastries from the basket."

Joseph said, "The three baskets are three days. In three days Pharaoh will lift your head from your body, and birds will come and eat your flesh."

It happened that three days later, on his birthday, Pharaoh gave a banquet for his courtiers, and he freed the butler and hanged the baker. But the chief butler, restored to his place, forgot Joseph.

Two years later, Pharaoh dreamed dreams that troubled his spirit. In the morning, he called for the magicians and wise men of Egypt and told them his dreams, but no one could interpret them. Then the butler said, "I am at fault. When I was in prison with the baker, we dreamed dreams and were troubled. A young Hebrew, the slave of Potiphar, interpreted our dreams, and as he interpreted them, so it was."

Pharaoh sent at once for Joseph, who was rushed from the prison. He shaved, changed his clothes, and entered the great hall. He was amazed by what he saw. Pharaoh sat on a high golden throne, dressed in shining gold robes, wearing a crown of many precious stones.

Joseph bowed, and Pharaoh descended from his throne and said to him, "My servant tells me that you are a discerning person. When you hear a dream, you can tell its meaning. Speak to me as you did to my butler—without flattery or fear. Explain my dream."

"But it is not in me," Joseph protested. "It is God who will protect Pharaoh."

Pharaoh said, "In my dream, I was standing on the bank of the river. Out of the Nile walked seven fat, plump cows, and they ate grass. Then seven lean, hungry cows came out of the river and ate the seven fat cows, but after eating they were as hungry as before. I awoke with a start. I fell asleep and dreamed again. In my dream, I saw seven full ears of grain on one stalk. Then seven withered ears, scorched by the east wind, sprung up on the same stalk and devoured the seven fat ears. My magicians interpreted the cows and the grain as cities, women, sons."

Joseph said to Pharaoh, "The two dreams are one. They are repeated, for this is God's way of announcing to you what God intends. The seven fat cows and the seven full ears of grain are seven good years of harvest. The seven lean cows and seven thin ears are seven years of famine that will swallow up the abundance of the land. That Pharaoh has dreamt the same dream twice means it will happen soon. Let Pharaoh find a man, discerning and wise, to travel the land and gather and store the grain in the good years so that there will be food during the years of famine and the people will not starve."

Pharaoh turned to his courtiers and said, "Where can we find such a man who carries the spirit of God?" Then he said to Joseph, "Since God has shown you all this and there is no one as discerning and wise as you, I will make you governor. You will rule Egypt and provide for the people and only by my throne will I be higher than you." He gave Joseph his ring and breastplate and dressed him in fine, linen clothes. Together they rode in Pharaoh's chariot, and Pharaoh called Joseph Zaphenath-paneah, meaning "revealer of secrets."

At thirty Joseph became governor of Egypt. That year the high priest, Potiphera, invited him to his house and said to his daughter Asenath, "There is a man for you to meet." Asenath understood what her father intended and said, "I will not marry a Hebrew slave." But when Joseph entered their palace, tears came into her eyes. She had never seen a man whose entire being shone with light. She went to greet him and said, "May the high God of Egypt bless you."

Joseph answered, "May El Shaddai from whom all blessings come bless you."

Asenath did not know this god, but she could not take her eyes from Joseph. She watched him at dinner. She listened to him speak, and that night she took off her clothes and put on sackcloth. She prayed that she would know Joseph's god. For seven days and nights, she remained in her room. On the eighth day, an angel appeared to her and said, "Put away your sackcloth and ashes. Dress yourself in your royal robes. You will marry Joseph and be his wife for all time. Your new name is City of Refuge." As soon as the angel left, it was announced that Joseph had arrived. Asenath washed and went to greet him. Not recognizing her, for she had become radiantly beautiful, he asked her name.

"I am Asenath, your servant. A messenger told me today that my new name is City of Refuge and that I am to marry you and to ask if a messenger also spoke with you."

Joseph's eyes filled with tears, "El Shaddai has blessed us both. I set out from my palace this morning intending to go see Pharaoh but when an angel told me I would find refuge today, without considering my direction, I drove to your father's house!"

Pharaoh had a magnificent palace built for them. Joseph sat in its great hall on a golden throne, inlaid with gold, silver, and precious stones that represented the land of Egypt.

In the years of abundance, he traveled throughout the land and gathered so much grain that it could not be counted. Then he stored it in grain houses in the cities. During this time, Asenath bore Joseph two sons. He named the first son Manasseh, meaning "God has made me forget the suffering of my father's house." The second son he named Ephraim, meaning "God has made me fruitful in the land of my affliction."

At the end of seven years, the famine began in all the lands, and it was severe. When the people cried to Pharaoh for bread, he replied,

"Go to Joseph. Do what he tells you." Joseph opened the storehouses and sold grain.

In Canaan, when Jacob heard that there was grain in Egypt, he said to his sons, "Why are you looking at each other? Go to Egypt and buy grain so we do not die. I will keep Benjamin with me so no harm comes to him."

The ten brothers entered the great palace of the governor of Egypt and bowed their faces to the ground. They did not recognize Joseph because of the grandeur of the palace and his beard and clothes and Egyptian speech. Joseph recognized his brothers at once, and at the same moment he remembered his dream. But he acted like a stranger and disguised his voice and spoke to the translator who said, "From where do you come?"

They answered, "We are brothers. We come to buy grain."

"No!" Joseph said, "You are spies! You came to spy on the naked-ness of the land. When men come to buy grain, they go directly to their place of business. For three days, you've been wandering about the city."

Judah said, "We are honest men. We are twelve brothers, sons of the same man. One brother is missing, and the youngest is at home in Canaan with our father, who would not let him leave. We have been searching for the one who is missing. We—"

"You are lying," Joseph interrupted. "Throw them in prison. They will not leave until their youngest brother arrives."

After three days, Joseph released them, saying, "I fear God. Let one brother stay in prison, and the others bring back grain so your family does not starve. Then return with your youngest brother so I know you are speaking the truth."

Not knowing that anyone but the translator could understand them, the brothers spoke among themselves. Judah said, "All this has happened because we heard the anguish of our brother when he called to us and we were silent."

"I warned you not to harm the child," Reuben said. "Now we will pay!" Joseph went out of the room and wept. Then he motioned to one of the guards to seize Simeon, the second oldest, and take him away. He ordered his steward to fill the men's sacks with grain and to restore the silver with which they had paid for the grain.

On their way to Canaan, when they stopped to rest and Simeon's twin brother, Levi, opened his sack to feed his donkey, he saw that it was filled with silver and the brothers were afraid and wondered, "What has God done to us?" Then, when they returned home and told their father about the governor of Egypt and emptied their sacks and found that each one's sack was filled with silver, they all trembled.

Jacob said, "Joseph is no more. Simeon is no more. Now you would take Benjamin. No. I will not let Benjamin go with you. His brother is dead. He alone is left. If I lose him, you will send me to my grave." But after a year, when they had eaten all the grain, and the little ones went to their grandfather and begged for bread, Jacob said to his sons, "Go down to Egypt and buy grain."

Reuben said, "Father, we cannot go without Benjamin. Give me Benjamin, and if I do not bring him back, you may kill my two sons."

"What foolishness you speak," Jacob said. "Are your sons not my sons as well? Why did you tell the man you had another brother?"

Judah answered, "Father, he kept asking about us. Is your father alive? Do you have another brother? Father, give me the youngest so that we and our children can live and not die. I will be a guarantee for Benjamin, and if anything happens to him, I will carry the blame forever."

"If it must be, then go," Jacob said. "Take double the money to pay for the grain in case there has been a mistake. Take gifts to the ruler of Egypt—honey, myrrh, balm, almonds—and do not let Benjamin out of your sight. May El Shaddai soften the heart of the governor of Egypt."

Joseph arrived in court. When he saw Benjamin with the brothers, he said to his servant, "Take these men home and prepare a feast. I will eat with them at noon."

The steward offered the brothers water to wash their feet and fodder for their animals. But the brothers were afraid and said, "When we came last time, we paid for the grain with silver. When we returned home, we found our silver returned to us and we do not know who did this. We have come to bring you back the silver and to buy new grain."

The steward said, "God did it; your own God hid the treasure in your sacks." And he brought them Simeon who was round and fat.

At noon the brothers eagerly presented the governor of Egypt with their gifts and bowed to the ground. Joseph asked them, "Is the old man, your father, well? And is he alive?"

"Yes," they answered. Joseph looked up and saw Benjamin, his mother's son, his own brother, and he asked, "Is this one your youngest brother?"

And before they could answer, Joseph said to him, "May God look on you kindly," and then because his heart was filled with feelings for his brother, he rushed from the room and wept. Tears poured out of his eyes. After a time, Joseph washed himself and calmed himself and returned. He held up his silver goblet and looked into it as if reading from it. Then he seated the brothers according to their ages and sent Benjamin five times the amount of food that everyone else ate.

That evening Joseph said to his steward, "Fill the men's sacks with grain, return their money, and put my silver goblet into the sack of the youngest one."

At dawn the brothers set out with Simeon. When they had gone a short distance, Joseph said to his steward, "Go, ride after them and say, 'Why did you return kindness with ill intent? Why did you take my master's silver goblet that he uses for divining?' "

The steward followed Joseph's orders. He caught up to the men and asked, "Why did you return kindness with ill intent? Why did you take my master's silver goblet that he uses for divining?"

"But why would we do such a thing?" the brothers answered. "We brought back the silver we found in our sacks. If any of us took your master's goblet, let him die, and we will all become your master's slaves!" Each of them eagerly opened his sack and the steward inspected each sack, starting with Reuben, the oldest. When he came to the sack of the youngest—Benjamin—he found the governor of Egypt's silver goblet.

"Return to Canaan," the steward said to the brothers, "I will take the youngest back to Egypt."

"No!" the brothers said with one voice. "We will not leave Benjamin." Then they tore their clothes in grief and wept, and every one of the brothers reloaded their donkeys and returned to the city. As they walked, they berated Benjamin, accusing him. "Your mother Rachel stole her father's gods. Why did you do the same as your mother? Now you've brought shame on all of us!"

When they saw Joseph, all eleven brothers fell to the floor with their faces pressed to the ground. Joseph said to them, "What have you done? Did you imagine that I would not know what you intended?"

Judah said, "What can we answer you? How can we prove our innocence? God has shown you our guilt. We are all your slaves."

"No," Joseph answered, "Only the one in whose sack the cup was found will remain and be my servant. The others may return peacefully to your father."

Judah stepped forward. He said, "My lord, I beg you, open your ear and do not let your anger flame up against me. When we came to you, you asked us who we were, and we said, 'We are twelve brothers, one is missing and the youngest is with our father.' You said, 'Bring me the youngest so I may set my eyes on him,' and we said, 'The boy cannot leave his father or his father will die.' You insisted. We went home and told our father and he said, 'My wife gave me two sons. One went out from me and I said, "Surely, he is torn to pieces," and I have not seen him again. If you take this one from me and he meets with disaster, you will send me to my grave.' My lord, the one you would keep is this one, the youngest."

"The one whose sack held my goblet is the one who will be my servant," Joseph replied.

"You have no mercy," Judah said. "You do not obey the law of the land. According to our law, a thief can pay double the value of what he has stolen. We will pay double the value of the goblet. Our brother is a free man. He must not become a slave."

"You speak well," Joseph said, "But why are you the only one to speak?"

"I gave my pledge to my father for the boy. I promised I would bring him back or be blamed for all time. Our father's life is bound up in the soul of this child. If he does not see the boy, he will die and I will have brought my father to his grave. I beg you, let the boy go with his brothers and I will remain in his place and serve you. I cannot return to my father again without his son and see the grief he would suffer."

Then Joseph could no longer contain himself. He asked everyone in the hall to leave but the eleven brothers. When only the brothers stood before him, he said to them, "Is the brother of Benjamin dead?"

"Yes," they said.

"Did you throw dirt on his corpse?"

"No," they said.

"Joseph is not dead," he said. "Joseph is living. He is alive. You sold him and I bought him. He is here. I will call him now. Joseph! Joseph! Joseph, son of Jacob!"

The brothers looked about the room. They turned in every direction. They saw no one but each other and the governor of Egypt who was staring at them. "Why do you look around you? Do you not know me?" he asked them. Then Joseph spoke in Hebrew and said, *"Ani Yosef.* I am your brother, Joseph."

The brothers could not move. They were terrified. Joseph said, "Come closer. I am Joseph, the brother you sold into slavery. But do not be afraid. God wished it to be this way so that I might preserve life. There will be five more years of famine. Go home and tell my father, 'Your son Joseph is alive. He is the ruler of Egypt and he asks you to come down to Egypt without delay. He will take care of you and your children and your children's children and your flocks and herds and all that you have,' and tell my father of the honor I have. Tell him that the words came from my mouth and you saw me with your own eyes, and return quickly with my father."

Then Joseph came down from his throne and opened his arms and held Benjamin, and they wept. He kissed all his brothers, and they wept. A great cry rose up from the brothers for all that they had held inside for so many years.

The servants who were listening outside the door said, "Joseph's brothers have come." They went to Pharaoh, and Pharaoh said to Joseph, "Invite your father and your brothers to settle here in Egypt. I will give them the fertile land of Goshen."

When the brothers returned to Canaan laden with gifts and food, they worried how their father might react to the news that Joseph was alive. They decided to ask Serach, the daughter of Asher, to go to her grandfather and play the harp and sing for him so his soul might be prepared. With the sweet voice of a child, Serach sang for her grandfather, "My uncle Joseph lives. My uncle Joseph rules Egypt. My uncle Joseph lives."

Then the brothers went to their father and said, "Father, Joseph is alive. He is governor of Egypt." And even though he had already heard this, Jacob's heart went numb. Then, when they told him all that Joseph had said, and he saw the wagons that Joseph had sent, his spirit revived and Jacob said, "Enough. My son is alive. I will go and see him before I die."

Jacob journeyed to Egypt with his wives and children and grandchildren and servants. They were seventy people, and he sent Judah before him to prepare the way. Joyously, Joseph set out in a chariot to meet his father. From a distance, Jacob saw Joseph wearing a golden crown on his head; and at the same moment, Joseph recognized his father and ran to him and held him. The two wept without stopping, for they had not seen one another for twenty-two years. Then Jacob said, "Now I may die, for I have seen your face and you are alive."

Then Joseph said to his father and brothers, "I will go to Pharaoh and tell him that you have come and that you are shepherds and wish to stay in Goshen."

Joseph presented five of his brothers to Pharaoh, who asked them, "What is your occupation?"

"We your servants are shepherds," they answered. "We and our fathers before us. We ask your permission to stay a time in Goshen, for the famine is great in Canaan."

Pharaoh allowed them to stay in Goshen and put the brothers in charge of his livestock. When Joseph brought his father to the palace, Pharaoh asked Jacob, "How many are the years of your life?"

"The years of my wandering are one hundred and thirty years," Jacob answered. "They have been hard and filled with sorrow. In my youth, I fled from the place of my birth because I quarreled with my brother. Now in my old age, I again have been forced to leave the place of my birth. I want to bless you and give you half of the life that remains to me. May the Nile overflow its banks and make the land fertile." With these blessings, Jacob left Pharaoh.

Joseph settled his father and brothers and their families in Goshen and nourished them. But the famine increased, and the Egyptian farmers had to sell their cattle and then their land and then their labor so they could buy grain and live. Joseph bought all the land for Pharaoh.

For seventeen years, Jacob lived in Goshen peacefully. When he knew he would die, he called Joseph to him and said, "Place your hand under my thigh and swear to me that when I die you will bring me out of Egypt and bury me in the field of Machpelah in the cave Abraham bought for Sarah."

Joseph swore. Several days later, Jacob again called Joseph to him and said, "When I was returning from Haran, your mother Rachel died on the road before we reached Bethlehem. Bring me her grandchildren so I may bless them. I never expected to see your face, and God has let me see the face of your children."

Joseph's sons bowed to the ground before Jacob. Then Joseph held his older son Manasseh in his left hand and his younger son Ephraim in his right so his father would bless Manasseh first. Jacob kissed them and then reached out his arms and crossed them, putting his right hand on Ephraim's head and blessing him first.

"No, Father, not so," Joseph said. "Manasseh is the firstborn."

"Yes, my son, yes, I know. But it is Ephraim who will be the greater. I will take your two sons as my sons. God, who has been my shepherd from my birth to this day; my angel, who has redeemed me from harm, bless my children. May my name be known through them." And he blessed Joseph, saying, "God will be with you and take you again to the land of your ancestors." Jacob then gathered together his sons and blessed them and foretold to each of them what was before him.

Jacob put his feet on the bed, and the Shechinah came and kissed Jacob on the lips and took him to heaven. Joseph flung himself on his father and wept and kissed him and closed his eyes. Asenath came, and she and all the women wept. Joseph had his father embalmed, and the people of Egypt wept for Joseph's father for seventy days.

Then Joseph sent word to Pharaoh, saying, "My father bound me with an oath to bury him in the cave of Machpelah in Canaan. Give me permission to go there and I will return." Pharaoh said, "You are bound to the oath you have made to your father. Go." And he sent the nobles and courtiers of Egypt as well as the people to accompany Joseph's father to his burial place.

When they crossed the Jordan, a loud wailing went up for Jacob. For seven days, his sons grieved for him. Kings came from many countries and thirty-six crowns were placed on Jacob's coffin. The twelve brothers buried their father in the cave of Machpelah next to his wife Leah. Then they returned to Egypt.

After this, the brothers were afraid that Joseph would remember the harm they had done to him and hate them. So they sent word to him, saying, "Before our father died, he commanded us to say to you, 'Forgive the transgressions of your brothers and the harm they did to you.' We too beg your forgiveness."

Joseph wept hearing these words. He sent for his brothers. They fell to the ground before him and said, "We are prepared to be your slaves."

"Do not be afraid," Joseph said. "Am I in God's place? What you intended for harm, God intended for good. I will nourish you and sustain you and your children. Only swear to me that when God remembers you and you leave Egypt, you will take my bones and bury them in Canaan." Joseph lived to the age of one hundred and ten. He held his grandchildren and great-grandchildren on his knees. When he died, he was embalmed and put in a coffin.

Many years later, when the children of Jacob left Egypt, they did not forget their promise. They placed Joseph's bones in an ark and carried the ark with them into the wilderness. In the desert, they were given another ark, containing the teachings.

For forty years, the Hebrews wandered in the desert, carrying the two arks. When other tribes who met them asked, "Why do you carry the bones of a dead man side by side with an ark containing the covenant?" they answered, "The man whose bones we carry fulfilled every one of the commandments in the living covenant."

About the Stories

Judith

The army of the great Nebuchadnezzar terrorizes all of the Near East. One by one, each country capitulates. When the invading army surrounds the tiny Judean village of Bethulia for three months and four days, a righteous widow named Judith turns to God for help. Three years and four months before this, her husband had died. Three and four is seven. The number seven is symbolic of completion in the Bible, and Judith's mourning is over. When news of her town's imminent surrender reaches her, she imagines a solution for her people and then, without asking any earthly assistance, acts as God's instrument to bring about their rescue.

Judith doesn't ask permission. She leaves her reclusive sanctuary and takes command. She is beautiful, rich, independent, and she assumes all her powers. She seductively walks into the enemy camp where she could easily be murdered or raped by any of the foot soldiers and carries out her plans with such assurance and pure intention that the enemy continually seeks to help her. She plans and, with the help of one other woman, single-handedly executes a successful military campaign and rescues all of Judea. She stops evil by letting it follow its own inclinations. As Holofernes' servant Bagoas says, "One—*one* woman destroyed the house of Nebuchadnezzar."

The striking aspect of the story is not just that a woman brought about the defeat of an army but that one person, just one, decided that with imagination and the help of God, she would defeat evil, and she did.

At the story's ending, Judith further confirms her purity of intention. The Hebrew soldiers gather the plunder of the Assyrian army for themselves. When the people reward Judith with all the glorious treasures of Holofernes, she brings them to the Temple in Jerusalem—to God who listened to her prayer and guided her in her journey.

Wise, holy, alluring, courageous, compassionate, independent—

Judith can be seen as the mature Shulamith who wore the necklace of the warriors (The Song of Songs). Judith dances the Dance of the Two Armies, embodying the qualities of the Warrior/Love Goddess who liberates her people and brings them stability as well as treasures.

The Maccabees

The story of *The Maccabees* raises many questions, constantly challenging the reader as to who the enemy is. The Hellenized Jews want to be free to choose which god they serve and when. The traditional Jews want to follow their previous ways of worship and to protect Judaism from extinction. The Syrian Greeks want no trouble from their subjects. Who has the right to determine the other's belief system? Is violence justified in the face of extermination? Is violence ever justified?

Unable to negotiate a way to live with the traditional Jews, the Hellenized Jews betray their relatives and steal the authority of the high priest by making a deal with the Seleucid emperor Antiochus. The traditional Jews try to retreat, but there is no retreat, for Antiochus' soldiers insist on complete obedience. Although there is no reasonable chance for survival if he disobeys, Mattathias Maccabee refuses to live in a way that is not true to his beliefs. In the moment that he chooses to risk his life, he binds his inner beliefs to his outer actions.

Mattathias' impulsive, spontaneous stand for liberty is heartfelt. Then comes the grit: He is forced to confront the paradoxical decisions a leader must make. He is forced to decide if he should compromise his principles, acting like the enemy, so that his people can survive. When he gives the leadership to his son, he advises Judah to pray to the Shechinah for guidance. Since the Shechinah dwells close to the Torah, to the place of study where these knotty questions and dilemmas are continually being explored, Mattathias is advising his son to remain humble, flexible, and open to debate and inspiration.

Each situation, each story, each life has its own rules and context. It is my understanding that this story, like the story of Josiah, is rooted in history. People are acting the best they can fathom, but this does not mean they are following the core teachings, which clearly say Do Not Murder. In the face of the extinction of his people, when ninety percent of the Jews had converted, Judah Maccabee became more extreme than his father and attacked those Jews who were not keeping the covenant. Some may say that the dire situation demanded extreme action: A community needed to be saved. Others may point to Judah's descendants, the Hasmoneans, who became as corrupt as the Hellenized Jews they had oppressed.

Whenever violence is committed, a price is paid. In the biblical narratives, those who destroy are destroyed. Those who harm, sooner or later, are harmed. Sarah throws out her husband's concubine and son Ishmael and to this day the tribes of the Ishmaelites (Hagar's descendants) and the Israelites (Sarah's descendants) are at war. Jacob steals his brother Esau's birthright and, centuries later, Jacob's offspring are nearly annihilated by Esau's descendant, Haman. It is not possible to harm others without being harmed oneself.

There is no perfect justice on earth. There is a covenant with the intent to care for others, all others: the stranger, the widow, the orphan, the slave, the impoverished, the land. Every seven years, according to the Torah, debts are to be released so that the debtor may start again. Every seven years, the land is to be left fallow to renew itself. Every seven years, slaves are to be freed with sufficient goods to begin their lives as freed people. The basic intention of the Torah is for the well-being of all the people as well as the land.

In defending his right to study the Torah and live by God's laws, Mattathias defended the right of each person and all groups to worship as they choose. Mattathias brought the question of religious freedom to the front of Western consciousness. We are still dealing with its implications.

Joseph

Mattathias's and Judith's situations are without exit: an army six times their size and an army one hundred times their size corner them. Joseph's story is similarly shocking and overwhelming. His own brothers overpower him, throw him into a pit with poisonous animals, and then sell him. And there is worse: Joseph is stolen from his own land, taken to a foreign country, and then bought by one of Pharaoh's officials.

Just when it seems that Joseph has been rendered powerless, we enter a seemingly unrelated story. With no transition, we follow the life of Joseph's brother Judah, who has everything—three sons, an inheritance, cattle. He exudes power. But then two of Judah's sons and then Judah's wife die, and he offers a cult prostitute his symbols of power so he might be comforted. Suddenly, the lack of transition in the story is made clearer. Both brothers journey from power to vulnerability, from hubris to humility, from arrogance to fear and reverence.

About the Stories

As the two brothers fall from their favored positions of power, we
learn that the lowliest of people—Tamar—a childless widow whose powerful father-in-law, Judah, has ceased to protect her and instead has broken his promises—has made her own plans. In her time of darkness,
Tamar conceives a bold plan. Disguising herself as a cult prostitute, she
seduces her father-in-law so she might conceive.

At the moment Judah discovers that Tamar is pregnant with his child,
he has a choice. He has the option to lie. He lied to his father concerning
the supposed death of his brother Joseph. Wouldn't it be as easy to lie
again? Who would take the word of an impoverished widow against his?
What an extraordinary act of courage it is to reveal to his own community
that he had lost control, that he was guilty of unwittingly having had
intercourse with his own daughter-in-law! Such an act is the beginning of
his repentance, of reclaiming his integrity.

Moses brought God's covenant to the people, who agreed to follow a
new way of living. Judah's example gives the people the inspiration to
understand that as difficult as the covenant is to adhere to, each person is
capable at any moment of reclaiming it by courage. In one of the greatest
acts of courage in the Bible, Judah confesses to his kinsmen, "She is more
right than I." And he changes his ways. Judah experiences how fragile
one's dreams of power are, how vulnerable each person is, how quickly life
and power change. Judah had hated Joseph for his hubris before he
encountered his own.

Joseph knows nothing of the fate of his brothers. After they sell him
into slavery and he is brought to a foreign land, it seems that nothing
worse could happen. But it does. He too runs into a woman—Zuleika, the
wife of his master, who does everything she can to seduce him. Judah goes
along with Tamar's seduction. Joseph refuses. As a result of refusing the
sexual advances of his master's wife, Joseph is not even permitted to live on
earth as a slave. He is thrown into a dungeon *under* the earth. He becomes
a prisoner. But once again, he thrives and even flourishes.

How is it that Joseph survives under such impossible odds? He does
not cry, "Betrayal, vengeance!" or dwell on past anguish. Rather, he holds
on to his faith in God. He triumphs over darkness by connecting to his
inner light, and because of this, others are continually drawn to him. By
holding on to his faith, Joseph flourishes.

Joseph had inappropriately vaunted his power before his brothers and
was brought low to understand the true source of power. Yet, he continued in Egypt to vaunt his beauty, and again, through the same object—a
cloak—God teaches him wisdom and discretion. When dreams begin to

manifest, he is prepared. Previously he told his brothers, you will bow down to me. Now he tells Pharaoh, if God wishes, dreams may be revealed.

Twenty years pass between the time Joseph was thrown into the pit in Canaan and when he becomes governor of Egypt. Next to Pharaoh, he is the most powerful man in the realm. Why should he risk his well-being to concern himself with the family who betrayed him? Despite his material wealth, his heart craves the restoration and unity of his family. The most adept of administrators, Joseph places his brothers in the same situation they had been in previously. Will they abandon a son of Rachel a second time? Will they betray their father a second time? The brothers who once had seen themselves as warring, competing entities now see themselves as one family that cannot live divided. Judah, who willingly speaks for the others, is the one who publicly acknowledges his failures and is willing to give his life so that his brother Benjamin may live.

In one of the most satisfying scenes in the Bible, Joseph reveals his identity to his brothers, and for a glorious moment there is brotherly love without rivalry. After twenty-two years, the family is reunited. And when Jacob once again reaches out and blesses a younger son rather than the older, the potential for envy returns. This time, however, the older son does not act upon it.

Nebuchadnezzar nearly destroyed the world. Joseph, Judah, and Judith nearly put it together.

The Seleucid ruler Antiochus forbids the Jews to follow the covenant they had made with their God. Nebuchadnezzar attacks all of the Near East. Joseph's brothers sell him into slavery. But no Parent/Protector appears to defend the children of Israel. God has taken them only so far and now they are being tested. Do they fearlessly find a way of believing in God's presence and protect themselves? Or do they give up their faith in God because fortune has turned against them and God is hidden?

On Mount Sinai, when describing the building of the tabernacle to Moses, God spoke of two lights: the eternal light of the covenant and the daily light of the menorah. Judith and the Maccabees fought overwhelming external powers to protect the daily light of the menorah so their people might be able to continue their spiritual practices. Judith and the Maccabees defeat oppression by the use of force. Joseph carries within him the eternal light of the covenant; and instead of retaliating when confronted by his brothers' violent deeds of darkness, he raises their spiritual level. He offers his brothers food and gifts and the opportunity to act differently. Joseph's devotion never wavers. Despite what is happening in the external world, Joseph chooses to dwell in the Shechinah's light and protection and offers his own light and goodness to whoever is open to receive it.

We, too, have a choice in driving out the darkness. We can try to defeat the enemy or we can try to bring peace within our own homes. Either task demands tremendous will and courage. In the story of Hanukkah, one cruse of oil brings light that lasts for eight days. The miracle reminds us that God's world is larger than nature. But if we can change our habits, our habitual inclinations, we can rise to a higher level of awareness and action and go beyond nature and participate in God's creation.

PURIM

About Purim

Purim celebrates deliverance: Esther and the Jewish people's deliverance from extinction at the hands of the Persian king's prime minister, Haman. The holiday begins the day before the full moon of the last month of the Jewish year (February or March). All that day people fast in observance of the Fast of Esther. At nightfall, the Book of Esther, also called the Megillah ("scroll"), is read. Then raucous celebrations begin and continue for twenty-four hours.

The Book of Esther, upon which Purim is based, is a literary piece and a mixture of Persian, Babylonian, Greek, biblical, and Jewish influences. Its protagonists, Esther and Mordecai, have the same names as the Babylonian deities Ishtar and Marduk, who were worshiped by the Babylonians at the time that Esther was written. The word "Purim" (derived from the Assyrian word *puru*, meaning "lots" (dice) refers to the lots that the Akkadian kings threw to determine the Babylonian New Year. It also refers to the lots that Haman threw to decide the fate of the Jews.

Scholars cannot confirm the historical time and characters of the story. Therefore many believe that the story is fictitious, but that its underlying plot—how to prevail in exile, how to survive a tyrant who seeks your annihilation—is based on the very real concerns directly confronting the authors who lived during the time of the Jewish opposition to the Seleucid emperor Antiochus IV.

On Purim the Bible commands the people to celebrate by feasting, giving gifts to the poor, sending food to one other, and listening to every word of the Book of Esther. Throughout the centuries, different Jewish communities in Europe and the Middle East created their own local Purim festivals in response to their individual miraculous deliveries from annihilation. To be delivered from near extinction brings on joy and giddiness, and so the customs surrounding Purim are filled with merriment.

People prepare and eat three-cornered pastries filled with poppy seed or fruit preserves named *hamantaschen*, after Haman, and enjoy gobbling down the villain. From the time of the second century Jews dressed up in costumes, the more outrageous the better, and created plays that made fun of their own religious traditions as well as those of the cultures in which they lived. In the Middle Ages, a yeshiva boy would be chosen as rabbi for the day. He would carefully prepare a long funny speech that mimicked the rabbi and ridiculed the endless Talmudic debates that took place in his school. For Purim, anything and everything can be spoken.

The word "Purim" is contained in "Yom Kippurim," the name of the most important day of the Jewish calendar. "Yom Kippur," referred to in the Bible as "Yom Kippurim," can be translated as a "day" (*yom*) "like" (*ki*) Purim. In fact, Yom Kippur mirrors Purim. Before Yom Kippur we eat as much as possible and then fast for the twenty-four hours of the holiday. On Yom Kippur, we come close to God through fasting, contemplating, and praying. Before Purim, we fast and then on Purim we hold a great banquet (*seudah*) and eat and drink past the boundaries of sobriety. On Purim we reach oneness through rejoicing, playing and drinking. In fact, we are supposed to drink so much wine that we enter a world of oneness in which we do not know the difference between Mordecai, the protector, and Haman, the enemy.

Because of the topsy-turvy mardi gras spirit of the holiday, many Jews view Purim as a holiday for children. But others see the transforming aspect of "play" as an opportunity for inner development. Amichai Lau-Levi, a New York rabbi, told me that when he was a child growing up in Israel, during Rosh Hashanah and Yom Kippur he would ponder the parts of himself he was afraid of or disliked. Then, as soon as Yom Kippur was over, he would begin preparing the Purim costume that would embody those aspects. If during the Days of Awe we find what we most fear or despise in ourselves, and if we then choose to create and manifest that part six months later at Purim, we give ourselves the opportunity of joining with our shadow self and creating a fuller being.

It was the story of Esther that began my life as a storyteller. In 1965, while studying pantomime in Paris, I taught Sunday school at Temple Copernic. As the months went by, I realized that what I most looked forward to during the week was not my classes in pantomime but the preparation and telling of Bible stories to nine- and ten-year-old children. And the one they loved the most was Esther.

The experience of telling stories to children and the children's delight in Esther made me yearn to tell similar kinds of stories. Upon returning to the United States, I found work telling stories at the Unitarian Church on Sundays. Over the years, I went from telling biblical stories to telling folk tales and then world myths. While researching stories about the Sumerian goddess, Inanna, I discovered that the beautiful, courageous Queen Esther, whom the children and I so loved, was an avatar, a spiritual descendant, of Ishtar/Inanna, the queen of heaven. Esther's Persian name is Ishtar, the goddess of love and war, the same goddess as the beautiful Sumerian Inanna, the goddess of love, war, and fertility. Inanna defends her people, passes through the seven gates of the underworld, and brings her people back a new vision. Similarly, the beautiful Esther delights the king, walks through the seven gates to the king's forbidden territory, rescues her people, and changes their perceptions of the possible.

The circle has come round. Esther brought me to stories and storytelling. Knowledge of the queen of heaven revealed to me a deeper appreciation of the essence of Esther as well as other biblical stories.

Esther

The Opposite Happened

In this topsy-turvy satire, the king becomes the servant and the beauty queen the political ruler of Persia. The weak triumph and the powerful topple. The opposite of our expectations takes place or we realize that there are no opposites. It is all one. We are all one. And only by caring for one another shall we survive.

The last commandment of Purim is to listen to the reading of the book of Esther *during the evening service and then again during the next day's morning service. Yet there is a tradition of making loud raucous noises each time the name of the villain Haman, who cared for no one but himself, is mentioned. The tradition continues, but so does the commandment that states: Listen! Listen to every word of the book of Esther!*

I've retold Esther's story combining biblical text, oral legends, and a few of my own musings.

*I*n the days of King Ahasuerus—who ruled one hundred and twenty-seven countries from India to Ethiopia—in the third year of his reign, the king moved his capital from Babylon to Susa and invited his nobles, army officers, and governors to a great banquet. He wanted them to admire his new throne as well as his wealth and power. The banquet lasted one hundred and eighty days. Ahasuerus' kingdom was so large that it took some governors many months to reach Susa. And once they arrived, what happened?

Every morning at the banquet, Ahasuerus appeared before his guests wearing the embroidered cape and gold breastplate that had once belonged to the high priest in Jerusalem. Every afternoon, he displayed another extraordinary treasure that his father-in-law, King Belshezzar, had stolen from Jerusalem. And every evening, the king's cook concocted a new dish to impress the guests.

When the banquet for the provinces was over, the king made a smaller banquet of seven days for the men of Susa. He invited the nobles as well as the servants. The banquet was held in the garden of the palace courtyard among blossoming bushes and fruit trees. A gentle breeze fluttered the purple-and-white linen canopies. Silver and gold couches were scattered over rose-colored marble floors. Royal wine was served to the guests.

The guests could drink as little or as much as they wanted. Moreover, they could drink *whatever* they wanted, and no waiter could disapprove, for the king had given orders that each guest was to be served according to his pleasure. Furthermore, no one needed to be rushed, for there was an abundance of gold goblets in the pantry. It was a perfect banquet, and the drinking went on night after night.

On the seventh night it occurred to the king, who was extremely merry with wine, that what he really wanted was for everyone to admire not only his wealth, but his wife. So he whispered orders to his servants that the queen was to appear "wearing only the royal turban." The servants went to Queen Vashti, who was giving a feast for the women. They arrived drunk and said, "Your Majesty, the king wishes you to wear only your royal turban and to dance at his banquet naked!" The mouth of every woman in the room dropped open. The queen took a breath and replied, "I am the granddaughter of King Nebuchadnezzar, the daughter of King Belshezzar. I will not dance naked at a drunken party! Tell the king *no!*"

When the servants reported that Vashti had said *no*, the king was furious. He spumed. He fumed, but he didn't know what to do. So he turned to his seven ministers. He had one for each day of the week.

(One good day of thinking was all these sages could manage.) The king asked them, "According to the law, what is to be done with the queen when she does not obey the king's order?"

The youngest minister, Memukan, answered first so he would not be influenced by what the others said. "Your Majesty, the queen has not only offended the king; she has offended the entire kingdom, for if one woman disobeys, all women will disobey. And this will not take long, for the moment the women leave the banquet, they will tell the others, 'The queen refused to obey her husband!' When the others hear this, throughout your kingdom, women will begin to think for themselves. That would be dreadful! Your Majesty, I advise the king to make an edict that is written into the laws of Persia and Media stating that Vashti may never again appear before the king. Then, the king can choose a better wife; and when the king's edict is heard throughout the empire, every woman, regardless of her status, will show proper respect to her husband." The king and his ministers agreed. So letters were sent to one hundred and twenty-seven countries stating that every man was to be master in his house, and *his* language rather than his wife's was to be spoken and obeyed.

The next morning Ahasuerus awoke, calling, "Vash-ti!"

His servant answered, "Your Majesty, did you forget that the queen has been banished and is not to appear again before the king?"

"Oh, then I had better go back to sleep," the king said. But as he turned over, his servant whispered in his ear, "Remember what your minister advised?"

"What was that?"

"Choose a better woman! Your Majesty, if scouts are sent to each of your provinces and they find the most beautiful young women, Hegai, your harem-keeper, can prepare them for you. Then you can choose the one who pleases you the most to be queen in Vashti's place."

This advice appealed to the king, so he followed it.

In the capital of Susa, there lived a Jew by the name of Mordecai. He had been exiled from Jerusalem to Babylon, and from there he had moved to Susa and become one of the king's advisors. His sister had died, and he had adopted his niece and brought her up as his own daughter. Her name was Hadassah, meaning "sweet-smelling myrtle."

On the night that Vashti was banished, Mordecai returned from the king's banquet to find Hadassah waiting for him. "My child," he said, "Tonight you will have a new name. You will no longer be called Hadassah. Your new name will be Esther, meaning in Hebrew 'secret' or 'concealed.' And if anyone asks, you are not to reveal who your people are." Esther was then given lessons in Persian as well as in singing and dancing. She was very beautiful, and her teachers said to her, "You are like your Persian namesake Ishtar, the shining morning and evening star, the goddess of love and war."

Many people spoke of Esther's beauty and charm, and a year later she was chosen as the most beautiful young woman in Susa and brought to Hegai, the harem-keeper of the palace. Other young women had been chosen from each province in the empire. They spent a year in preparation. The first six months they were oiled with myrrh. The second six months, they were perfumed. After twelve months, they were ready to go before the king. Hegai, the harem-keeper, who was fond of Esther, gave her seven servants of her own and allowed her uncle Mordecai to visit her every day.

Four years passed and in the winter of the seventh year of the king's reign, it was Esther's turn to go to the king. She wore the clothes and perfume that Hegai suggested and put pink roses in her hair. The king was standing in the corner of the room with his arms folded. She wondered about this man who had taken such a long time to find a queen. He looked lonely. She walked up to him and folded her arms in the same way as his were folded. She tilted her head and smiled at him. A rose fell from her hair to the floor. She picked up the rose and put it in the king's curly hair. He laughed, and she said, "Laugh again. I like your laugh." He laughed, and without consulting his seven advisors, he placed the royal turban on her head and said, "You, my radiant one, shall be queen." So Esther, who was once Hadassah, took Vashti's place, and became the queen of Persia.

The king held a banquet and invited his nobles and officials to meet Esther. He distributed gifts throughout the provinces and declared that in the queen's honor no taxes were to be paid that year. Before the feast, he asked Esther about her people, but following the advice of Mordecai, she said that she was an orphan and did not know her origins. When he asked her again, she answered, "A true king knows patience. In time, all is revealed." Ahasuerus was pleased by Esther's wisdom as well as by her beauty.

However, not all the people in the kingdom were equally pleased with her. Two relatives of Vashti plotted to poison the king. They conspired together in their native language, Tarsian, certain that no one could understand them. But Mordecai, who spoke seventy languages, overheard them and told Esther to inform the king. When the matter was investigated and found to be true, the conspirators were caught and hanged on the gallows. The names of the two conspirators and Mordecai's name were then written down in *The Book of Records* in the king's presence.

After this scare, the king chose Haman, the fierce Agagite, a descendant of Amalek, to be prime minister over his other ministers. Not wanting to share his power, Haman dismissed all the king's advisors and for the first time in Persia, the kingdom was ruled by one rather than many advisors. Whenever Haman walked through the palace, all the servants were forced to go down on their knees and prostrate themselves before him. But Mordecai refused.

When, time after time, the arrogant minister walked through the palace and Mordecai refused to bow to him, Haman made inquiries. When he found out that Mordecai was a Jew, Haman determined to kill every Jew in Persia. On the thirteenth day of the first month of the year, Haman gathered his sons together and they threw *pur,* which in Persian means "lot" or "fate." They threw *pur* to find out which day would be the most auspicious day to kill all the Jews. The *pur* fell on the thirteenth day of the last month of the year.

Haman went to the king with a large sack of silver. He placed the sack on the table and said, "Your Majesty, in your kingdom there is a certain group of people scattered among your lands. Their customs are different from ours. They eat differently. They drink differently. They follow different laws. It is of no benefit to the king to tolerate them. If Your Majesty will write a law to destroy them, I will happily put ten thousand silver talents into the royal treasury to cover the expense of ridding the kingdom of these people."

"I know of whom you speak," replied the king. "And I know of their power. King after king has tried to destroy them. Consider what happened to my father-in-law, Belshezzar, and to his father, Nebuchadnezzar. Some wise men say that the world exists because of their law."

"Yes, yes," said Haman, humoring the king. "That was when their God was young, but now their God is old and spends most of his time sleeping. You do not need to worry that they will rebel—they can never agree on anything." Haman pushed the sack of silver toward the king. The king gave Haman his signet ring and said, "It is your silver. Write the decree you wish."

On the thirteenth day of the first month of the year, the king's secretaries wrote what Haman ordered. Letters were sent to the governors of one hundred and twenty-seven countries, each in its own script and language, written in the name of King Ahasuerus and sealed with his royal signet ring. The order was to kill, destroy, and exterminate all Jews, young and old, including women and children, on the thirteenth day of the twelfth month of the year. And those who killed the Jews were to be rewarded with their property.

At the king's command, the messengers went out quickly. The king and Haman sat down to drink, and all of Susa was thrown into a terrible confusion.

When the Jews read the proclamation, some in panic begged their neighbors to take their children as slaves so they would not be killed, but the law forbade such an action. Mordecai put on sackcloth. He went into the streets and wailed a loud, bitter wail. He came upon a young child and asked him, "What are you studying?"

The child answered, "It is from Isaiah. It says, 'When your hair turns white, I will care for you. I made you. I will sustain you. I will rescue you.'" The thought that children would no longer study or pray made Mordecai wail even louder. Then he cried out, "All the gates are closed, but the gates of tears."

When Esther heard that her uncle was wandering the streets in sackcloth, she sent her servant to him with new clothes. Mordecai gave her servant a copy of the edict and wrote a letter to Esther that said: "My dear Esther, We have been sold by Haman for ten thousand silver talents to be killed, destroyed, and exterminated. Go to the king now and plead for the lives of your people."

Esther read the letter and wrote back to Mordecai: "Every person in the kingdom knows that anyone who dares to go through the seven gates to the king's inner courtyard without the king's permission will be killed with no exceptions unless the king extends his scepter, allowing them to live. The king has not sent for me for thirty days. If I go now and am killed, what use will I be? It is better that I wait until the king sends for me."

Mordecai sent a reply: "My dear Esther, long ago when I lived in Jerusalem, a wise woman told me that one day my niece would be queen of Persia. I thought that that was impossible, but when Vashti was banished, it seemed as if the impossible were coming into being. Who knows if it is not for just this moment that you have been made queen? Do you think that because you live in the palace you are safer than the other Jews? There is no time to wait. Already in the provinces, they are taunting Jews and some of our people are being killed. If you are silent, help will come from another place, but you and your father's house will perish."

Esther looked out the window. It was dusk. Just then the evening star appeared alone in the heavens. She thought of her ancestors. Sarah had gone alone to Pharaoh so that her husband might live; Rachel had whispered secrets to Leah so that her sister would not be humiliated. But she was being asked to save not the pride or life of one person. She was being asked to save the lives of *all* her people. If she were to save their lives, she needed their help.

Esther sent word to Mordecai, saying, "Dear Mordecai, my servants and I will fast and not eat or drink for three days. Gather all the Jews in Susa together and ask them also to fast and pray for three days. After this time, I will go to the king. And if I perish, I will perish."

Mordecai spoke to the Jews. They united. Ancient feuds among families ended. Even though Passover was to be celebrated at the full moon, the Jews did not celebrate Passover. For three days, they did not eat or drink. They actively repented. They prayed that Esther would be given the strength she needed. Even the children fasted.

For three days and nights, Esther lay on the floor of her room, praying. Then she heard the priests blowing the rams' horns outside the palace. She washed and bathed. Her servants perfumed her with the scent of roses. She put on her finest gold dress and the royal turban. Alone, she walked toward the throne room. Just before the seventh gate, she stopped. Again, from outside the palace she heard the rams' horns. She pushed open the last gate.

The king turned at the sound of unsummoned footsteps. Who would dare to risk his life to see him? It was Esther and her face was shining with light. He extended his gold scepter to her and said, "My queen, my radiant wife, what is your wish? What is your request? Speak! Do not be afraid. You will not die. Up to half the kingdom is yours."

Esther approached and touched the scepter. She smiled at the king and said, "Your Majesty, if I have pleased you, I ask that you and Haman come to a banquet I am preparing for you tonight. Then I will tell you my wish."

The king and Haman went to Esther's party. Esther sat close to the king. While they were drinking wine, the king said, "My beautiful wife, what is your wish? It will be given to you. What is your request? Remember, up to half the kingdom is yours."

Esther answered in a soft voice, "Your Majesty, if I have pleased you, my wish and my request is for you and Haman to come tomorrow to another wine party in my room and then I will reveal to the king what he wishes to know."

Haman, who had once been a lowly barber, nearly pranced through the halls of the palace with pride as servant after servant bowed down to him. But when he walked out through the King's Gate, standing in the street was Mordecai. Mordecai did not bow down to him. He did not even look at him.

Furious, Haman controlled himself until he arrived home. Then he sent for his friends and his wife and said to them, "I am the richest man in the kingdom next to the king. I have ten sons and great honors. This very day I was invited to the queen's party. Tomorrow too I am invited to the queen's party, but all of this is worthless to me, for every time I see that Jew Mordecai at the King's Gate and he does not bow to me, my happiness is stolen!"

Haman's wife, Zeresh, advised him, "Get rid of the source of your troubles. Build a great gallows from a high tree. Speak to the king in the morning before Esther is awake and let them hang your enemy Mordecai. Then, when you dine with the queen in the evening, you can think of your wealth, of your position, of your sons, and you will be content."

Haman found gallows builders who began work at once. His sons joined them, hammering nails and singing. The noise woke the king, who called for his servant to read to him from *The Book of Records*. The book was so boring it usually put him to sleep immediately, but this night in his sleeplessness, he heard that Mordecai, the Jew at the King's Gate, had reported a plot by two of the king's servants, who had intended to poison him.

"I live because of Mordecai," the king said. "What great honor was given to him for saving my life?"

The servant looked at the book and answered, "No honor, your Majesty. No honor or promotion."

At this moment, there was a sound outside the king's court. Haman, who could not wait for morning, had come before dawn to get permission to hang Mordecai. The king said, "Haman, I need your advice. Tell me, what shall be done for a man whom the king wishes to honor?"

Certain the king was referring to himself, Haman closed his eyes to fully imagine this moment of glory. Then he answered, "Your Majesty, let the royal clothes the king wore for his coronation be brought. Let the royal horse the king rode in his coronation be brought. Then, let the noblest prince in the kingdom dress the man of honor in your royal clothes and lead him on your royal horse through the main street of the capital, proclaiming: 'This is what the king does for the man he wishes to honor!' "

"Excellent!" agreed the king. "Haman, you are our noblest prince. Go at once to Mordecai the Jew, who sits at the King's Gate. Dress him in the royal manner. Lead him on my royal horse through the streets. And do not leave out anything that you have suggested!"

The next day, since all the shops were closed because of the parade, Haman had to bathe, wash, and shave Mordecai. Then he had to lead him in the grand parade. There were two thousand buglers, five thousand drummers, and twenty thousand musicians with tambourines. Mordecai sat on the king's white horse, singing:

> *Praise the Lord who loosened my sackcloth,*
> *Praise the Lord who decorated my cloak with joy,*
> *Praise the Lord who changed my grief to dancing,*
> *Praise the Lord who restored my soul.*

With each burst of song, Haman's head sunk lower. As the parade approached his house, Haman's nearsighted daughter was certain that the man whose head was down was the miserable Mordecai. So she ran and got the chamber pot, full of the morning slop, and, as the two passed in front of her window, she poured the slop directly on her father's head.

Haman rushed home after the parade covered in shame and told his wife and friends what had happened. "What am I to do?" Haman asked. But just then, the king's guards arrived to take him to Esther's party.

The king and Haman drank wine. Then the king asked Esther for the third time, "Queen Esther, my beautiful wife, what is your wish? What is your request? Remember, up to half the kingdom is yours."

The queen bowed to the king. She paused, and then she said, "Your Majesty, if I have pleased you, my wish is for my life and my request is for my people's lives. If we had been sold as slaves, I would have been silent, for the adversary is not worthy of your attention. But we have been sold to be killed, destroyed, and exterminated!"

"Who?" King Ahasuerus cried, "Who dared do such a thing?"

Esther pointed to Haman and said, "He—he is the adversary—Haman!"

Flustered, the king left the party and went out into the garden. He had counted on Haman to protect him. Terrified the king would kill him, Haman rushed to the queen who was lying on a couch and blubbered, "Your Majesty, please, spare my life, my—"

Just then as the king entered the room, Haman stumbled and fell on top of the queen. "What?" the king cried. "He dares do this too? In my presence, in my house, he attacks the queen! What is to be done?"

One of the servants said, "Haman made gallows for Mordecai. They are fifty feet high and empty!"

"Hang him from his gallows!" the king proclaimed. So Haman was hanged on the gallows that had been prepared for Mordecai. And that same day King Ahasuerus gave Haman's house and all his wealth to Queen Esther. Esther brought Mordecai to the king. The king gave Mordecai his signet ring, which he had taken back from Haman, and Esther gave Mordecai Haman's property.

Two months later Esther dared to go again to the king. She fell at his feet and wept. The king held out his gold scepter and asked, "What is your request?"

Esther touched the scepter and answered, "Your Majesty, if I have pleased you, my request is for the lives of my people. The decree Haman dictated ordering the extermination of my people has not been stopped, and I cannot live when my relatives are being killed at this very moment."

The king said to Queen Esther and Mordecai, "What is written in the king's name and sealed with the king's signet ring cannot be changed. That is the law."

Esther looked at the king. She did not take her eyes from the king until the king had an idea. Then the king said, "The decree cannot be changed. But, a new law can be made!" And he said to Mordecai, "Write a new decree."

So the king's secretaries were summoned, and an edict, written as Mordecai dictated, sealed with the king's signet ring, was sent to one hundred and twenty-seven countries, to each land in its own script and to each people in its own language. The letters gave the Jews permission to assemble and defend themselves on the thirteenth day of the last month of the year against any armed group who might attack them and take their property.

At the king's command, messengers riding the fastest horses rushed from the palace to post the edicts. As the law was proclaimed in Susa, Mordecai went out of the palace wearing a gold turban and a royal cloak of purple and white linen. At last, for the Jews there was light and gladness, joy and honor. And some people in fear and awe of the Jews converted and became Jews themselves.

On the thirteenth day of the last month of the year, on the day the Jews thought they would be killed, the opposite happened. The Jews defended themselves against those who attacked them in the provinces as well as in Susa. The king then went to Esther and asked, "In Susa the Jews have killed five hundred men as well as Haman's ten sons. What is your wish now? What is your request?"

Esther answered, "If I have pleased the king, let the Jews in Susa continue fighting one more day. Let the bodies of Haman's sons be hung as a warning for all to see, so no one group who is different will ever again be singled out to be harmed." The king gave the order. The fighting in Susa continued another day. The Jews killed the three hundred men who attacked them, but they took no property. In the provinces, the Jews killed the seventy-five thousand people who attacked them, and they took no property. Then, on the fourteenth and fifteenth days, friends and neighbors ran from door to door, from home to home, rejoicing. In every house, there was feasting. There was celebrating. There was great relief.

Mordecai sent letters to the Jews in the one hundred and twenty-seven countries, urging them to continue to celebrate the fourteenth and fifteenth days of the last month of the year and to call these days Purim, for on these days the fate of each person was changed. Mordecai became second to the king and was honored among the Jews and respected by the Persians for he remained a humble man. Wherever he went in the capital, he greeted everyone in a friendly manner. He looked for peaceful solutions to conflict and spoke of the necessity for peace.

Esther herself wrote letters to the Jews in the one hundred and twenty-seven countries, urging them to remember not only the days of feasting, but the days of fasting, the days when they had lived in fear and joined with her, united as one people. Because of what they had witnessed, the Jews agreed as a community to continue the custom they themselves had begun of celebrating on the full moon of the last month of the year. Since then, in every family, in every generation, in every city and in every country, Jews have celebrated the holiday of Purim by feasting, by sending food to friends, by helping the needy, and by listening to each word of the story of Esther.

About the Story

In Esther, everything turns upside down. The arrogant prime minister, Haman, is hanged. The lowly Jews create their own feasts, sending food to *all* who are needy. And the king, who had treated his queens as slaves, seeks Queen Esther's advice, giving her spiritual and political power.

The story's plot is put into motion by Haman, a descendant of Amalek—who could not bear the happiness of others. Haman wishes to rid the Persian kingdom of the Jews. His pride is so large that he can see nothing beyond his own need to be acknowledged. When Mordecai presses his niece, Esther, to speak to the king regarding Haman's decree to destroy the Jews, she at first is reluctant. But then she realizes that no king can make the decision about how she will live her life. She is the one with that power.

With her newfound power, she does not blindly obey Mordecai's demands; she sets her own terms. Before Esther will go to the king, she insists that all the people for whom she is risking her life join her in fasting and praying for three days. She unites everyone in a common goal. And later when Ahasuerus asks Esther for her request, she does not follow Mordecai's instructions, which could bring about a direct and disastrous confrontation. Rather, she waits for the right moment, delaying her answer by means of an ingenious ploy. She brings the enemy into her camp by inviting Ahasuerus *and* Haman to a feast. By not answering immediately, Esther makes the king eager to know and eager to grant her request. And by cleverly inviting Haman to both of her feasts, she plants suspicion in the king's mind as to why she, the queen, is including Haman at their intimate party.

As Mordecai had requested, Esther informs Ahasuerus of Haman's actions. The king protects her and gives her all the material wealth she could wish for. Without Mordecai's prodding, Esther returns to the king and risks her life again to ask that Haman's decree be repealed so the Jews who have been unjustly accused will not be killed. Just as Moses told God, "If you cannot forgive the people, do not include me in the book you are writing," Esther says, "I do not want to live if my people are being destroyed." How could this extraordinary act of selflessness not appeal to a king who wishes to be seen as a great ruler?

With the acknowledgment of a woman's power to speak her mind, the tacit hierarchy of absolute power is broken. At the end of the story the king goes to Esther and asks if *she* is satisfied: "In Susa, five hundred men have been killed as well as Haman's ten sons. What is your wish now?" Esther requests that the bodies of Haman's sons be displayed. Mordecai had warned Esther that if she did not act, she and her father's house would perish. Esther is broadcasting to future generations: Beware, do not ever again weed out a minority to destroy them! Freedom in the household brings freedom in the nation.

Esther is beautiful, and she is also a warrior. In Persian her name means Ishtar. Ishtar, the goddess of love and war, is the same goddess as Inanna who, after daring to enter the fearsome gates of the underworld, returns to her people with a new understanding. Inanna's understanding brings an equality and a separation of masculine and feminine. Esther's understanding offers an integration.

Midrash links Esther and Sarah through the number one hundred and twenty-seven that occurs in both of their stories. Sarah dies at the age of one hundred and twenty-seven. Esther's kingdom, we are repeatedly informed, has one hundred and twenty-seven countries. Both women were taken into the palaces of foreign kings against their wishes, yet were able to serve their people. Sarah was forced to serve Pharaoh and Abimelech until God released her. Esther, who embodies the alluring and assertive qualities of Ishtar/Inanna, releases herself and her people from the will of the Persian king. Sarah had spiritual status; Esther has spiritual and political power. Esther brings Sarah's powers to fruition and changes the course of history for her people and those who read her story.

Something new is revealed with Esther. The something new is the sharing of power both between the leaders and between the leaders and their people. In the story told at Passover, after God chooses Moses to liberate the Hebrew people from slavery in Egypt, Moses becomes so close to the Shechinah that he did not share his power with his priestess wife or with his prophetess sister. In the story told at Purim, after freeing her people, Esther chooses to share the power the king explicitly gave to her, with

Mordecai. Mordecai, who is logical and stubborn, and Esther, who is intuitive and flexible, complement each other. It is Mordecai who alerts Esther to the need to speak to the king and Esther who intuits the best way to get the results they need: All the people must pray, repent, and give themselves over entirely to God. Mordecai organizes the people and they do as Esther asks. The people's unity and Esther's meditations empower Esther so that when she goes before the king she is radiant. Unlike the Hebrews in the desert who complained and rebelled against their leaders, the Persian Jews actively agree to pray, fast, and cooperate. The Jews prevail because by their prayers—three days and nights of meditation—they join themselves to God, and they help to bring about the king's change of heart.

God initiates Passover by instructing Moses to command the people celebrate their deliverance. Esther and Mordecai invite the people to celebrate a new holiday. Before, it was God who rescued the people, brought them out of slavery, and saved them from exile. Since God is no longer speaking directly with them (God's name is not mentioned in the biblical text of the Book of Esther), Esther, Mordecai, and the people ask for God's support and unite to defend themselves. Previously, the Shechinah dwelt close to the teachings, the ark of the covenant, between the embracing male and female cherubim. Now, in the place where man and woman extend their arms toward each other, in that place where there is closeness to the teachings and to one another, the Shechinah dwells.

The name Esther in Hebrew means "hidden," "concealed." The great joy of Purim is the revelation of the secret: the goodness of God, the potential for change that is in each of us. Moses' God, whose name means "the place whose name is mystery," *can* be found. Although God is seemingly hidden from us, we can find the divine when we are ready.

"If you seek him with all your heart and soul you will find him there," Deuteronomy says.

"Where is there?" the Hasidic rabbi Simchah Bunam asks. And he answers, "In your heart."

Afterword

More than thirty years have passed since Shlomo told me to wait. The ripened apple has fallen into the earth and I have discovered a new story. It is the story of the Jewish calendar which reflects the developing relationship between the Jewish people and their God: At Passover, God rescues the people from slavery. At Shavuot, the people and God exchange vows. At Tisha B'Av, the people break their vows and God exiles them. At Rosh Hashanah, the people ask for forgiveness and take responsibility. At Yom Kippur, God returns (in the form of the teachings) and the people draw closer to God. At Sukkot, the people build homes and honeymoon with their Beloved. At Simchat Torah, they rejoice in their Beloved, the Torah. At Hannukah, they defend themselves so they can live by the teachings. And at Purim, with God's teachings internalized, the community (man and woman) works together to bring about their own redemption. When the story begins, there are two: God and the people; at the story's end, God and the people are one.

In the process of working on this book, I have been considering the many questions I asked Shlomo. I am grateful for his inspiration that led me to walk on the path of his ancestors and mine and to learn of the wisdom of Judaism. And now I realize that what I truly wanted to know—the question behind all the questions—was: Could I also know and love the God he loved so deeply?

In exploring the biblical stories and midrash, I've come to understand that they are large enough, balanced enough, to include all people: men and women, our children and grandchildren. But they need to be told in a way that we can grasp today. They need to be told as dialogues that honor all of us, that pierce our hearts with their human dilemmas and surprise our mindsets with their questions.

According to Jewish belief, the fullness of the human being is to breathe in the inner power and light and return it with service to others. In my eight-year journey working on *Treasures of the Heart,* I have come to understand my roots more fully. The stories in *Treasures* are very human stories; they speak of reality and our struggle with others and with God. I cannot say that I met Shlomo's God, but I have come to understand that the joy he was filled with and the boundless love he was continually expressing were the result of his seeing God in everything and rejoicing that he was able to carry out God's wishes as he understood them. He wanted to give peace and joy to everyone; he was always eager to share God's love.

My belief in a force that binds, surrounds, and animates all things has increased. I do not define it as Shlomo's God or a uniquely Jewish force. My sense of God changes as I change. My intellectual self thrills at the Voice Job heard in the Whirlwind. I can imagine that if God's Majesty were to speak, these would be God's words. My emotional self breaks open in the story of Ruth on the road from Moab to Judah when loving-kindness fills the world. My soul place comes to life when Moses speaks with God, whether pleading for the lives of his people (*The Covenant*) or asking to live as a little bird who flies each day to a different place and sings God's praises (*The Death of Moses*). My austere self believes that neither stories nor words can begin to describe the Mystery Beyond Life and Death. My child self, in emergencies (and on holidays), calls out the Hebrew name she heard growing up. And my knowing self understands that all these are manifestations of the Infinite.

The stories in *Treasures of the Heart* are venturing out toward you. I hope they will be a comfort, an inspiration, a blessing.

Sources and Notes for the Stories

In choosing oral legends, my chief source was Louis Ginzberg's seven-volume book *The Legends of the Jews*. His comprehensive, erudite yet lively compilation of two thousand years of written Jewish legends, culled from both Jewish and Christian sources, is without parallel. I also used Angelo Rappoport's *Myth and Legend of Ancient Israel*, volumes of *midrash rabah* when available, and *The Zohar*. In the instances in which I heard a particular legend from a teacher in a Bible class or a lecture, I do not always have an attribution. Whenever I have created the midrash, I identify it as my own.

When there are choices of midrash, I used my intuition honed from years of researching and telling stories. For example, although the midrash of Moses finding Joseph's bones in the sea is more well-known, I chose the legend of Moses finding Joseph's bones in the earth by the sense of smell (Mekh. Beshallah 1). I did so because I wanted to bring Serach, who appears in the next to last story in *Treasures of the Heart* (*Joseph*), into the first story (*Exodus*) to emphasize continuity. At the same time, I wanted to emphasize the importance of smell and fragrance. In *The Covenant*, we find out that the people smell the fragrance of the Shechinah when receiving the tablets and that God's favorite offering is the sweet-smelling fragrance of the thanks-offering. We cannot see or fathom God. Fragrance is a reminder of the invisible essence that nourishes the soul.

Foreword

Hieros gamos (the Mesopotamian sacred marriage rite) and the Sumerian cuneiform tablets: see S. N. Kramer's *The Sumerians* and Diane Wolkstein and S. N. Kramer's *Inanna, Queen of Heaven and Earth*.

Talmudic term, Shekina, its origin and development: Raphael Patai's *Hebrew Goddess, The Zohar*.

Oral tradition passed on for 40 generations: Mordecai Munk's *The Wisdom in the Hebrew Alphabet*.

Sources and Notes for the Stories

About Passover

Passover, Shavuot, and Sukkot are observed for an extra day outside of Israel; Rosh Hashanah has the extra day even in Israel. Until around 400 C.E., the first day of each month was determined by witnesses who came before the rabbinical court in Jerusalem to testify that they had seen the new moon. When their testimony was accepted, the court sent runners to all Jewish settlements to let them know the first day of the month. However, as runners often did not reach a community before a holiday occurred in that month, Jews in those communities extended holidays by an extra day to be certain to observe the holiday on the correct day. Since the advent of the fixed Jewish calendar, Jewish communities outside Israel still keep the tradition of adding an extra day to holidays. See Glossary, calendar.

Exodus

I follow the biblical text Exodus 1:15 and interweave legends from Ginzberg, vol. 2, in creating this rendition. According to Ginzberg, Pharaoh's three advisors were Balaam, Jethro, and Job. Despite my predilection for linking characters, I thought it would be too distracting and shocking for readers to begin *Exodus* by reading about Job. I also consulted Rappoport, vol. 2, for Amram's remarriage and for Bithiah's naming Moses.

Although there is very little text about Miriam in the Bible, her importance to the people is known because when she was sick they refused to leave her (Num 12:15). I enlarged Miriam's role in *Exodus* by having her teach Moses his family history, address the people as Moses' spokesperson, and instruct the women. Her prophecy of Moses' leading the people from Egypt is a well-known Talmudic midrash, *BT* Sot, 12a, to which I added the detail of the white stone that came to me in a dream. To the account in *Mekh.* Amalek 3 of Moses and Zipporah in Midian, I created details about Zipporah's relationship to Moses and Jethro recalling his time at Pharaoh's court. The staff that Jethro gives Moses is a well-known midrash (see Glossary, Jethro). The wonderful midrash of God telling Moses that there is no time for long prayers comes from *Mekh.* Beshallah 4, and God not wanting to hear singing when the Egyptians drown is from *BT* San 39b as well as *BT* Sot. 37a.

The Red Sea is a conventional but not accurate translation of the Hebrew *sup* which means "rush" or "reed." There is no identifiable location for the Reed Sea (or for Mount Sinai).

There is a discrepancy in the dating of the amount of years the Hebrews were slaves in Egypt. The biblical account Gn 15:13 and Ex 12:40 give the time of oppression as 400 to 430 years. The well-known Talmudic scholar Rashi, when commenting on Ex 12:40, suggests that this dating of 400 years was to be determined from Isaac's birth (rather than Jacob's going down to

Egypt). Based on the life span of the generations, Rashi's explanation of the supposed 210 years of slavery in Egypt fits some modern scholars' approximation of 1450 to 1250 B.C.E. as the time of slavery in Egypt.

The Song of Songs

I have closely followed the biblical text of The Song of Songs. I broke the text into different voices and abbreviated the length by taking out repetitions and a few lines from different sections.

Josiah

I followed the biblical text II Kings 22–23 and added the biblical texts: "You heard God's voice but saw no form" (Dt 4:15–19); "When God brings you into the land" (Dt 8:11–19); "Such a Passover has not been celebrated" (II Chr 35); and II Chr 35:20–27 for the death of Josiah. I consulted Buck's *People of the Lord* and Miller and Hayes's *A History of Ancient Israel and Judah* regarding Josiah's reason for opposing Pharaoh Neco's entry into Israel. Midrash is from Ginzberg, vol. 4.

About the Stories

Texts of Inanna, the goddess of fertility: Wolkstein and Kramer's *Inanna*, "The Courtship of Inanna and Dumuzi."

Male and female aspects of God: *The Zohar*.

Literary analogies of The Song of Songs with Sumerian literature: Marvin Pope's *Song of Songs*.

Asherah worshiped with Yahweh: Ackerman's *Under Every Green Tree*, Hadley's *The Cult of Asherah*.

Seventy names of God: *The Zohar*.

The place whose name is mystery: Chagigah 5b.

About Shavuot

Ashkenazic Jews come from Eastern Europe; Sephardic Jews come from Spain and the Middle East.

Sephardic marriage contract of God and Jewish people: Waskow's *Seasons of Our Joy*, p. 194, Philip Goodman's *The Shavuot Anthology*, JPS, pp. 99–101.

The Covenant

The biblical text on which *The Covenant* is based is Exodus 16–40. I consulted Ginzberg, vol. 3, in composing this story. He offers the midrash of God admitting to the mistake of speaking to Adam rather than Eve first. He also offers wonderful midrashim explaining the 10 Commandments. My rendition of the 10 Commandments is based on Ginzberg and my own phrasings. Many of Ginzberg's phrases of explanation help the reader to connect to the intent behind the teaching. Ginzberg uses the analogy of the seven days of genesis in the midrash of the 10 Commandments and also suggests that the completion of the tabernacle resembles the creation of the world. I've adapted both analogies.

In addition to Ginzberg, I've consulted Ex. R. Tanhuma, vol. 2, speaks of the delicious taste of the animals that ate the manna and Jethro's acknowledgment of the greatness of God. Amalek 1–4 offers other midrash about Amalek and Jethro. PRE 41–46 is the reference for Amalek's anger; descriptions at Mount Sinai; the women refusing to give their earrings; Miriam's son, Hur; Moses arguing with God; the celebration of the new moon; and the ram's horn blowing at Elul.

The wave of perfume emanating from the tablets is from *The Zohar*, Ex. 227a; the word becoming a voice from *The Zohar*, Teruma 146a; and the letters flying into the air and disappearing from *BT* Pes. 87b. The concept of the embracing cherubim is from Patai's Hebrew Goddess, Num R. 4:13, and *BT* Yoma 54a. Miriam's speeches to the people and the women are my own. I abbreviated the Song of the Sea (Ex 15:1–21).

Ruth

I closely followed the biblical text of the book of Ruth. I used *BT* Sotah 42a for Orpah's children, *BT* Baba Bathra 91a for the recent death of Boaz' wife, *BT* Yebv 63a comparing Ruth to Abraham, *BT* Sanh. 19b for Naomi raising Obed, and *BT* Baba Bathra 91b for Ruth watching Solomon rule Israel. The law forbidding Israelites to live with or marry Moabites is from Dt 23:4–5 and Neh 13:2. My own musings can be found in Ruth and Orpah's weddings, Ruth remembering Boaz' gifts, Ruth preparing to meet Boaz, and Ruth's grief at Boaz' death. The fertility cult aspect of the celebrants at the threshing floor was inspired by Kluger's *A Psychological Interpretation of Ruth*. Rabbi Arthur Waskow suggested I create a conversation between Ruth and Boaz at the threshing floor. I based their conversation on Gn 19 and 38. I am grateful to Aviva Zornberg for her brilliant lecture on Ruth and grandparenting at Hebrew Union College (HUC) in New York City.

Ezekiel

In the preface to the story of Ezekiel, God's placing his left hand on Ezekiel is a midrash from *The Zohar*.

Ezekiel is a direct translation of the biblical book of Ezekiel 1:1–28.

Sources and Notes for the Stories

About the Stories

Moses as shaman bringing back a stone from vision journey: Speech by Luis
  Yglesias at Exodus program at American Museum of Natural History in
  New York City.

God as changing character: Jack Miles's *God: A Biography*.

Naomi falling into the underworld: Kluger.

The wisdom of the grandmother: Zornberg's lecture on Ruth at HUC.

Kabbalistic teachings: Kaplan's *Meditation and the Bible; Book of Yetzirah*; talks
  and lectures with Rabbi Shlomo Carlebach, Rabbi Meyer Fund, Rabbi
  Zalman Schachter-Shalomi, and *The Zohar*.

The Spies

I followed the biblical text Num 13, 14:1–38 in composing *The Spies* and
interwove parts from Ginzberg, vol. 3. Changing Joshua's name is from Munk
p. 131. The devouring fire and the Anakites is from Dt 9:2–3. *M. Ta'anit* 4:8
speaks of the people being forced to dig their own graves. The concept of the
minimum commandments can be found in the Glossary.

Rachel and the Shechinah

In the mid-eighties at a peace conference held in Westchester, New York,
Rabbi Arthur Waskow told the legend about Rachel pleading with God to
save her people. A woman's voice changes God's heart! I never forgot his
telling of the story. I framed the horrific story of the destruction of the First
Temple with Rachel's compassion.

The biblical material for *Rachel and the Shechinah* comes from: 11 Kings
23:31–36, 24, 25, Jer 8.13–9.20; 22:13–17; Psalm 137:1 "By the waters of
Babylon"; and Jer 31:15–17 "A Cry is Heard in Ramah." I used Ginzberg,
vol. 4, and Pesik. Rab. 26:71 for Jeremiah following the people toward Babylon. I consulted Miller and Hayes' *A History of Ancient Israel and Judah* for the
alliance of six nations and Nebuchadnezzar's invasion.

The Bible gives two locations for Rachel's burial: Ramah (Jer 31:15–17)
and near Ephrath, "which is Bethelehem" (Gn 35:19). The *Anchor Bible Dic-
tionary* states that some scholars believe this later gloss, "which is Bethelehem," is incorrect.

Lamentations

In order to make the text more of a story, I abbreviated and freely translated the biblical book of Lamentations.

Sources and Notes for the Stories

Destruction of the Second Temple

I often heard this story told on Tisha B'Av. The core of the legend comes from *BT* Git. 56a–57a. Ben Zakkai and Vespasian comes from Lam. R. 1:31. Titus and the Zealots from Farmer's *Maccabees, Zealots, and Josephus*. Rabbi Tzadok from Freiman's *Who's Who in the Talmud*. I added the sections on Rabbi Hillel.

Job

It was very difficult to leave out any of the beautiful poetry of the Book of Job. For the purpose of shaping Job more into a story, I condensed many of Job's speeches and combined his friends' many speeches into one speech for each friend. The legends of Job's caring for the widows himself, his wife selling her hair, his marrying Dinah, his daughters seeing the Shechinah, and the poor mourning for Job are all from Ginzberg, vol. 2.

About the Stories

Steven Mitchell speaks about the importance of Job giving his daughters names in the introduction to his book, *The Book of Job*.

Ben Zakkai's advice to continue planting: Avot de Rabbi Natan, 31b from Solomon Schecter's *Avot de Rabbi Natan*, 1967, p. 67.

About Rosh Hashanah

Each person can change their fate during Rosh HaShanah: *BT* Rosh Hash. 16b.

Abraham, God, and the ram's horn are from *BT* Rosh Hash. 16a; MT Gn. 4:46.

Abraham and Sarah

The text of Abraham and Sarah is included in Gn 11–21. Gn 21 includes the birth of Isaac. For Sarah's spiritual powers, I followed Teubal's ideas in *Sarah the Priestess* and portrayed Sarah as a Mesopotamian priestess. *BT* Baba Bathra 91a speaks of Abraham's mother's birth and the infant Abraham. I created the conversations between the mothers and between Abraham and Sarah, Sarah dreaming, Abraham naming Isaac. Hadley's *The Cult of Asherah* connects the worship of the goddess with oak trees. Other midrashim come from Ginzberg, vol. 1, Gn. R, and PRE 30 and 32. *The Book of Yashar* recounts Abraham's visiting Ishmael (21:20–48); Abraham not making a sacrifice to God for twenty-six years (22:51–53).

Sources and Notes for the Stories

The Binding of Isaac

I interwove midrash with Genesis 22 and 23 in composing *The Binding of Isaac*. All references to Satan are legends from the *Book of Yashar* 23 (as well as *BT* San. 89b), and Ginzberg, vol. 1. PRE 31, 32 gives midrash on Isaac asking to be bound, the journey to Mount Moriah, Sarah's soul ascending to heaven.

Hannah

I Samuel is the biblical text for *Hannah*. I Samuel 1 includes the birth of Samuel. Struck by Hannah's faith and strength of character, I chose to make her the protagonist of the birth of Samuel and so began the story with her. Professor A. J. Levine at Vanderbilt University, Nashville, Tennessee, suggested to me that the image of Samuel wearing the coat that Hannah made for him when he rises from the grave to speak with Saul would allow Hannah's presence to return at the end of the story. The first half of *Hannah*, until Samuel becomes the priest at Shiloh, follows the biblical text; the second half condenses large sections. Ginzberg, vol. 4, PRE 43:6 (Hannah urging Elkanah to marry) and Pesik. Rab. 43:7 (Each time Hannah gives birth, one of Peninah's children dies) provide the midrash for Hannah. In crafting Hannah's song, I included the lines "I ask all peoples, all nations" from Bib. Ant. 51:15; and for the last stanza of her song, lines from Bib. Ant., 51:25, 51:32. Samuel meditating on the cherubim is from Kaplan's *Meditation and the Bible*, p. 61.

About Yom Kippur

Moses brought the second set of tablets on Yom Kippur: PRE 46.
Dancing, lovemaking, and matchmaking followed: M. Ta'anit 4:8.
A man who gives charity in secret: *BT* Baba Bathra 9b.

The Holy of Holies

The Holy of Holies is from Mishnah Yoma. The story describes a ritual thousands of years old. Because it continues to be told, we know it has a great significance, but there is clearly missing information. In an attempt to understand the high priest's mysterious recitation of the numbers when throwing the blood, I introduced the concept of God's attributes. I have used Phillip Birnbaum's *High Holiday Prayer Book*, Hebrew Publishing Co., New York, 1951, pp. 812–26. The expression "Ten generations after," the paragraph "O God, you gave life to our ancestors," and the last paragraph "Now that the Temple is gone" are mine.

Sources and Notes for the Stories

Jonah

Jonah follows the biblical book of Jonah for Jonah's prophetic career. I begin Jonah's story with his childhood to bring out his spiritual initiation. Elijah and the widow is adapted from I Kings 17:8–24; Elijah giving the spirit to Elisha from II Kings 2; and Elisha commissioning his disciple to anoint Jehu from 11 Kings 9:1–14. My Hebrew teacher Anath Zahini at Hebrew University, in Jerusalem, pointed out to me that the Hebrew word for "fish" is first masculine and then feminine. I interwove midrash from Ginzberg's *Legends of the Jews*, vol. 4, throughout *Jonah*.

About the Stories

Counting God's attributes: *The Zohar.*

About Sukkot

Joyous singing, dancing, lighted torches, and acrobatics: *BT* Sukk. 53b.
Rejoicing at the place of drawing water: *BT* Sukk. 51b.
Different aspects of freedom: Seidman's *The Glory of the Jewish Holidays.*

The Etrog

I heard Rabbi Shlomo Carlebach tell the story of *The Etrog* several times. Rabbi Abraham Twersky, a direct descendant of Menahem of Chernobyl, owns the *tefillin* of the Baal Shem Tov. When I asked him the name of Nahum's wife, he graciously and dramatically told me his family's version of *The Etrog*. My rendition combines both tellings.

Solomon and the Demon King

This story is composed of many different legends and a small portion of biblical text, I Kgs 8:2–30 and I Chr 22:5–13. The gates beating Solomon and most of the legends in the story are based on Ginzberg, vol. 4. Several midrash are from *BT*: the shamir and Benaiah capturing Asmodeus: *BT* Git. 68b; Ruth in Solomon's kingdom: *BT* Baba Bathra 91b. Jane Enkins suggested using the question of "truth and illusion" from "The Beggar King" in Howard Schwartz's *Elijah's Violin*. Once I read Schwartz' wonderful telling, I added the use of Solomon's staff as a divining rod. My musings include King David giving his ring to Solomon and Solomon considering giving his ring to his son, the meeting of Solomon and Naamah, and their conversations. I based some of their conversations on the text in The Song of Songs: "You have awakened my soul," 4:9; "Let my spices flow," 5:16; "Set me as a seal on your arm," 8:6; "Love is as strong as death," 8:6.

Sources and Notes for the Stories

Kohelet

I shaped and condensed the biblical text of Ecclesiastes so that it reads more like a story. The first four sections follow Eccles 1–4. The fifth section is a combination of Eccles 7 and 9. The proverbs are selected from Eccles 5–11. The sixth and seventh sections are based on Eccles 12. The translation of *hebel* as breath—"all is the breath"—is from *The Zohar* 59A.

About the Stories

We stop for funerals and weddings: Munk, p. 139.
Union of God's masculine and feminine soul: *The Zohar.*

The Death of Moses

The Death of Moses is based mainly on Ginzberg, vol. 3. The Hebrew word for soul, *neshamah*, is feminine.

Joshua

To give the necessary context for the oak of Moreh as well as Joseph's bones being buried in Shechem, I begin the story of *Joshua* with the story of the oak of Moreh (Gn 12:6) and Dinah and Shechem (Gn 34). I condensed the biblical book of Joshua and consulted Ginzberg, vols. 3 and 4, as well as the *Book of Yashar* 33. Joshua marrying Rahab is a well-known midrash. The mark of the fish on Joshua refers to his name in Aramaic, which means "fish" (Gn R 97:3). The love stories of Dinah and Shechem and Rahab and Joshua are my own as are the grieving of the earth (see also Hos 4:3), the Canaanite woman naming Joshua the son of Nun, Rahab's conversations with her parents, Joshua staying with Rahab's family, and the Shechinah counseling Joshua to help those who are distant. Ginzberg states that Joshua is a hangman. When I asked Rabbi Zalman Schachter-Shalomi about Joshua's profession, he told me that oral tradition says that Joshua was a tax collector. Hamlin's *Inheriting the Land*, pp. 99–101, proposes that the oppressed Canaanite peasants joined the invading Hebrews. For the minimum commandments, see Glossary. The Shechinah's choices regarding war are based on Dt 20:10.

Genesis

In the Hebrew word *lev*, meaning "heart," the Hebrew letters *b* and *v* are interchangeable.

I followed the biblical text Gn 1:1–31 closely and added the midrash of Shimon bar Yochai that is in Munk, p. 109.

Sources and Notes for the Stories

About the Stories
No archeological evidence of battle during time of Joshua: Hamlin.
Information on Egyptian God, Nun: R. T. Rundle Clark, *Myth and Symbol in Ancient Egypt.*
The horrific crimes of the Canaanites/Sodomites: Noah, *Book of Yashar.*

Judith
    I condensed the text from the Apocrypha in *The Jerusalem Bible* for Judith. I added Judith changing her way of living after her husband's death, the character of Ora, the love scene of Holofernes and Judith, the interchange between Judith and Achior, and the shaping of Judith's victory song.

The Maccabees
    I begin and end *The Maccabees* with the Temple and the presence of the Shechinah to contrast with the horrors of war. I wove *The Maccabees* from many different sources. The primary one is Maccabees I and II as well as the Talmud. The description of the Temple and the cherubim is from Patai's Hebrew Goddess, pp. 101–36. Life under Greek rule is from Bickerman's *From Ezra to the Last of the Maccabees.* The battle scenes and war strategies from Pearlman's *The Maccabees.* The laws of the covenant for battle are from Dt 20:5–9. The last paragraph regarding the lighting of the menorah is mine.

Joseph
    Joseph follows the biblical text Gn 37–50. Throughout the text, I interweave Ginzberg, vol. 2, and Gen. R. Joseph's bones traveling with the Hebrews in the desert is from *Mekh.*, Beshallah.

About the Stories
Changing habitual inclinations: Teaching of Rabbi Shlomo Carlebach on Hanukkah.

Purim
Assyrian word *pur(u)*: "The First Purim" by William W. Hallo. *Biblical Archaeologist*, Winter 1983, pps. 19–29.

Esther
    Esther follows the biblical text with much interweaving from Culi's *The Book of Esther*, and Ginzberg, vol. 4. Yoram Hazony in *The Dawn* suggests that

Haman became the only advisor to the king. The following legends come from PRE 50: Mordecai spoke seventy languages; Jews do not celebrate Passover; Mordecai, a man of peace. Esther mimics the king is from Wolkstein's *Esther's Story*. Esther staring the king down until he changes his mind is also mine.

Some modern translators say Haman is impaled, I've retained the earlier translation of "hung" because it adds to the topsy-turvy atmosphere of the story.

About the Story
Esther claims her power, appeals to the king: Hazony.
Midrash linking Sarah and Esther: Rabbi Shlomo Carlebach; Gen. R. 58:13.
"Where God resides:" Munk, pp. 144–45.

Traditional Sources
BT—Babylonian Talmud. The Talmud is a multivolume collection of law and legend made up of 2 parts: the Mishnah, which tries to explain what is in the Torah, and the Gemara, which tries to further clarify. There are 2 versions of the Talmud, the more frequently cited and more extensive Babylonian Talmud, which was completed around the 5th century C.E., and the Jerusalem Talmud, also known as the Palestinian Talmud, which was completed around the 4th century C.E.

Gen. R.—Genesis Rabbah. Collection of midrash on the book of Genesis, thought to have been edited ca. 425 C.E.

Lam. R.—Lamentations Rabbah. Collection of midrash on the book of Lamentations, including proems and exegesis. This collection is thought to have been edited around the 4th and 5th centuries C.E.

LoJ—*Legends of the Jews*, by Louis Ginzberg. A 7-volume work published between 1909 and 1938 that brought together as a continuous narrative Jewish midrashim on biblical text preserved in a wide range of sources, including the Talmud, midrashic collections, Kabbalistic works, and early Christian writings.

Mekhilta—Midrash on Exodus, based on draft from school of Rabbi Ishmael, thought to be one of the earliest collections, probably compiled in the 1st and 2nd centuries C.E.

Mishnah—The collection of Oral Torah that explains the material contained in the Torah, probably completed around 200 C.E. The Mishnah, comprised 6 orders that are divided into tractates and, together with the Gemara, form the main body of the Talmud text.

M. Ta'anit—Mishnah Ta'anit. The tractate of the Mishnah that deals with fasts.

Sources and Notes for the Stories

MT—Midrash Tanhuma. Group of midrashim that includes material from other sources, possibly dates as early as 4th century C.E., though thought by some scholars to be no earlier than 9th century C.E.

Pesik. Rab.—Pesikta Rabbati. Rabbinical commentaries on texts read for festive days and Sabbaths, accounts of lives of rabbis, composed in Palestine in the 4th and 5th centuries C.E.

PRE—Pirke De Rabbi Eliezer. A midrash on Genesis and the beginning of Exodus that is generally attributed to a 1st-century C.E. teacher named Rabbi Eliezer ben Hyrcanus. Thought to have been compiled in the 8th century C.E.

Zohar—The Zohar is the classic 13-century work of Jewish mysticism.

Glossary

This glossary is intended to be supplemental and helpful; it is not definitive. Entries are offered when there is information to supplement the introductions or stories. Pronunciation note: *ch* in Hebrew is pronounced as the *ch* in Loch Ness.

Aaron (possibly Egyptian origin) AIR-un
Tribe: Levi; father: Amram; mother: Yocheved; brother: Moses; sister: Miriam; wife: Elisheba; sons: Nadab, Avihu, Eleazar, Ithamar. Spokesman for Moses and first high priest. Loved people, gave over teachings with great humility, never criticized anyone, and sought to bring peace to families. Because of his merit, clouds of glory followed the Hebrews during their wanderings and disappeared at his death. Died on Mount Hor at age 123. His sons Nadab and Avihu were consumed by fire from the holy of holies; his son Eleazar inherited his priestly office and garments.

Abraham (origin unknown) A-brah-ham
Father: Terah; mother: Emtelai; brothers: Nahor, Haran; wives: Sarah, Hagar (Keturah); sons: Ishmael and 6 other sons with Hagar, Isaac with Sarah; nephew: Lot. Father of the Ishmaelites and Hebrews; one of 3 patriarchs. Tenth generation from Noah; studied in Ur with Noah and Shem (when Abraham was 58, Noah died at age of 950). Left Ur with father to go to Haran. At God's command journeyed from Haran to Canaan; built many altars to God. Divided land in Canaan with Lot. At age 99, God changed his name from Abram (high) to Abraham. Agreed to God's covenant: land of Canaan will belong to his descendants; he is to circumcise all males in his tribe at 8 days old and descendants are to follow God's teachings. Pleaded with God not to destroy Sodom and Gomorrah. Sent away Hagar and Ishmael at Sarah's command. Agreed to God's command to sacrifice Isaac. Bought cave of Machpelah in Hebron to bury Sarah. Married Hagar and had 6 more sons; gave them wealth, sent them to the east. Gave Isaac his blessing and title to land. Died at age

of 185 on the day Jacob bought Esau's birthright (Bava Bathra 16b). All his sons, including Isaac and Ishmael, attended his funeral. Buried in cave of Machpelah with Sarah. Mourned for a year by relatives, people of Canaan, especially children.

Adonai (Hebrew: "Lord") Ah-doe-NYE

Name of God meaning "My Lord." Also used as a substitute term for Yahweh. Adonai represents God's merciful qualities.

afikoman (Greek: "dessert") Ah-fee-KOE-man

The half of the middle matzah of 3 matzahs that represents the Passover lamb; traditionally last thing eaten at Passover Seder so its taste and recollection will remain strongest.

aggadah (Hebrew: "narration") ah-GAH-dah

Sayings, proverbs, legends, and narrations of rabbinic literature. Some examples of aggadah: "We enter the world with our hands closed, we leave with our hands open." "Whoever seeks a friend without faults will remain friendless." Thirty percent of Babylonian Talmud is aggadic literature, the remaining 70 percent is halakhah, pertaining to legal matters and rules of conduct.

Ahasuerus (origin unknown) Ah-hahs-VAY-russ

Wives: Vashti, Esther. Possibly the historical Xerxes, 486–465 B.C.E. According to book of Esther, the king of the Persian Empire. Accepted bribe from his prime minister Haman to kill all Jews in Persia; persuaded by Esther to allow Jews to defend themselves against genocide.

Amalekites (origin unknown) Uh-MAH-leh-kites

Name of group of people. Nomads descended from Amalek who was grandson of Esau and the son of Eliphaz and Timna. Represented archetypal enemy of Israel; attacked Hebrews' entry into Promised Land (Num 14:44–45). Also said to exist from time before the Flood (Zohar 1:25b). Saul lost kingship of Israel because he did not follow Yahweh's command to destroy all Amalekites but let Agag live. According to tradition, Haman is descendant of Agag. The last Amalekites were destroyed in time of Hezekiah. Associated with land of Edom.

Amram (Hebrew: "The Divine Kinsman is exalted") AHM-rahm

Tribe: Levi; father: Kohath; wife and aunt: Yocheved; children: Miriam, Aaron, Moses. A leader of his generation (Sot. 12a). One of the 7 righteous who brought the Shechinah back to earth. Thought to have died free of sin at age 137.

Apocrypha (Greek: "secret," "hidden") Ah-PAH-krih-fah

Name of books of ethical content, such as Judith and the Maccabees, written by Jews during Second Temple but not included in Hebrew Bible.

Glossary

Asher (Hebrew: "fortunate," "happy," or derivation of Asherah, name of Canaanite Goddess) AH-sher

Father: Jacob; mother: Zilpah (Gn 30:12–13); wife: Hadurah; stepdaughter: Serach. Last son of Jacob to die. Endowed with riches, blessings, and beautiful daughters. At death, revealed name of redeemer, which Joseph had told him, to his stepdaughter Serach.

Asherah (Assyrian: "shrine") Ah-SHER-ah

Goddess, wooden image, tree pole. Powerful Canaanite goddess whose consort is El. Inscriptions link name to Yahweh; numerous cultic objects of Asherah found in sanctuaries of Yahweh; said to have 400 prophets (I Kgs 18:19). Canaanite shrine consisted of stone pillar and sacred tree (asherah). Subsequently became literary construct Lady Wisdom.

Azazel (Hebrew: origin unknown) Ah-zah-ZELL

(1) Name of Angel. Rebelled against God for creating humans because he knew humanity would sin; sent to earth with angel Uzza for testing but failed. He was no more immune to sin than mortals. Azazel and Uzza took wives and had children, the nephilim the spies meet in Canaan (Gn 6:4). The two angels taught sorcery and revealed God's ineffable name; punishment was exile. In some legends, exiled to earth; in others, left suspended between heaven and earth. (2) Name of demon. At Yom Kippur a goat is offered to Azazel to atone for the sins of the people. (3) Name of place in wilderness thought to be rugged, precipitous, and habitat of demons.

Balaam (Hebrew: origin unknown) BAH-lahm

Ancestor: Kemuel; father: Beor. Sorcerer, diviner, advisor, prophet. Understood that all evil contains spark of holiness (Zohar 2:69b). Learned sorcery from father who learned from angels Azazel and Uzza (Zohar 1:126a). Advisor to pharaoh. Called by king of Moab to curse Israelites, but God caused him to bless them instead (Num 22–24). Prophesied Israel's victory over Moab and Edom and downfall of other nations. Killed in battle between Israelites and Midianites.

Boaz (Hebrew: "of sharp mind" or "in him there is strength") BOE-az

Tribe: Judah; ancestors: Joshua, Rahab; wife: Ruth; son: Obed. Respected landowner in Judah. Related to Naomi's husband, Elimelech. Boaz' first wife's funeral was on day Ruth arrived in Judah (Baba Bathra 91b). Supported the Moabite Ruth, who came to glean in his field; later married her at age of 80. Died day after wedding.

breastplate

One of 8 garments worn by high priest. Made of double piece of woven, embroidered fabric; set with 4 rows of 3 stones; each stone inscribed with

Glossary

name of one of 12 tribes of Jacob. High priest said to gaze at 12 stones in meditative mode close to prophecy and to perceive which letters the urim and thummin inside the breastplate were illuminating. See urim and thummin.

Caleb (Hebrew: "dog") KAY-leb

Tribe: Judah; father: Jephunneh; brother: Kenaz (descendant of Esau, Gn 36:15); wife: Miriam? Friend and spokesman for Joshua. Sent by Moses to bring reports back from Promised Land (I Chr 2:18–20). In Canaan forced fearful Hebrew spies to bring fruit back to people in wilderness. Because of his favorable report, God promised him land (Num 24:14) that Joshua gave him near Hebron. Defeated Anakites in Hebron. Cared for Miriam in her illness (Rashi).

calendar

The Hebrew calendar combines a solar and lunar cycle. The sun determines the years, the moon the months. Each month begins at the new moon or the dark of the moon, and the 15th night of the month is the full moon. The calendar is adjusted by intercalating an extra month, after the last month, 7 times during 19 years. Each new month had been determined by observation and calculation; in the 4th century, astronomical observation fixed the Jewish calendar internationally. The names of the Hebrew months are based on the Babylonian months. Thirtieth day of the month became 1st day of new month.

cherubim (Hebrew: k'ruvim, from the Akkadian) CHAIR-uh-bim

Beings with large wings, human heads, and animal (often lion) bodies. Servants of God, guardians of a sacred place. The holy of holies had 2 facing gold cherubim forming one piece with ark cover. Their outstretched wings protected the ark and acted as God's throne. King Solomon's cherubim, made of olive wood covered with gold, were 15 feet high; their inner wings touched. Philo attributes masculine and feminine aspects of God to each of the cherubim. Talmudic tradition reports that in Second Temple cherubim were intertwined in marital embrace and during festivals priests rolled up veil, allowing people to witness this divine love.

Dathan (Hebrew: "law") DAY-than and **Abiram** (Hebrew: "father is exalted") Ah-BEER-um

Hebrew slaves. Represent divisive and rebellious quality of Hebrews who left Egypt. Dathan's quarrel with Egyptian taskmaster, who consorted with his wife, precipitated Moses striking the taskmaster (Ex R. 1:28); he quarreled with Abiram following day. Reported Moses' killing Egyptian to Pharaoh (Yalkut shimoni). Rebelled at Reed Sea. In wilderness hoarded extra manna, which rotted. When Hebrews rebelled in wilderness, they wanted to appoint Dathan in Moses' place and Abiram in Aaron's place. Both perished in wilderness with Korath; swallowed up by the earth for defying Moses.

David (Hebrew: "beloved") DAY-vid

Tribe: Judah; father: Jesse; mother: Nizbeth; wives: 18; children: 6. King of Israel, known as exceptional political and military leader (Lev. R 1:4), poet, (BT Ber. 10a), harpist (BT Ber. 3b), and scholar (Lev. R. 35:1, BT Ber. 4a). A shepherd who fought giant Goliath and prevailed, captain in Saul's army but later feared and hated by Saul (I Sam 18:10–24:22; 26:1–31:13). After Saul's death became king (II Sam 2:4). Book of Psalms attributed to him (BT Pes. 117a; Eccl. R. 7:19). According to legend, sent Uriah to be killed in battle in order to marry his wife, Bathsheba; as a result not permitted by God to build the Temple. When Temple gates accepted ark of covenant in David's name, David's sin was forgiven. Born and died second day of Shavuot, the holiday associated with his great-grandmother Ruth.

Dinah (Hebrew: "judge") DEE-nah

Father: Jacob; mother: Leah. Tragic figure who loved an outsider. Placed in chest when father went to meet his brother Esau, so Esau would not lust after her. Raped by Shechem and according to legend bore a daughter by him, who was abandoned in Israel. The daughter, who was given a protective amulet by her grandfather, Jacob, was carried to Egypt, raised by Potiphar, and named Asenath (Yalkut shimoni, Vayishlach 134). Daughter gave amulet to Joseph when she met him. Many legends about Dinah's fate: married Simeon who brought back her bones from Egypt and buried her in Canaan, married Job and had 10 children by him.

Eliezer (Hebrew: "God is my help") El-ee-EH-zer

Abraham's steward. Put in furnace by Nimrod; survived and given by Nimrod as gift to Abraham (Sefer ha-Yashar Noah 42). Accompanied Abraham to rescue Lot. Hoped Isaac would marry his daughter, but faithfully brought Rebekah back from Haran to marry Isaac (Gn 24). As reward, freed by Abraham and given land of Basham; took the name Og (PdRE16).

El Shaddai (Hebrew: "breast" or "God of the mountain." Greek: "self-sufficient," "omnipotent," "nourishing" or "all-powerful") EL-Shah-DIE

Name for God. In Torah, God appeared to Abraham, Isaac, and Jacob as El Shaddai (Ex 6:3).

Eliphaz (Arabic: "my God triumphs") EL-ee-fahz

Father: Esau; mother: Adah; concubine: Timnah; son: Amalek. Friend of Israelites. Defied Esau's wishes regarding the fate of Jacob and helped Jacob's people (Mid. Ag., Gn 28:20).

Elkanah (Hebrew: "God has created") EL-kah-nah
Wives: Hannah, Peninah; sons: 16, including Samuel. Righteous leader of Israel. Made 4, rather than usual 3 yearly pilgrimages to Shiloh; always took different route; encouraged many people to join him. People cast lots 4 times to choose him as a judge but refused appointment because did not want to take on people's sins (Bib. Ant. 49:5). God promised that one of his sons would be priest and rule Israel.

Elohim (Hebrew: "the powers," "the forces") El-oh-HEEM
Name for God. God created the world as Elohim. According to Kabbalah, the hidden aspect of God is Ein Sof, which leads to the house of the beginning and from this house the creator Elohim emerges. According to Kabbalah, the upper Shechinah or supernal mother aspect of God; divine justice and strength. Person stands before Elohim in fear and trembling or with sense of reverence or piety. Root for "*El*," god, is also the root for "*elon*," oak tree.

Esau (Hebrew: "hairy") EE-saw
Father: Isaac; mother: Rebekah; twin brother: Jacob; wives: Judith, Adah, Basemath (daughter of Ishmael); sons: 6, including Eliphaz; grandson: Amalek. Father of tribes of Edomites and Amalekites; a hunter. Isaac's favorite son. Shot Nimrod in the fields and believing he would be killed by Nimrod's men, agreed to sell birthright to brother Jacob, who later tricked him out of his father's blessing. Asked his grandson Amalek to take revenge on Jacob's children (Yalkut shimoni, chukas 764). Reconciled with Jacob at father's deathbed, but then followed brother into cave of Machpelah saying, "Now that my father is dead, I will kill Jacob." Jacob's son Judah saw Esau crawl into cave and shot him with an arrow from behind (Shocher Tov 18:2).

Esther (Hebrew: "secret"; Akkadian: "Ishtar," Goddess of love, war, fertility)
Husband: Ahasuerus; father died when she was conceived; mother died when she was born (Meg. 13a). Prophetess and queen; considered, along with Sarah, Rahab, and Abigail, one of the most beautiful women in the Bible. Raised by Mordecai, uncle/cousin (?). Chosen for king's harem as most beautiful girl in Susa. Became queen of Persia. When lives of Jews in Persia threatened, cleverly appealed to king to amend death decree, thus giving Jews a chance to defend themselves against total annihilation. Legend says her son was Cyrus, who conquered Babylon and allowed the Jewish exiles to return to Jerusalem to rebuild the Temple.

Ezekiel (Hebrew: "God will strengthen me") Eh-ZEE-kee-el
Father: Buzi. A temple priest and prophet. Taken by Nebuchadnezzar in first exile to Babylon, 597 B.C.E. Preached in Babylon near Nippur,

593–571 B.C.E. during reign of Zedekiah. Buried in Israel next to Baruch, Jeremiah's disciple.

Gabriel (Hebrew: "God is my warrior") GAY-bree-el

Along with Michael, one of 2 angels named in Hebrew Bible. According to midrash, one of 4 angels guarding throne of God, along with Michael, Uriel, and Raphael (Num. R. 2:10). Said to be made of fire (Jb 25:2; Deut. R. 5:12). Identified as one of 3 anonymous strangers who visited Abraham after his circumcision (Gn. R. 48:9) as well as the figure who wrestled with Jacob at the Jabbok River (Gn. R. 78:1) when Jacob was returning to Canaan.

Gemara (Arabic: "to learn") Geh-MAHR-ah

Interpretations and commentaries on the Mishnah. Compiled by rabbis in Babylon and Palestine between third and sixth centuries. Part of Talmud.

Goliath (Origin unknown) Guh-LIE-uth

Mother: Orpah (BT Sot. 42b). Philistine warrior from Gath. Regarded as a *Rafah*, a people thought to be giants (II Sam 21:19–20; Dt 2:11). Greatly feared by Israelites because of his height, armor, and weapons; taunted Israelites for forty days. Killed by young shepherd David with slingshot (I Sam 17:4–51).

Hagar (Sabean: "splendid village" or town) Hah-GAHR

Father: pharaoh; mother: a concubine; husband: Abraham; sons: 7, including Ishmael. Married Abram at Sarai's request. (Note: In Babylon, if a man's wife was childless after ten years, he was allowed to take a concubine to have children [Yev. 6:6]. According to Mesopotamian legal practices, a woman could hire a slave-girl to bear her husband children and those children would be considered the wife's.) During pregnancy fled from Sarai's harshness and saw angels at well in wilderness (Gn. R. 45:7); one of whom spoke to her. First person in Bible to name God. After death of Sarah, sent for by Abraham and married him; name was then Keturah meaning she had bound herself to good deeds.

Haggadah (Hebrew: "telling," "recounting") Ha-GAH-dah

The text used at Passover Seder. Includes prayers, benedictions, scriptural passages, commentaries, poetry, songs, and instructions as described in the Mishnah (Pes. 10). Although the order and primary texts for the most part remain the same, style and interpretation vary across generations and from one Haggadah to another.

halakhah (Hebrew: "guidance," Talmudic law) ha-LACH-hah

Examination of Jewish legal tradition, rules of conduct; first compilation made by Rabbi Akivah was used as a basis for the Mishnah.

Hannah (Hebrew: "graciousness," "favor," "compassion") HAH-nuh

Husband: Elkanah; children: 6, including Samuel. Prophetess. One of 7 biblical prophetesses (Meg. 14a). Suggested Elkanah marry another woman so he might have children; tormented by cowife Peninah. Her manner of prayer to God—moving lips, fervent, silent—became the exemplary way to pray. Conceived at age of 130. When son Samuel was age 4, brought him to Temple to be raised by priests. Hannah, Sarah, and Rachel conceived children on Rosh Hashanah (Berachos 29a).

Hasidism (Hebrew: *hasid*, "goodness," "kindness," "piety")

Modern movement started by the Baal Shem Tov (1700–1760) as a reaction to intellectual, legalistic approach to Judaism in eastern Europe and Poland. It began at a time of great oppression toward Jews and reached out and appealed to the poor. Emphasized that God's presence is everywhere and available to everyone. Stories, music, dance, prayers, walks in nature were considered ways of reaching God as valid as study: "Before you can find God, you must lose yourself." Stressed inspiration, kindness, and serving God with joy and happiness, especially when carrying out mitzvot (God's commandments). Leaders of different branches of Hasidism called *tzaddikim* or rebbes.

hesed (Hebrew: "loving-kindness") HEH-sed

Loving-kindness, loyalty, faithfulness, compassion.

high priest

Aaron, who was from the tribe of Levi, was the first high priest. (All male descendants of Aaron are called Kohens; the firstborn sons served as high priests. The rest of the tribe of Levi served as Temple musicians, attendants, teachers, scribes. Jews not of the tribe of Levi are called Israelites. (To this day certain responsibilities in the synagogue service and in Jewish life can only be fulfilled by Kohanim and Leviim.) High priest was considered conduit allowing God's energy to flow through God's aspects (the sephirot) to earth. During time of First Temple, religious office appointed by Israel's king. When Israel became vassal state, religious office appointed by foreign king. In Greek times, political as well as religious head of Israel. At time of Second Temple, high priest determined calendar and regularly convened sanhedrin, a group of 70 rabbis, to make legislative and judicial decisions. The high priest and temple priests were supported by sacrifices and tithes from the people. Position of high priest ended when Second Temple was destroyed.

Hillel

Sage and founder of religious academy. Born in Babylon. Lived between first century B.C.E. and first century C.E. Traveled to Palestine at 40, studied for 40 years suffering much hardship, at 80 became spiritual head of Israel. Known for his patience, humility, exemplary life. Core teaching: love your neighbor. Believed soul is a guest on earth toward whom we must offer charity and loving-kindness. Sayings include: "If I am not for myself, who will be for me? If I am only for myself, what am I?" "If I am here, so says God, everyone is here, if I am not here, nobody is here." His sayings are in book *Ethics of Fathers*. Died at age of 120.

Hineni (Hebrew: "I am here") HEE-nay-nee

Traditionally taken to be righteous person's response to God, meaning "I am here."

Huldah (Arabic: "beauty mark"?) HULL-dah

Ancestors: Joshua and Rahab; husband: Shallem, relative of Jeremiah. Prophetess. Josiah consulted Huldah rather than Jeremiah because he thought she would intercede with God and be more compassionate (Meg. 14b). Huldah's husband Shallem was said to be a *tzaddik*. He sat by the roadside and gave water to whoever was thirsty. One of 7 biblical prophetesses.

Inanna (Sumerian: queen of heaven) In-NAH-nah

Great Sumerian goddess of love, war, fertility, and the morning and evening star (the planet Venus); connected iconographically to stars, serpents, bulls, trees. Prototype for queen of heaven (2800–1900 B.C.E.). Ritual offerings included animals, grain, cakes, flowers, beer. Married shepherd king (Dumuzi, Tammuz) in sacred marriage rite (*hieros gamos*); brought back attributes of civilization from Eridu to her city, Uruk (biblical Erech); journeyed to underworld and opened communications with its deity. Later (1200–200 B.C.E.), syncretized with Akkadian goddess Ishtar and Canaanite goddesses Astarte, Asherah, Anat.

Isaac (Hebrew: "he will laugh") EYE-zick

Father: Abraham; mother: Sarah; half-brother: Ishmael; wife: Rebekah; sons: Jacob, Esau. One of three patriarchs known for his strength and devotion. Brought by father to Mount Moriah to be given as burnt offering. (Note: Binding of Isaac is called in Hebrew "The Akedah.") Eyes weakened after experience of binding. After returning from Mount Moriah, studied with Shem. Tricked by Rebekah into blessing younger son, Jacob, rather than older son, Esau. Sent Jacob to Haran to find a wife. United his father with Hagar (Keturah) after Sarah's death; mourned death of half-brother Ishmael many days. Summoned sons to deathbed and begged them to reconcile. Died at age 180, buried by sons.

Ishmael (Hebrew: "God will hear") ISH-my-ell

Father: Abraham; mother: Hagar; half-brother: Isaac; wives: Meribah, Malchut; sons: 12; daughter: Mahalath. Father of Ishmaelites. Before his birth, God predicted that "he will be a wild ass of a man; his hand will be against everyone and every man's hand against him" (Gn 16:12). Played roughly with half-brother Isaac; he and Hagar were sent away by Abraham. Betrothed daughter to nephew, Esau. At father's advice, divorced Egyptian wife; his marriage to Canaanite woman blessed by Abraham. Reconciled with his father. He and Isaac bury Abraham. Died at age 137.

Jacob (Hebrew: "he will supplant," later called Israel—"wrestler") JAY-cub
Father: Isaac; mother: Rebekah; brother: Esau; wives: Leah, Rachel; concubines: Bilhah, Zilpah; sons: 12; daughter: Dinah. Father of 12 sons each of whose descendants became one of 12 tribes of Jacob; one of three patriarchs. Tricked brother Esau out of birthright (Gn 25:29–34) and father's blessings (Gn 270). According to midrash, studied with Shem and Eber until age 50 when Shem died. Traveled north from Beersheba to Bethel, where he dreamt of a ladder with angels coming and going from heaven (Gn 28:10–22). In Haran, married Leah, then Rachel; took Bilhah and Zilpah, servants of Rachel and Leah, as his concubines. After working 20 years as shepherd for father-in-law, Laban, returned to Canaan (Gn 29–31). At Jabbok, wrestled with angel who blessed him: "Your name will no longer be Jacob but Israel, for you have wrestled with God and with men and have persevered" (Gn 32:29). Reconciled with Esau (Gn 32–33). Settled in Hebron. Separated from favorite son, Joseph. During famine in Canaan, sent sons to bring grain from Egypt; when summoned by Joseph, set out for Egypt and made offering in Beersheba, his birthplace; settled in Egypt (Gn 37–47). Buried in cave of Machpelah. Born and died on Sukkot at age of 137.

Jeremiah (Hebrew: "God established") Je-re-MY-ah
Ancestors: Joshua, Rahab; father: Hilkiah (a priest); son: Sira? Prophet during time of First Temple. God spoke to him at age 13; studied in Jerusalem under Shaphan. Began prophesying in 627 B.C.E. during reign of Josiah; preached that Israel owed everything to God's love and that people needed to be loyal and obedient, and to repent their betrayal of the covenant. After Josiah's death, preached that each person's deeds, not merely Temple attendance and sacrifices, were at core of Judaism. Mocked by people, rejected by priests who barred him from entering Temple, forced to go into hiding. His disciple, Baruch, read his teachings in Temple for him. Avoided execution by King Jehoiakin; commanded by God to go to Anathoth because God could not destroy Jerusalem in his presence. After capture of Judah, taken to Egypt where he died. Disciple, Baruch, taken captive and imprisoned in Babylon. After Baruch's death, Baruch's disciple Ezra brought people back from Babylon to rebuild the Temple in Jerusalem. Credited with writing Lamentations, 640–587 B.C.E.

Glossary

Jesse (origin unknown) JEH-see

Father: Obed; wife: Nizbeth; sons: 8, including David. One of eight messianic princes (BT Suk. 52b). Taught Torah to the masses (BT Yev. 76b). When Nizbeth saw that he was about to seduce a slave, she disguised herself as that slave, and Jesse slept with her. They conceived David. Encouraged David to slay Goliath to protect King Saul.

Jethro (Origin unknown) JEH-throe

Wife: Jael; daughters: 7, including Zipporah; son-in-law: Moses. Originally named Jether, renamed Jethro because of his good deeds. As priest, taught his people the wisdom of the Hebrews. When he left Egypt, took sapphire staff that God had given to Adam that passed from the patriarchs to Joseph; buried staff in garden. Moses able to pull out staff (Amalek 3).

Jonah (Hebrew: "dove") JOE-nah

Father: from tribe of Zebulun; mother: from tribe of Asher. Prophet. Disciple of Elijah, anointed by Elisha, who sent him to anoint Jehu, king of Israel (Bamidbar 14:1). Called by God to tell Ninevites to repent; instead fled to Jaffe and took boat to escape God's will. Thrown into sea by sailors during storm and swallowed by huge fish. Prayed to God, saved, obeyed God's wishes. Angry that God forgave the Ninevites when city of Nineveh repented.

Joseph (Hebrew: from verb "to add"; "may the Lord add another son to me") JOE-sef

Father: Jacob; mother: Rachel; brothers: 11; sister: Dinah; wife: Asenath (daughter of Potiphera, the priest of On); sons: Ephraim, Manasseh. Governor of Egypt. Father's favorite son, sold by brothers to traders. Became steward to Potiphar in Egypt; refused advances of Zuleika, his master's wife. Thrown in prison for 10 years. Interpreted dreams for Pharaoh; raised to governor of Egypt; sold grain to his brothers; reconciled with his family. Died on last day of Sukkot at age 110, bones buried in Shechem by Joshua.

Joshua (Hebrew: "God is my salvation") JOSH-oo-ah

Tribe: Joseph; wife: Rahab; daughters: 8. Leader and general of Israelites. Fought Amalek. Name changed by Moses from Hosea to Joshua. Assumed leadership of Hebrew people after death of Moses; led them into Canaan. Supported by God in all his battles to conquer the land; defeated Jericho when shouts of Hebrews destroyed city's walls; during battle of Ai when he cried out, "Stand still, O sun at Gibeon, O moon in the valley of Aijalon" (Jos 10:13), both heavenly bodies stood still. Set up tabernacle at Shiloh and apportioned land. Died in land of Ephraim at age 110.

Josiah (Hebrew: "God will support") JOE-zie-ah
Father: Amon; mother: Adidah. King and reformer who united Judah and Israel. Lived during the time of Assyrian occupancy of Judah; brought reform to Judah when Book of Moses (Dt 32) was found in Temple in 622 B.C.E. Because of prophecy of Huldah, hid ark, container of manna, Aaron's staff (Yoma 52b). Fought Egyptians in their war against Babylon and died in 609 B.C.E. at age 39.

Judah (Hebrew: "praise" or "give thanks") JOO-dah
Name of Person. Father: Jacob; mother: Leah; brothers: 11; sister: Dinah; wife: Aliyath; sons: 5, including Perez and Zerah. Son of Jacob, head of most powerful Hebrew tribe. Suggested selling his brother Joseph into slavery; acknowledged illegitimate sons by his daughter-in-law Tamar. Willing to sacrifice his life for his brother Benjamin's freedom. Had great strength; according to midrash, when he became angry, the hairs on his chest burst through his clothes (Gn. R. 6, 7). Died at age 119. Name of Place. After the division of Solomon's kingdom, Judah became the name of the southern kingdom. Known as Judea in Latin during Persian and Roman times and as Palestine after 74 B.C.E.

Judith (Hebrew: a "Judean" woman) JOO-dith
Tribe: Simeon; father: Merari; husband: Manasseh. Wise woman and daring warrior. Wealthy, righteous widow risked her life to rescue her people; entered enemy camp alone with one servant, beguiled and killed Nebuchadnezzar's general, Holofernes, who intended to annihilate all Israelites. Her story is from the Apocrypha. Died at age 105.

Kabbalah (Hebrew: "received") Kah-BAH-lah
Esoteric, mystical teachings belonging to many centuries, that are based on the Torah, Talmud, and Jewish oral traditions; passed on from master to student, from mouth to ear. Its foremost book is the Zohar, published in the thirteenth century. According to Kabbalah, there are three levels of interpretation: outer, inner, and innermost. Kabbalistic teachers devised metaphors and meditations to guide practitioners in their quest, which was to be close to God. Kabbalah's underlying belief is in the unity of the universe: as above, so below; as humans reside in God, God resides in humans.

kitel (Yiddish: garment) KEH-tel
A simple linen robe worn by orthodox on wedding, Passover, Yom Kippur, and for burial.

Leah (Hebrew: "cow") LAY-ah
Father: Laban; twin sister: Rachel; husband: Jacob; sons: Reuben, Simeon, Levi, Judah, Issachar, Zebulun, daughter: Dinah. One of four matriarchs. Wept so much at idea of marrying Esau that her eyes became

"tender" looking (Tanhuma vayeitzei 12). Through son Judah, progenitor of the Davidic line of kingship and through son, Levi, connected to the Aaronic priesthood. The rivalry between Leah's descendants, the tribe of Judah, and Rachel's descendants, the tribe of Ephraim, continued in clashes between the southern kingdom, Judah, and the northern kingdom, Israel. Died in Hebron at age 51.

Lech l'cha (Hebrew: "go" or "go into yourself") LEHKH-leh-hah
Go, set out. Most important occurrence of phrase is when God commands Abraham to leave Haran to go to a land he does not know (Gn 12).

Mahlon (Hebrew: "sickness") MAH-lahn and **Kilyon** (Hebrew: "destruction") KILL-yahn
Father: Elimelech; mother: Naomi (Ruth 1:2). Mahlon's wife: Ruth; Kilyon's wife: Orpah. Mahlon was thought to have committed acts of profanity, Kilyon to have been condemned to destruction by God. Brothers sinned by leaving the land of Israel during famine in time of Judges (BT Baba Bathra 191b).

manna (Hebrew: "what is it?") MAN-nah
Bread that fell from heaven and because of the merit of Moses fed Hebrews during the 40 years they wandered in desert. Described as fine, white coriander but tasted differently to each person. Gathered by Aaron and put in ark of covenant for future generations; disappeared after destruction of Temple.

matzah (Hebrew: origin unknown) MAH-tzah
Unleavened bread made of flour and water, mixed by hand or machine, then baked within 18 minutes of being mixed. It is a flat, square- or oval-shaped wafer. Referred to as the bread of affliction (Dt 16:3). Eaten at Passover as a remembrance of the Hebrews' hasty departure from Egypt at the time of the Exodus, when there was no time for dough to rise (Ex 12:34).

midrash (Hebrew: "study," "interpretation") MIH-drash
Jewish stories, teachings, and sayings created to elucidate biblical text. Includes halakhah (study of laws), and aggadah (exploration of stories). Each generation created and continues to create midrash to explain, explore, challenge and open content of biblical text.

minimum commandments (Noachian Precepts)
The 7 principles, known as Noachian Precepts, imposed on descendants of Noah. These hold for all non-Jews as the minimum requirements of right action and ethical behavior rather than a forced creed; based on belief in a divine Creator. They are 1. No idolatry, 2. No murder, 3. No theft, 4. No blasphemy, 5. No incest, 6. No eating the flesh of a live animal, 7. promotion of justice.

Miriam (Hebrew: "bitter water"; Egyptian: "beloved of Ammon") MIH-ree-um

Tribe: Levi; father: Amram; mother: Yocheved; brothers: Moses, Aaron; possible husband(s): Hur, Caleb; son: Hur? Prophetess, midwife, and leader. Only biblical mentions of Miriam are in Book of Exodus when she convinced Egyptian princess to allow Moses to be nursed by his blood mother, and when she sang at the Reed Sea; and in Numbers, when she complained to God that Moses was neglecting his wife and was punished by leprosy but not abandoned by people. Midrash associates her with Puah, one of 2 midwives whom Pharaoh summoned. Had vision of Moses as liberator. Her merit brought a well in the shape of a beehive that accompanied the Hebrews as they journeyed through wilderness; may have known how to bring water forth through song. Passed her wisdom on to her descendant Bezalel, who built the tabernacle. Taken to heaven by the kiss of the Shechinah. Buried by Aaron and Moses at age 86.

Mishnah (Hebrew: "teaching") MISH-nah

A compendium of legal and religious teachings, believed to be explanations that Moses gave concerning the Bible that were passed from parent to child and teacher to disciple. Later scholars contend that these were the teachings of 80 to 120 rabbis who lived in Israel between 50 and 200 C.E. during the time of the Roman occupation; they based their compendium on Rabbi Akiva's systematic collection of oral law.

Moabites (Hebrew: "from my father") MOE-ab

Ancient people who settled in land east of Jordan River and Dead Sea area in 14th century B.C.E. After destruction of Sodom and Gomorrah, Lot's daughters, believing themselves the last people on earth, got their father drunk and slept with him (Gn 19:37). One of the sons was called Moab meaning "from father" from whom the Moabites are descendants. Chemosh was their chief god.

Mordecai (Akkadian: "Marduk") MORE-deh-kie

Tribe: Benjamin; father: Jair; mother: from the tribe of Judah. Lived during the time of Ahasuerus (Xerxes I, 486–465 B.C.E.). Exiled to Babylon with King Jehoiakim in 597 B.C.E., returned to Jerusalem, then exiled a second time; raised Esther as a daughter and sought peace. Knew 70 languages.

Moses (Egyptian: "son," "child") Hebrew: "to draw out") (?) MOE-zuhz

Ancestor: Levi; father: Amram; mother: Yocheved; brother: Aaron; sister: Miriam; wife: Zipporah; sons: Gershom, Eliezer. Prophet, lawgiver, and general. Born in Egypt, raised by Pharaoh's daughter. After killing an Egyptian taskmaster, fled from Egypt at age 40 to Midian and tended sheep for 40 years. At God's command returned to Egypt to lead Hebrews out of Egypt. Brought Torah (teachings) from God to people. While regarded as being humble and wise, also criticized for his temper. Not permitted by God to enter Promised Land, but allowed to stand on top of Mount Pisgah and glimpse it. Died in Land of Moab at age 120. Taken to heaven by kiss of Shechinah. Buried by God (Sot. 14a) in grave prepared for him on sixth day of creation (Pes. 54a).

Nahshon (Hebrew: "little serpent") NAH-shone

Tribe: Judah; father: Amminadab; sister: Elisheva (wife of Aaron); son: Salmah; grandson: Boaz. First to enter Reed Sea, an act that showed his great faith in God. Upon seeing his example, tribe of Judah followed him (BT Sotah 37a). Helped Moses take census. First to give gifts and offerings for Tabernacle.

Naomi (Hebrew: "pleasant") NAY-oh-mee

Tribe: Judah; grandfather: Nahshon; husband and cousin: Elimelech; sons: Mahlon, Kilyon. Mother-in-law of Ruth. Left Judah for Moab with husband and 2 sons; returned to Judah with daughter-in-law, Ruth. Advised Ruth to seek Boaz as husband/redeemer; became foster grandmother of Ruth's son, Obed.

Nephilim (Hebrew: from the verb "to fall") neh-FEE-lim

"Sons of gods," children of fallen angels. Rebellious angels "fell" from God's grace, bringing sin to earth. Because of their evil nature, God decreed they would massacre one another. These "sons of gods" (Gn 6:1–2) (angels such as Uzza and Azazel) took mortal wives and produced divine offspring. According to legend, their descendants were violent and corrupt and brought about the flood in which most of them perished. Those who remained became a race of giants who lived in Canaan and were seen by the spies sent by Moses (Num 13:33).

Nimrod (origin unknown) NIM-rod

Grandfather: Ham; father: Cush. Adam's garments, which were stolen by Nimrod's grandfather from Noah were given to Nimrod; these clothes made him a great hunter and fearsome warrior. Built cities of Erech and Babylon in Sumer. Appointed Terah one of his princes. Threw Abram and his older brother Haran into fire; Haran perished, Abram lived; rewarded Abram with presents and servant, Eliezer. Killed by Esau who cut off his head with sword. (Book of Yashar, 7–12; 27:1–8)

Nun (Egyptian: "abyss," "primeval waters") NOON

(1) Egyptian god of the primeval waters. According to Egyptian mythology, one of the 3 manifestations of the Creator God: Khepri (the morning—the beetle, the rising sun), Atum (the day—the high hill), Nun

(the evening—the serpent, the old man). From Nun arose all of life: the four beings (Nothingness, Inertness, Infinity, Invisibility) as well as the gods Shu and Tefnut, who represented air and water, life and order. (2) Joshua's epithet is son of Nun; scholars do not know whether the epithet refers to Joshua's biological father or the Egyptian god.

offering
(1) burnt offering (Hebrew: *olah*—"to go up," "to go up in smoke"). Oldest and most common form of animal sacrifice for community and individual. Offered to God at Temple, morning and afternoon, and on Sabbath, new moon, and festivals. Expressed a person's submission to God and intention to devote life to God's service; request for forgiveness for not keeping commandment, or as thanks offering. Three kinds of male animals offered: bull, sheep/goat, or fowl. Priest dashed animal's blood against altar and, with exception of the hide, burnt rest of offering until it turned into smoke and ashes. (2) thanks, meal, peace offering (Hebrew: *todah*—"thanks"). An animal or unleavened grain sacrifice offered to celebrate a happy national event—a successful military campaign (I Sam 11:15) an end of famine or pestilence (II Sam 24:25); or a personal occasion—a family reunion (I Sam 20:6). Unlike burnt offering, portions of peace offering were reserved for priests and leftovers were eaten at communal meal.

Orpah (Hebrew: "nape" or "back of the neck") OR-pah
Father: Eglon; husband: Kilyon; sons: 4 giants, including Goliath (Ruth R. 2:20). Daughter-in-law of Naomi. Her name evokes posture of her "turning her back" on Naomi, choosing not to go with her from Moab to Bethlehem (Ruth R. 2:9). Killed by David's general Abishai while protecting one of her sons (Sanh. 95a).

Phinehas (Egyptian: "dark complexion") FIN-e-has
Tribe: Levi; grandfather: Aaron; mother's father: Jethro; father: Eleazar; son: Eli. High priest, general, and spy. Slew Hebrew man Zimri and Midianite woman Cozbi who were cohabitating (Num 25:7–16). Accompanied Caleb to spy on land at Moses' command (Num 21:32). Lost his divine inspiration because he would not make the effort to absolve Jephthath from his vow when he unwittingly offered God whatever first came out of his house to meet him if God would bring him victory. His only daughter came out to greet him (Gn. R. 60:3, Jgs 11:30–31).

Plony Almony (equivalent of English "John Doe") PLOE-nee Al-MOE-nee
(1) Name used to indicate person whose name is not known. (2) father: Nahshon; brother: Elimelech. Naomi's uncle who refused to marry Ruth (*BT* Baba Bathra 91a).

Queen of Heaven, *See* Inanna

Glossary

Rachel (Hebrew: "ewe") RAY-chul

Ancestor: Nahor; father: Laban; mother: Adinah; twin sister: Leah; husband: Jacob; sons: Joseph, Benjamin. One of four matriarchs. Described as beautiful of face and figure (Gn 29:17). Met Jacob at well in Haran and gave him water; he kissed her. Forced to wait 14 years to marry Jacob because her father forced Jacob to marry her sister. Waited many years to have a child. When they left Haran for Canaan, stole father's household gods (small statues called *terafim*). Died at age 45, giving birth to Benjamin en route from Bethel to Hebron. Buried in Ramah near roadside. After death, according to midrash, prayed to Shechinah to have compassion on her descendants. Rachel's descendants thought to be more powerful in battle because their tribes (Joseph and Benjamin) did not harm their brothers.

Rahab (Hebrew: "broad," "wide," "boisterous," "generous," "grasping") RAH-hab

Ancestor: Jethro; husband: Joshua; daughters: 8, who were the ancestors of prophets including Baruch, Ezekiel, Jeremiah, Huldah. Woman of courage and convert to Judaism. Lodged Caleb and Phinehas when they came to spy on Jericho. Practiced harlotry until age 50, then converted. Rahab was considered the most beautiful woman in the Bible along with Esther, Abigail, and Sarah.

Rashi RAH-shee

Solomon ben Isaac, 1040–1105, born in Troyes, France. Leading commentator on the Bible and the Talmud. Educated by father, studied in Mainz. Founded a school in Troyes; his three daughters's husbands and their children were his best students.

Rebekah (origin unknown) Re-BECK-ah

Ancestor: Nahor; father: Bethuel; brother: Laban; husband: Isaac; twin sons: Esau, Jacob. One of four matriarchs. Decisive, clear of vision; grew up in Haran (Paddan-aram); chose to go with Abraham's servant Eliezer to marry Isaac in Canaan. Persuaded son Jacob to trick his father into giving him rather than his brother Esau his blessing. Died at age 133.

redeemer

Custom of levirate marriage guarantees family line. "If brothers live together and one dies and has no son . . . the husband's brother shall marry the widow (Dt 25:5)." The purpose of the levirate marriage was to keep property in family. Duty of marrying childless widow was not enforced in ancient times but refusal regarded as disgraceful.

Reed Sea/Red Sea

The correct translation from the Hebrew is Reed Sea, not Red Sea. Scholars do not agree on its location.

Rehoboam (Hebrew: "the people are extensive") Reh-Hoe-BOE-um
Tribe: Judah; father: Solomon; mother: Naamah (the Ammonite); wives: 18, sons: 28, daughters: 60. Son of Solomon and king of Judah. Proclaimed king in Shechem at age 41. Cruel to subjects: for example, when asked to lighten harsh labor that his father had imposed, he answered, "My father flogged you with whips, I will flog you with scorpions" (I Kgs 12:11). During his reign Israelites living in north rebelled and kingdom became divided; people in Judah built numerous shrines to foreign gods; shrines were "on every high hill and under every leafy tree" (I Kgs 14:23–24). Ruled 17 years; buried in Jerusalem with his fathers.

Ruth (Hebrew: "friendship") ROOTH
Ancestor: Moab; father: Eglon; father-in-law: Elimelech; mother-in-law: Naomi; husbands: Mahlon, Boaz; son: Obed; great-grandson: David, great-great-grandson: Solomon. Courageous and righteous convert to Judaism. Left birthplace, Moab, and went with mother-in-law to Judah despite knowing that she might not be welcomed there. Gleaned in fields of Boaz.

Samuel (origin unknown) SAM-yoo-el
Tribe: Judah; father: Elkanah; mother: Hannah; sons: Joel, Abijah. Priest, judge, and prophet. Raised by Hannah. Became priest at sanctuary in Shiloh. Last of judges. Became prophet at time when there was corruption and no prophecy in Israel. Did not reprimand his sons who were corrupt. When asked by Israelites for a king, anointed Saul and then David. Helped organize tribes into one political and religious kingdom. Killed Agag, whose sword was said to render women childless. Remained committed to God and holiness all his life. According to midrash, the tunic his mother wove for him grew as he grew. Died at age of 52.

Sarah (Hebrew: "princess"; Akkadian: "Sarrat," one of the names of the Moon Goddess)
Father: Terah; brothers: Milcah, Haran; husband and half-brother: Abraham; son: Isaac. Prophetess, mother of Jewish people, one of four matriarchs. Only woman in Bible that God speaks to directly. Considered, along with Esther, Rahab, and Abigail, one of most beautiful women in Bible. Agreed to be called Abraham's sister in Egypt and in Philistine to protect him from danger; Pharaoh gave her gold, silver, land of Goshen, and daughter, Hagar. Gave birth to Isaac at age 90; had enough milk in breasts to nurse all infants (those who nursed at Sarah's breasts later converted to Judaism, Gn. R. 53:9). Sent away Hagar and Ishmael out of jealousy and fear for her own son's safety. Remained beautiful and vigorous until her death. After hearing news of Isaac's being

given as burnt offering, died in Hebron at age 127; buried in cave of Machpelah.

Seder (Hebrew: "order") SAY-dur

A home-based service held on first two nights of Passover in communities outside Israel, on one night in Israel. Special foods are eaten and a selection of prayers, songs, narratives, and commentaries from the Haggadah are read and sung in a certain order to fulfill commandment to teach one's children about the Exodus from Egypt.

sephirot (Hebrew: "story," "counting") Seh-FEER-oat

According to 12th-century Kabbalists, sephirot are God's 10 attributes. Kabbalists conceived of God as Ein Sof as ineffable, nameless, combining opposites, beyond intellectual understanding. In order to know Ein Sof, which cannot be conceived, they attributed 10 emanations or attributes, known as sephirot, to reveal God. Descending from infinity to creation, from heaven to earth, they are

Awakening—will, crown (*keter*)

Insight—wisdom, father (*chochmah*)

Understanding—wisdom, mother (*binah*)

Loving-kindness—mercy (*hesed*)

Judgment—strength (*gevurah*)

Beauty—(*tiferet*)

Victory—endurance (*netzach*)

Glory—(*hod*)

Foundation—(*yesod*)

Kingdom—Shechinah (*malkhut*)

Serach (origin unknown) Seh-RACH

Father: Malkiel; mother: Hadurah. Beautiful, wise, and long-lived granddaughter of Jacob. Adopted at 3 years by stepfather, Asher. Given extraordinarily long life as reward for gently informing grandfather Jacob that his son Joseph was still alive. Her life spanned time of patriarchs through Exodus to entry into Promised Land. Keeper of vital information: for example, knew words true redeemer would use at time of redemption; identified Moses as true redeemer; knew location of Joseph's bones which Moses had to find before Israelites left Egypt. Entered paradise alive.

shamir (Hebrew: "to guard") Sha-MEER

A tiny worm that could cut through stone. According to legend, created by God at twilight of 6th day, along with ram that was sacrificed instead of Isaac; disappeared after destruction of Second Temple.

Shechinah (Hebrew: *shakhan*, "to dwell" or "abide") Sheh-CHEE-nah

The divine presence; aspect of God that is perceived visibly and audibly by people; later, the feminine aspect of God. Kabbalistic sign is sovereignty and kingdom (Malchut). Kabbalistic names are Atara, the diadem, the apple orchard. When united with partner, compassion (*tiferet*), there is harmony and balance in the world and a soul is born. Of the foremothers, identified with Rachel (the moon), whose partner was Jacob (the sun). In Kabbalah known as the Torah and the great sea into which all rivers flow. Associated with images of light and radiance (Hul. 59b–60a; Ex. R. 32:4). In tabernacle and First and Second Temples, dwelt in holy of holies above ark of the covenant; after destruction of Temples, is said to be present when ten are gathered for prayer, when there is learning of Torah, or when a person carries out God's commandments (Ber. 6a). When pronounced (Sheh-CHEE-nah) sounds like wind gently pouring through a hollow tube.

Shem (Hebrew: "name") SHEM

Great-great-grandfather: Enoch; great-grandfather: Methusaleh; father: Noah; mother: Naamah; brothers: Japheth, Ham; great-grandson: Eber. Teacher and ancestor of Israelites. Born circumcised. Inherited Adam's priestly clothes that had been passed from Adam to Seth to Methusaleh to Noah. After flood, covered father's nakedness when he became drunk, and gave offering to God because Noah had wounded himself. Learned Torah from Enoch, who had been taught by Seth who had learned from Adam. Prophesied for 400 years; circumcised Abraham and Ishmael. Began legal court that became a school. Isaac studied three years with Shem after the Akedah. Chose place for Abraham to be buried. Died at age of 600.

Sheol (origin unknown) Shee-OLE

Place of dead; under the earth, dark, gloomy; all souls go there. God is also there.

Sh'ma (Hebrew: "hear") ShMAH

Declaration of Jewish faith: "Hear O Israel, the lord, our God, the lord is one. *Sh'ma Yisrael, Adonai eloheinu, adonai echad.*" Part of a prayer of three paragraphs that is recited morning and evening (Dt 6:4–9). First prayer to be taught to Jewish child. Recited at death. "The lord is one": The numerical value of the Hebrew word "one" is thirteen, which has same numerical value as the word for love. By saying God is one, a Jew is proclaiming the connectedness of the universe; such a concept implies justice, holiness, and love.

shofar (Ugaritic: "horn," Sumerian: "wild goat") SHO-fahr

A ram's horn blown as a trumpet for religious services and in battle. On Rosh Hashanah blown 100 times; close of Yom Kippur, blown once. In month preceeding Rosh Hashanah, blown every day at morning service to prepare for Rosh Hashanah. In synagogue, the prescribed notes— *Tekiah:* one sustained note, *Teruah:* nine staccato notes, *Shevarim:* three short notes—are blown at specific times during service accompanying recitation of biblical verses. The shofar blown in synagogue for the Jubilee Year (every 50 years) is straight, not curved, to symbolize freedom. (Rosh Hashanah 26b.)

Solomon (Hebrew: "shalom," "peace" or "wholeness") SOL-eh-mahn
Ancestor: Judah; father: David; mother: Bathsheba; son: Rehoboam, wives: 700; concubines: 300. King and writer. Credited as author of Song of Songs, Proverbs, and Ecclesiastes. Appointed king of Israel and Judah by David; anointed king during David's lifetime by prophet Nathan and priest Zaddok. Ruled for 40 years from the Euphrates River to Egypt. Built first Temple in Jerusalem. Ushered in a time of peace and prosperity: "All the days of Solomon, Judah and Israel from Dan to Beersheba dwelt in safety, everyone under his own vine and fig tree" (I Kgs 5:5). Known for his wisdom; queen of Sheba visited Solomon and tested his wisdom with riddles. In later years, he enslaved foreigners and exacted forced labor from people to build palace, fortifications. Angered God by building shrines for his foreign wives. Punishment was loss of kingdom by his son. Died at age of 52; buried with his father in Jerusalem.

tabernacle (Latin: "tent" or "hut") TAB-uhr-nak-uhl
Portable sanctuary constructed by Hebrews in wilderness at God's command. Referred to as God's dwelling place in Israel (Ex 25:9) or Tent of Meeting where God is revealed (Ex 28:43). Its innermost sanctuary, called the holy of holies, contained the ark of the covenant. Made of variety of materials contributed by the people. After Hebrews' entry into Promised Land, lodged in Gilgal for 14 years; then housed in Shiloh; after Eli's death, moved to Gibeon by Samuel; brought into Temple in Jerusalem by Solomon. Destroyed when Temple was destroyed.

Talmud (Hebrew: "teaching") TAHL-muhd
Combination of Mishnah and Gemara. The Palestinian Talmud was finalized in 370 C.E. and the Babylonian in 500 C.E. The Babylonian Talmud, which is 12 volumes, is considered vast and referred to as the ocean of the Torah. It encompasses religion, ethics, ritual, law, philosophy, medicine, history, literature, geography, politics. . . .

Tamar (Hebrew: "date palm") Tah-MAHR
Ancestor: Shem; husbands: Er, Onan; twin sons: Zerah, Perez. Determined, strong Canaanite woman. After husband Er's death, married

his brother. After Onan's death, father-in-law, Judah, did not allow her to be redeemed. So as not to remain childless, disguised self as a cult prostitute and seduced Judah. To clear name and children's patrimony, sent Judah his staff and ring which he confessed were his.

Targum Onkelos, TAR-gum ON-ke-lus

Translation of Masoretic Bible into Aramaic during first to fourth centuries in Palestine and Babylon. Edited with commentary to teach the masses so they could understand Torah reading in synagogue.

tefillin (Hebrew: "prayer") Teh-FEEL-ehn

Small leather boxes containing sacred passages from the Bible that are placed on the forehead and wrapped around the arm during morning prayers.

Torah (Hebrew: "teachings," "directions;" "to point the way") TOE-rah

The five books of Moses or the Pentateuch (which was translated into Greek in Alexandria) also referred to as entire Hebrew Bible. Consists of religious laws, ethics, narratives, prayers, and songs. Writings can be understood on 4 different levels: literal, homilectic, allegorical, and esoteric. According to Kabbalah, the Torah, formed of sacred letters that are the primal spiritual forces of creation, existed before the world began. Five books of Moses are said to have existed in written form from time of Josiah (622 B.C.E.); read publicly at time of Ezra and afterwards yearly on Sukkot. The Prophets were later included in the Bible and the Writings by second century C.E. Those who bind themselves to Torah bind themselves to God. Perceived by rabbis as wisdom (the sage is one who is so immersed in Torah that all his actions and thoughts express Torah) and the feminine embodiment of God. Study of Torah has replaced the offerings given at the Temple altar; in Temple times during Sukkot, people circled the altar, now they circle the Torah.

tzaddik (Hebrew: "righteous") TSA-dik

Humans who sustain and protect the world, and are thought to know God's will. Biblical *tzaddikim* include Abraham, who offered humanity the concept of a divine creator, and Joseph, who nourished the world with food and his moral strength.

urim and thummin (Hebrew: "lights" and "perfection") OOR-eem, TOO-meen

Sacred objects used only by king or high priest for divination and oracles. Possibly dice, sticks, or stones that were kept inside pouch of high priest's breastplate. Given by Moses to Aaron who as high priest was Yahweh's representative. Possibly caused particular stones in breastplate to light up and/or protrude, thus forming words which priest interpreted. Used by

Glossary

high priest Eleazar at time of entry into Promised Land to announce which tribe would inherit which land; his pronouncements were confirmed by drawing lots. No longer used after destruction of Temple. (See breastplate.)

Uzza (origin unknown) OO-zah

Angel who protected Egypt; also called the prince of the sea. Eventually thrown into the sea, paralleling fate of Egypt at Reed Sea.

Yнwн (four-letter acronym of God's divine name) YAH-weh

Translated as, I will become who I will become, I am who I am, or I am. Original pronunciation is unknown. Personal name of God known as the Tetragrammaton. Represented by 4 consonants that make up name in Hebrew. According to Kabbalistic tradition, each letter of the Hebrew alphabet contains a spiritual power that is a manifestation of God's power. In the name Yahweh:

Yod represents judgment, insight (*chochmah*)

Hay represents understanding, wisdom (*binah*)

Vav represents compassion (*tiferet*) and the other five sephirot

Hay represents sovereignty, kingdom, the Shechinah (*malchut*)

In English, the *v* changed to *w* (Yнvн—Yнwн) from the German transcription. Because of sacred nature of name, was uttered only on Yom Kippur by high priest within holy of holies (M. Yoma 6:2) and by priests in Temple when reciting priestly benediction (Sot. 7:6). Observant Jews avoid speaking this name, believing that its invocation would be too overwhelming for the speaker. The word Adonai has been substituted for Yнwн. The numerical equivalent of the 4 letters is 186, which is the Hebrew word for "place," referring to God's omnipresence.

Yochanan ben Zakkai (Hebrew: *tzaddik*, "righteous one")

Forty years businessman, 40 years student, 40 years leader of Israel. Lived in Galilee at time of Jesus. Youngest and most distinguished of 80 students of Hillel; studied mystical texts leading to closeness to God. Shared leadership of Sanhedrin with Simeon ben Gamaliel II. During Roman conquest, sought peaceful negotiations with Romans. Like Jeremiah, warned against war; after destruction of Jerusalem, his small academy at Yabneh replaced Sanhedrin and ruled on ritual, ethical, and legal questions; advised Jews to replace Temple sacrifices with acts of kindness and mercy. When opposed by Gamaliel, rather than quarrel, relinquished leadership and set up another academy. Died at age of 120.

Yocheved (Hebrew: "God is my glory," "divine splendor") Yo-CHE-vehd

Father: Levi; mother: Otah; brothers: Kohath, Merari; husband and nephew: Amram; children: Miriam, Aaron, Moses. Midwife. Born as

Jacob's family entered Egypt from Canaan; divine light came from her forehead; thought to be the midwife Shifrah, who saved lives of hundreds of Hebrew infants at time of Exodus. Born on same day as husband, Amram.

Zealots

Believed in importance of Temple ritual. During time of Nero, wanted to rid Israel of foreign rule so burned warehouses with food to incite people to fight Romans; burned palaces and archives to destroy bonds of moneylenders. After fall of Jerusalem, fled to Masada.

Zipporah (Hebrew: "little bird") Tsih-POR-ah

Father: Jethro; husband: Moses; sons: Gershom, Eliezer. Priestess. Rescued Moses from snake on their way to Egypt. Grieved at not singing at the Reed Sea with the other women and so promised by God that her soul would be reborn in prophetess Deborah, who would sing a great song of salvation. (Exodus Rabba 27)

Zohar (Hebrew: "splendor," "flash") ZOE-har

Compendium of mystical teachings from different times. Central work in literature of Kabbalah. Gives meditations on ascending the sephirot of the Tree of Life. Composed in Spain in 13th century by Moses de Leon, who attributed his work to second century author Rabbi Shimon Bar Yohai. During Roman times, Bar Yohai hid in cave for 13 years; at entrance to cave by carob tree the prophet Elijah revealed secrets hidden in the Torah; Bar Yohai then revealed these secrets to a group of disciples. Bar Yohai's teachings were used as a framework for the Zohar.

Compiled by Rabbi Beth Appel, Freema Gottlieb, Deb Hoffman, and Diane Wolkstein.

Bibliography

I am deeply grateful to these authors, their scholarship, and their convictions. Their ideas have provoked my own and I could not have written the commentaries without our lively, mute conversations. The Sources acknowledges their specific ideas, and the listing in the Bibliography acknowledges general concepts and ideas. I hope the reader will be interested in the topics they explore and enjoy reading the fullness of their explorations.

Ackerman, Susan. *Under Every Green Tree: Popular Religion in Sixth Century Judah.* Harvard Semitic Monographs, no. 46. Atlanta, Ga.: Scholars Press, 1992.
———. *Warrior, Dancer, Seductress: Women in Judges and Biblical Israel.* New York: Doubleday, 1998.
Aharoni, Yohanan, and Michael Avi-Yonah. *The Macmillan Bible Atlas.* New York: Macmillan, 1968.
Bickerman, Elias. *From Ezra to the Last of the Maccabees, Foundations of Post-Biblical Judaism.* New York: Schocken Books, 1962.
Birnbaum, Philip. *A Book of Jewish Concepts.* New York: Hebrew Publishing, 1975.
Bloch, Abraham P. *The Biblical and Historical Background of the Jewish Holy Days.* New York: Ktav Publishing House, 1978.
Burns, Rita J. *Has the Lord Indeed Spoken Only through Moses? A Study of the Biblical Portrait of Miriam.* Atlanta, Ga.: Scholars Press, 1980.
Cassuto, U., *A Commentary on the Book of Genesis.* Part 1. Trans. Israel Abrahams, 2 Vol. Jerusalem: Magnes Press, The Hebrew University, 1961.
Chasidai, Yishai. *Encyclopedia of Biblical Personalities.* Anthologized from the Talmud, Midrash, and Rabbinical writings. Brooklyn: Noble Book, 1994.
Cook, Joan E. *Hannah's Desire, God's Design: Early Interpretations of the Story of Hannah.* Sheffield: Sheffield Academic Press, 1999.
Craven, Toni. *Artistry and Faith in the Book of Judith.* Chico, Calif.: Scholars Press, 1983.

Bibliography

Culi, Yaakov, *The Book of Esther: MeAm Lo'Ez*. New York and Jerusalem: Moznaim Publishing, 1978.

Day, John. *God's Conflict with the Dragon and the Sea: Echoes of a Canaanite Myth in the Old Testament*. Cambridge: Cambridge University Press, 1985.

Exum, Cheryl J. *Tragedy and Biblical Narrative: Arrows of the Almighty*. Cambridge: Cambridge University Press, 1992.

Farmer, William Reuben. *Maccabees, Zealots, and Josephus: An Inquiry into Jewish Nationalism in the Greco-Roman Period*. New York: Columbia University Press, 1956.

Fox, Everett, trans. *Genesis and Exodus*. New York: Schocken Books, 1990.

Frieman, Shulamis. *Who's Who in the Talmud*. Northvale, N.J.: Jason Aronson, 1995.

Gaster, Theodore H. *Festivals of the Jewish Year: A Modern Interpretation and Guide*. New York: William Sloane Associates, 1953.

Ginzberg, Louis. *The Legends of the Jews*. 7 vols. Trans. Henrietta Szold, Paul Rabin, Boaz Cohen. Philadelphia: Jewish Publication Society, 1975.

Gunn, David M., and Danna Nolan Fewell. *Narrative in the Hebrew Bible*. Oxford. Oxford University Press, 1993.

Hadley, Judith M. "From Goddess to Literary Construct: The Transformation of Asherah into Hokmah." In *A Feminist Companion to Reading the Bible*, edited by Athalya Brenner and Carole Fontaine. Sheffield, England: Sheffield Academic Press, 1997.

———. *The Cult of Asherah in Ancient Israel and Judah: Evidence for a Hebrew Goddess*. Cambridge: Cambridge University Press, 2000.

Hamlin, E. John *Inheriting the Land: A Commentary on the Book of Joshua*. Grand Rapids, Mich.: Eerdmans, 1983.

Hazony, Yoram. *The Dawn: Political Teachings of the Book of Esther*. Jerusalem: Genesis Jerusalem Press, 1995.

Jacobs, Louis. *The Schocken Book of Jewish Mystical Testimonies*. New York: Schocken Books, 1997.

The Jerusalem Bible. Garden City, NY: Doubleday, 1966.

Kaplan, Aryeh. *Meditation and the Bible*. Maine: Samuel Weiser, 1981.

———. *Innerspace: Introduction to Kabbalah, Meditation, and Prophecy*. Brooklyn: Moznaim, 1991.

Kaufmann, Yehezkel. *The Biblical Account of the Conquest of Canaan*. Jerusalem: Magnes Press, 1985.

Kluger, Yehezkel, and Nomi Kluger-Nash. *A Psychological Interpretation of Ruth in the Light of Mythology, Legend, and Kabbalah; and Standing in the Sandals of Naomi*. Einsiedeln, Switzerland: Daimon, 1999.

Koehler, Ludwig, and Walter Baumgartner. *The Hebrew and Aramaic Lexicon of the Old Testament*. E. J. Brill, Leiden, 1996.

Bibliography

Kramer, Samuel Noah. *The Sumerians: Their History, Culture, and Character.* Chicago: University of Chicago Press, 1963.

Mendenhall, George. *The Tenth Generation: The Origins of the Biblical Tradition.* Baltimore: Johns Hopkins University Press, 1973.

Miles, Jack. *God: A Biography.* New York: Knopf, 1995.

Miller, J. Maxwell, and John H. Hayes. *A History of Ancient Israel and Judah.* Philadelphia: Westminster Press, 1986.

Mitchell, Stephen. *The Book of Job.* New York: Harper Perennial, 1992.

Munk, Michael L. *The Wisdom in the Hebrew Alphabet: The Sacred Letters as a Guide to Jewish Deed and Thought.* Brooklyn: Mesorah Publications, 1986.

Neusner, Jacob. *A Life of Yohanan Ben Zakkai, ca. 1–80 CE.* 2d ed. Leiden: E. J. Brill, 1970.

Niditch, Susan. *Oral Word and Written Word: Ancient Israelite Literature.* Louisville: Westminster John Knox Press, 1996.

Noah, Mordecai Manuel, trans. *The Book of Yashar.* New York: Hermon Press, 1972.

Pardes, Ilana. *Countertraditions in the Bible: A Feminist Approach.* Cambridge: Harvard University Press, 1992.

Patai, Raphael. Hebrew Goddess. New York: Ktav Publishing House, 1967.

Pearlman, Moshe. *The Maccabees.* New York: Macmillan, 1973.

Pope, Marvin, trans. *Song of Songs.* Garden City, N.Y.: Doubleday, 1977.

Rappoport, Angelo S. *Myth and Legend of Ancient Israel.* 3 vol. New York: Ktav, 1966.

Rowlett, Lori L. *Joshua and the Rhetoric of Violence: A New Historicist Analysis.* Sheffield, England: Sheffield Academic Press, 1996.

Sailhamer, John H. *The Pentateuch as Narrative: A Biblical-Theological Commentary.* Grand Rapids: Zondervan Publishing House, 1992.

Sarna, Nahum M. *On the Book of Psalms: Exploring the Prayers of Ancient Israel.* New York: Schocken Books, 1993.

———. *Exploring Exodus: The Origins of Biblical Israel.* New York: Schocken Books, 1996.

Scherman, Nosson. *The Complete Art Scroll Machzor.* Brooklyn: Mesorah Publications, 1986.

Schneidau, Herbert N. *Sacred Discontent: The Bible and Western Tradition.* Berkeley and Los Angeles: University of California Press, 1976.

Seidman, Hillel. *The Glory of the Jewish Holidays.* New York: Shengold Publications, 1969.

Sperling, Harry, and Maurice Simon. *The Zohar.* 5 vol. New York: Soncino Press, 1984.

Soggin, Alberto J. *A History of Ancient Israel.* Trans. John Bowden. Philadelphia: Westminster Press, 1984.

Bibliography

Strassfeld, Michael. *The Jewish Holidays: A Guide and Commentary*. New York: HarperCollins, 1985.

Tanakh. Philadelphia: Jewish Publication Society, 1985.

Teubal, Savina J. *Hagar the Egyptian: The Lost Tradition of the Matriarchs*. San Francisco: Harper & Row, 1990.

Teubal, Savina J. *Sarah the Priestess: The First Matriarch*. Athens, Ohio: Swallow Press, 1984.

Waskow, Arthur. *Seasons of Our Joy: A Modern Guide to the Jewish Holidays*. Boston: Beacon Press, 1982.

Winkler, Gershom. *The Soul of the Matter*. New York: Judaica Press, 1981.

Wolkstein, Diane. *Esther's Story*. New York: Morrow, 1996.

Wolkstein, Diane, and Samuel Noah Kramer. *Inanna, Queen of Heaven and Earth: Her Stories and Hymns from Sumer*. New York: Harper and Row, 1983.

Ziff, Joel. *Mirrors in Time: A Psycho-Spiritual Journey through the Jewish Year*. Northvale, N.J.: Jason Aronson, 1996.

Zornberg, Aviva Gottlieb. *The Beginning of Desire, Reflections on Genesis*. New York: Image, 1995.

Acknowledgments

My thanks to the people at Schocken, my editors Altie Karper and Rahel Lerner, who took such loving care of *Treasures of the Heart;* Archie Ferguson and Peter Andersen who watched over the cover and the design; Tony da Luna for his care and advice; Timothy DeVinney for his fine copyediting.

Over the past eight years, I've told the stories in *Treasures of the Heart* hundreds of times—in libraries, homes, and performance centers throughout the world. I can remember almost every telling and am grateful to those who were kind enough to share their reactions that then led me to reconsider or appreciate different aspects of the stories.

Many friends helped by listening, reading, and contributing their reactions. I am grateful for their love, encouragement, and discernment. They are all a part of *Treasures:* Barbara Abrash, Olivier Bernier, John Boe, Elizabeth Borsodi, John Flattau, Rabbi Steven Geller, Jill Golden, Rabbi Ed Greenstein, Jill Hammer, Eve Ilsen, Anna Ivara, Elena-Beth Kaye (computer advisor), Franklin Kiermeyer, Jeri Kroll, Amy-Jill Levine, Alicia Ostriker, Peninah Petruck, Adina Popescu, Margaret Powell, Eli Rarey, Lorna Roberts, Rabbi Zalman Schachter-Shalomi, Laura Simms, Kate Smith, Alan Stewart, Arthur Strimling, Gioia Timpanelli, my brother, Gary Wolkstein, and my daughter, Rachel Zucker.

Other dear friends appeared in the knick of time to wrestle. They held me down, forcing me to say what it was I was coming to believe in. My deep appreciation to Cass Dalgliesh, Jane Enkins, Rabbi Meyer Fund, Alec Gelcer, Judy Kroll, Rabbi Justin Lewis, Kaye Lindauer, Willow Hearth, Melissa Heckler, Jinx Roosevelt, Diane M. Sharon, Susanne Sklar, Susan Thomas, and especially Andrea Curley, who has been my editor for fifteen years.

Special thanks to the libraries and staff of Jewish Theological Seminary, New York University, and Union Theological Seminary.

Translators: Freema Gottlieb, Rabbi Ray Scheindlin (The Song of Songs), Diane Wolkstein, Anath Zahini.

Index

Index

charity, 158

cherubim, 53, 72, 146, 165–66, 177, 190, 259–60, 308, 314, 317, 320, 326

circumcision, 11, 75, 262
  of Abraham, 130, 149–50
  of the Israelites, 224–25
  of Shechem's tribe, 221
  by Zipporah, 235

compassion, 35, 56–57, 73, 76, 88, 92, 95, 110, 116, 145, 149, 174–76, 178, 201, 204, 282, 315, 339
  binah, 177
  Hannah, 330
  hesed, 330
  tiferet, 342, 345

conversion, 61, 73, 221

covenant
  acceptance of, at Shavuot, 71–72, 76, 314
  destruction of the temple, 78
  failures of, 116–19
  minimum commandments, 57, 83, 228, 335
  reception of, on Mount Sinai, 45, 50–58, 314
  Ten Commandments, 31, 50–58

creation story, xiv, 162, 178, 232–34, 240–41, 320

Dance of the Two Armies, 283

Dathan, 9, 326

David, 67, 147–48, 186–87, 319, 327

Day of Atonement. *See* Yom Kippur

Days of Awe, 124

Deuteronomy, 206–7, 209, 308

"The Diamond" (Rabbi Nachman of Bratislav), 79

dietary customs
  Hanukkah, 246
  Passover, 2–4, 341
  Purim, 290–91
  Shavuot, 42
  Tisha B'av, 79

Dinah, 319, 327
  in Job, 115
  in Joshua, 219–21, 240

Dreamtime of Australian aboriginals, 208

Dumuzi, 37

Ecclesiastes, xvii, 194–99, 202–3, 319

Egypt/Mitzraim, 2–18

Eleazar, xviii

Rabbi Eleazar, 158

Eli, the high priest, 141–42, 145–47

Eliezer, son of Moses, 10–11, 327

Eliezer, servant of Abraham, 128, 136

Elijah, 3, 169–70, 318

Eliphaz, 47, 104, 105, 114, 324, 327

Elisha, 170, 318

Elkanah, 140–142, 317, 328

Elohim. *See* God, names of

El Shaddai. *See* God, names of

Ephraim, 272, 280

Er, 269

Esau, 284, 328

Esther, xvi–xvii, 290–308, 321, 328
  niece of Mordechai, 296
  chosen as queen, 296
  saves her people, 299–305
  holiday observances, 305

Esther, 290, 293, 321

The Ethics of the Fathers, 43

etrog, 12, 183–85, 318

Exodus, 5–18, 36, 235, 312–13
  departure of the Jews from Egypt, 17–18
  Jewish calendar, xx
  Moses's story, 5–11
  plagues of Egypt, 11–16
  reception of the covenant, 45, 50–58, 314
  retrieval of Joseph's bones, 16–17
  Songs of the Sea, xiv

Ezekiel, 68–70, 74–76, 315, 328–29
  covenant with God, 71
  Tree of Life, 74–75
  visions of Shechinah, 69–70, 74, 241

Ezra, 122–23, 163, 320, 332, 344, 347

famine
  in Abraham and Sarah, 127
  in The Destruction of the Second Temple, 98–99
  in Exodus, 5–6
  in Lamentations, 94
  in Ruth, 59–60, 62,64
  in Rachel and the Shechinah, 88

feminine visions of traditional stories, xiv–xvii
  portrayals of women, xv–xvi
  role of God, xvi–xvii
  role of the Goddess, xv

fertility, 177

Festival of Lights. *See* Hanukkah

354

Index

Five Books of Moses. *See* Torah

food. *See* dietary customs

foreign deities. *See* Mesopotamian and Sumerian deities

forgiveness, 123–24, 177–78

fragrance. *See* smell

Gabriel, 8, 18, 216–17, 329

Gemara, xviii, 329

Genesis, xiv, xix, 207, 232–34, 320

Ginzberg, Louis, 311

God, names of

  Adonai, 95, 101, 146, 172–74, 251, 254–55, 324

  Elohim, 31, 39, 94–95, 171–73, 328

  El Shaddai, 61, 64, 69, 105, 125–32, 134, 138, 150–51, 273, 275, 327

  in Exodus, 36, 39–40

  in the Kabbalah, 39

  speaking the name, on Yom Kippur, 163–67, 176–77

  thirteen names of mercy, 56–57

  YHWH, 178, 345

goddesses, xv–xvi

  Inanna, xv, 37, 292, 331

  Ishtar, 290, 292, 296, 307

  sacred marriage rite, 177

golden calf, 38–39, 54–55, 71, 158, 182

Goliath, 61, 329

Greek culture, 258–66, 283–84

haftorot, xvii

Hagar, 128–30, 132–33, 149–50, 284, 329

Haggadah, xviii, 3, 329

halakhah, xviii, 329

Haman, 284, 290, 293, 297–306, 321

Hannah, xvi, 125–33, 140–48, 152–55, 330

  infertility, 141

  prayer of, 141–142

  birth of Samuel, 142

  song of joy, 144

Hanukkah, 243–84, 309, 320

  dreidel, 246

  hanukkiah, 245–246

  Joseph's story, 266–81, 284–86

  Judith's story, xvi, 247–57, 282–83

  Maccabees, 258–65, 283–84

  menorah. See hanukkiah

harvest celebrations. *See* Shavuot; Sukkot

Hasidism, 330

Hasmoneans, 265, 284

hebel, 202

The Hebrew and Aramaic Lexicon of the Old Testament, 237

Hebrew Goddess (Patai), xvi

hesed, 60, 63, 330

high priests, 58, 88, 158, 161–167, 177–179, 330

Rabbi Hillel, 101, 245, 330–31

hineni, 10, 113, 135, 137, 146, 267, 331

holidays

  ordering of, xx–xxi

  readings for, xvii–xviii

Holocaust, 78

Holofernes, 248–50, 252–57, 282, 320

holy of holies, 161–68, 176–79, 259–60, 317–18

Hoshanna Rabbah, 185

Huldah, 31, 331

Hur, 53–54, 314

idolatry, xv–xvi

  destruction of the Temples, 78, 88–91

  golden calf, 38–39, 54–55, 71, 158

  invasions by Assyria and Babylon, 86–91

  Jeremiah's story, xv, 31, 39

  Josiah's story, 30–33, 38–39

  at Mount Sinai, 53–54

  under the Seleucid Empire, 259–62

Inanna, xv, 37, 292, 331

Inanna, Queen of Heaven and Earth (Kramer), xv

Isaac, xix, 36, 162, 316–17, 331

  binding of, 135–39, 150–52

  birth of, 125–34

  destruction of the First Temple, 90–91

Ishmael, 331–32

  banishment of, 132–33, 149, 284

  binding of Isaac, 136–37

  birth of, 130

  visits with Abraham, 133–34, 150

Ishtar, xv, 290, 292, 296, 307

Israel, Najara, 44

Jacob, 6, 36, 85, 162, 284, 332

  death of, 280

  descendants in Egypt, 6–18, 221

  destruction of the First Temple, 90–91

  marriage to Rachel, 91

  migration to Egypt, 278–80

  story of Dinah, 219–21

355

Index

Index

Index

Index

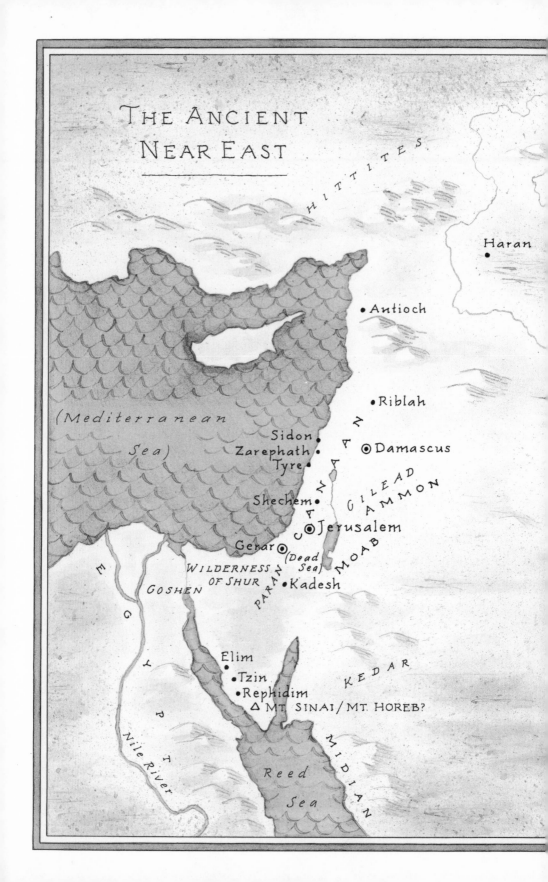

THE ANCIENT NEAR EAST

HITTITES

Haran

(Mediterranean Sea)

• Antioch

• Riblah

Sidon
Zarephath
Tyre

⊙ Damascus

C A N A A N

GILEAD

AMMON

Shechem

⊙ Jerusalem

Gerar ⊙

(Dead Sea)

MOAB

WILDERNESS
OF SHUR

PARAN

• Kadesh

E
G
Y
P
T

GOSHEN

Elim
• Tzin
• Rephidim
△ MT. SINAI / MT. HOREB?

KEDAR

Nile River

MIDIAN

Reed Sea